S0-BJM-980

Comparative National Balance Sheets

Raymond W. Goldsmith

Comparative National Balance Sheets

A Study of Twenty Countries, 1688–1978

The University of Chicago Press
Chicago and London

RAYMOND W. GOLDSMITH is professor emeritus of economics at Yale University. He is the author of many books, including *The National Balance Sheet of the United States, 1953–1980*, also published by the University of Chicago Press.

The University of Chicago Press, Chicago 60637
The University of Chicago Press, Ltd., London

Printed in the United States of America
92 91 90 89 88 87 86 85   5 4 3 2 1

Library of Congress Cataloging in Publication Data

Goldsmith, Raymond William, 1904–
Comparative national balance sheets.

Bibliography: p.
Includes index.
1. National income—Accounting. I. Title.
HC79.I5G64 1985 339.3 84-16277
ISBN 0-226-30153-2

Contents

List of Tables

In Text

1. Always benchmark dates; for actual years see table 33

2. Tables 38–47 and 54–59 show information, where available, for benchmark dates between 1850 and 1978 for 20 countries.

3. Tables 60, 62, 63, 64, 66, and 67 also show information for the United States in 1900.

Appendix A

4. In all tables in Appendix A (except A15, A20, and A21) only earliest and latest benchmarks dates are indicated.

Appendix B

Preface

This is the first comparative study of national and sectoral balance sheets. It is based (1) on the national balance sheets of 20 countries, including all the large ones with the exception of Brazil and the People's Republic of China, going back to the late 19th century or beyond for 10 of the countries; and (2) on the sectoral balance sheets of six large countries (France, Germany, Great Britain, India, Japan, and the United States) in the postwar period. While balance sheets I constructed earlier for some of the countries for all or part of the period (Belgium, Germany, India, Japan, Russia/USSR, Switzerland, the United States, and Yugoslavia) could be used, most of the balance sheets had to be developed for this study, often from fragmentary and heterogeneous data.

This pioneering character will, I hope, excuse some of the deficiencies of the study, such as the inclusion of only two less developed countries (India and Mexico), and the limited amount of analysis of the data. Regarding the first deficiency, one cannot construct national or sectoral balance sheets in the absence of data on the value of land, of the reproducible capital stock, and of the main financial instruments oustanding. The mainly descriptive character of the study, on the other hand, reflects the fact that no theory of national balance sheet structure has as yet been proposed.

The purpose of this study is twofold. It is, first, to complete the system of national accounts that now exists for the 20 countries, although in most cases those accounts do not yet go back as far as the national balance sheets used in this study. The second purpose is to provide an essential part, though certainly not all, of a quantitive basis for the analysis of the long-term financial development of these countries for which the national balance sheets go back to at least the eve of World War I. I am fully aware that this study represents only a first step in both directions.

This study is based on about 3000 entries, each measuring the value of one type of tangible or financial asset or liability at one benchmark date in one of 20 countries. Many, if not most, of these entries could be improved by the use of additional known sources or the discovery of new ones, by reexamination of primary or secondary data, by development of alternative techniques of estimation, and by closer adherence to standard definitions. But proceeding in this way would soon encounter decreasing returns in terms of altering the major features of intertemporary changes and international differences in national balance sheets, and thus of modifying conclusions drawn from the imperfect data as they now stand. Additional efforts would be better directed, it seems to me, to extend the period covered by the estimates back to the late 19th century in countries for which they now start at the eve of World War I or the end of World War II—Australia, Canada, Mexico, Russia and Sweden—or, more important, to develop national balance sheets for some of the few developed countries now omitted, primarily the Netherlands and Spain, and for a few important less developed countries of a different type such as Argentina and Brazil; Algeria, Egypt, and Nigeria; and Indonesia and the People's Republic of China.

To conform as far as practicable to the principle of reproducibility, the source or derivation of each estimate has been described briefly in the notes to the country tables in Appendices A and B. To have given the reasons for using one source rather than another possible one; to have justified, or even described exhaustively, the techniques of adjustment applied in each individual case, such as the interpolation or extrapolation; or to have set forth the background of the, unfortunately, not too rare cases of figures labeled "rough estimates," would have increased the size of Appendix A beyond its possibly already excessive length.

The number of countries whose statistical offices now publish their national and sectoral balance sheets, in all cases only for a few recent years, is still very small—France, Great Britain, and Japan—though in a few others—at least Germany, Norway, Sweden, and the United States—official estimates of the reproducible capital stock and flow-of-funds statistics provide the necessary information for most components of national and sectoral balance sheets on an annual basis. It is to be hoped that in a few years a substantially larger number of countries will adopt the scheme proposed several years ago by the United Nations, or at least a somewhat simplified version of it, and will produce national and sectoral balance sheets, if not annually then at short intervals. Studies such as this one will then have a mainly historical interest, and individual workers will be able to concentrate on the analysis of the figures rather than on the construction of the basic data, here national and sectoral balance sheets, as they have been able to do in the case of the other components of the system of national accounts—income and product accounts, input-output tables, and flow-of-funds accounts—during the last one or two decades.

Because of rounding, some subtotals and totals differ slightly from the sum of components.

Thanks are due, first, to many colleagues in the statistical offices and the central banks in most of the countries covered, excluding, of course, the Soviet Union though not Hungary. I do not name them lest they be regarded as accomplices in some of the statistical shortcuts or legerdemains I have committed. Thanks are due also to Franco Modigliani, the organizer of the seminar of the International Economic Association held in Bergamo in June 1980, in which an earlier version of this study, limited to 17 countries (not including Denmark, Mexico, and Switzerland), was presented, and to some of the participants of that seminar. I am indebted to Salvatore Zecchini for collaborating in the construction of the national balance sheet of Italy. Thanks are due, last but not least, to Mrs. Anne Tassi, without whose skill in deciphering my handwriting and in typing the tables this manuscript would never have reached the editor.

Most of the work on the manuscript was done in 1979/80, which will explain why no balance sheets are shown for years later than 1978, and why with few exceptions nothing published after mid-1981 has been taken into account.

Readers not interested in definitional niceties or data problems may disregard Chapter 2 and Appendix C. I hope, though, that they will not entirely neglect Appendix A as it provides, in the case of four countries for which the estimates go back to the late 19th century and have not previously been published—Denmark, France, Great Britain and Italy—as well as for Mexico, an idea of the problems involved in the historical statistics of national balance sheets, and supplies a brief discussion of the development of these countries' infrastructure of national wealth and of their financial superstructure over the last century.

RAYMOND W. GOLDSMITH

New Haven, Connecticut
February 1983

1
The Quintessence

1. Summa Summarum

This section is for readers who are not interested in details, qualifications, and the origins of the estimates on which this study is based; and who trust the author to have made the appropriate allowance for the limitations of his sources in formulating this summary.

National (or sectoral) balance sheets are intended to reflect the structure of tangible and financial assets of a country (or sector) at a point of time, and changes in that structure over time. What then do the balance sheets of the 20 countries, covering between 15 and nearly 300 years of their history, and now accounting for approximately three-fourths of the world's product and wealth, tell us directly about these matters and indirectly about economic and financial development?

1. In the late 1970s tangible assets, usually called national wealth, accounted for nearly three-fifths of the value of planetary assets, and financial assets accounted for fully two-fifths. Land, about equally divided between agricultural land and that used for other purposes, represented fully one-fourth of tangible assets. Dwellings constituted one-fourth of the stock of reproducible assets, nonresidential structures about one-third, equipment approximately one-fifth, inventories and livestock about one-eighth, and consumer durables about one-twelfth. Monetary and other claims against financial institutions represented one-third and their short- and long-term loans were equal to about one-fifth of all financial assets, government securities accounted for about one-tenth, corporate securities for about one-seventh, trade credit for about one-twelth, and foreign investments for approximately one-twentieth. There were, of course, substantial differences among countries, considerably

larger between developed and less developed and between market and centrally planned economies than among developed market economies.

2. The structure of national balance sheets has undergone considerable changes over the past century, changes which can be measured only for the developed market economies, which account for well over two-thirds of planetary assets. The most important of these changes are the sharp reduction in the share of farm land and livestock in national wealth from over two-fifths to less than one-tenth, a change which reflects the declining importance of agriculture, the rise of the share of financial in total assets from approximately one-fourth to one-half, and the increase in the share of financial institutions in total financial assets from about one-eighth to one-third. These increases were offset by declines in the share of government securities, mortgages, and trade credit. This means that the relative size of the financial superstructure has doubled and that it has become increasingly institutionalized.

3. The creation of a modern financial superstructure, not in its details but in its essentials, was generally accomplished at a fairly early stage of a country's economic development, usually within five to seven decades from the start of modern economic growth. Thus it was essentially completed in most now-developed countries by the end of the 19th century or the eve of World War I, though somewhat earlier in Great Britain. During this period the financial interrelations ratio, the quotient of financial and tangible assets, increased fairly continuously and sharply. Since World War I or the Great Depression, however, the ratio in most of these countries has shown no upward trend, though considerable movements have occurred over shorter periods, such as sharp reductions during inflations; and though significant changes have taken place in the relative importance of the various types of financial institutions and of financial instruments. Among less developed countries, on the other hand, the financial interrelations ratio had increased substantially, particularly in the postwar period, though it generally is still well below the level reached by now-developed countries early in the 20th century.

4. National balance sheets by themselves cannot answer the crucial question of the role of the financial superstructure in economic growth. They indicate, however, that modern economic growth has been accompanied in all market economies in the early and intermediate stages of their development by a substantially more than proportionate expansion of their financial superstructure. This suggests that this expansion is a necessary concomitant of economic development in countries of this type until they reach financial maturity, which is reflected in a financial interrelations ratio of the order of unity, i.e., the approximate equality of the value of financial and tangible assets. In a mature modern market economy, on the other hand, a parallel expansion of the size of the real

infrastructure and of the financial superstructure apparently is compatible with sustained economic growth.

5. Within the financial superstructure the importance of financial institutions, measured by their share in total financial assets, has increased in almost all market economies. In this case the trend has continued in most countries into the postwar period. As a result, financial institutions now are either holders or issuers of at least one-half of all financial instruments, and their share exceeds four-fifths in a few market economies, as it does in Soviet-type economies. Among financial institutions, the originally dominating position of the banking system, particularly as the issuer of money, has generally declined at the expense of thrift and insurance organizations but the banking system remains the most important single group of financial institutions.

2. The Planetary Balance Sheet

a) The Global Picture in the Postwar Period

In the late 1970s a planetary balance sheet, rough as it must be, would present approximately the picture shown in table 1, if the balance sheets of the different countries are based on market values, or in the case of most components of reproducible assets on replacement cost, and are combined using the value of their total assets at purchasing power parities as weights. It then appears that in this planetary balance sheet tangible assets, i.e., national wealth, accounted for nearly three-fifths of the planetary assets, and financial assets accounted for two-fifths.

Land, about equally divided between agricultural and other land, represented fully one-fourth of tangible assets and nearly one-sixth of planetary assets. Slightly more than one-half of the stock of reproducible assets had the form of nonresidential structures and equipment, divided approximately in the ratio of two to one. Dwellings accounted for one-fourth of all reproducible assets—their share including the underlying land in all tangible assets is about the same—and (including land) about one-seventh of planetary assets. The shares of inventories (including livestock) and of consumer durables, with one-eighth and one-twelfth of reproducible assets, and with 5½ and 3½ percent of planetary assets, were much smaller.

The monetary and other claims against financial institutions were the largest single component of financial assets accounting for over one-third of the total. Short- and long-term loans of these institutions constituted another fourth of all assets, well ahead of government and corporate securities with fully one-tenth and one-seventh, respectively, and trade

Table 1 **Structure of the Planetary Balance Sheet, 1950 and 1978[a] (National Weights)**

	1950[a]							1978[a]						
	Market Economies			Centrally Planned Economies				Market Economies			Centrally Planned Economies			
	Developed (1)	Less Developed (2)	All (3)	Developed (4)	Less Developed (5)	All (6)	World (7)	Developed (8)	Less Developed (9)	All (10)	Developed (11)	Less Developed (12)	All (13)	World (14)
I. Tangible assets	51.3	69.7	54.6	76.0	91.4	81.2	58.1	50.8	65.0	53.1	77.6	91.4	80.6	57.4
1. Land	13.0	30.3	16.1	25.6	51.4	34.4	18.5	13.6	14.9	13.8	17.7	51.4	25.0	15.5
a) Agricultural	6.0	27.2	9.8	22.2	47.4	30.6	12.5	3.6	9.3	4.6	10.9	47.4	18.7	6.8
b) Other	7.0	3.1	6.3	3.4	4.0	3.7	6.0	10.0	5.6	9.2	6.8	4.0	6.3	8.7
2. Reproducible assets	38.3	39.4	38.5	50.3	40.0	46.8	39.6	37.2	49.9	39.4	59.9	40.0	55.6	41.8
a) Dwellings	11.4	7.9	10.7	13.1	9.8	12.0	10.9	11.2	11.1	11.2	9.7	9.8	9.7	10.9
b) Other structures and equipment	17.8	16.9	17.7	20.8	16.9	19.5	17.8	18.4	29.8	20.3	36.1	16.9	32.0	22.1
c) Inventories	4.3	6.1	4.6	11.2	6.9	9.7	5.3	3.6	4.5	3.8	9.0	6.9	8.5	4.5
d) Livestock	0.8	4.9	1.6	2.6	3.4	2.8	1.8	0.4	1.1	0.5	1.5	3.4	1.9	0.8
e) Consumer durables	4.0	3.6	3.9	2.6	3.0	2.7	3.8	3.6	3.3	3.6	3.7	3.0	3.5	3.5

II. Financial assets	47.2	30.3	44.2	24.0	8.6	18.8	40.9	46.4	35.0	44.6	22.4	8.6	19.4	40.5
1. Monetary metals	0.8	0.2	0.7	0.2	0.0	...	0.6	0.4	0.4	0.4	0.3	0.0	0.2	0.4
2. Claims against financial institutions	14.5	8.2	13.3	7.2	1.8	5.4	12.3	16.1	10.7	15.2	12.1	1.8	9.9	14.1
3. Loans by financial institutions[b]	4.1	3.3	4.0	6.2	1.8	4.7	4.1	6.4	5.5	6.2	8.0	1.8	6.6	6.3
4. Mortgages	2.4	3.4	2.6	0.2	...	0.1	2.3	4.5	...	3.7	0.2	...	0.2	3.2
5. Government debt	11.0	3.0	9.6	5.6	0.6	3.9	8.9	5.5	3.4	5.1	...	0.6	0.1	4.4
6. Corporate bonds	1.3	0.3	1.2	...	...	...	1.0	1.8	...	1.5	...	...	...	1.3
7. Corporate stock	7.2	6.0	7.0	...	...	...	6.1	5.5	5.7	5.5	...	...	...	4.7
8. Trade credit	3.2	4.8	3.5	4.8	4.4	4.7	3.6	3.4	3.7	3.5	1.8	4.4	2.4	3.3
9. Other	2.7	1.2	2.3	...	...	...	2.0	2.9	5.7	3.4	...	...	...	2.9
III. Foreign assets[c]	1.5	...	1.2	...	...	...	1.0	2.8	...	2.3	...	...	...	2.0
IV. National assets	100.0	100.0	100.0	100.0	100.0	100.0	100.0	100.0	100.0	100.0	100.0	100.0	100.0	100.0

[a]Standard benchmark dates; for actual years see table 33.

[b]Excluding mortgages.

[c]Gross or net if positive.

Source:

The structure ratios for individual countries shown in Appendix A are weighted by the value of their national assets in dollars of 1970, which are obtained by applying the asset-product ratios in cols. 1 and 8 of the 15 developed market economies; in cols. 2 and 9 those of India and Mexico; in cols. 4 and 12 those of the Soviet Union in 1950 and 1977; and in cols. 5 and 12 that of the Soviet Union in 1928. The estimates of national products in dollars of 1970 are for market economies those of Summers, Kravis, and Heston (1980). Those for the centrally planned developed economies are based on the relation of their assets to those of the United States (Block, 1979, 122). That for centrally planned less-developed economies is a very rough estimate assuming purchasing power to be three times as high as exchange rate, a ratio well below in 1950 but about equal in 1977 to that of the Indian Subcontinent (Summers, Kravis, and Heston 1980).

credit with about one-twelfth. Foreign investments represented on a worldwide scale approximately 5 percent of all financial assets and 2 percent of planetary assets.

Over a quarter century of far-reaching changes in the world economy one might expect substantial alterations in the structure of the planetary balance sheet. Table 1, however, shows the changes between the middle of the century and the late 1970s to have been moderate, though not insignificant. Thus the fundamental relation between tangible and financial assets hardly changed as the planetary financial interrelations ratio (financial and foreign assets divided by tangible assets) rose only from 0.72 to 0.74, a negligible change given the margins of uncertainty in the data. There were, however, some significant changes within tangible and financial assets. One of them was the reduction in the share of agricultural land and livestock in tangible assets from about one-fourth to one-eighth, evidence of the continuing decline of the importance of agriculture in the world economy. The increase in the share of nonresidential structures and equipment in tangible assets from fully 30 to nearly 40 percent, a rough indicator of the progress of industrialization, was another. Among financial assets, the claims against and the loans (including mortgages) by financial institutions continued their secular upward trend, rising from nearly two-fifths to nearly one-half of the total. The share of government debt declined sharply from over one-fifth around 1950, when recent war debts bulked heavily, to one-tenth in the late 1970s, a movement which in part reflected the reduction of the weight of old debt through inflation. The doubling of the share of foreign assets from about 2½ to over 4½ percent (both figures slightly understated because of the unavailability of data for the smaller developed market and the less developed market, and for the centrally planned economies) was moderate in view of the rapid expansion of international lending and investment during the postwar period, and probably failed to restore the ratio to the level it had in the late 19th and early 20th centuries.

The similarity between the planetary balance sheets of the mid-century and the late 1970s was due, on the one hand, to the absence of substantial differences in the share of the main groups in planetary assets and, on the other, to the generally moderate, though more pronounced, changes in the structure of the combined balance sheets of the four groups.

It has not been possible to construct a planetary balance sheet for any date before World War II. The combined balance sheets for between five and 10 developed market economies discussed in the following section permit, however, the observation of changes since the middle of the 19th century in the balance sheet structure of that segment of the world economy, which accounted in terms of national product or national assets for at least one-half of the planetary total.

There is probably more interest for purposes of economic and financial analysis in similarities and differences in national balance sheet structure among the four broad groups of countries and among individual countries in each group. Since the latter subject will be studied in some detail in Chapter 3, the discussion will be limited here to some important features of differences in the structure of the combined balance sheets of the four groups of countries.

The differences between developed and less developed market economies, which can be followed in more detail in table 1, were as expected: the share of tangible assets, particularly agricultural land, nonresidential structures, inventories, and livestock was higher, and that of dwellings lower in less-developed countries. Among financial assets, the shares of most financial instruments were lower except for trade credit and miscellaneous claims. Astonishingly the share of corporate stock was about the same, the result of using Mexico as one of the two countries on which the group average for less developed market economies is based. Differences were, of course, pronounced between market and centrally planned economies even though the weight of less developed countries was not too different in the two groups, one-sixth among market and more than one-fifth among planned economies.

The share of tangible assets was much lower and that of financial much higher in market economies, in the ratio of about 1⅛ to one for market and four to one for centrally planned economies, implying widely different financial interrelations ratios of approximately 0.88 and 0.24, respectively. Among tangible assets, agricultural land accounted for slightly less than one-tenth in market economies, but for nearly one-fourth in centrally planned economies. Dwellings represented one-fifth of tangible assets in market economies, but only one-eighth in centrally planned economies, while the share of inventories and livestock with one-eighth was much higher in the latter compared to one-twelfth in the former. The differences were, as might be expected, much more pronounced among financial assets. Four categories of financial instruments (mortgages, government debt, and corporate bonds and stocks) which accounted for approximately one-third of all financial assets in market economies were virtually absent in centrally planned economies. On the other hand, the claims against and the loans by the monobank, which is common to all planned economies following the Soviet model, accounted for nearly seven-eighths of their financial assets compared to about 45 percent in market economies.

The distribution of planetary assets and their main components among the four broad groups of countries near mid-century and in the late 1970s can be followed in table 2. At both dates the developed market economies held 70 percent of planetary assets, the less developed market economies about 15 percent, and the centrally planned economies the

Table 2 **Regional Distribution of Planetary Assets, 1950 and 1978[a] (% of World Total)**

	1950[a]						1978[a]					
	Market Economies			Centrally Planned Economies			Market Economies			Centrally Planned Economies		
	Developed (1)	Less Developed (2)	All (3)	Developed (4)	Less Developed (5)	All (6)	Developed (7)	Less Developed (8)	All (9)	Developed (10)	Less Developed (11)	All (12)
I. Tangible assets	63	18	81	12	7	19	62	17	79	16	5	21
1. Land	49	25	74	13	3	16	61	14	75	14	11	25
a) Agricultural	32	33	65	17	18	35	37	20	57	20	23	43
b) Other	82	10	92	5	3	8	80	9	89	9	2	11
2. Reproducible assets	69	15	84	11	5	16	62	17	79	18	3	21
a) Dwellings	75	10	85	11	4	15	71	15	86	11	3	14
b) Other structures and equipment	71	14	85	10	5	15	58	19	77	20	3	23
c) Inventories	58	17	75	19	6	25	56	15	71	24	5	29
d) Livestock	34	43	77	14	9	23	37	22	59	26	15	41
e) Consumer durables	76	14	90	6	4	10	71	13	84	13	3	16

II. Financial assets	83	11	94	5	1	6	80	12	92	7	1	8
1. Monetary metals	85	15	100	0	0	0	75	15	90	10	0	10
2. Claims against financial institutions	84	10	94	5	1	6	78	11	89	10	1	11
3. Loans by financial institutions[b]	74	11	85	13	2	15	71	13	84	15	1	16
4. Mortgages	86	13	99	1	0	1	99	0	99	1	0	1
5. Government debt	89	5	94	6	0	6	88	12	100	0	0	0
6. Corporate bonds	96	4	100	0	0	0	100	0	0	0	0	0
7. Corporate stocks	85	15	100	0	0	0	82	18	100	0	0	0
8. Trade credit	63	19	82	12	6	18	72	16	88	7	5	12
9. Other	79	21	100	0	0	0	70	30	100	0	0	0
III. Foreign assets	100	0	0	0	0	0	100	0	0	0	0	0
IV. National assets	70	16	86	9	5	14	70	15	85	12	3	15

[a]Standard benchmark dates; for actual years see table 33.
[b]Excluding mortgages.
Source: As for table 1.

remaining 15 percent, of which two-thirds around 1950 but four-fifths in the late 1970s were accounted for by the developed economies in the group. It may be unexpected that the distribution of planetary assets among the four groups was virtually the same at the beginning and the end of a quarter century of rapid and varied economic development.

The distribution differed substantially among the two main components of planetary assets. The share of developed market economies was only slightly above three-fifths for national wealth, while that of less developed market and of centrally planned economies was close to one-fifth each. On the other hand, the developed market economies held about four-fifths of all financial assets, the less developed a little more than the centrally planned economies somewhat less than one-tenth. This difference, which did not change substantially over the period, is the necessary consequence of the fact that the share of tangible in total assets was considerably lower and that of financial assets much higher among developed market economies than it is in the three other groups.

The differences in and the deviations from the share in planetary assets was much more pronounced for some of the components of tangible and of financial assets. The share of market economies was necessarily at or close to 100 percent for corporate securities, government debt, and mortgages because these financial instruments do not exist or are of negligible importance in centrally planned economies. On the other hand, trade credit, which had to be very roughly estimated in many countries, was less unequally distributed among the four groups than any other financial instrument.

Among tangible assets, deviations from the share in planetary assets were most pronounced, and hence the distribution among the four groups least unequal, in the case of agricultural land and livestock. In the late 1970s the share of the developed market economies in these two assets was somewhat in excess of one-third, while less developed market economies and developed and less developed centrally planned economies each accounted for about one-fifth. Land, moreover, is one of the few cases in which the distribution changed substantially between mid-century and the late 1970s, as the share of the less developed market economies declined from one-third to one-fifth in the process of industrialization. The share of centrally planned economies in planetary inventories was well above that in all tangible assets, their relative large size being a well-known characteristic of their system. At the other extreme, the share of dwellings and particularly of nonagricultural land in reproducible assets in developed market economies, considerably exceeded at both dates that in all tangible assets, reflecting the higher proportion of these two components in the balance sheet of these economies.

Up to this point the reader has been asked to take the figures of tables 1 and 2 on trust. Some explanation of the derivation of these tables and some discussion of the limitations of the figures is therefore overdue. Essentially two problems are involved: the representativeness of the countries whose balance sheets have been combined to produce the totals for the four groups, and the adequacy of the weighting system used.

There is little doubt that the 15 (14 in 1950) developed market economies whose balance sheets have been combined are entirely representative of the group, since they account for over nine-tenths of its national product (in dollars of 1970); and there is no indication that the dozen smaller countries not included, the most important of which are the Netherlands and Spain, have a balance sheet structure or asset-product ratios that significantly differ from those of the 15 countries. Although the combined balance sheet of the developed centrally planned economies is based solely on the balance sheet structure of the Soviet Union, it should be quite representative for that group. The national product of the Soviet Union accounted for over three-fifths (1950) or more than two-thirds (1977) percent of the group's national product, and it is likely, and indeed known in the case of Hungary, that the structure of the balance sheet of the satellites of the USSR is similar to its own, partly as a result of economic and financial policies common to all members of the bloc.

Representativeness is, however, a serious problem for the group of less developed market economies. The structural coefficients for that group shown in tables 1 and 2 are a combination of the balance sheets of India and Mexico. In this combination Mexico was allocated a weight corresponding to the share of the national product in terms of purchasing power of all Latin American and Caribbean countries in that of all less developed market economies—one-third in 1950, two-fifths in 1977—while India was used to represent the less developed market economies in Asia and Africa, except that the share of Indian gold and silver hoards, which are known to be nonexistent in other countries of that group, were disregarded. This is, of course, a risky procedure. India accounted for only two-fifths percent in 1950 and one-third in 1977 of the aggregate national product of this subgroup on a purchasing power basis, and the corresponding ratios were even lower—about one-sixth—for Mexico.

There are no comprehensive data to establish whether and how the national balance sheet structure of the other countries in these two subgroups deviate from those of the two countries used here to represent them; and, possibly even more serious, to what extent the asset-product ratio differs. All that can be said is that the real national product per head of the two countries is close to the average for the subgroup which they represent in the case of Mexico, and only about one-fourth below it in that of India.

In the case of the less developed centrally planned economies, it is not the representative character which is at stake since one single country, the People's Republic of China, has been estimated to account for about seven-eighths of the group's aggregate national product (Block 1979, 122). The difficulty rather is that no estimate exists of the structure of China's national wealth or financial assets. In this situation the structure of the national assets of the Soviet Union in 1928, when that country was near the beginning of its process of industrialization, though its real national product per head was substantially above that of China in the late 1970s, has been used as a substitute. Use of the structure ratios of the Soviet Union in 1937, which may be preferable, would not make a substantial difference in the weighted average of all centrally planned economies and would hardly be noticeable in the world total because of the low weight—about 5 percent of the planetary total—of the less developed planned economies, and because the differences between the Soviet structure ratios of 1928 and 1937 are not radical.

It thus appears that the use of the balance sheet structure of 15 countries for all developed market economies and of the Soviet Union for all developed centrally planned economies is not likely to result in figures significantly different from those that would be obtained if national balance sheets were available for all countries in these two groups. Since these two groups account for approximately four-fifths of the planetary total, the structure of the national balance sheets of the less developed countries which represent the remaining one-fifth would have to deviate radically from those of India, Mexico, and the Soviet Union in 1928, respectively, which have been used here as their representatives, to result in planetary balance sheets whose structure would be significantly different from the picture shown in tables 1 and 2. If, to take an extreme case, the share of agricultural land in national assets in less developed planned economies were either 50 percent higher or 50 percent lower than estimated in table 1, its share in the planetary assets would rise to 7.1 percent or fall to 6.4 percent compared to the share of 6.8 percent of table 1.

The weights applied to the 20 countries to derive the balance sheets structure ratios for the four groups and their combination into the planetary balance sheet were obtained by multiplying their national products in dollars of 1970 (as estimated for market economies by Summers, Kravis, and Heston 1980) by the asset/product ratios for the countries regarded as representative for each group. The procedure, therefore, assumes that the asset/product ratios for the other countries in the group on the average did not deviate from those of the countries treated as representative. This assumption seems, as just explained, justified for developed market and centrally planned economies, but is doubtful for the two groups of less developed countries. If one wants to avoid this assumption one may use as weights the national products of the individual countries, at exchange rates or purchasing power parities, because statistics permit the determination of the share of the representative countries in the total national product of their group, a ratio which is not known for national assets. This approach avoids one assumption undoubtedly subject to a considerable margin of error for the less developed countries, but it ignores the undoubtedly significant differences in the asset/product ratios among the four groups. A comparison between the structure of the national balance sheet using these three different weighting systems, which is provided in table 3, therefore seems not without interest.

It will be seen that the differences in the structure of the planetary balance sheet under the three weighting systems were moderate. In the balance sheets using purchasing power parities, the types of assets which are relatively more important in less developed market and in centrally planned economies—particularly agricultural land, nonresidential structures and equipment, and inventories—had lower shares in the planetary balance sheet based on each group's assets than in that based on their national product because of the lower asset/product ratios of these countries. For the same reason financial assets, which are relatively more important in developed market economies, showed higher shares in the planetary balance sheet using asset weights. The difference was most pronounced in the case of mortgages, government debt, and corporate securities, in part because these types of assets are virtually absent from the balance sheets of centrally planned economies. The differences were in the opposite direction when the planetary balance sheets using national product weight on the basis of either exchange rates or purchasing power parities are studied. Now the assets which are relatively more important in less developed markets and in centrally planned economies showed higher shares in the planetary balance sheet calculated on the basis of the purchasing power equivalent of their national product, while the shares of those of less importance for them were lower. As a result of these offsetting tendencies the differences in the structure of the planetary balance sheet using, on the one hand, asset purchasing power weights and, on the other, exchange rate national product weights were small, indeed almost negligible, in view of the roughness of most of the estimates, except for agricultural land, government debt, and corporate stock.

The differences among the changes in the structure of the planetary balance sheet between mid-century and the late 1970s among the three weighting systems were similarly moderate.

Finally, a word of caution. The figures in tables 1 and 2 cannot be better than the estimates of the balance sheet structures of the 20 countries whose qualifications and limitations are discussed in some detail in Chapter 2, and will be evident in the notes and comments to the basic country tables in Appendix A. Indeed, they must be worse because the problems of representativeness and weighting introduce margins of uncertainty additional to the limitations of the basic country balance sheets. On the other hand, some of the errors in the balance sheets of the

Table 3 **Structure of the Planetary Balance Sheet under Different Weighting Systems, 1950 and 1978**[a]

	1950			1978		
		National Product			National Product	
	Assets (1)	Exchange Rates (2)	Purchasing Power (3)	Assets (4)	Exchange Rates (5)	Purchasing Power (6)
I. Tangible assets	58.1	58.7	61.9	57.4	59.0	61.5
1. Land	18.5	18.5	21.4	15.5	16.4	17.0
a) Agricultural	12.5	12.7	15.7	6.8	7.7	9.3
b) Other	6.0	5.9	5.7	8.7	8.7	7.7
2. Reproducible assets	39.6	40.3	40.4	41.8	42.6	44.5
a) Dwellings	10.9	11.1	10.9	10.9	10.7	10.8
b) Other structures and equipment	17.8	18.0	17.9	22.1	22.9	24.3
c) Inventories	5.3	5.7	5.9	4.5	4.7	5.0
d) Livestock	1.8	1.8	2.1	0.8	0.8	0.9
e) Consumer durables	3.8	3.7	3.7	3.5	3.5	3.5
II. Financial assets	40.9	40.3	37.3	40.5	39.2	37.0
1. Monetary metals	0.6	0.6	0.5	0.4	0.2	0.2
2. Claims against financial institutions	12.3	12.2	11.2	14.1	14.2	13.4
3. Loans by financial institutions[b]	4.1	4.2	3.9	6.3	6.2	6.2
4. Mortgages	2.3	1.7	1.7	3.2	3.0	2.5
5. Government debt	8.9	9.0	7.8	4.4	3.9	3.5
6. Corporate bonds	1.0	0.9	0.8	1.3	1.2	1.0
7. Corporate stocks	6.1	5.8	5.3	4.7	4.3	4.2
8. Trade credit	3.6	3.7	3.9	3.3	3.3	3.2
9. Other	2.0	2.2	2.1	2.9	2.8	2.8
III. Foreign assets	1.0	1.0	0.8	2.0	1.8	1.5
IV. National assets	100.0	100.0	100.0	100.0	100.0	100.0

[a]Standard benchmark dates; for actual years see table 33. [b]Excluding mortgages

Source: For cols. 1 and 4 table 1; for cols. 3 and 6 same procedure omitting multiplication of national product totals by asset/product ratios; for cols. 2 and 5 national products at current exchange rates are used as weights; for 1978 from The World Bank, *World Development Report, 1980* 110 ff.

individual countries offset each other in the combination group balance sheets and ultimately into the planetary balance sheet. Nevertheless, the entries for less developed centrally planned economies should not be regarded as figures in their own right but only as stopgaps necessary for the derivation of balance sheet structure coefficients of all centrally planned economies and for the world as a whole. Since the less developed planned economies, i.e., essentially the People's Republic of China, can hardly account for as much as one-tenth of planetary assets, inappropriate figures for this group cannot, as has already been stressed, significantly affect the structure of the planetary balance sheet.

b) Developed Market Economies, 1850–1978

For these countries, which now account for well over two-thirds of the world's assets, though numbering only about two dozen out of 150-odd members of the United Nations and accounting for less than one-fourth of the world's population, we are on firmer ground, as the 15 countries for which national balance sheets are available for the postwar period hold well over nine-tenths of the total assets or national product of the group. Figures are lacking to determine the proportion of the then-developed market economies represented by the six to 10 countries for which national balance sheets are available for the benchmark dates between the middle of the 19th century and the eve of World War II. There is little doubt, however, that they also accounted throughout the period for about nine-tenths of all countries which could then be regarded as developed market economies, and thus would have to exclude Russia and the countries in the Balkan and Iberian peninsulas. Moreover, there is no reason to assume that the structure of the national balance sheets of the countries not covered, the only important ones of which are the Netherlands and Austria-Hungary—already a borderline case—differed sufficiently from that of the six to 10 countries included to affect the combined balance sheet significantly. There is, therefore, again no question of representativeness.

In tables 4–6 the seven (four in 1850) developed European market economies are separated from the United States, whose share in the group's aggregate national product increased from not much over one-fifth in 1850 to about one-half since the end of the century. (The share of the United States would be slightly lower in the interwar period, but substantially so up to 1913, on the basis of the purchasing power of assets, because the asset/product ratio of the United States has always been lower than that of the European countries, though the difference has been diminishing over time.) The purpose of this separation is to permit ascertaining to what extent the average for the eight (five in 1850)

Table 4 Combined National Balance Sheet of Eight Developed Market Economies, 1850, 1875, and 1895[a]

	1850			1875			1895		
	Four European[d]	U.S.A.	Five	Seven European[c]	U.S.A.	Eight	Seven European[e]	U.S.A.	Eight
Weights (%)[b]	78.0	22.0	100.0	65.7	34.3	100.0	51.0	49.0	100.0
	(1)	(2)	(3)	(4)	(5)	(6)	(7)	(8)	(9)
I. Tangible assets	75.2	68.1	73.5	62.9	60.9	62.3	48.4	58.5	53.4
1. Land	34.4	28.1	33.0	27.8	18.9	25.1	17.4	20.4	18.9
a) Agricultural	30.0	24.4	28.8	24.0	11.9	20.4	14.0	9.6	11.9
b) Other	4.4	3.7	4.2	3.8	7.0	4.8	3.4	10.8	7.0
2. Reproducible assets	40.6	40.0	40.5	35.6	42.0	37.2	31.0	38.0	34.4
a) Dwellings	11.3	7.4	10.4	9.2	7.7	8.8	7.6	10.4	9.0
b) Other structures and equipment	20.5	19.2	20.3	17.9	18.8	18.1	16.7	17.0	16.9
c) Inventories	4.1	5.6	4.4	3.9	8.8	5.4	3.3	4.5	3.9
d) Livestock	2.7	5.0	3.2	2.4	2.8	2.5	1.8	2.1	1.9
e) Consumer durables	2.2	2.8	2.3	1.7	3.8	2.3	1.6	4.0	2.8

II. Financial assets	23.5	31.4	25.3	31.9	38.3	33.6	43.2	40.8	42.0
1. Monetary metals	1.5	1.4	1.5	1.3	0.9	1.2	0.9	0.9	0.9
2. Claims against financial institutions	3.0	4.0	3.2	6.5	5.3	6.2	10.3	8.3	9.3
3. Loans by financial institutions[c]	1.0	3.6	1.6	2.5	2.8	2.6	4.4	4.2	4.3
4. Mortgages	5.0	2.0	4.3	5.5	2.6	4.6	6.2	4.5	5.4
5. Government debt	6.7	3.3	5.9	6.8	4.9	6.2	6.5	2.2	4.4
6. Corporate bonds	1.2	2.5	1.5	2.4	4.2	3.0	3.1	3.4	3.2
7. Corporate stocks	1.9	5.8	2.8	3.2	9.2	5.0	8.5	9.1	8.8
8. Trade credit	3.2	6.5	3.9	3.5	5.5	4.1	3.5	3.8	3.6
9. Other	0.0	2.3	0.5	0.0	2.8	0.9	0.0	4.3	2.1
III. Foreign assets	1.4	0.5	1.2	5.2	0.8	3.9	8.4	0.7	4.6
IV. National assets	100.0	100.0	100.0	100.0	100.0	100.0	100.0	100.0	100.0

[a]Standard benchmark dates; for actual years see table 31.
[b]Gross national product in $ of 1970.
[c]Excluding II.4.
[d]France, Germany, Great Britain, and Italy.
[e]Also, Denmark, Norway and Switzerland.
Source of basic data: Country tables in Appendix A.

Table 5 **Combined National Balance Sheet of Eight Developed Market Economies, 1913, 1929, and 1939**[a]

	1913			1929			1939		
	Seven European	U.S.A.	Eight	Seven European	U.S.A.	Eight	Seven European	U.S.A.	Eight
Weights (%)[b]	54.2	45.8	100.0	49.2	50.8	100.0	46.6	53.4	100.0
	(1)	(2)	(3)	(4)	(5)	(6)	(7)	(8)	(9)
I. Tangible assets	49.3	54.7	51.6	52.7	43.7	48.1	49.5	43.1	46.0
1. Land	14.6	19.3	16.7	12.2	11.8	12.0	10.0	10.2	10.1
a) Agricultural	10.6	10.5	10.5	7.6	3.6	5.6	5.8	2.7	4.1
b) Other	4.0	8.8	6.1	4.6	8.2	6.4	4.2	7.5	6.0
2. Reproducible assets	34.6	35.4	35.0	40.5	32.0	36.2	39.5	32.9	35.9
a) Dwellings	8.4	8.4	8.4	10.4	9.3	9.8	10.0	9.9	9.9
b) Other structures and equipment	19.3	16.9	18.2	22.5	14.3	18.5	22.7	15.7	18.9
c) Inventories	3.6	3.7	3.7	3.4	3.3	3.3	3.3	2.9	3.1
d) Livestock	1.8	1.9	1.8	1.7	0.7	1.2	1.2	0.6	0.9
e) Consumer durables	1.5	4.5	2.8	2.6	4.4	3.5	2.3	3.7	3.0

II. Financial assets	42.2	43.7	42.9	43.7	54.1	49.0	47.3	52.8	50.3
1. Monetary metals	1.0	0.8	0.9	0.6	0.5	0.5	0.3	2.3	1.4
2. Claims against financial institutions	11.7	9.2	10.6	12.6	9.2	10.9	15.1	16.4	15.8
3. Loans by financial institutions[c]	4.8	4.8	4.8	5.3	4.7	5.0	5.4	2.3	3.7
4. Mortgages	5.5	4.0	4.8	2.8	4.8	3.8	4.2	4.1	4.2
5. Government debt	6.1	1.9	4.2	10.9	3.4	7.1	9.8	7.7	8.7
6. Corporate bonds	2.8	4.8	3.7	1.4	3.9	2.7	1.1	3.7	2.5
7. Corporate stocks	7.0	12.5	9.4	7.1	19.4	13.4	8.1	11.7	10.0
8. Trade credit	3.3	2.7	3.1	3.0	2.7	2.9	3.3	1.7	2.4
9. Other	0.1	3.1	1.4	0.0	5.4	2.7	0.0	3.0	1.6
III. Foreign assets	8.5	1.6	5.5	3.6	2.2	2.9	3.1	4.0	3.6
IV. National assets	100.0	100.0	100.0	100.0	100.0	100.0	100.0	100.0	100.0

[a]Standard benchmark dates; for actual years see table 33.
[b]Gross national product in $ of 1970.
[c]Excluding mortgages.
Sources: As for table 4.

Table 6 **Combined National Balance Sheet of 15 Developed Market Economies, 1950, 1965, and 1978**[a]

	1950			1965			1978		
	Seven European	U.S.A.	Fourteen[c]	Seven European	U.S.A.	Fifteen[c]	Seven European	U.S.A.	Fifteen[c]
Weights (%)[b]	32.1	50.5	100.0	32.3	47.2	100.0	32.7	42.1	100.0
	(1)	(2)	(3)	(4)	(5)	(6)	(7)	(8)	(9)
I. Tangible assets	56.8	46.0	51.3	47.9	43.8	47.3	50.9	50.2	50.5
1. Land	13.6	9.0	13.0	9.4	10.7	13.0	10.4	12.5	13.1
a) Agricultural	7.5	2.4	6.0	4.6	2.4	4.0	3.8	2.7	3.4
b) Other	6.1	6.6	7.0	4.8	8.3	9.0	6.6	9.8	9.7
2. Reproducible assets	43.2	37.0	38.3	38.5	33.1	34.3	40.5	37.7	37.4
a) Dwellings	12.9	12.0	11.4	10.8	9.6	10.0	14.5	11.1	11.3
b) Other structures and equipment	21.6	15.6	17.8	19.0	15.3	16.3	18.8	17.6	18.5
c) Inventories	4.9	3.7	4.3	3.9	3.8	3.7	3.4	4.2	3.6
d) Livestock	1.0	0.6	0.8	0.6	0.3	0.5	0.4	0.3	0.4
e) Consumer durables	2.7	5.0	4.0	4.2	4.1	3.7	3.4	4.5	3.6

II. Financial assets	43.0	51.6	47.2	50.3	54.1	51.1	45.0	47.3	46.8
1. Monetary metals	0.3	1.3	0.8	0.5	0.2	0.3	0.5	0.3	0.4
2. Claims against financial institutions	13.6	15.7	14.5	17.1	13.5	15.4	19.3	13.3	16.2
3. Loans by financial institutions[d]	4.8	2.5	4.1	6.2	4.8	5.9	5.8	5.5	6.5
4. Mortgages	2.0	3.3	2.4	3.4	5.9	4.1	4.3	6.6	4.5
5. Government debt	10.5	12.7	11.0	6.8	6.6	6.2	5.2	6.2	5.5
6. Corporate bonds	0.5	1.9	1.3	1.0	2.1	1.8	0.6	2.4	1.8
7. Corporate stocks	6.6	8.0	7.2	11.2	15.8	12.4	4.3	7.3	5.5
8. Trade credit	4.1	2.4	3.2	3.4	2.2	3.1	3.6	2.2	3.4
9. Other	0.5	3.8	2.7	0.6	2.9	1.9	1.4	3.4	2.9
III. Foreign assets	0.3	2.4	1.5	1.8	2.1	1.6	4.3	2.5	2.6
IV. National assets	100.0	100.0	100.0	100.0	100.0	100.0	100.0	100.0	100.0

[a]Standard benchmark dates; for actual years see table 33.

[b]Gross national product in $ of 1970.

[c]Also includes Australia, Belgium, Canada, Israel, Japan, South Africa, and Sweden in 1965 and 1978.

[d]Excluding II.4.

Source: As for table 4.

countries is representative for both of its main components. It will be seen that the differences in structure are in general small, particularly from 1875 on. Exceptions, fairly pronounced, e.g., in the two types of land and particularly in corporate stock can be followed in tables 4–6. The structure of the national balance sheets thus shows significant and generally common trends over the period of nearly a century.

The most important of these trends are the sharp decline in the share of agricultural land and livestock in both national assets and national wealth from one-third to 4 percent of the former and from well over two-fifths to 8 percent of the latter and the doubling in the share of financial in national assets from one-fourth to one-half. Within financial assets the main changes were the increase of the assets of financial institutions from one-eighth to one-third; the decline of the share of government debt from nearly one-fourth to not much over one-tenth; that of mortgages from one-sixth to one-twelfth and that of trade credit from 15 to 6 percent. The share of corporate stock was the same—not much over one-tenth—at the beginning and the end of the period, after having reached a peak of about one-fourth in 1929 at the end of the stock market boom of the 1920s. Turning to national wealth, we find that the shares of dwellings with about one-tenth of national and one-fourth of reproducible assets and those of other structures and equipment with about one-fifth of the former and about one-half of the latter were approximately the same at the beginning and the end of the period. Among the smaller components the share of inventories declined moderately, while that of consumer durables increased substantially. Changes, or lack of them, may, of course, reflect either changes in the structures of individual countries' national balance sheets, or changes in the weight of these countries, or a combination of both factors which may reinforce their effect or offset each other.

Changes in the structure of the combined national balance sheets of the 15 developed market economies between mid-century and the late 1970s—when it was very similar to that of the eight covered for the preceding century—were quite small. Among the more important ones were the continued decline in the share of agricultural land and the rise of that of other land approximately offsetting each other; another rise in the share of assets and loans of financial institutions; a sharp decline in the share of government debt, as increasing inflation reduced the weight of wartime borrowings; and a substantial reduction in the share of corporate stock in the second half of the period as stock prices failed to keep pace with inflation. The crucial financial interrelations ratio was approximately the same at the beginning and the end of the period—0.95 and 0.98, respectively, after having reached 1.09 in the mid-1960s. For claims alone, however, the ratio showed an upward trend from 0.76 to 0.81.

The similarity or difference among the shares of the various assets among the eight or 15 developed market economies is illustrated in table 7 for the eight or three benchmark dates by their coefficients of variation. The coefficient is lowest, i.e., differences are least pronounced, for the shares of the three large components of all tangible, reproducible, and financial assets. They are lower for the components of reproducible assets, except livestock, and for nonagricultural land (partly because of the method of estimation of the latter) than for agricultural land. Among financial assets they are considerably lower, indicating more structural homogeneity, for total assets and loans of financial institutions and for trade credit than for the shares of monetary metals—very small in absolute terms—of mortgages, of government debt, and of corporate securities. This indicates that differences in the financial superstructure are primarily reflected in the relative importance of these three types of financial instruments. The level of the coefficients for the three benchmark years 1950, 1965, and 1978 is fairly similar for the group of eight and 15 countries suggesting that the original eight and the supplementary seven countries have a similar national balance sheet structure.

No clear trends are visible in the coefficients of variation over the century among the eight countries shown in table 7. Among the 17 types of assets being distinguished, 12 show a decrease and five an increase in their coefficients of variation between the beginning and the end of the period, the prevalence of declines being pronounced for tangible assets (six of seven types), but the net differences are generally small and the movements between the eight benchmark dates far from regular. There is therefore at best a slight tendency among developed market economies to become more similar in national balance sheet structure, a tendency which is considerably more pronounced among tangible than among financial assets. This may reflect the greater importance of technological factors for the structure of national wealth than for that of the financial superstructure, but it would require intensive statistical and institutional analysis before proposing such a hypothesis.

3. The Growth of National Assets

A first impression of the expansion of national balance sheets over the past century for each of the up to 20 countries is provided in table 8 in the form of the average annual rates of growth of national assets in current prices between every two balance sheet dates, usually separated by one to two decades as well as, when the figures are available, for three longer time spans, namely, for the four decades of pre–World War I normalcy, for the nearly four decades of the very heterogeneous interwar period, for the nearly three decades of the post–World War II period, as well as in the case of 11 countries for the entire century. In this section all qualifica-

Table 7 **Similarity of National Balance Sheet Structures in Developed Market Economies Measured by the Coefficient of Variation, 1875–1978[a]**

	Standard Benchmark Year										
	Eight Countries								15 Countries		
	1875 (1)	1895 (2)	1913 (3)	1929 (4)	1939 (5)	1950 (6)	1965 (7)	1978 (8)	1950 (9)	1965 (10)	1978 (11)
I. Tangible assets	0.18	0.26	0.22	0.28	0.27	0.24	0.12	0.13	0.20	0.12	0.13
1. Land	0.28	0.55	0.36	0.32	0.40	0.47	0.25	0.32	0.70	0.64	0.47
a) Agricultural	0.39	0.63	0.53	0.58	0.78	0.74	0.58	0.67	0.94	0.67	0.65
b) Other	0.30	0.50	0.32	0.26	0.26	0.25	0.25	0.27	0.52	0.80	0.50
2. Reproducible assets	0.16	0.20	0.19	0.29	0.27	0.19	0.12	0.12	0.21	0.19	0.18
a) Dwellings	0.44	0.43	0.34	0.39	0.35	0.37	0.33	0.34	0.43	0.37	0.35
b) Other structures and equipment	0.27	0.19	0.20	0.33	0.31	0.22	0.24	0.23	0.24	0.26	0.28
c) Inventories	0.48	0.28	0.27	0.26	0.41	0.33	0.27	0.37	0.31	0.26	0.31
d) Livestock	0.63	0.67	0.82	0.54	0.73	0.64	0.73	0.60	0.60	0.69	0.59
e) Consumer durables	0.40	0.46	0.56	0.41	0.32	0.38	0.57	0.38	0.45	0.45	0.35
II. Financial assets	0.26	0.22	0.17	0.23	0.20	0.28	0.10	0.08	0.22	0.11	0.12
1. Monetary metals	0.64	0.34	0.47	0.77	1.24	1.38	1.05	0.81	1.34	1.09	0.86
2. Claims against financial institutions	0.46	0.34	0.30	0.30	0.17	0.32	0.18	0.25	0.27	0.17	0.25
3. Loans by financial institutions[b]	0.31	0.23	0.21	0.32	0.39	0.40	0.46	0.41	0.43	0.41	0.44
4. Mortgages	0.84	0.76	0.78	0.90	0.79	0.88	0.73	0.70	0.82	0.67	0.68
5. Government debt	0.76	0.77	0.53	0.71	0.63	0.60	0.67	0.60	0.52	0.61	0.57
6. Corporate bonds	0.83	1.10	1.02	0.87	1.02	0.86	0.52	0.66	0.87	0.57	0.65
7. Corporate stocks	0.75	0.76	0.63	0.70	0.68	0.64	0.51	0.49	0.64	0.61	0.50
8. Trade credit	0.32	0.30	0.26	0.19	0.36	0.33	0.26	0.50	0.44	0.48	0.52
9. Other	0.07	0.32	0.42	0.90	0.51	0.88	1.22	1.00	0.70	0.87	0.73
III. Foreign assets	0.72	0.80	0.93	0.90	0.64	1.00	0.84	0.89	0.82	0.75	0.98

[a]For actual dates see table 33.

[b]Excluding mortgages.

Source: Individual country balance sheets in Appendix A.

Table 8 **Growth Rates of National Assets, 1850–1978 (% per year)**

	Standard Benchmark Period[a]												
Country[b]	1851 to 1875 (1)	1876 to 1895 (2)	1896 to 1913 (3)	1914 to 1929 (4)	1930 to 1939 (5)	1940 to 1950 (6)	1951 to 1965 (7)	1966 to 1978 (8)	1876 to 1913 (9)	1914 to 1950 (10)	1951 to 1978 (11)	1876 to 1978 (12)	1914 to 1978 (13)
1. Australia	...	...	...	...	...	...	8.5	12.3	...	...	10.6	...	...
2. Belgium	3.5	1.4	3.8	15.3	−0.7	13.8	6.3	11.3	2.6	10.1	8.2	6.7	9.3
3. Canada	...	...	...	...	...	...	7.6	12.5	...	...	10.4	...	...
4. Denmark	...	3.8	5.4	5.5	2.7	8.0	8.0	13.6	4.4	5.5	10.4	6.6	7.7
5. France	2.5	1.4 (cols. 2–3)		10.9	15.5 (cols. 5–6)		12.9	13.0	1.4	13.5	13.0	9.0	13.3
6. Germany[c]	3.8	1.4	5.0	(1.1)	−0.4	(−2.0)	13.1	10.1	3.3	(−0.3)	11.2	(4.0)	(4.4)
7. Great Britain	2.5	1.4	2.1	5.2	2.0	6.0	6.0	13.3	1.7	4.5	9.0	4.7	6.5
8. Hungary	...	...	...	...	...	...	...	8.4	...	...	...	...	...
9. India	3.5	2.0	3.1	5.5	0.4	8.2	6.0	12.4	2.5	4.9	9.8	5.2	6.9
10. Israel	...	...	...	...	...	...	22.6	29.4	...	25.3	...	...	...
11. Italy	2.7	1.4	3.0	12.0	2.8	37.5	9.1	15.3	2.3	17.7	12.4	13.4	19.6
12. Japan	...	7.8	5.8	7.8	10.6	38.7	17.2	16.8	6.9	18.7	17.0	14.6	18.1
13. Mexico	...	...	...	...	4.8	19.8	14.0	20.3	...	...	16.7	...	...
14. Norway	...	2.5	4.4	5.3	3.0	9.3	7.5	12.9	3.3	6.1	10.0	6.1	7.6
15. Russia/USSR[c]	...	...	...	(0.8)	15.0	10.8	9.8	6.6	...	(7.6)	8.9	...	(8.1)
16. South Africa	...	...	...	3.3	5.9	9.6	7.2	13.1	...	6.4	10.5	...	7.8
17. Sweden	...	...	...	...	...	...	...	10.6	...	...	...	...	...
18. Switzerland	...	2.4	5.0	4.5	0.9	4.3	7.3	9.1	3.4	3.5	8.1	4.9	5.6
19. United States	6.1	4.4	5.9	7.1	−1.1	9.0	6.4	9.2	5.0	5.4	7.7	5.9	6.5
20. Yugoslavia	...	...	...	...	...	...	12.2	19.9	...	...	16.9	...	...

[a]For actual dates see table 33.

[b]Boundary changes which are particularly important in lines 6, 9 and 15 are disregarded in this and similar tables.

[c]Bracketed figures disregard devaluations.

Source of basic data: Country tables in Appendix A.

tions of the figures as well as a discussion of the components of the balance sheets are omitted; they can be found in reasonable detail in Chapters 2 and 3.

For the century as a whole the rate of growth of national assets in current prices has, as table 8 shows, varied between 4 percent for Germany and 15 percent for Japan, with an average for the 11 countries of a little over 7 percent. These figures disregard the German hyperinflation following World War I. Allowance for it would increase the secular growth rate for Germany by 23 percent and raise the average to 9 percent. The rates, however, lie between 4 and 7 percent for the eight of the 11 countries (seven of 10 if Germany is excluded), other than the three countries whose secular growth rate of national assets in current prices have been affected by a period of rapid inflations after World War II (Japan) or after world wars (France and Italy).

The variations of the growth rates of national assets in current prices among interbenchmark periods as well as the longer spans are substantial, but what is more significant is that the rhythm of the variations, though not their absolute size, are similar for most countries. Thus all seven countries for which the relevant data are available show a substantial decline in the rate of growth of national assets between the third and the fourth quarters of the 19th century. Over the following two decades before World War I the rate increased in nine of 10 countries. The rate further increased between 1913 and 1929 in nine of 11 countries (10 if the German devaluation is not disregarded), Switzerland being the sole exception. The rate declined sharply during the 1930s in 10 of 13 countries, even becoming negative in three of them (Belgium, Germany, United States). The inflation accompanying World War II led to a sharp increase in the rate of growth of national assets in 13 of 14 countries, and became the highest rate of any interbenchmark period in four (Belgium, France, Italy, Japan). The similarity in the rhythm of growth persisted in the postwar period. Among the 17 countries, the rate of growth of national assets was higher in the second than in the first half of the period in all but one (Japan), where the difference was insignificant.

Comparing the approximately four decades before World War I and the quarter century starting around 1950 it is found that national assets grew more rapidly in the postwar period in all 11 countries for which the comparison can be made, the average rising sharply from 3.4 to 10.5 percent. While only one country (Japan) had an annual growth ratio exceeding 5 percent before World War I, the rate was above 10 percent in five of the 11 countries in the postwar period.

For a better understanding of the meaning of the growth rates of national assets, it is necessary to eliminate the influence of changes in the price level. This can be attempted by reducing the current value of assets by means of the national product deflator, thus ignoring deviations in the price movements of different types of assets from those of the general price level.

The growth rates of real national assets, i.e., reduced to constant prices by the gross national product deflator shown in table 9, are of course lower in most periods that the rates in current prices. Similarly, some of the period-to-period changes as well as some of the intracountry differences are altered, and sometimes profoundly so, particularly for periods of sharp inflations. Many of the movements over time and differences between countries, however, that appeared in the growth rates in current prices are also visible in those reduced to constant prices, particularly before World War I when differences in the rate of price changes among countries and periods were much smaller than in the interwar or postwar years.

For the century ending in the late 1970s, the unweighted average rate of growth of real national assets was 2.7 percent for the 11 countries for which the data go back far enough and the weighted average would be of the same order. This was also the growth rate for the third quarter of the 19th century, the average for which is limited to seven countries, including all the ones then of major importance. If the century, or 1¼ century, is divided into three periods of between 38 (63), 36, and 28 years (on the basis of standard benchmark years), significant differences appear. In the pre–World War I period, which is as long as the two following ones combined, the ratio averaged about 2¾ percent with only small differences among the three subperiods. In the interwar period it was sharply lower at about 1½ percent. This was the result of a ratio close to 2 percent in the 1914–29 and 1930–39 subperiods and one of less than one-half of 1 percent for the 1940s. The latter average, however, was strongly influenced by the large negative rate of growth of Germany, but, even if it is excluded, the average of 1¼ percent remains the lowest for any of the eight subperiods. The average for the postwar years was sharply higher, nearly 5¼ percent for the 11 countries and nearly 5¾ percent if the seven additional countries, for which earlier data are unavailable, are included, the high ratios of Israel, Mexico, and the Soviet Union accounting for most of the difference. The unweighted average for the 18 countries was considerably higher for the first half of the postwar period, with 6.1 percent compared to 5.2 percent for the second half. There was thus a pronounced U-shaped long-term movement in the rate of growth of real national assets, the interwar period, and particularly the 1940s, constituting a trough between the preceding and the following periods, and a definite upward secular trend.

Intercountry differences, however, were substantial. Among the 11 countries for which the data go back to the late 19th century, the secular average rate of growth stretches from 1.8 for France to 4.5 percent for Japan, but one-half of the ratios keep within a range of 2.0 and 2.6,

Table 9 **Growth Rates of Real (Deflated)[a] National Assets, 1850–1978 (% per year)**

Country	Standard Benchmark Period[b]												
	1850 to 1875 (1)	1876 to 1895 (2)	1896 to 1913 (3)	1914 to 1929 (4)	1930 to 1939 (5)	1940 to 1950 (6)	1951 to 1965 (7)	1966 to 1978 (8)	1876 to 1913 (9)	1914 to 1950 (10)	1951 to 1978 (11)	1876 to 1978 (12)	1914 to 1978 (13)
1. Australia	...	...	...	...	...	...	4.0	3.9	...	...	3.9	...	...
2. Belgium	2.2	2.9	2.7	0.4	0.7	−1.6	4.5	4.9	2.8	−0.1	4.5	2.2	1.8
3. Canada	...	...	...	...	...	...	5.5	5.2	...	...	5.3	...	...
4. Denmark	...	4.4	4.8	2.2	1.0	0.6	3.5	4.5	4.6	1.4	3.9	3.2	2.8
5. France	1.9	1.4		−0.1	−1.5		4.1	7.4	1.2	−1.0	6.9	1.8	2.3
6. Germany	2.2	2.2	3.7	−1.3	−1.8	−6.5	10.5	5.9	2.9	−2.3	7.0	2.0	1.5
7. Great Britain	1.8	1.9	1.8	1.0	2.3	0.4	3.0	3.2	1.9	1.2	3.1	1.9	2.0
8. Hungary	...	...	...	...	...	...	...	6.8	...	...	...	...	...
9. India	2.9	0.7	1.4	3.8	3.4	4.3	−3.0	4.7	1.0	3.8	1.5	2.2	2.7
10. Israel	...	...	...	...	...	...	13.1	12.2	...	...	12.8	...	...
11. Italy	1.7	1.8	1.4	1.4	3.0	1.9	5.5	5.0	1.6	2.0	5.2	2.5	3.0
12. Japan	...	3.3	2.1	4.7	4.3	−0.8	12.2	9.2	2.8	2.6	10.6	4.5	5.2
13. Mexico	...	...	...	...	1.7	6.4	11.4	7.5	...	...	9.7	...	...
14. Norway	...	2.2	3.2	2.9	0.8	3.6	5.7	4.8	2.6	2.7	5.2	3.3	3.7
15. Russia/USSR	...	...	...	...	...	...	8.0	7.2	...	...	7.4	...	...
16. South Africa	...	...	...	1.6	6.4	3.0	4.3	3.4	...	4.3	3.8	...	4.1
17. Sweden	...	...	...	...	...	...	...	3.1	...	...	...	...	...
18. Switzerland	...	1.6	3.0	1.5	2.6	−0.6	5.2	3.5	2.2	1.2	4.5	2.5	2.7
19. United States	5.5	5.3	4.0	4.0	0.2	2.8	3.5	3.5	4.8	2.7	3.5	3.6	2.5
20. Yugoslavia	...	...	...	...	...	...	4.9	5.6	...	...	5.4	...	...

[a]Gross national product deflator.

[b]For actual dates see table 33.

Source of basic data: Table 8 and gross national product deflator (for cols. 1–6 mostly from Mitchell 1975, 1982; for cols. 7 and 8 from *IFSYB* 1981).

including the only less developed country in the group (India). The similarity in rhythm was pronounced after World War I when the rates moved in the same direction in most countries: downward (nine of 11) in the 1914–29 period compared to that of 1896–1913, downward (eight of 12) in the 1940s, upward (12 of 13) in the first half of the postwar period, and downward (14 of 18) in its second half. It was only in the 1930s that the number of countries with increasing or declining rates was approximately equal. The range among the growth rates of the 18 countries during the postwar period was somewhat wider, running from 3 percent for Great Britain to over 10 percent for Israel and Japan, but for eight of them it remained between 4 and 5½ percent.

Since the differences in the rate of growth of population among countries and over time were considerably smaller than those in the price level, the rates of growth of real national assets per head, the most appropriate basis of comparison, shown in table 10, differed less from those of aggregate real national assets than did the latter in comparison with the rates of growth of national assets in current prices. Intercountry and intertemporal differences are similar to those of table 9.

The secular rate of growth of real assets per head for the 11 countries averaged just under 2 percent, ranging from slightly less than 1½ percent in France and in Great Britain to 3¼ percent in Japan, with eight ratios between 1½ and 2½ percent and the United States very close to the average. The range thus was somewhat narrower in absolute terms but larger relative to the average than for the growth rates of total real national assets.

As is the case with total assets, the average for the 11 countries was considerably lower in the interwar period, with about 1 percent, than in the pre–World War I period, with nearly 1¾ percent, which in turn was far below the 4¼ percent of the postwar period. The postwar average for 18 countries of 4¼ percent was equal to that of the 11. It is of some interest that the average rates of growth were quite similar in the three subperiods of the prewar period, the two subperiods of the interwar period, and the two subperiods of the postwar period, which are thus shown to have been fairly homogeneous in this respect, while the 1940s with their average of zero stand alone. For the century ending with the late 1970s the (unweighted) average rate of growth for 11 countries was close to 2 percent with a spread from 1.4 (Great Britain) to 3.3 (Japan), but an interquartile range of only 1.7 to 2.1.

Only a slight connection appears on a secular scale between the rate of growth with real income per head at the starting point of around 1880. Of the two countries which then were at the bottom of the range, Japan showed the highest rate of growth among the 11 countries, while India kept slightly below the average. On the other hand, the two countries

Table 10 **Growth Rates of Real (Deflated) National Assets per Head, 1850–1978 (% per year)**

Country	Standard Benchmark Period[a]												
	1850 to 1875 (1)	1876 to 1895 (2)	1896 to 1913 (3)	1914 to 1929 (4)	1930 to 1939 (5)	1940 to 1950 (6)	1951 to 1965 (7)	1966 to 1978 (8)	1876 to 1913 (9)	1914 to 1950 (10)	1951 to 1978 (11)	1876 to 1978 (12)	1914 to 1978 (13)
1. Australia	...	...	...	...	...	...	1.8	2.7	...	...	2.0	...	...
2. Belgium	1.9	1.9	1.7	0.0	−0.2	−1.3	3.9	4.5	1.8	−0.4	4.0	1.6	1.6
3. Canada	...	...	...	...	...	...	3.2	3.8	...	...	3.5	...	...
4. Denmark	...	3.3	3.5	0.8	0.2	−0.4	2.8	4.0	3.4	0.3	3.3	2.2	1.7
5. France	1.7	1.1		−0.3	−2.6		6.5	5.4	1.1	−7.2	6.0	1.5	1.8
6. Germany	1.5	1.2	2.2	−1.1	1.2	−4.0	9.6	5.7	1.7	−1.5	6.2	1.7	1.8
7. Great Britain	1.4	1.0	0.8	1.2	1.9	−0.2	2.5	2.3	0.9	0.9	2.5	1.4	1.6
8. Hungary	...	...	...	...	...	...	...	6.4	...	...	...	...	...
9. India	2.7	0.3	1.0	3.2	2.1	4.8	3.7	2.1	0.6	3.4	2.7	1.3	2.0
10. Israel	...	...	...	...	...	...	9.6	9.2	...	...	9.4	...	...
11. Italy	1.1	1.1	0.7	0.5	2.3	1.2	4.7	4.3	0.9	0.9	4.5	1.8	2.3
12. Japan	...	2.4	0.9	3.4	3.2	−2.3	11.2	7.9	1.7	1.2	9.4	3.3	4.0
13. Mexico	...	...	...	...	−0.1	3.3	7.9	3.8	...	...	6.1	...	...
14. Norway	...	1.3	2.4	2.1	0.2	2.7	4.8	4.1	1.8	1.9	4.4	2.5	2.9
15. Russia/USSR	...	...	...	...	...	...	7.7	6.3	...	...	6.0	...	...
16. South Africa	...	...	...	0.1	3.6	0.9	3.3	0.7	...	2.3	1.5	...	1.8
17. Sweden	...	...	...	...	...	...	...	2.5	...	...	...	...	...
18. Switzerland	...	0.7	1.8	1.2	2.1	−1.4	3.7	2.9	1.3	0.7	3.3	1.7	1.2
19. United States	2.8	3.1	2.0	2.5	−0.6	1.5	1.8	2.4	2.7	1.3	2.1	2.1	1.6
20. Yugoslavia	...	...	...	...	...	...	3.8	4.6	...	...	4.3	...	...

[a]For actual dates see table 33.

Source of basic data: As for table 9; population figures for cols. 1–6 mostly from Mitchell 1975, 1982; for cols. 7 and 8 from *IFSYB* 1982.

with the highest starting real national product per head—France and Great Britain—had the lowest secular rate of growth of real national assets. The rate for the United States of 2.1 percent was slightly above the average for the 11 countries.

A comparison between the growth rates of real national assets per head in the pre–World War I and post–World War II periods is provided in table 11. It shows that the average rate of growth was more than 2½ times as high in the later period; and that the absolute and relative differences varied greatly among countries. The increases were largest in descending order in Japan, France, and Germany. Only in two countries was the postwar rate of growth of real national assets per head below that prevailing before World War I—the United States and Denmark. As a result, the United States fell from second to last place among the 11 countries. The range of the country growth rates was considerably wider in the more recent period, with more than 7 percent compared to one of less than 3 percent, though the coefficient of variation declined slightly from 0.49 to 0.45.

Table 12 compares the average rates of growth of the three main components of national real assets per head—tangible, reproducible, and financial assets—over long periods. These figures, however, must be interpreted with great caution in the case of total assets and of reproduci-

Table 11 **Comparison of the Growth of Real National Assets per Head in the Pre–World War I[a] and the Post–World War II[b] Periods in 11 Countries**

	Growth Rate		Difference	
	A[a] (1)	B[b] (2)	Absolute (3)	Relative (4)
1. Belgium	1.79	3.55	+1.76	1.98
2. Denmark	3.41	3.29	−0.12	0.96
3. France	1.06	5.98	+4.92	5.64
4. Germany	1.67	6.16	+4.49	3.69
5. Great Britain	0.91	2.53	+1.62	2.78
6. India	0.59	2.72	+2.13	4.61
7. Italy	0.86	4.50	+3.64	5.23
8. Japan	1.69	9.38	+7.69	5.55
9. Norway	1.76	4.43	+2.67	2.52
10. Switzerland	1.32	3.33	+2.01	2.52
11. United States	2.73	2.09	−0.64	0.77
12. Average (unweighted)	1.62	4.36	+2.74	2.69

[a]Benchmark dates 1875–1913; for actual years see table 33.
[b]Benchmark dates 1950–78; for actual years see table 33.
Source of basic data: As for table 10.

Table 12 **Long-Term Rate of Growth of the Main Components of Real (Deflated) National Assets per Head, 1875–1978 (% per Year)**

Country	Standard Benchmark Periods[a]											
	Tangible Assets				Reproducible Assets				Financial Assets			
	1875 to 1913 (1)	1914 to 1950 (2)	1951 to 1978 (3)	1876 to 1978 (4)	1876 to 1913 (5)	1914 to 1950 (6)	1951 to 1978 (7)	1876 to 1971 (8)	1876 to 1913 (9)	1914 to 1950 (10)	1951 to 1978 (11)	1876 to 1978 (12)
1. Australia	...	...	2.45	...	...	...	2.69	...	...	...	1.44	...
2. Belgium	0.93	−0.25	3.50	1.26	1.40	−0.25	3.51	1.44	3.26	−0.51	3.62	2.07
3. Canada	...	...	3.63	...	...	...	3.25	...	...	...	3.42	...
4. Denmark	2.94	0.64	3.34	2.23	3.44	1.16	3.24	2.56	3.83	−0.02	3.20	2.25
5. France	0.33	−0.38	4.96	1.79	2.04	−0.19	4.04	1.71	1.26	0.01	4.92	1.75
6. Germany	1.01	−0.88	4.99	1.35	1.55	−0.93	5.18	1.58	2.90	−2.57	8.09	2.20
7. Great Britain	−0.21	1.14	3.18	1.21	0.50	1.29	3.30	1.56	1.77	0.85	2.11	1.55
8. India	0.84	3.14	2.45	1.63	0.06	3.47	3.95	1.81	−0.05	3.94	3.28	1.77
9. Israel	...	...	6.12	...	...	...	5.88	...	...	...	8.62	...
10. Italy	0.90	1.01	3.06	1.52	1.13	0.62	6.85	2.44	1.24	1.50	3.60	1.96
11. Japan	0.90	1.32	8.05	2.76	3.57	0.95	11.19	4.12	1.14	0.10	9.79	2.66
12. Mexico	...	...	6.13	...	...	...	6.72	...	...	...	6.06	...
13. Norway	1.06	1.76	4.26	2.16	15.9	2.11	4.71	2.59	3.14	2.03	4.63	3.06
14. Russia/USSR	...	...	6.08	...	...	...	6.69	...	...	...	5.69	...
15. South Africa	...	1.68	1.29	...	...	1.74	1.74	...	...	3.12	0.38	...
16. Switzerland	0.79	0.94	2.69	1.42	0.86	1.56	2.84	1.71	1.73	3.87	1.94	2.04
17. United States	2.39	0.25	3.10	1.90	2.03	0.78	3.18	1.99	3.08	2.53	1.39	2.33
18. Yugoslavia	...	...	1.91	...	...	...	2.31	...	...	...	8.83	...

[a]For actual years see table 33.

Source of basic data: As for table 10.

ble tangible assets, because the current values have been reduced to constant prices by means of the national product deflators which are not identical with, and at times may substantially deviate from, the price indices of the relevant types of tangible assets. Such indices are not yet available, though the implicit deflators of capital expenditures from the national accounts provide an approximation in the case of reproducible assets. This problem is discussed below in Chapter 2, 2.d.ii. The reservations are less serious for financial assets if one is interested in their purchasing power, and the relevant rates are shown in table 13 for each of the 12 periods.

Among the three components, the (unweighted) rates of growth over the past century for the 11 countries for which they can be calculated were slightly in excess of 2 percent for reproducible tangible and for financial assets, but were substantially lower for land, with the result that the average rate for all tangible assets is reduced to 1¾ percent.

The secular growth rates for reproducible assets lie between 1.4 percent (Belgium) and 4.1 percent (Japan), with an interquartile range of 1.6–2.5 percent. Generally the rates are highest for late starters (Italy, Japan, Denmark, Norway) and lower for early starters (Great Britain and Belgium being at the bottom). However, the rate of Germany is only fractionally (and not significantly) higher than that of Great Britain and below that of France, both of which started earlier, possibly because of the effects of the two world wars. Differences in the rates of growth over time were pronounced. For the 11 countries the average rate of growth of real reproducible national assets per head declined from 1.6 percent in the pre–World War I period to 1.0 percent in the interwar period, but increased sharply to 4.7 percent in the postwar period, well above the average of 3.3 percent for the other nine countries. Here too the difference among the three subperiods are large. For the 11 countries the average declined from 2.1 percent for the pre–World War I period to only 0.9 percent in the interwar period and was sharply higher at 4.2 percent for the postwar period.

For the century as a whole, the growth rate of real (deflated) financial assets per head has averaged slightly more than 2 percent for the 11 countries for which the data go back far enough, with a range from 1¾ percent for Great Britain to fully 3 percent for Norway, the rates for the five large developed Western countries keeping between 1.6 and 2.3 percent. The average for these 11 countries was highest in the postwar period with 4.1 percent—only slightly below the 4½ percent for 18 countries—lowest in the interwar period with 0.4 percent, and with 2.2 was close to the secular average in the pre–World War I period.

The estimates in table 13, which distinguish eight rather than only three subperiods, do not suggest an easy explanation for the intercountry

Table 13 **Growth Rates of Real (Deflated) Financial Assets per Head, 1851–1978 (% per year)**

Country	Standard Benchmark Period[a]											
	1851 to 1875 (1)	1876 to 1895 (2)	1896 to 1913 (3)	1914 to 1929 (4)	1930 to 1939 (5)	1940 to 1950 (6)	1951 to 1965 (7)	1966 to 1978 (8)	1876 to 1913 (9)	1914 to 1950 (10)	1951 to 1978 (11)	1876 to 1978 (12)
1. Australia	...	...	...	...	...	...	1.62	1.30	...	...	1.44	...
2. Belgium	3.15	3.15	3.37	−0.23	0.61	−2.21	3.55	3.72	3.26	−0.51	3.62	2.07
3. Canada	...	...	...	...	...	...	3.15	3.63	...	...	3.42	...
4. Denmark	...	3.78	3.90	0.94	−0.65	−0.97	2.57	4.03	3.83	−0.02	3.20	2.25
5. France	1.37	1.94		0.86	2.55		2.29	6.60	1.26	0.01	4.92	1.75
6. Germany	3.46	3.35	2.41	−3.74	4.13	−5.80	12.60	5.52	2.90	−2.57	8.09	2.20
7. Great Britain	2.14	2.67	0.77	1.74	2.15	−1.42	1.60	2.84	1.77	0.85	2.11	1.55
8. Hungary	...	...	...	...	...	...	...	10.60	...	...	...	...
9. India	1.38	−0.37	0.27	2.56	3.93	5.97	1.54	4.45	−0.05	3.94	3.28	1.77
10. Israel	...	...	...	...	...	...	8.14	9.35	...	...	8.62	...
11. Italy	0.24	0.66	1.67	0.52	1.91	2.33	3.27	3.89	1.24	1.50	3.60	1.96
12. Japan	...	2.13	0.02	1.14	3.94	−3.53	9.32	10.19	1.14	0.10	9.79	2.66
13. Mexico	...	...	...	...	4.05	4.09	7.60	4.09	...	...	6.06	...
14. Norway	...	2.81	3.59	3.26	−1.78	3.06	4.69	4.57	3.14	2.03	4.63	3.06
15. Russia/USSR[c]	...	...	...	...	...	...	5.34	6.52	...	...	5.69	...
16. South Africa	...	...	...	1.20	5.42	3.75	1.86	−0.73	...	3.12	0.38	...
17. Sweden	...	...	...	...	...	...	...	3.20	...	...	...	...
18. Switzerland	...	1.81	1.61	1.37	1.97	−2.19	4.09	3.59	1.73	0.49	3.87	1.94
19. United States	3.50	3.36	2.63	3.76	−0.64	4.46	1.31	1.51	3.08	2.53	1.39	2.33
20. Yugoslavia	...	...	...	...	...	...	13.36	6.21	...	...	8.83	...

[a]For actual dates see table 31.

Source of basic data: As for table 10.

differences observed. Some of the early starters in financial development show relatively low secular rates of growth of real financial assets per head, e.g., France and Great Britain, but so do some late starters, e.g., Italy and India. As might be expected, some late starters have relatively high rates of growth, e.g., Japan, Denmark, and Norway, but so do the United States and Germany, which cannot be regarded as late starters from a secular point of view.

4. Asset/Product Ratios

Probably the most effective simple way of assessing the growth of national assets and their components as part of an economy is to express them as a proportion of gross national product, the handiest even if not a perfect measure of its size.

It is seen then in table 14 that the ratio of national assets to national product exhibits large differences among countries as well as substantial changes over time. For the nine now- and then-developed countries for which the ratio can be followed for a full century—all except the United States located in Europe—both the average and the median have declined over this period, but only moderately, and they have increased for nearly as many countries as for which they have declined. The scatter of the country ratios, however, has been narrowing the coefficient of variation, declining from 0.68 to 0.41 if Switzerland is included, but from 0.45 to 0.11 if it is excluded. The ratio for the 20 countries in the 1970s with 8.1 is slightly lower than for the nine with 9.1. There is among the 17 market economies no obvious relation to factors like nominal or real national product per head, while the ratios for the three centrally planned economies are substantially lower with an average of hardly six.

The 20 countries differ considerably, not only in the level of the ratio but also in its movement over the periods of about three decades. These variations which can be followed in table 14 do not exhibit marked uniformities, and their explanation would require the analysis of each country's economic and financial history. One of the few common features is the relatively low level of the ratio during or following rapid inflations or currency reforms that is visible in the cases of Belgium, Germany, Japan, and Italy at mid-century. Understanding of the intercountry and intertemporal differences in the asset/product ratio is, however, helped by the study of the corresponding ratios for the two main components—financial and tangible assets—and the further split of the latter between reproducible assets and land.

It is then immediately seen that in contrast to the relative stability of the total asset/product ratio the ratio of financial assets to national product, which can be followed in table 15, shows a secular upward trend,

Table 14 **National Assets/Gross National Product Ratio, 1850–1978**

	Standard Benchmark Year[a]								
	1850 (1)	1875 (2)	1895 (3)	1913 (4)	1929 (5)	1939 (6)	1950 (7)	1965 (8)	1978 (9)
1. Australia	...	...	...	...	...	...	4.22	7.84	7.35
2. Belgium	10.62	9.50	10.75	10.59	8.67	9.55	7.53	7.87	8.05
3. Canada	...	...	...	...	...	...	7.49	8.05	8.92
4. Denmark	...	6.72	8.33	9.98	10.51	8.98	8.00	7.43	8.77
5. France	10.72	12.47	...	10.74	7.01	...	6.43	5.88	7.27
6. Germany	10.84	9.46	10.26	11.18	8.91	7.01	5.31	6.41	8.48
7. Great Britain	12.89	9.06	9.65	8.62	9.81	9.87	8.36	8.49	9.45
8. Hungary	...	...	...	...	...	...	...	6.00	7.56
9. India	3.65	3.87	4.56	4.65	7.60	8.52	5.49	6.72	8.10
10. Israel	...	...	...	...	...	...	4.16	6.44	9.04
11. Italy	6.51	7.97	9.19	7.71	7.12	7.91	6.80	7.21	8.37
12. Japan	...	8.11	8.32	8.68	10.92	9.97	6.19	7.97	9.16
13. Mexico	...	...	...	...	3.99	3.29	3.25	3.68	4.48
14. Norway	...	8.10	9.40	10.74	9.24	8.45	8.43	8.36	9.20
15. Russia/USSR	...	...	...	9.50	7.24	2.94	3.42	5.24	6.22
16. South Africa	...	...	...	8.91	7.46	7.98	8.99	8.12	7.44
17. Sweden	...	...	...	...	...	...	...	7.36	7.95
18. Switzerland	...	14.44	11.65	11.19	11.66	14.77	11.89	11.94	14.12
19. United States	4.44	6.36	7.67	7.62	9.98	9.20	7.15	7.41	7.67
20. Yugoslavia	...	...	...	...	...	...	7.02	5.63	3.87

[a]For actual dates see table 33.
Source of basic data: Country tables in Appendix A.

Table 15 **Ratio of Financial Assets to Gross National Product, 1850–1978**

	Standard Benchmark Year[a]								
	1850 (1)	1875 (2)	1895 (3)	1913 (4)	1929 (5)	1939 (6)	1950 (7)	1965 (8)	1978 (9)
1. Australia	...	...	...	...	...	...	3.14	3.20	2.70
2. Belgium	2.15	2.70	4.01	5.02	3.95	4.73	3.23	3.36	3.73
3. Canada	...	...	...	...	...	...	4.06	4.36	4.74
4. Denmark	...	3.64	4.70	5.84	5.87	5.01	4.30	3.80	4.61
5. France	2.52	5.08	...	6.31	3.79	...	1.72	3.26	3.29
6. Germany	1.88	2.69	4.09	5.02	2.66	2.46	1.53	2.00	3.83
7. Great Britain	4.95	3.44	6.41	5.70	6.96	7.54	5.71	4.77	6.64
8. Hungary	...	...	...	...	...	...	...	0.96	2.42
9. India	1.41	1.25	1.31	1.18	1.74	2.33	2.05	2.35	2.82
10. Israel	...	...	...	...	...	...	1.51	2.87	4.24
11. Italy	1.09	2.26	2.85	2.49	2.90	3.44	2.23	3.60	4.28
12. Japan	...	1.90	2.13	3.40	6.05	5.84	2.19	4.09	4.68
13. Mexico	...	...	...	...	1.03	1.55	1.33	1.48	1.85
14. Norway		2.14	3.04	3.73	5.00	3.39	3.73	3.67	4.25
15. Russia/USSR	...	...	...	2.64	0.63	0.64	0.82	0.99	1.31
16. South Africa	...	...	...	2.71	2.92	3.80	4.32	4.32	3.30
17. Sweden	...	...	...	...	...	...	...	3.73	4.44
18. Switzerland	...	8.90	8.10	9.82	8.05	9.65	7.97	6.98	9.27
19. United States	1.33	2.29	4.61	3.47	5.61	5.17	3.90	4.42	3.90
20. Yugoslavia	...	...	...	...	...	...	1.36	2.21	2.34

[a]For actual dates see table 33.

Source of basic data: As for table 14.

the average for the nine developed countries rising between 1880 or thereabouts and the late 1970s from 3.6 to 4.5, or from less than two-fifths to nearly one-half of the broader ratio, and advancing in all but one of the nine countries (France)—and in most of them substantially. In this case the ratio for all 20 countries in the late 1970s with 3.7 was substantially below that of the nine developed countries, for which the data span the entire century (4.5), as well as that of all 15 developed countries (4.2), because of the much lower level of the ratio for the two less developed market economies (2.9) and the three planned economies (1.8). Here, too, intercountry and intertemporal variations are substantial, and the effect of rapid inflation or currency reforms in reducing the ratio is even more evident in the case of Germany and Japan in 1950. Here, too, the scatter of the ratios among the nine developed countries was substantially lower at the end than at the beginning of the century, the coefficient of variations (excluding Switzerland) declining from 0.25 to 0.14.

The movements of the broader form of the capital-output ratio which includes land can be followed in table 16. The average for the nine developed countries declined in the last century from 5.5 to 4.4, which at the end of the period is only slightly above the average of 4.2 for the 20 countries. A downward trend is evident in all but two of the nine developed countries, the ratio showing no change in the United States and increasing substantially in Denmark whose 1880 ratio had been far below the average. Here too the ratios were considerably closer together in the late 1970s than a century earlier, the coefficient of variation for the nine developed countries declining sharply from 0.38 to 0.03. Even for the 20 countries the coefficient was only 0.16, and one-half of the ratios was concentrated between 4.1 and 4.8, though the range stretched from 1.8 to 5.3.

A comparison of the broad with the intermediate capital-output ratio which is limited to reproducible assets and is shown in table 17 reveals that the decline in the broad ratio was due entirely to that in the ratio of land, essentially that of agricultural land, to national product, which over the century fell on the average for the nine developed countries from 2.3 to 0.7. The average of the intermediate ratio for these countries actually increased slightly from 3.4 to 3.7, rising in five and declining in four countries. The average for the 20 countries in the late 1970s of 3.5 was only insignificantly different, and the scatter was relatively narrow with a coefficient of variation of only 0.15 and an interquartile range of 3.1 to 4.0.

Some economists might argue that the economically relevant capital-output ratio should be limited to so-called productive assets, i.e., broadly speaking tangible assets used in business and by government to support business. The available data do not permit calculation of this ratio. It is,

Table 16 Broad Capital/Output Ratio,[a] 1850–1978

	Standard Benchmark Year[b]								
Country	1850 (1)	1875 (2)	1895 (3)	1913 (4)	1929 (5)	1939 (6)	1950 (7)	1965 (8)	1978 (9)
1. Australia	...	...	...	...	...	...	4.03	4.53	4.46
2. Belgium	8.45	7.09	7.31	5.55	4.79	4.82	3.90	4.50	4.41
3. Canada	...	...	...	...	...	...	3.42	3.76	4.18
4. Denmark	...	3.26	3.68	4.14	3.79	3.97	3.84	3.63	4.18
5. France[c]	9.89	9.11	...	6.47	4.69	...	3.11	2.62	3.95
6. Germany	9.29	7.12	5.68	6.58	6.91	4.35	3.78	2.17	4.32
7. Great Britain[d]	7.30	4.70	3.27	2.91	2.84	2.79	3.23	3.18	5.96
8. Hungary	...	...	...	...	...	...	...	5.20	5.55
9. India[e]	2.21	2.64	3.26	3.48	5.87	6.19	4.31	4.39	5.23
10. Israel	...	...	...	...	...	...	2.27	3.42	3.82
11. Italy	5.29	5.74	6.34	5.33	4.30	4.71	5.35	4.24	4.21
12. Japan	...	6.25	6.22	5.35	4.93	4.13	4.01	5.08	4.58
13. Mexico	...	...	...	...	2.90	2.38	1.81	2.20	2.60
14. Norway	...	5.85	5.50	5.21	4.84	4.61	4.71	4.68	4.88
15. Russia/USSR	...	...	...	6.77	6.68	2.30	2.60	4.61	4.80
16. South Africa	...	...	...	5.19	4.20	4.12	3.80	3.80	4.32
17. Sweden	...	...	...	...	...	...	...	3.61	3.49
18. Switzerland	...	8.12	5.05	6.55	4.89	6.07	5.25	4.60	5.08
19. United States[f]	2.83	3.56	4.56	4.17	4.36	3.91	3.32	3.45	3.93
20. Yugoslavia	...	...	...	...	...	...	5.76	3.00	1.95

[a]Net tangible assets (excluding gold and silver): year-end rate of gross national product.

[b]For actual dates see table 33.

[c]In addition 1815: 6.25.

[d]In addition 1688: 5.97; 1760: 8.33; 1800: 7.56; 1830: 6.76.

[e]Including gold and silver hoards: 3.15; 3.44; 4.06; 4.04; 6.40; 6.90; 4.85; 4.81; 5.70.

[f]In addition 1805: 2.17.

Table 17 Intermediate Capital/Output Ratio, 1850–1978[a]

Country	Standard Benchmark Year[b]								
	1850 (1)	1875 (2)	1895 (3)	1913 (4)	1929 (5)	1939 (6)	1950 (7)	1965 (8)	1978 (9)
1. Australia	...	...	...	...	...	...	3.36	3.97	3.92
2. Belgium	3.84	4.82	5.47	4.52	3.99	4.05	3.17	3.18	3.61
3. Canada	...	...	...	...	...	...	2.82	2.82	3.17
4. Denmark	...	2.04	2.61	3.05	2.82	3.11	3.40	3.07	3.60
5. France	4.29	4.48	...	4.32	3.45	...	2.40	2.05	3.03
6. Germany	5.04	4.26	3.79	4.82	5.52	3.61	2.71	1.66	3.25
7. Great Britain	5.12	2.82	2.25	2.27	2.34	2.30	2.66	2.19	5.08
8. Hungary	...	...	...	...	...	...	...	3.66	4.05
9. India	1.43	1.64	1.84	1.61	2.38	2.35	2.24	2.99	3.92
10. Israel	...	...	...	...	...	...	1.77	2.73	3.11
11. Italy	2.80	2.97	3.23	3.24	3.01	3.23	3.88	3.39	3.50
12. Japan	...	3.38	3.32	3.10	2.67	2.71	1.39	1.74	2.27
13. Mexico	...	...	...	...	2.02	1.78	1.24	1.71	2.09
14. Norway	...	3.37	3.48	3.75	3.51	3.58	3.68	3.75	4.11
15. Russia/USSR	...	...	...	2.61	2.93	1.41	1.72	3.03	3.49
16. South Africa	...	...	...	3.73	3.18	3.13	2.96	2.95	3.52
17. Sweden	...	...	...	...	...	...	...	3.01	2.95
18. Switzerland	...	5.04	3.43	4.17	3.66	4.86	4.16	3.80	4.20
19. United States	1.66	2.45	2.91	2.69	3.09	2.99	2.67	2.61	2.95
20. Yugoslavia	...	...	...	...	...	...	4.27	2.15	1.59

[a]Net reproducible tangible assets: year-end rate of gross national product.

[b]For actual dates see table 33.

however, possible to derive a related ratio, the quotient of all nonresidential structures, equipment, inventories and livestock, and national product. The numerator of this ratio exceeds the desired value by government "nonproductive" capital, particularly military structures and equipment, which while not negligible generally constitute only a moderate fraction of what should be included. The level of the ratios so calculated are thus too high, but their movements over time and their differences among countries should not be misleading. This narrow capital-output ratio is shown in table 18. In the United States the ratio for military structures and equipment averaged about one-tenth, but for most countries, except the Soviet Union, and for most dates, except during and immediately after both World Wars, it was certainly considerably lower.

There are only five countries, all developed, for which the narrow capital-output ratio can be approximated back to the middle of the 19th century. For these countries the ratio averaged between 1850 and 1939 about 2¼ without clear trend, while the values for the three benchmark dates in the postwar period are at a considerably lower level though rising from 1.6 to 1.8. The average for 18 countries in the postwar period is slightly higher, but also shows a rising trend, in this case from 1.8 to 2.2. The range of the values for individual countries is fairly wide, extending in the late 1970s from 1.3 to 3.3, with an interquartile range from 1.6 to 2.7. The scatter, however, has considerably narrowed, the coefficient of variation falling from 0.26 around 1950 to 0.11 in the late 1970s. No association is evident between the level of the ratio and a country's real national product per head or another indicator of its economic development or its financial characteristics. Thus the small groups of less developed market and of planned economies include countries with the lowest and nearly the highest ratios. The ratio of the United States is well below that of other developed countries which have considerably lower real income per head, e.g., Great Britain and Italy; and the ratios for the three Scandinavian countries, which have similar income levels and similar economic and social structures, vary from one of the lowest (Denmark) to the highest (Norway) among the 20 countries. It is thus clear that table 18 poses more questions than it answers, even allowing for the substantial margins of error in the calculation of not a few of the ratios. This is true also, though to a lesser extent, of the movements over time of the ratios of individual countries. In some countries the ratio has exhibited considerable stability over long periods, or at least no definite trend and no sharp jumps, e.g., in Great Britain from 1895 to 1965, in Italy from 1861 to 1977, in Japan from 1885 to 1939, in Norway from 1880 to 1965, and in the United States from 1880 to 1939. Others have shown a sharp downward shift between the full half century before World War I and the postwar period, e.g., France and Germany. Some movements

Table 18 **Narrow Capital/Output Ratio, 1850–1978**[a]

Country	Standard Benchmark Year[b]								
	1850 (1)	1875 (2)	1895 (3)	1913 (4)	1929 (5)	1939 (6)	1950 (7)	1965 (8)	1978 (9)
1. Australia	...	...	...	...	...	...	2.32	2.89	2.87
2. Belgium	...	...	...	...	...	...	...	1.82	2.03
3. Canada	...	...	...	...	...	...	1.81	1.93	2.08
4. Denmark	...	...	...	...	...	...	2.56	2.21	2.36
5. France	2.56	2.72	...	2.98	2.28	...	1.50	1.28	1.44
6. Germany	4.20	3.29	2.70	3.42	3.68	2.48	1.88	1.06	1.87
7. Great Britain	3.77	2.11	1.66	1.70	1.61	1.45	1.70	1.76	3.31
8. Hungary	...	...	...	...	...	...	...	2.46	2.81
9. India	...	...	...	...	...	...	1.59	1.84	2.98
10. Israel	...	...	...	...	...	...	1.04	1.66	1.86
11. Italy	1.41	1.57	1.93	2.27	2.14	2.38	2.14	1.79	1.77
12. Japan	...	2.16	1.98	2.17	1.99	2.12	7.09	1.16	1.68
13. Mexico	...	...	...	...	1.39	1.16	0.87	1.14	1.31
14. Norway	...	2.09	2.19	2.52	2.46	2.41	2.51	2.80	3.10
15. Russia/USSR	...	...	...	1.97	1.99	0.99	1.18	2.29	2.72
16. South Africa	...	...	...	3.13	2.53	2.47	2.24	2.20	2.72
17. Sweden	...	...	...	...	...	...	...	1.75	1.79
18. Switzerland	...	...	...	...	...	3.63	3.09	2.79	3.09
19. United States	1.24	1.78	1.81	1.71	1.82	1.75	1.44	1.53	1.73
20. Yugoslavia	...	...	...	...	...	...	3.31	1.60[c]	1.50[c]

[a]Nonresidential structures, equipment, inventories, and livestock: year-end rate of gross national product.
[b]For actual years see table 33.
[c]Based on rough division of structures and equipment among residential and others.

seem easily explainable, such as the sharp increases in the ratio during the postwar period in India, Japan, and Mexico, and the sharp decline between 1940 and 1955 in Japan.

It must always be kept in mind that countrywide capital-output ratios are weighted averages of sectoral ratios or of ratios for different types of capital and that these ratios and their weights are likely, and to some extent are known, to show substantial differences among countries and variations over time. Countrywide unsectorized ratios such as those shown in tables 16–18 therefore are only of limited analytical value. It has been said that "we cannot expect a great deal of wisdom from staring at capital-output ratios for many countries over long periods of time," and "only close detailed analysis of a particular national economy at a particular time is likely to provide reasonable insight into the multiple variables determining the level of changes in its incremental capital-output ratio" (Rostow 1980, 282), a statement which equally applies to most of the other ratios used in this study as well as for most ratios and parameters employed by economists.

It is tempting to try to explain the levels and the intercountry and intertemporal variations of the broad, intermediate, and narrow capital/output ratios by basic economic and financial factors, but the absence of the required data for a sufficient number of countries and dates makes this impossible within the scope of this study. It may, however, be worth pointing out that capital-output ratios are positively related to the share of property income in national product and negatively related to the level of yields on the different types of tangible assets. The generally downward trend in the share in property income and the upward trend in interest rates together with the declining share of land, the yield on which is commonly lower than that on other tangible assets, may thus help to explain the fact that the capital-output ratios are generally lower in the postwar period than in the 60 years before World War I. In the case of the ratio of financial or total assets to national product, the level of the financial interrelations and intermediation ratios provide additional explanatory information.

5. The Financial Interrelations Ratio

The broadest, and for financial analysis the most important, relation that can be derived from the national balance sheet is the financial interrelations ratio, i.e., the quotient of financial and tangible assets, the ratio which measures the relative size of an economy's financial superstructure. While the ratio and its changes over time are a significant, and even the most important single indicator of the level and trend of financial development, it cannot be used for that purpose without consideration of other characteristics of the financial superstructure and of the real infrastructure of the economy, such as a country's monetary history, its international financial relations, its rate of economic growth, and breaks in its economic development. These are matters that can only be alluded to occasionally but cannot be given adequate consideration.

Table 19 permits a few conclusions that may be summarized without spelling out all the necessary qualifications and without pointing out the occasional exception.

First, the financial interrelations ratio has shown a secular upward trend until World War I or the 1930s in all six developed countries for which the data go back to the mid-19th century or beyond, as well as for the four additional countries for which they are available since 1880. In the middle of the 19th century the ratios, not eliminating interfinancial claims and hence slightly higher than on a net basis, were in the order of one-fifth to one-fourth in Belgium, France, Germany, and Italy, which at that time were at or only slightly beyond the start of their modern economic and financial development. A similar level had been reached in the United States a few decades earlier and in Great Britain probably as far back as the early 18th century, reflecting in the latter case an earlier development of modern financial instruments, particularly a public debt which became the most important single financial instrument. The Indian ratio was at a comparable level if the public's hoards of gold and silver are excluded but increased very little until World War II, but it was much higher but declining if the hoards are included, a special case too complicated to be considered here (see Goldsmith 1983, chap. 1). At the eve of World War I the ratio had risen sharply to between three-fourths and unity in Belgium, France, Germany, and the United States, a level that could then be considered standard for developed countries, and was considerably higher in Denmark and Switzerland and particularly in Great Britain. The British ratio reached unity already in the 1880s, and since the turn of the century was close to or in excess of two reflecting the country's role as the first to develop most modern forms of financial instruments and financial institutions as well as the extraordinarily high ratio of foreign to domestic financial assets. Japan, whose modern financial development started only in the 1870s, attained the same level during the 1920s, while Italy lagged.

Second, the strong, and among developed countries common, upward trend, has not continued beyond World War I or the 1930s. Instead the ratio has in most countries shown substantial variations, the largest ones generally reductions which reflected the destruction of old fixed claims through inflation or currency reform and their reconstitution after stabilization. The lower ratios of 1950 in France, Germany, Italy, and Japan

Table 19 Financial Interrelations Ratio, 1850–1978

Country	Standard Benchmark Year[a]									
	1850 (1)	1875 (2)	1895 (3)	1913 (4)	1929 (5)	1939 (6)	1950 (7)	1965 (8)	1973 (9)	1978 (10)
1. Australia	...	...	...	...	...	...	0.78	0.72	0.83	0.60
2. Belgium	0.25	0.38	0.55	0.90	0.82	0.98	0.83	0.75	0.99	0.85
3. Canada	...	...	...	...	...	...	1.19	1.18	1.20	1.13
4. Denmark	...	1.11	1.28	1.41	1.55	1.26	1.12	1.04	1.25	1.10
5. France[b]	0.25	0.56	...	0.98	0.81	...	0.55	1.24	0.92	0.83
6. Germany	0.20	0.38	0.72	0.76	0.39	0.56	0.40	0.92	0.85	0.89
7. Great Britain[c]	0.68	0.93	1.96	1.96	2.45	2.70	1.77	1.50	1.29	1.11
8. Hungary	...	...	...	...	...	...	...	0.15	0.21	0.36
9. India[d]	0.64	0.47	0.40	0.34	0.30	0.38	0.45	0.54	0.57	0.54
10. Israel	...	...	...	...	...	...	0.66	0.74	0.84	1.11
11. Italy	0.21	0.39	0.45	0.47	0.68	0.73	0.42	0.85	1.16	1.04
12. Japan	...	0.30	0.34	0.64	1.23	1.42	0.55	0.81	0.92	1.02
13. Mexico	...	...	...	...	0.36	0.64	0.74	0.68	0.75	0.71
14. Norway	...	0.37	0.55	0.72	1.03	0.74	0.79	0.78	0.87	0.87
15. Russia/USSR	...	...	...	0.40	0.09	0.28	0.32	0.22	0.22	0.29
16. South Africa	...	...	...	0.52	0.69	0.92	1.14	1.14	1.04	0.76
17. Sweden	...	...	...	...	...	...	...	1.03	1.24	1.27
18. Switzerland	...	1.11	1.60	1.50	1.65	1.59	1.29	1.52	1.61	1.82
19. United States[e]	0.47	0.64	0.71	0.83	1.29	1.32	1.17	1.28	1.11	0.99
20. Yugoslavia	...	...	...	...	...	...	0.24	0.74	1.01	1.20

[a]For actual dates see table 33.

[b]In addition 1815: 0.18.

[c]In addition 1688: 0.17; 1760: 0.40; 1800: 0.57; 1830: 0.76.

[d]Excluding gold and silver: 0.15; 0.13; 0.13; 0.15; 0.19; 0.23; 0.29; 0.40; 0.45; 0.42.

[e]In addition 1774: 0.28; 1805: 0.32.

(in the first two countries also in 1929) reflect these events, although only in attenuated form since the two waves of war inflation ended well before the benchmark dates of 1929 and 1950. Between the mid-century and 1973, when the great postwar boom ended, the ratio increased in 17 countries, and substantially in most of them. It declined in only three, substantially in Great Britain and the Soviet Union and fractionally in the United States. The almost uniform decline of the ratio for developed countries between 1973 and the late 1970s seems to be connected with the acceleration of inflation, but also to be influenced by the accompanying sharp rises in real estate prices. Of the 13 countries for which the ratio can be calculated for 1913 as well as for the late 1970s, it increased in eight cases and declined in five. Four of the five countries in which the ratio declined are European countries which already had a fully developed financial superstructure before World War I, the particularly sharp fall in the case of Great Britain being in part due to the declining importance of foreign investments. The reduction in the case of Russia reflects the shift from a market to a centrally planned economy and the accompanying elimination of corporate and government securities. Four of the eight countries in which the ratio rose—India, Italy, Japan, and South Africa—are economies in which the financial superstructure was still relatively small in 1913. In the four others—Germany, Norway, Switzerland, and the United States—the increase was small. The unweighted average for the 13 countries was somewhat higher in the late 1970s with 0.93 compared to 0.88 in 1913, and the median of 0.87 was substantially higher than that of 0.76 in 1913. The interquartile range narrowed from 0.52 to 0.98 to 0.68 to 1.09, reflecting a tendency toward convergence among market economies.

Third, the movements of the ratio in Great Britain are idiosyncratic, combining a long upward swing from 0.40 at the start of the industrial revolution to a peak of 2.70 before World War II—the highest level in any country—followed by a marked continuous downward swing during the next 40 years, which has brought the ratio in the late 1970s down to the level of a century earlier. The international activities of the British financial system and the relatively large public debt certainly played an important role in accounting for the high level of the ratio until World War II while the relatively high ratio of postwar inflation contributed to the decline in the ratio since 1940, but these two factors leave a good deal to be explained.

Fourth, with India and Mexico as their sole representatives, table 19 cannot say much about the levels and trends of the financial interrelations ratio of less developed countries. The failure of the ratio (excluding hoards) to increase between the middle of the 19th century and World War I and the modest rise in the interwar period observed in India are not likely to be representative of the bulk of less developed countries, at least not for Latin America. The low level of the ratio compared to that of developed countries, on the other hand, is a common characteristic of less developed countries before World War II. Similarly, the sharp increase of the Indian ratio in the postwar period, still leaving it below that of developed countries, is probably shared by most developing countries, though the fact that the Mexican ratio has failed to increase substantially since the late 1930s suggests caution.

Fifth, and finally, the level of the financial interrelations ratio is very low in Communist developed as well as less developed countries. In the Soviet Union, whose financial statistics leave much to be desired, the ratio appears to have remained between 0.22 and 0.32 for most of the last 40 years. While this is close to the level of the ratio of Western European countries a century ago, it must be remembered that one important type of financial instrument—corporate securities—does not exist in these countries and that a second one—government securities—is of negligible size. If attention is limited to credits by financial institutions and trade credit, the Soviet ratio of fully one-fourth of tangible assets is not significantly below that of developed market economies. Hungary and Yugoslavia deviate from this pattern. The Hungarian ratio more than doubled between 1959 and 1978 from 0.15 to 0.36. The rise was particularly pronounced in the 1970s, and in part reflected a move away from a rigid Soviet-type financial organization. The movement is much more pronounced in Yugoslavia, which abandoned that system in the 1950s and now has a financial interrelations ratio similar to those found in developed market economies.

These are the statistical facts. Some contribution to their explanation can be made by a formula which identifies some of the measurable determinants of the financial interrelations ratio. The formula is, like the quantity equation of monetary theory, an identity; but like the quantity equation it is no less informative in its ability to distinguish quantitatively important and secondary components of the level and movements of the ratio. The formula, developed elsewhere (see, particularly, Goldsmith 1969, chap. 2 and 7; and Goldsmith 1970), is:

$$FIR_t = [(\delta + \phi + \xi)\ (1 + \nu)\ \alpha\beta_t^{-1}]\ \tau + \rho.$$

In the formula δ, ϕ, and ξ are the net issue ratios (net issues:national product) of domestic nonfinancial, domestic financial, and foreign issues over the period from $t - n$ to t; ν and ν' are the ratios of valuation changes to the period's issues and to assets at the beginning of the period, respectively, which depend on the share of price-sensitive assets, i.e., corporate shares, and their price trend; α is the multiplier of nominal national product over the period ($\alpha = \gamma^{-1} + 1$), where γ, the rate of growth of national product, is made up of γ', the rate of growth of real national product per head, ψ that of population and π that of the price level; β_t the capital-output ratio at the end of the period; τ the truncation ratio $(1 - 1/e^{-\gamma n})$ which ranges from zero to unity and takes account of the fact that the summation of issues extends only over the period from $t - n$ to t rather than from zero to t; ρ is the residual or carryover ratio, equal to $F_{t-n}(1 + \nu')/W_t$ where F_{t-n} is the value of financial assets at the beginning of the period and W_t that of tangible assets at its end.

The nonfinancial domestic issue ratio δ can usefully be split into ratios for private debt issues (δ_{cp}), government debt issues (δ_{cg}), and the issues of corporate shares (δ_e), the latter calling for an accompanying ratio for valuation changes. The analytic value of these ratios is considerably increased if they can be divided into the capital formation ration (k/y) and the external financial ratio (d/k), where d is the value of issues). Similarly, the domestic financial issues ratios can be divided into ratios for the issues of financial institutions (ϕ_f) and of nonfinancial sectors (ϕ_o). Understanding of that ratio is enhanced by splitting it into the financial intermediation ratio, the quotient of financial to nonfinancial issues ($\phi/\delta + \xi$), and the nonfinancial issue ratio.

It is evident from the formula that the financial interrelations ratio is positively related to the issue ratios, and therefore to the capital formation, external financing and financial intermediation ratios, and the residual, and is negatively related to the rate of growth of nominal national product and its three components, in particular the price level, as well as to the capital-output ratio.

In implementing the formula with the help of national balance sheet data and data on national product it has been necessary to combine δ_e and ν_e, i.e., to include valuation changes on stocks with their net new issues; to ignore ν', which is usually small; and to measure $(\alpha^{-1} + 1)$ by the ratio of the period's national product to its terminal rate, thus failing to separate the effects of γ, ψ, and π on α though the values of the three components can be found in table 23. The formula actually used in tables 20, 24, and 25 then is

$$FIR = (\delta_{cp} + \delta_{cg} + \delta_e + \phi + \xi)\ \bar{\alpha}\beta^{-1} + \bar{\rho}$$

where $\bar{\alpha} = \sum^{t} y/y_t$ and $\bar{\rho} = F_{t-n}/W_t$. While it has not been possible to divide each of the three domestic nonfinancial issue ratios into the corresponding capital formation and external financing ratios, the split has been attempted for the aggregate of domestic nonfinancial issues. Limitation of data has prevented a systematic separation of ϕ_b from ϕ_o. The financial intermediation ratio is not explicitly shown in tables 20, 25, and 26 but can be calculated from the values of ϕ and δ shown in the tables and is discussed in Chapter 3, 2.a rather than here.

All the parameters of the equations shown in tables 20, 25, and 26 have been derived from the absolute figures underlying the country tables in Appendix A. The numerators of the issue ratios are the differences between the amounts outstanding at the appropriate benchmark dates, which implies that they include valuation changes that generally are important only for the relatively small amounts of corporate stock; the denominators are the figures for gross national product shown at the bottom of the country tables for benchmark dates or the sums of gross national product for the periods between benchmark dates.

In comparing the calculated and the observed values of the financial interrelations ratio in tables 20, 25, and 26 it is necessary to realize that the differences are due mostly to three facts: (1) the use of rates of growth of national product derived from only the first and last years of the period in calculating, and of a summation formula that uses only these two years as the basis of the denominator of the issue ratios; (2) the ommission from the simplified formula of ν because it is difficult to calculate and generally small (Goldsmith 1969, 85, 328); (3) the omission of τ, which, while not too difficult to approximate, is also generally small, rarely being below 0.90 for the periods of several decades which are covered in tables 24 and 26 (Goldsmith 1969, 332). The two omitted factors almost always tend in the opposite directions, ν slightly increasing the value of the financial interrelations ratio and τ slightly reducing it. It is in part this largely offsetting character of ν and τ which explains the generally small differences between the calculated and the observed values of the financial interrelations ratios.

The main determinants of the financial interrelation ratio can be followed in table 20 for 11 countries, including all most important ones, for a period of about three decades before World War I, a period long enough not to be unduly influenced by ephemeral events; hardly affected by war or inflation; and a period of particular interest because it witnessed the emergence of most countries' modern economic and financial systems, which antedates the middle of the 19th century only in Great Britain.

In 1913 the unweighted averages of the observed financial interrelations ratio was 1.05 for the 11 countries, but 1.13 for the Big Four (France, Germany, Great Britain, United States), and extended from 0.34 (India) to 1.96 (Great Britain), with an interquartile range of approximately 0.50–1.50. Table 21 shows—and this is the essential point—that these ratios are the result of quite different and partly offsetting determining factors.

For financial analysis probably the most interesting factors are the five issue ratios, which measure the volume of net issue of financial instruments emitted by domestic nonfinancial and financial and by foreign issuers in relation to national product. Their total averaged 17 percent for the pre-1913 period, varying from less than 2 percent in India and from 7 percent in Italy to 29 percent in Switzerland, but keeping between 13 and 21 percent among the Big Four. The issues of domestic nonfinancial

Table 20 **Determinants of the Financial Interrelations Ratio in the Pre–World War I Period**

	Period	New Issue Ratios (%)						Multi-plier[a]	Output Capital Ratio[a]		Resid-ual	Financial Interrelations Ratio[a]	
		δ_{cp}	δ_{cg}	δ_e	ϕ	ξ	ϵ[b]	α	β^{-1}	$\epsilon\alpha\beta^{-1}$	ρ	Calcu-lated	Ob-served
	(1)	(2)	(3)	(4)	(5)	(6)	(7)	(8)	(9)	(10)	(11)	(12)	(13)
1. Belgium	1876–1913	8.6	2.5	2.8	4.1	3.9	21.9	19.0	0.18	0.75	0.20	0.95	0.90
2. Denmark	1881–1913	10.8	1.4	3.6	9.0	0.4	25.2	18.4	0.24	1.11	0.30	1.41	1.41
3. France	1881–1913	3.7	1.4	1.6	3.4	2.6	12.7	22.9	0.18	0.52	0.44	0.96	0.98
4. Germany	1876–1913	8.3	2.1	2.0	6.6	1.6	20.6	19.1	0.16	0.63	0.14	0.77	0.76
5. Great Britain	1876–1913	3.1	0.5	3.8	2.2	4.6	14.2	24.9	0.34	1.20	0.75	1.95	1.96
6. India	1876–1913	1.0	0.2	0.2	0.4	−0.8	1.8	23.4	0.29	0.12	0.17	0.29	0.34
7. Italy	1881–1914	2.1	1.5	0.2	3.3	−0.3	7.1	20.0	0.19	0.27	0.19	0.46	0.47
8. Japan	1886–1913	9.4	1.8	2.8	7.6	−0.3	21.6	13.9	0.19	0.58	0.06	0.64	0.64
9. Norway	1881–1913	7.7	1.3	2.0	5.4	−0.1	16.4	21.2	0.16	0.56	0.16	0.72	0.72
10. Switzerland	1881–1913	7.0	2.6	4.1	9.8	5.7	29.2	16.7	0.22	1.07	0.42	1.49	1.50
11. United States	1881–1912	7.7	0.4	5.3	3.9	1.0	18.3	15.4	0.24	0.68	0.15	0.83	0.83

[a]At end of period.

[b]Sum of cols. 2–6, excluding col. 6 in lines 6–9 because it represents issues floated abroad.

Source of basic data: Absolute figures underlying country tables in Appendix A; for col. 13 see table 19.

Table 21 **Average[a] Financial Interrelations Ratio and Its Main Components, 1876–1978**

	Prewar (1876–1913)[b]	Interwar (1914–50)[b]	Postwar (1951–78)[b]	
	(1)	(2)	(3)	(4)
I. New issue ratio (ϵ)	0.173	0.291	0.452	0.466
1. Domestic private debt	0.063	0.075	0.165	0.162
2. Domestic government debt	0.014	0.070	0.045	0.047
3. Domestic equities	0.026	0.036	0.032	0.036
4. Domestic financial issues	0.051	0.095	0.183	0.183
5. Foreign issues	0.019	0.015	0.026	0.038
II. Multiplier (α)	19.7	12.7	8.4	9.0
III. Capital/output ratio (β^{-1})	0.22	0.25	0.25	0.23
IV. Carry-over ratio (ρ)	0.27	0.15	0.07	0.07
V. Financial interrelations ratio, end of period				
1. Average	0.96	0.99	0.88	1.01
2. Median	0.83	1.10	0.95	0.93
3. Range				
a) Total	0.35–1.95	0.41–1.87	0.34–1.82	0.54–1.82
b) Interquartile	0.52–0.98	0.51–1.15	0.76–1.14	0.83–1.15
VI. Number of countries	11	9	20	11

[a]Unweighted averages.
[b]Standard benchmark dates; for actual years cf. table 33. Figures in lines III–V refer to end of period.
Source of basic data: Tables 20, 25 and 26.

units, i.e., essentially business and government, were in all countries substantially larger than domestic financial or foreign issues. The ratio of domestic nonfinancial to financial issues varied between less than 1½ (Italy, Switzerland) and about 3½ (Great Britan, India, United States), with an average of little over 2. The distribution of nonfinancial issues can be followed in table 22. Debt issues of the private sector, i.e., business and households, are shown to have accounted in the pre–World War I period on the average for one-half of all nonfinancial issues, government debt issues for one-eighth, and domestic equity and foreign issues for nearly one-fifth and one-sixth, respectively. The share of equity issues is, however, considerably overstated as it includes the appreciation in their prices over the period. Excluding appreciation, their share is likely to have been below one-tenth, while that of the other three types of issues would be increased slightly. Deviations from the averages are, however, substantial, particularly for government and foreign issues. Thus the share of domestic government issues ranged from less than 5 percent in Great Britain and the United States to over one-third in Italy compared to an average of 13 percent and an interquartile range of 9–14 percent. Foreign issues were the largest component in Great Britain, with nearly two-fifths of all nonfinancial issues, but exceeded one-fifth of the total also in Belgium, France, and Switzerland. The high Indian ratio reflects the accumulation of gold and silver hoards rather than as in the other countries where it predominantly evidences the acquisition of foreign securities.

The level and distribution of the issue ratios are the result of numerous influences, particularly the methods of financing the private sectors' capital expenditures, the size of the government's deficit, and the structure of the balance of payments. There is no room to discuss these problems here, if only because most of the necessary basic data are lacking. It is, however, possible to provide an idea of the level and the intercountry differences of the two components of the issue ratios of domestic nonfinancial issues, unfortunately only for the aggregate of private and government debt and of equity issues, namely, the national gross capital formation ratio ($\kappa = k/y$) and the external financing ratio ($\eta = d/k$, where d = net issues). The latter ratio reflects not only, as one would wish, the extent to which capital expenditures are financed externally but also the use of external funds for other purposes, such as the acquisition of financial assets, the financing of private consumption, and in the case of governments the meeting of current deficits. The external financing ratio as measured here is also overstated to the extent that the numerator includes the appreciation of corporate shares.

The distribution of the issue ratio of nonfinancial issues during the interwar period is characterized by the high share of the government of

Table 22 **Distribution of Net New Nonfinancial Issues, 1875–1978 (%)**

	Pre–World War I Period (1875–1913)[a]				Interwar Period (1914–50)[a]				Postwar Period (1951–78)[a]			
	Domestic				Domestic				Domestic			
	Government debt (1)	Private debt (2)	Equities[b] (3)	Foreign[c] (4)	Government debt (5)	Private debt (6)	Equities[b] (7)	Foreign[c] (8)	Government debt (9)	Private (10)	Equities[b] (11)	Foreign[c] (12)
1. Australia	...	...	...	...	...	...	...	...	20.1	57.8	12.0	10.1
2. Belgium	14.1	48.2	15.7	22.0	43.6	30.7	13.8	11.9	32.4	34.8	7.7	25.1
3. Canada	...	...	...	...	...	...	...	...	17.0	62.5	11.6	8.9
4. Denmark	8.9	66.2	22.2	2.7	24.5	56.8	13.6	5.1	8.1	74.8	11.3	5.8
5. France	14.7	40.0	17.4	27.9	21.5	56.9	20.2	1.4	5.8	61.6	17.5	15.1
6. Germany	15.0	59.3	14.2	11.5	...[d]	...[d]	...[d]	...[d]	12.9	52.7	18.0	16.4
7. Great Britain	4.3	25.3	32.1	38.3	52.4	21.7	25.3	0.6	18.9	41.8	13.7	25.6
8. India	9.2	46.5	7.4	36.9	13.7	46.0	8.4	31.9	14.1	60.0	5.4	20.5
9. Israel	...	...	...	...	...	...	...	...	33.0	60.7	5.6	0.7
10. Italy	37.1	51.0	3.8	8.1	44.9	41.3	12.6	1.2	44.1	47.9	5.0	3.0
11. Japan	12.5	65.3	20.0	2.2	...[d]	...[d]	...[d]	...[d]	7.3	79.9	11.6	1.2
12. Mexico	...	...	...	...	...	...	...	...	10.1	46.4	43.2	0.3
13. Norway	11.9	69.1	17.9	1.1	28.5	66.9	3.9	0.7	28.8	62.9	8.1	0.2
14. South Africa	...	...	...	...	31.6	33.3	34.0	1.1	20.2	51.4	15.2	13.2
15. Sweden	...	...	...	...	...	...	...	...	9.4	78.9	5.6	6.1
16. Switzerland	13.2	36.4	20.9	29.5	15.7	36.2	26.5	21.6	5.1	38.7	17.6	38.6
17. United States	2.9	53.3	36.6	7.2	37.3	33.8	19.0	9.9	15.9	56.0	21.5	6.6

[a]For actual dates see table 33.
[b]Includes valuation changes.
[c]Includes monetary metals.
[d]Omitted because of hyperinflation or currency reform.
Source of basic data: Absolute figures underlying country tables in Appendix A.

nearly one-third—more than double the share of the preceding full half century—which, of course, reflects the financing of the large deficits most countries incurred during both world wars and the Great Depression. In contrast the share of foreign issues was cut in half. Those of equities and of domestic private debt issues, on the other hand, were only moderately reduced. The pattern of distribution during the postwar period returned to one closer to that of the period before World War I, though shares of government and of private debt issues were somewhat higher and those of equities and of foreign issues were by about three-tenths below the earlier levels.

In table 23 the issue ratios of the nonfinancial domestic sectors are broken down into their two components, the capital formation ratio ($k = K/y$) and the external financing ratio (d/k).

Table 23 **Two Components[a] of the Issue Ratios of Nonfinancial Domestic Sectors**

	Standard Benchmark Period[b]					
	Pre–World War I (1875–1913)			Postwar (1951–78)		
Country	η (1)	κ (2)	δ (3)	η (4)	κ (5)	δ (6)
1. Australia	...	...	...	0.67	0.26	0.17
2. Belgium	...	...	...	0.67	0.20	0.14
3. Canada	...	...	...	1.32	0.24	0.31
4. Denmark	1.40	0.11	0.16	1.04	0.24	0.25
5. France	0.48	0.14	0.07	0.91	0.24	0.22
6. Germany	0.59	0.21	0.12	0.73	0.25	0.18
7. Great Britain	1.06	0.07	0.07	1.55	0.19	0.29
8. Hungary	...	...	...	0.24	0.35	0.09
9. India	0.25	0.06	0.01	0.91	0.19	0.17
10. Israel	...	...	...	1.41	0.30	0.43
11. Italy	0.32	0.12	0.04	1.23	0.22	0.27
12. Japan	0.78	0.18	0.14	1.32	0.34	0.45
13. Mexico	...	...	...	1.11	0.22	0.24
14. Norway	0.66	0.17	0.11	0.92	0.32	0.29
15. Russia/USSR	...	...	...	0.14	0.30	0.04
16. South Africa	...	...	...	0.74	0.28	0.21
17. Sweden	...	...	...	1.44	0.23	0.33
18. Switzerland	...	...	...	0.92	0.26	0.24
19. United States	0.64	0.21	0.13	1.07	0.19	0.21
20. Yugoslavia	...	...	...	0.78	0.40	0.31

[a] $\eta = d/k$, $\kappa = k/y$ and $\delta = d/t$ where d = net domestic nonfinancial issues, k = gross capital formation excluding consumer durables, and y = gross national product.

[b] For actual dates see table 33.

Source of basic data: see text.

For the nine countries, for which the relations can be estimated for the period before World War I, the domestic nonfinancial issue ratio averaged fully 9 percent of gross national product. Since the actual gross capital formation ratio averaged 14 percent, the average external financing ratio was in the order of 70 percent or, if some allowance is made for the overstatement of the new issue ratios because of inclusion of share appreciation, of approximately 60 percent. Since part of the issues were used for purposes other than capital expenditures, the ratio of gross capital expenditures financed externally was on the average probably closer to one-half. Intercountry differences were obviously large. As measured, and hence somewhat overstated, the external financing ratio ranged from one-fourth in India and less than one-third in Italy to more than unity in Great Britain and Denmark, staying between nearly one-half and fully three-fourths in France, Germany, Japan, Norway, and the United States. While the ranking of the different countries is not unreasonable in view of their financial structure and financing methods in the Victorian era (except for Denmark), the figures must be interpreted very cautiously.

Among the other determinants of the financial interrelations ratio (shown in table 20), the output-capital ratio (β^{-1}) at the eve of World War I averaged 0.22—i.e., the more familiar capital-output ratio averaged 4.5—with an interquartile range of 0.18–0.24 and extremes of 0.16 and 0.34. This ratio is a basic characteristic of the real side of the economy and must be treated as exogeneous in financial analysis. This is also true of the multiplier (α) and at least two of its three components, the rates of growth of population and of real national product per head. For the three to four decades before World War I the multiplier averaged 20, implying an average rate of growth of nominal national product of 5 percent, with a range from 14 to 25. The two countries for which rises in the price level were most pronounced because they were on the silver standard during part of the period—India and Japan—showed one of the highest and the lowest multiplier reflecting differences in the rate of growth of real national product. Rapid growth of real national product was responsible for the low multiplier of the United States and slow growth for the high multipliers of France and Great Britain. The contribution of the three components to the value of the multiplier can be followed in table 24. On the average real national product per head accounted for nearly one-half of the rate of growth in nominal national product, which determines the value of the multiplier; population growth for nearly one-third; and changes in the price level—slightly negative for three countries—for one-fifth.

The carry-over ratio, averaging fully one-fourth, is generally positively related to the multiplier. Its particularly high value in Great Britain

Table 24 **Components of Growth Rate of Nominal Gross National Product**

	Prewar Period (1851–1913)[a]				Interwar Period (1914–1950)[a]				Postwar Period (1951–1978)[a]			
		Share of				Share of				Share of		
	Growth Rate[b] (1)	Price Level (2)	Population (3)	RPH[c] (4)	Growth Rate[b] (5)	Price Level (6)	Population (7)	RPH[c] (8)	Growth Rate[b] (9)	Price Level (10)	Population (11)	RPH[c] (12)
1. Australia	...	...	...	...	...	...	...	...	10.55	57	19	24
2. Belgium	2.28	−10	44	66	11.16	91	3	6	7.38	47	6	47
3. Canada	...	...	...	...	...	...	...	...	9.51	50	19	31
4. Denmark	3.25	−2	34	68	6.15	65	19	16	10.07	62	6	32
5. France	1.88	10	9	81	15.93	91	1	8	11.23	53	7	40
6. Germany	2.84	14	43	43	...	...	...	...	9.44	44	8	48
7. Great Britain	1.84	−8	51	57	4.60	72	5	23	8.83	70	4	26
8. Hungary	...	...	...	...	...	...	...	...	7.33	21	5	74
9. India	2.01	72	22	6	3.82	68	24	8	8.23	39	25	36
10. Israel	...	...	...	...	...	...	...	...	21.95	61	16	23
11. Italy	2.40	29	30	41	18.05	88	4	8	11.48	59	6	35
12. Japan	6.62	60	16	24	19.66	80	7	13	14.92	39	7	64
13. Mexico	...	...	...	...	...	...	...	...	15.42	41	22	37
14. Norway	2.39	26	36	38	6.79	50	11	39	9.60	47	8	45
15. Russia/USSR	...	...	...	...	...	...	...	...	6.62	22	20	58
16. South Africa	...	...	...	...	6.55	34	30	36	10.84	55	28	17
17. Sweden	...	...	...	...	...	...	...	...	10.04	73	6	21
18. Switzerland	4.35	29	22	49	3.33	70	14	16	7.38	53	15	32
19. United States	4.38	5	45	50	5.53	49	22	29	7.36	51	18	31
20. Yugoslavia	...	...	...	...	...	...	...	...	19.85	55	5	40

[a]For actual dates cf. table 33.
[b]Percent per year.
[c]Real gross national product per head.
Source of basic data: *YNAS* (var. issues); *IFSYB* (1980); Mitchell (1975); Goldsmith (1983a, 1983b).

reflects the fact that the country's financial superstructure was in 1875 already further developed than elsewhere.

The picture for the interwar period, which is shown for individual countries in table 25 and in the form of unweighted averages in column 2 of table 21 is in the most countries determined by the inflations during the two world wars, particularly evident in the low financial interrelations ratios of France, Germany, Italy, and Japan which would have been even lower immediately after the war. The average close to mid-century was only slightly above that of 1913, but the spread was somewhat narrower, as was the interquartile range. For the nine countries for which the financial interrelations ratio can be broken down into its main components, the (calculated) average of 0.99 is the result of a new issue ratio of nearly 0.30, a multiplier of nearly 12, an output-capital ratio of 0.25, and a residual of 0.15. In comparison to the financial interrelations ratios of 1913 for the same countries, which are based on the full half-century starting around 1860, the average of the new issue ratios for the following nearly four decades is considerably higher, while the multiplier is much lower reflecting the inflation during the two world wars; the output-capital ratios is slightly higher; and the carry-over ratio is much lower, again a result of inflation.

Turning from averages to individual countries, the financial interrelations ratios for the mid-20th century are in most cases somewhat below those of 1913—on the average by 0.10 or one-tenth of their 1913 level—but the changes in their determinants are much larger. There were only three countries in which the financial interrelations ratio was higher than in 1913—India, Norway, and the United States—but for different reasons, in the United States in part because of the much higher government debt issue ratios. In general, the new issue ratios for the interwar period are considerably higher than those for the three to four decades before World War I and the multipliers considerably lower. These changes reflect the more rapid rise in the price level, which on the average accounted for over two-thirds of the rate of growth of nominal national product, leaving one-eighth for the growth in population and only one-fifth for that of real product per head. On the other hand, the output-capital ratios are only slightly higher, averaging 0.26 against 0.21. The details can be followed in table 25.

In the late 1970s the (unweighted) financial interrelations ratio for 10 developed market economies averaged 1.01, hardly different from its 1913 value of 0.96, and only slightly different from the average of 0.84 for all 20 countries and of 0.93 for the 17 market economies. The ratio increased in seven countries by on the average 0.26 or fully one-third of the 1913 value, and declined in four of them by an average of 0.30, or nearly one-fourth in the process reducing the average absolute deviation

Table 25 **Determinants of the Financial Interrelations Ratio in the Interwar Period**

		New Issue Ratio (%)						Multiplier	Output Capital Ratio		Residual	Financial Interrelations Ratio[a]	
	Period (1)	δ_{cp} (2)	δ_{cg} (3)	δ_e (4)	ϕ (5)	ξ (6)	ϵ (2−6) (7)	$\bar{\alpha}$ (8)	β^{-1}[a] (9)	$\epsilon\bar{\alpha}\beta^{-1}$[a] (10)	$\bar{\rho}$ (11)	Calculated (12)	Observed (13)
1. Belgium	1914–48	10.0	14.0	4.5	14.0	3.9	46.4	7.1	0.24	0.79	0.03	0.82	0.83
2. Denmark	1914–48	8.1	3.5	1.9	10.5	0.7	24.7	14.2	0.26	0.91	0.19	1.10	1.12
3. France	1914–50	...	...	...	...	...	...[b]	...[b]	0.32	...[b]	0.01	...[b]	0.55
4. Germany	1914–50	...	...	...	...	...	...[c]	...[c]	0.26	...[c]	0.00	...[c]	0.40
5. Great Britain	1914–48	4.1	9.8	4.7	8.7	0.1	27.4	16.4	0.33	1.48	0.39	1.87	1.77
6. India	1914–50	3.6	1.1	0.7	2.1	2.5	10.0	14.7	0.26	0.38	0.06	0.44	0.47
7. Italy	1915–51	11.6	12.6	3.5	13.8	0.3	41.8	4.9	0.20	0.41	0.00	0.41	0.42
8. Japan	1913–55	...	...	...	...	...	...[c]	...[c]	0.25	...[c]	0.00	...[c]	0.55
9. Norway	1914–53	9.5	4.0	0.6	10.5	0.1	24.7	13.8	0.21	0.72	0.07	0.79	0.79
10. South Africa	1914–55	9.2	8.7	9.3	9.8	0.3	37.3	11.1	0.21	0.87	0.06	0.93	1.14
11. Switzerland	1914–48	5.8	2.5	4.3	8.9	3.5	25.0	18.6	0.20	0.93	0.42	1.35	1.29
12. United States	1913–50	5.9	6.4	3.3	7.6	1.7	24.9	13.9	0.30	1.04	0.13	1.17	1.17

[a]At end of period.
[b]Omitted because absence of estimates of gross national product.
[c]Omitted because of hyperinflation or currency reform.
Source: As for table 20.

from the mean from 0.36 to 0.19. This similarity, however, hides large and significant changes in the value of the determinants of the ratio. Thus the new issue ratio in the postwar period with 0.47 was almost three times as high as the 0.17 value of the pre-1913 period. In contrast, the multiplier averaged 9.0 compared with nearly 20 in the earlier period, reflecting a much accelerated rate of growth of nominal national product due chiefly to a much more rapid rise in the price level; and for the same reason the average carry-over ratio was radically lower at 0.07 compared to 0.27 in 1913. On the other hand, the output-capital ratios were practically the same at 0.22.

Differences were also substantial though less radical in the structure of the new issue ratios. First, the share of domestic financial issues with nearly two-fifths was considerably higher than the almost 30 percent of the pre–World War I period. Second, the share of government in all domestic financial issues with one-fifth was much larger than it had been in the pre–World War I period, while that of equity issues (including valuation changes) was reduced from about 25 to 15 percent—not much higher relative to national product than it had been half a century earlier—and the share of private debt issues was slightly in excess of three-fifths in both periods. The share of foreign in all nonfinancial issues rose slightly from about 15 to 18 percent, but changed its content from mainly publicly offered bonds and stocks to direct investments and bank loans. Finally, both components of the domestic nonfinancial issue ratio of 0.09 and 0.24 increased in approximately equal proportions, the gross capital formation ratio (excluding consumer durables) from 0.14 to 0.23 and the external financing ratio (including appreciation of corporate stock) from 0.69 to 1.03. This indicates that in the more recent period a larger proportion of the growing gross capital formation was financed externally by debt and to a declining extent by corporate stock issues.

The components of the multiplier also were quite different. In the postwar period one-half of the rate of growth of nominal national product was due to inflation compared to only one-fifth in the three to four decades before 1913. Population growth accounted for only one-eighth against nearly one-third, leaving nearly two-fifths against almost one-half to real product per head.

These averages, of course, again hide considerable differences among countries, which can be followed in table 26, but whose description, let alone explanation, would far transcend the scope and possibilities of this study as it would require an analysis of the past century's economic and financial history of a dozen countries.

Some comments are, however, in order on the differences in the level and determinants of the financial interrelations ratio in the late 1970s of the 20 countries.

Table 26 **Determinants of the Financial Interrelations Ratio in the Postwar Period**

	Period (1)	New Issue Ratio; percent δ_{cp} (2)	δ_{cg} (3)	δ_e (4)	ϕ (5)	ξ (6)	ϵ (7)	Multiplier α (8)	Output Capital Ratio β^{-1}[a] (9)	(7)×(8)×(9) $\epsilon\alpha\beta^{-1}$ (10)	Residual ρ[a] (11)	Financial Interrelations Ratio[a] Calculated (12)	Observed (13)
1. Australia	1948–77	11.0	3.8	2.3	12.9	1.9	31.8	8.56	0.21	0.57	0.05	0.62	0.60
2. Belgium	1949–76	6.4	5.9	1.4	16.4	4.6	34.7	9.52	0.23	0.76	0.09	0.85	0.85
3. Canada	1956–78	21.4	5.8	4.0	16.7	3.1	50.9	8.32	0.24	1.02	0.12	1.14	1.13
4. Denmark	1949–78	19.5	2.1	2.9	24.1	1.5	50.1	8.65	0.24	1.04	0.06	1.10	1.10
5. France	1951–76	16.1	1.5	4.6	12.8	3.9	38.9	8.21	0.25	0.80	0.03	0.83	0.83
6. Germany	1951–77	11.3	2.8	3.9	15.0	3.5	36.5	9.93	0.22	0.80	0.03	0.83	0.89
7. Great Britain	1949–77	16.2	7.3	5.3	21.0	9.9	59.7	8.20	0.24	1.17	0.11	1.28	1.11
8. Hungary	1960–77	8.5	...	...	9.1	...	17.6	9.60	0.19	0.32	0.04	0.36	0.36
9. India	1951–75	13.0	3.0	1.2	6.8	4.4[b]	28.4	9.07	0.19	0.49	0.05	0.54	0.54
10. Israel	1952–76	26.1	14.2	2.4	68.5	...	111.2	3.77	0.26	1.09	0.00	1.09	1.11
11. Italy	1952–77	13.5	12.5	1.4	36.1	0.9	64.4	6.59	0.24	1.02	0.03	1.05	1.04
12. Japan	1956–77	36.6	3.4	5.3	19.3	0.5	65.1	7.06	0.22	1.01	0.02	1.03	1.02
13. Mexico	1949–78	11.3	2.4	10.5	12.3	...	36.5	5.03	0.38	0.70	0.01	0.70	0.70
14. Norway	1954–78	17.8	8.1	2.3	16.4	...	44.6	8.72	0.20	0.78	0.08	0.86	0.87
15. South Africa	1956–78	12.2	4.8	3.6	16.3	3.1	40.0	7.23	0.23	0.67	0.09	0.76	0.76
16. Sweden	1964–78	27.3	3.3	2.0	12.0	2.1	46.6	7.64	0.29	1.03	0.26	1.29	1.27
17. Switzerland	1949–78	15.4	2.0	7.0	24.1	15.3	63.8	12.98	0.20	1.66	0.16	1.82	1.82
18. United States	1951–78	12.4	3.5	4.7	8.9	1.5	31.0	10.36	0.25	0.80	0.13	0.93	0.99
19. U.S.S.R.	1951–77	4.1	...	...	5.2	...	9.3	13.60	0.21	0.27	0.03	0.30	0.29
20. Yugoslavia	1963–77	29.9	1.2	...	12.4	...	43.5	4.50	0.55	1.08	0.06	1.14	1.20

[a] At end of period.
[b] Mostly appreciation on holdings of gold and silver.
Source: As for table 20.

The new issue ratio, averaging 0.45 for the 20 countries, range from less than 0.10 in the Soviet Union to 1.15 in Israel, with an interquartile range of 0.35 to 0.50. The country ratios were negatively related to the multiplier, which was strongly influenced by the rate of inflation. As a result, since differences in the output-capital ratio were generally much smaller—16 of the 20 values lie between 0.19 and 0.25—and the carry-over ratio was generally small—in 15 of the countries below 0.10 with an average of 0.07—the range of the financial interrelations ratios of 0.30–1.82, was considerably narrower than that of the new issue ratios, which extends from 0.09 to 1.15. There remains, however, a definite though not close positive correlation between the new issue ratio and the financial interrelations ratio. To that extent, therefore, the new issue ratio and its main components, the capital formation ratio and the external financing ratio, which together determine the nonfinancial issue ratio and the financial intermediation ratio, may be regarded as the principal determinants of the financial interrelations ratio. These ratios, in turn, are the result of the complex interplay of numerous financial and nonfinancial factors, some of which are amenable to an explanation by economic theory while others depend on institutional peculiarities and historical accidents. A simple explanation of the level and movements of the financial interrelations ratio is therefore hardly to be expected.

The level of real national product per head is not among the determinants of the financial interrelations ratio distinguished in the formula. This means that the relative size of the financial superstructure is not regarded as directly determined by real product per head or as rising with increasing affluence. It is, however, possible that the level of real product per head indirectly influences the value of the financial interrelations ratio, e.g., if the capital formation ratio is positively correlated to real product per head. It therefore seems worthwhile to look at the relationships between the value of the financial interrelations ratio and the level of real product per head either among countries or over time.

There is some evidence that a positive association between the movements of national real product per head and the financial interrelations ratio existed among developed countries during the 19th century. Thus for the six countries for which the data go back to the middle of the century (Belgium, France, Germany, Great Britain, Italy, United States), the relations for the four relevant benchmark years (for actual dates see table 33) show the following picture:

	1850	1875	1895	1913
Unweighted average:				
Real national product per head; $1970[a]	542	817	1029	1282
Financial interrelations ratio[b]	0.34	0.55	0.85	0.98
Weighted average:[a]				
Real national product per head; $1970[a]	551	840	1178	1449
Financial interrelations ratio[b]	0.39	0.61	0.93	1.01

[a]Weighted by aggregate real gross national product (Maddison 1979, 426–29, multiplied by population).
[b]Table 19.

For this period the elasticity of the ratio to real national product, i.e., the quotient of the two growth rates (weighted averages), was very close to unity. The relation is also positive for three additional European countries (Denmark, Norway, Switzerland) for which the data start somewhat later as well as for Japan and India. It also holds for the two European countries (France and Great Britain) for which information is available for the first half of the 19th century.

In Great Britain the financial interrelations ratio is estimated to have advanced from 0.17 in 1688 to 0.68 in 1850 (table 19) a level reached by most other countries only late in the 19th century, while the increase in real national product per head is put at from $(1970)288 to 698 (Maddison 1979, 424–25) and thus was relatively less rapid than the former. The French ratio seems to have advanced from 0.18 in 1815 to 0.26 in 1850, about in line with the rise of real national product per head from $(1970) 377 in 1820 to 537 30 years later.

The positive correlation over time between financial interrelations ratio and real national product per head, however, breaks down for the period since World War I. In the late 1970s the (unweighted) average financial interrelations ratio for 10 developed countries of 1.05 was only insignificantly above the 1913 of 1.02, although the average real national product had almost quadrupled. If the ratio between the rate of growth of real national product and of the financial interrelations ratio, which prevailed before 1913, had continued, one would have expected instead an average ratio for the late 1970s of about five! Among the 10 countries, the ratio of the late 1970s was actually lower than that of 1913 in five (Belgium, Denmark, France, and considerably so in Denmark and Great Britain), and it was sightly above the 1913 ratio in four (Germany, Norway, Switzerland, United States). Even in the two countries in which the positive difference was substantial—Italy and Japan which in 1913 had the lowest ratios—the increase in the ratio was proportionately much smaller than that in real national product per head.

To test the intercountry relationship between the financial interrelations ratio and the level of real national product per head, tables 27 and 28 show the result of regressing the financial interrelations ratio on real national product per head for different groups of countries and different benchmark dates. The results of the calculations for nine developed countries and eight benchmark dates between 1875 and 1978 are reported in table 27. They show only a small degree of correlation, real national product per head explaining at most—in 1950 and 1965—fully one-fourth of the variance in the financial interrelations ratios, and on the average for the eight dates only one-seventh. Moreover, hardly any of the parameters are statistically significant. The results are equally negative for the relationship in the late 1970s for different groups of countries shown in table 28. Real national product per head explains the relatively largest, but still only a small, proportion of the variance of the financial interrelations ratios for five large developed countries and for the two groups of countries that include less developed and centrally planned economies having both relatively low financial interrelations ratios and real national product per head levels. It is thus evident that it is necessary to look

Table 27 **Correlation between the Financial Interrelations Ratio (x) and Real Gross National Product per Head (y; $000 of 1970)[a] in Nine Developed Countries,[b] 1875–1978**

Standard Benchmark Year[c]		Equation			R^2
1875	x =	0.258	+	0.052y	0.117
		(0.556)		(0.892)	
1895	x =	0.282	+	0.070y	0.161
		(0.418)		(1.071)	
1913	x =	0.296	+	0.063y	0.189
		(0.436)		(1.181)	
1929	x =	0.285	+	0.062y	0.168
		(0.320)		(1.101)	
1939	x =	−0.118	+	0.080y	0.192
		(−0.102)		(1.195)	
1950	x =	0.264	+	0.036y	0.266
		(0.523)		(1.474)	
1965	x =	0.353	+	0.023y	0.310
		(0.800)		(1.640)	
1978	x =	1.452	−	0.008y	0.038
		(2.015)		(−0.485)	

[a]Maddison (1979), 426–28.

[b]Belgium, Denmark, France, Germany, Great Britain, Italy, Norway, Switzerland, and United States.

[c]For actual dates, see table 33.

Table 28 **Correlation between the Financial Interrelations Ratio (x) and Real Gross National Product per Head (y; $000 of 1970)[a] in the Late 1970s[b] for Different Groups of Countries**

Country Groups	Equation				R²
1. Five developed countries[c]	x =	1.663	−	0.0136y	0.313
		(2.428)		(−0.954)	
2. Nine developed countries[d]	x =	1.452	−	0.0077y	0.038
		(2.011)		(−0.485)	
3. Ten developed countries[e]	x =	1.387	−	0.0066y	0.028
		(2.125)		(−0.451)	
4. Twelve developed countries[f]	x =	0.976	+	0.0013y	0.001
		(1.767)		(0.103)	
5. Sixteen market economies[g]	x =	0.624	+	0.0090y	0.209
		(3.181)		(1.852)	
6. Twenty countries[h]	x =	0.511	+	0.0012y	0.259
		(2.802)		(2.438)	

[a]Maddison (1979), 426–28.
[b]For actual dates see table 33.
[c]Belgium, France, Germany, Great Britain, United States.
[d]As for table 25.
[e]Group 2 plus Japan.
[f]Group 3 plus Australia and Canada.
[g]Group 4 plus India, Israel, Mexico, and South Africa.
[h]Group 5 plus Hungary, Sweden, USSR, and Yugoslavia.

beyond real national product per head to explain the level and movements of financial interrelations ratios, particularly after World War I and among developed market economies.

2

Conceptual and Statistical Problems

"Strict logic is a stern master, and if one respected it, one would never construct or use any national balance sheet," to adapt a statement Arthur Burns made half a century ago with respect to the less novel and controversial subject of production indices (Burns 1934, 262). And yet as empirical economists would not like to do without production indices and the even more complex tool of national income and product accounts, so economists and financial analysts find use for, and even need, national and sectoral balance sheets as the most comprehensive statement of nonhuman assets, of the structure of the capital stock, and of the essentials of financial structure.

1. The Function of National and Sectoral Balance Sheets

The construction of national and sectoral balance sheets serves two main objectives. The first, formal one, is to provide one of the main components of a system of national accounts, such as is outlined, e.g., in the United Nations schedules (1968, 1977). The second, substantive, objective is to provide a condensed picture of a country's or a sector's tangible wealth and of its superstructure of financial assets, liabilities, and net worth at one date and over time. In that role national balance sheets facilitate, or may even be essential for, the study of the structure of a country's capital stock, of its financial superstructure, and of the interrelations between the two; and of changes over time of differences among countries in these magnitudes and their interrelationships. Sectoral balance sheets provide a basis for similar analyses for the main sectors of the economy—households, financial and nonfinancial business enterprises, and governments—and for subsectors of them. They permit, in addition, comparisons among sectors of the structure of tangible and financial assets and of changes in them.

The statistical information contained in national and sectoral balance sheets is used in many fields of economic analysis beyond their primary application in the study of intertemporal changes and intersectoral or international differences in the structure of tangible and financial assets. Among such uses are, the order of listing not reflecting their importance or claiming to be exhaustive, the calculation of national and sectoral capital—output, capital-income and capital-labor ratios; the derivation of the financial interrelations ratio (financial: tangible assets) and the financial intermediation ratio (assets of financial institutions: total financial assets); the relation of reproduction costs of reproducible assets or preferably of the adjusted value of net worth to the market valuation of corporate stock; the separation of the effects of saving and valuation changes in the increase or decrease of the value of assets or of net worth between two dates; the calculation of leverage ratios, i.e., the rate of change in net worth per unit of change of price-sensitive assets, a ratio which depends on the share of price-sensitive in total assets and on the debt-asset ratio; and the use of individual components of national and sectoral balance sheets in econometric models, mainly reproducible tangible assets or parts of them, and among financial assets money and bonds. National and sectoral balance sheets have, last but not least, become of growing importance in monetary analysis, as monetary theory has increasingly adopted the portfolio approach.

2. Conceptual Problems

a) The Scope of National Balance Sheets

i) Standard Scope

The national accounting system of the United Nations (1968, 1977) may now be regarded as defining the standard scope of tangible and financial assets for national and sectoral balance sheets, and this study has generally adhered to it fairly closely, deviations generally being due to unavailability of data.

The system includes among tangible assets subsoil assets and forests (United Nations 1977, 27), two items which have had to be omitted from most national balance sheets used in this study, because even rough estimates are available only for a few countries and a few recent benchmark dates, information briefly reviewed in Chapter 3, 3.a. The United Nations scheme includes patents, trademarks, and copyrights among nonreproducible tangible assets, to the extent that they have been acquired by the owner through purchase (1977, 30). These items are omitted from this study for reasons explained in subsection ii.(*j*). On the other hand, the United Nations system relegates consumer durables to a supplementary table (1977, 38), while they have been included here among reproducible tangible assets as constituting an obvious and important component of national wealth. Both the United Nations system and this study exclude consumers' stocks of semidurables and perishables, and fail to include nonmonetary nonindustrial holdings of gold and silver bullion and coins—with the exception in this study for India—as well as holdings of precious stones and collectors' items. Attempts to indicate the order of magnitude of these two items are, however, made in Section 2.a.ii.(*d*).

The most important type of tangible assets whose inclusion is conceptually debatable are the stocks of military durables. They are excluded insofar as they are "put mainly to military uses" from the United Nations' balance sheet schedule (1977, 8), though without saying why. The argument for excluding them presumably is that they do not serve the ultimate purpose of all other components of wealth, i.e., current or future consumption. By that criterion, however, other tangible assets, such as jails and police barracks, also would have to be excluded. Conceptually the inclusion of military durables would seem to be the solution more in line with the logic of national accounting, since military durables are subject to the "measuring rod of money," and their value can be estimated, like that of all other reproducible tangible assets, by the perpetual inventory method, though the determination of length of life, prices, and quality changes may be more difficult. The economic differences between military and civilian durables are, however, large enough to make it desirable to separate them in national and sectoral balance sheets. That unfortunately is not easy to do in practice. Most estimates of the stock of structures and of equipment either omit military durables or combine them with civilian ones, and do not even indicate how they treat military structures and equipment. This is a serious matter, since the amounts involved are in some countries substantial compared to the entire stock of structures and equipment, at least since the 1940s. For the United States, for example, military durables have been put at fully 3 percent of the civilian stock of structures and equipment in 1978 compared to less than 2 percent in 1929 and a peak of one-fourth in 1945 (Musgrave 1980, 35). Their ratio to total national assets is, of course, substantially lower, in 1978 slightly above 1 percent. The ratios are probably lower, at least since World War II, in the other countries covered in this study except in the Soviet Union and possibly in Israel. In this study military durables have been implicitly included in countries and for benchmark dates for which they are covered by the estimates of the capital stock of the government, which have been used in constructing national balance sheets of the 20 countries; they have been implicitly excluded, where these estimates do not cover them; but they have never been shown separately, which of course would have been impossible given the state of the basic data, except in the United States and in a few other scattered cases. The inconsistencies involved in their treatment should be of relatively small quantitative importance except in a few countries following the first benchmark date after World War II.

The scope of financial assets and liabilities in this study is identical with that of the United Nations' system with two exceptions, at least in principle, although in practice some minor types of financial instruments often escape the statisticians' attention. The first, and more important, exception is the disappearance of the equity in unincorporated business enterprises, which results from the consolidation of the balance sheets of the household sector with those of unincorporated business enterprises. This omission is motivated by the absence of data except for the United States (Goldsmith, Lipsey, and Mendelson 1963, vol. 2; Goldsmith 1982). The second omission concerns accruals and is due to unavailability of data as well as to conceptual considerations discussed in Section 2.a.ii.(*i*).

The national balance sheets constructed for and used in this study thus cover land and sometimes forests; reproducible tangible assets (structures, equipment, livestock, and inventories); monetary metals; claims; and corporate shares. The sectoral balance sheets also show debts and net worth.

ii) Marginal or Controversial Tangible and Financial Assets

The exclusion of most of these assets from almost all existing estimates or from the United Nations' standard system of national accounts is due more to difficulties of estimation, small size in modern economies in relation to other components of the national balance sheet, and limited analytical interest than to evident conceptual reasons. This section has nevertheless been included for two reasons: first, the neglect of these items in the literature; and, second, in order to provide an idea of the orders of magnitude involved in relation to the size of national assets conventionally measured.

(a) Forests: There is no conceptual reason to exclude forest land and standing timber from national wealth and assets, classifying the former with nonreproducible and the latter with reproducible tangible assets. Their valuation presents interesting and difficult theoretical and practical problems; and they constitute in many countries substantial components of national wealth. Their omission from most existing national wealth estimates, as well as from most of the balance sheets used in or constructed for this study, is therefore due mainly to the scarcity of the price and quantity data required for the estimation of their current value, and

to some extent to the neglect of the forestry sector by statisticians and economists. The few available data which will be discussed in Chapter 3, 3.a indicate that the value of forests in the two countries with the largest forest area—the U.S. and the USSR—is at the present time equal to about 3 percent (Goldsmith 1982, 187) and 6 percent (table A15), respectively. The ratio for the entire world is likely to be substantially lower, but still probably as high as 2 percent of tangible assets and about 1½ percent of national assets, and hence large enough to call for specific inclusion in the national balance sheet of many countries, particularly in Europe and North America (though not, e.g., in Australia, the Middle East, and North Africa.

(b) Subsoil assets: The arguments for the inclusion of subsoil assets are similar to and as strong as those for forests. Indeed, national balance sheets for about a dozen countries, fortunately not including any of the 20 countries covered in this study, are nearly worthless unless they include the value of subsoil assets, particularly oil and gas. Subsoil assets represent even now only small fractions of the tangible or total assets of the two largest producers—the United States and the Soviet Union—but would constitute the largest component in the national balance sheet of several other countries whose above-soil assets are relatively small in international comparison.

In the United States the value of subsoil assets in 1975 has been estimated at about 4 percent of that of suprasoil tangible assets, about two-thirds being contributed by oil and gas (Goldsmith 1982, chap. 7, 5). As a result of the sharp rise in the relative price of most minerals, the share should now be substantially above 5 percent. In 1977 in Great Britain the value of North Sea oil and gas reserves was put at a figure exceeding 5 percent of other tangible assets (*Fortune*, 17 March 1978, 82). Estimates for the Soviet Union indicate a ratio of subsoil assets of about 3½ percent in 1977 (Silaev and Shimov), which should now be well above 5 percent. For these three countries, which accounted in 1977 for over one-third of world wealth and also for one-third of world oil production, the share of subsoil assets in tangible assets should therefore at the present time be close to 5 percent and hence to about 3 percent of national assets. The share is, of course, much higher in the other large oil producers. In Mexico in 1978 it was estimated at about two-fifths on tangible and one-fifth of national assets (p. 263), and it may have been of a similar order of magnitude in Indonesia, Nigeria, and Venezuela. Among the Middle Eastern producers it was obviously much higher. Assuming an average share for these producers of one-half of oil in their suprasoil tangible assets and of about 6 percent in planetary suprasoil wealth, based on their share in planetary product (Block 1981, 33 ff.) their oil reserves would be equal to 3 percent of planetary tangible assets.

The corresponding share for the rest of the world is undoubtedly very low, probably well below 1 percent. Combining these rough estimates one obtains a share of oil in planetary tangible assets of about 5 percent, and a slightly higher share for all subsoil assets. The purpose of this exercise is only to suggest that the value of subsoil assets should not be omitted from a planetary balance sheet and *a fortiori* from the balance sheets of many individual countries, including about one-half of the 20 countries covered in this study (Australia, Canada, Great Britain, Mexico, Norway, South Africa, the United States and the USSR) and that its share is now large enough to justify separate estimation, and to call for much more attention by national accountants than has hitherto been given to the conceptual and statistical problems of their valuation.

(c) Consumer semidurables and perishables: In the United States semidurables, consisting mostly of apparel and footwear, have in the postwar period accounted for only about 3 percent of all tangible assets. The proportion is probably higher in less developed countries and is likely to have been higher in developed countries in earlier times.

Household stocks of perishables, essentially foodstuffs, constitute only a very small proportion of national wealth and assets in modern economies. Assuming expenditures on food at one-fourth of national product and food stocks equal to one week's consumption, such stocks would be equal to only about one-half of 1 percent of national product, not much over 0.2 percent of national wealth and less than 0.1 percent of national assets. While the ratios should have been higher in earlier phases of economic development, household food stocks are unlikely to have been in excess of a few percent of national wealth except in primitive agricultural communities. In developed countries the ratios are certain to have fallen since the industrial revolution under the influence of both the declining share of agriculture and of food preparation within nonagricultural households. This tendency may have been offset, at least in part, in the postwar period by the increased use of food freezers.

(d) Gold and silver: There is no conceptual problem here. Gold and silver should be included among national assets whether in the form of coins or bullion. When used in jewelry they should be accounted for among consumer durables. The exception is India where gold and silver jewelry is usually treated as part of the stock of financial assets, because it represents, particularly before World War II, a substantial part of household savings, especially that of women, and even of national assets.

The difficulties are entirely statistical. While the holdings of monetary authorities generally are exactly known, the Soviet Union being the main exception—though in the 1970s a shift from book to the much higher market value is required—gold coin and bullion holdings by the public, which are important in a few countries, particularly in France, would have to be very roughly estimated.

At the end of 1979 the world's stock of gold was estimated at slightly above $1200 billion (at an average price per ounce of $528; *Pick's Currency Yearbook: 1977–1979*, 742), of which government-held stocks were put at about $780 billion and private hoards at $430 billion, the two largest owners of private hoards being French and Indian households. As a result, France held about one-seventh and India well over 5 percent of the world's gold stock. The stock of the United States represented another one-eighth, and that of five other large European countries (Belgium, Germany, Italy, Netherlands, and Switzerland) where private holdings are small (except in Switzerland) as in the United States represented one-sixth more. At a price of about $500 per ounce the world's gold stock therefore was worth nearly $1000 billion. This was equal to about 1½ percent of the world's assets, and to approximately 2½ percent of its tangible wealth. The ratios were lower in most countries, amounting, e.g., in the United States to only about 0.8 percent of national assets, but significantly higher in France and India for which the share of gold in national assets may have been as high as nearly 4 and about 10 percent, respectively.

The recent extraordinary rise in the price of gold has restored the share of monetary metals in the world's tangible and financial assets to nearly the level prevailing before World War I, when that share was in the order of 1¼–1½ percent both in 1913 and in 1880 (Triffin's estimates [1964, 56] for monetary metals holdings). In 1950, on the other hand, when monetary gold stocks were worth $35 billion and private holdings were relatively smaller—though India's hoards alone were probably in excess of $5 billion and constituted about 5 percent of the country's assets (Goldsmith 1983a, table 3–56)—they had fallen to well below 1 percent of the world's tangible and financial assets.

These sketchy calculations should suffice to indicate that in the study of the world's tangible and total assets, their trends and their distribution, and still more in the case of a few individual countries, primarily India, the holdings of precious metals are too large to be ignored.

With the sharp recent rise of the price of silver, the value of the stocks of this metal may now again warrant consideration in national balance sheets as they did before World War I. In 1913 the world's stock of silver was valued at $3.5 billion, nearly one-half that of the gold stock (Triffin 1964, 56), and should then have represented between 0.2 and 0.3 percent of the world's assets, though a substantially larger share in India, where it was equal to about 7 percent of national assets in 1913 and possibly as much as 15 percent in 1875 (Goldsmith 1983a, chap. 1). Silver's share in planetary assets was at least twice as high in 1880 before the sharp decline in silver prices when the absolute value of the stock was slightly higher than in 1913. Since then silver has almost disappeared from monetary circulation, and hoards seem to have been small outside of India, where they may now have a value of as much as $50 billion at $10 per ounce, or as much as 5 percent of the country's total assets other than precious metals. No estimates of the world's present silver hoards has come to attention. If they are as large as the supposed Indian stock they would account for less than 0.1 percent of planetary assets and be equal to only one-tenth of the world's gold stock.

(e) Precious stones: Compared to the monetary and privately held stock of gold, that of gem diamonds, incorporated for the most part in jewelry, is moderate though not negligible. On the basis of the end of 1978 price (U.S. average import price of gem diamonds) of about $350 per carat and estimates of the world stock of gem diamonds of about 500 million carat (Epstein 1982, 252), the value of the stock is now in the order of $175 billion, assuming the U.S. import price to refer mostly to cut stones. A step-up is then necessary to allow for the difference between the import price and the price to the ultimate buyer, which appears to run between 50 and 100 percent (*New York Times Magazine*, 2 October 1980, 35 ff.). It is therefore likely that the market value of the world stock of gem diamonds at the end of 1979 was in the order of $300 billion, nearly one-half of which may have been in the United States. The stock would then represent somewhat less than one-half of 1 percent of planetary assets. The resale value would be considerably lower because of the wide spread between bid and asked prices (Epstein 1982, chap. 20). The ratio of the stock of diamonds to planetary assets would, of course, be considerably lower before the sharp rise in gem diamond prices, which started in the early 1970s after about two decades without substantial upward trend, and between 1970 and the end of 1978 amounted to 250 percent, or an annual 17 percent a year in absolute terms (Salomon 1980; U.S. average import price), and even in relative terms to about 10 percent compared to the rise in the price of gold at a rate of 25 percent a year. From the point of view of total assets, for the world or for individual countries most of these totals represent duplications, since the majority of the stock of diamonds is embodied in jewelry and therefore included—at least conceptually—in the estimates of consumer durables.

After a further substantial rise prices collapsed in 1981–82 and by the end of 1982 seem to have returned to their level of four years earlier. The prices of the very rare one-carat *D* flawless diamonds showed even wilder gyrations. They are reported to have risen from about $20,000 in 1978—approximately 20 times the average import price per carat (assuming a markup to retail price of about 100 percent)—to $62,000 late in 1980 and then to have fallen by over three-fourths to $15,000 in mid-1982. Taking the longer view, however, the 1982 price was still 8.4 times as high as it had been in 1967 and slightly more than twice its 1976 price, implying annual rates of growth of 15½ and of nearly 5 percent, respectively, the first 2.3 times but the second only two-thirds the rate of inflation (*Time*, 8 October 1982, 66). Going back to 1950 the increase of diamond prices on the basis of American average import prices of 5¼ percent per year compares to a rate of increase in the general price level of 4¼ percent, far below the rate of appreciation during this generation of gold of 8 percent and of collectors' items of, on the average, nearly 20 percent.

It has not been regarded as worthwhile to estimate even the order of magnitude of the much smaller stocks of other precious and of semi-precious stones or of pearls not embodied in jewelry and hence conceptually included in the value of consumer durables.

(f) Collectibles: There is again no conceptual reason to exclude these items—mainly movable works of art, rare books, coins, and stamps—from national wealth and assets, as they are in modern economies traded in competitive international markets.

No census of collectibles has been taken in any country, they are not covered in sample household balance sheets, and they cannot easily be estimated by the perpetual inventory method. Hence the only two methods of estimation available are the value of changes of hand through sales or gifts multiplied by the turnover ratio, both figures difficult to ascertain and subject to large errors of estimation; or in some countries like the United States through cumulated net imports adjusted for price changes.

The only indication of the worldwide value of sales of works of art by auction houses and dealers that has come to attention is one of about $1.55 billion in 1978, derived from an estimate that the sales of the Dorotheum in Vienna, a government auction house over 200 years old, of $25 million were equal to 1.6 percent of world sales (communication of Professor Herbst of Dorotheum). Consideration of changes of hand by gift and inheritance should increase the volume to at least $2 billion, and inclusion of other collectors' items (mainly books, coins and stamps) might further raise it to about $2-½ bill. If recent estimates (*New York Times*, 9 September 1979) of a turnover in the United States alone of over $1 billion in 1975 and $2–$3 billion in 1978 are correct, these figures would have to be at least doubled.

The very difficult problem then arises of estimating the velocity of turnover. Many if not most items are probably held from acquisition to the collector's death, i.e., for up to one generation. The considerable proportion acquired by public institutions has a practically zero velocity of turnover. The average turnover period is therefore unlikely to be less than 50 years. On that basis the value of the world's stock of collectors' items would be of the order of $125 billion, but of twice as much if the higher estimate based on alleged turnover in the United States is accepted. This would be equal to about 0.2 (0.4) percent of planetary assets, and to nearly one-tenth (one-fifth) of the world's gold stock. The figures are in any case sufficient to indicate that collectors' items constitute at present a minor but not negligible component of world wealth and assets. Because of their concentration in a few countries, collectibles constitute a considerably higher proportion of both totals in those.

For the United States an alternative, and probably superior, method is to revalue the net imports of "works of art and antiques" which are reported in the foreign trade statistics. If this is done, using the indices of art prices of table 29, the imports during the years 1951–79 would have had a value in 1979 prices of about $30 billion. Assuming that the price rise was small in the 1936–50 period, the price-adjusted value of imports for the last near half-century might then be about $40 billion. Putting exports at one-fifth of imports, net imports between 1936 and 1979 would be in the order, in 1979 prices, of $32 billion. It is difficult to argue that as much as one-half of the present stock of works of art and antiques has been acquired since 1936 if we consider the contents of our major collections, and a ratio of one-third seems equally defensible. The present stock of works of art in the United States would then have a value of between $65 and nearly $100 billion. This surmise receives some support from the estimate of the value of the collections of Yale University as being around $1 billion (*Yale*, May 1982) and a guess (by the author of that estimate) that the Yale collections represented about 1 percent of U.S. total, which may well be on the high side. This would suggest a value for all U.S. holdings of works of art to be in the order of at least $100 billion, or 0.5 percent of national assets.

To this a modest though not negligible amount, discussed in the following paragraphs, would have to be added for books, coins, and stamps. The total for all collectibles might then be equivalent to between 0.4 and 0.7 percent of national assets, or 0.8 and 1.3 percent of national wealth. If this estimate is nearer the truth than the one based on the estimated, or guessed, values of turnover and turnover ratios, it would provide support for the higher rather than the lower of the two estimates of the value of the world's stock of collectors' items.

The value of the world's stock of rare books is undoubtedly much smaller. There are only a few hundred scientific rare books which sell for $10,000 or more, and the number of copies in existence is small, again a few hundred on the average. The aggregate value of these books is therefore unlikely to exceed $1 billion. It is difficult to see how inclusion of the more numerous lower priced items would bring the total for all rare scientific books beyond $1½ billion. The value of the stock of literary rare books is not likely to be higher. There is thus little doubt that, even if these calculations seriously underestimate the value of the stock of rare

Table 29 **Prices of Collectibles, 1946–80 (% per Year)**[a]

	Period (1)	Rate of Increase (2)	Period (3)	Rate of Increase (4)
1. Old master paintings	1951–69	11.2	1970–80	13.4
2. Old master drawings	1951–69	18.7	...	...
3. Old master prints	1951–69	22.4	...	...
4. English pictures	1951–69	13.5	...	...
5. Impressionist paintings	1951–69	17.2	...	...
6. Modern pictures	1951–69	20.6	...	...
7. Old master paintings	1971–74	19.6	...	...
8. English paintings	1971–74	11.1	...	...
9. Impressionist paintings	1971–74	12.5	...	...
10. Modern paintings	1971–74	16.4	...	...
11. Paintings at auction Great Britain	1946–49	11.7	...	...
12. Paintings at auction United States	1965–68	8.0	...	...
13. Chinese ceramics	1951–69	19.4	1970–80	18.8
14. English silver	1951–69	12.6	...	...
15. English porcelain	1951–69	8.0	...	...
16. English glass	1951–69	13.0	...	...
17. French furniture	1951–69	9.4	...	...
18. Antiquarian books	1951–69	15.3	1970–80	16.1
19. Modern books	1951–69	13.0	...	...
20. Coins	1968–79	12.7	1970–80	16.0[b]
21. U.S. postage stamps	1956–65	5.4	1970–80	21.8

[a]All prices in col. 2 in £ except for lines 12, 20, and 21, which are in $; prices in col. 4 in $.
[b]United States coins.
Source of basic data:
Cols. 1, 2:
Lines 1–6, 13–19 Keene (1971), 48, 250 ff.
Lines 7–10 Cunneen and Barnes (1976).
Lines 11–12 Stein (1977), 1025.
Line 20 *New York Times*, Aug. 9, 1979; April 9, 1980.
Line 21 Scott U.S. Stampindex™ as reprinted in Joseph Kardwell, Inc., *Rare Stamps for the Investor*, 1980.
Cols. 3, 4:
Lines 1, 13, 18 Solomon (1980).

books, this component of collectors' items can for the time being be omitted from the evaluation of national assets. The same is probably true of the value of coin and stamp collections.

The international distribution of collectibles is certainly very uneven, and considerably more unequal than world product or planetary assets. There is little doubt that the bulk of collectors' items, possibly as much as nine-tenths, is concentrated in Western Europe and North America, which together account for only about one-half of planetary assets. For these countries, and particularly for France, Great Britain, Italy, and the United States, the share of collectors' items in total wealth and assets is therefore considerably above the world average, but even so remains a minor component of their national balance sheet. Since collectors' items are concentrated within nations in wealthier households, nonprofit institutions, and governments, they represent a higher share of the assets of these sectors, and in the first two of them may begin to represent a substantial component of their assets. The information now available is, however, insufficient to permit a quantification of these relationships.

While the margin of error in estimating the value of collectibles is very large, there is little doubt about the trend of prices; and because the quantities involved change very slowly, about the trend in the value of collectors' items. The price of practically all types of collectors' items has risen during the postwar period until 1980 considerably more rapidly than the general price level, and in all countries since the market is international. It is also very likely, though less certain, that the rise in the prices of collectors' items was more rapid than that of the other components of national assets before World War II back to at least the middle of the 19th century, though the difference probably was considerably smaller than it has been in the past few decades. A more rapid rise in the prices of collectors' items, of course, is not equivalent to a rise in their share in national wealth and assets, because their quantity increases much more slowly than that of tangible or financial assets.

It is evident from table 29 that the prices of all types of collectors' items have increased during the postwar period at rates far in excess of the rise in the general price level, at least until the late 1970s. The annual rates of price increase (in £) for the 21 types shown in table 28 range from 8 to 22 percent per year with an average for the period from the early 1950s to the mid-1970s of about 12 percent for old master paintings, probably the most important category, and of generally somewhat higher rates for the other categories, for an overall average in the order of 15 percent. This compares with increases over the same period in the British general price level of 6 percent. In real terms collectors' items therefore have increased over this exceptional quarter of a century at an average annual rate of almost 10 percent a year. At that rate—obviously not maintainable in the long run and equally obviously not duplicated in the past—the real price of collectors' items would double in less than eight years, quadruple in 15 years. In the last 10 years prices of five categories of collectibles have on the average increased by 17 percent a year (table 29), while the American price level has risen at a rate of 7 percent. The rate of increase in the real prices of works of art has thus averaged about 10 percent, probably below the rate of the preceding two decades. Comprehensive statistics are as yet lacking on the movements of prices of works of art in the early 1980s, but it seems that the upward trend in nominal prices has come to a halt or has even been reversed, certainly in comparison to the continuing though declining increase in the general price level.

If, as seems reasonable, it is assumed that in the postwar period the price of works of art has increased, on the average, at an annual rate of approximately 15 percent compared to an increase in planetary assets of probably not more than 10 percent a year, it would mean that if in 1948 the share of works of art in planetary assets was *x* percent, it would by 1978 have risen to nearly four times *x* percent, even before allowance for the increase, relatively moderate, in the quantity of art objects resulting from current production. Since the distribution of collectors' items is very unequal, most of them being owned by upper-wealth households and by the nonprofit sector and constituting a well-above-average proportion of their total assets, the share of collectors' items in their total assets must have gone up considerably, particularly in the case of upper-wealth households whose share in total household wealth has substantially declined in most if not all developed countries. To vary a popular saying of the 1920s, "Works of art are rich men's best friends," the more so because they do not produce taxable current income, and in many countries their appreciation is not subject to tax.

The prices of works of art probably also rose more rapidly than the general price level, i.e., they increased in real value, before World War II, though apparently much less so than since the 1950s. On the basis of 1730 paintings which came on the market twice or more often, the average annual rate of return between 1780 and 1970 has been put at slightly less than 4 percent (Anderson, unpublished paper, ca. 1972, table 2). This indicates that the upward trend in picture prices was much flatter before than since World War II, both in absolute terms and in relation to the general price level. Indeed the average rate of return is put at only 3.6 percent for the entire 19th century, and at 5.2 percent for the 1900–1914 period, not in excess of that of high-grade bonds. For the interwar period it is given—and this is difficult to believe—at −4 percent per year.

In the postwar period the prices of collectors' items other than works of art seem to have increased even more than those of the latter. Thus U.S. postage stamps are reported to have risen between 1970 and 1980 at an average rate of 22 percent a year, while U.S. coin and rare book prices advanced by 16 percent a year, implying real price increases by 15 and by 9 percent a year (table 29). In contrast to works of art, the appreciation—financial rather than aesthetic—seems to have accelerated in the late 1970s, the rate of increase in 1979–1980 being reported at 43 percent for U.S. stamps and 25 percent for U.S. coins—probably not representative of all nonartistic collectors' items—as rare books advanced by only 14 percent, all far ahead of an increase in the price level of 11 percent. Here too the early 1980s saw a break in the trend.

The increase in the nominal and real prices of collectibles other than works of art was, of course, much slower before the 1950s but still seems to have been substantial in some cases. Thus the prices of postage stamps are reported to have increased at an annual rate of about 7 percent per year between 1893 and 1936 (Kruse 1949, 108, 163). The rise was considerably more rapid in the period before World War I, when the index rose at an annual average of 8½ percent while the general price level in the United States advanced at a rate of not much over 1 percent, than in the following two decades when the rate of increase was below 5 percent, still about three times that of the general price level. The increase in the real price level then was about 7 percent per year before World War I but only 3½ percent in the interwar period. The real prices of postage stamps would have doubled within 10 years at the earlier and within 20 years at the later period's trend. Another calculation puts the increase in the average price (in gold francs) of 28 rare stamps issued before 1872 at 10 percent per year for the period 1878–1921 but only at less than 2 percent for the years 1921–1933, clearly showing the effects of the Great Depression (Loeser ca. 1947, 16–17). The Scott U.S. Stampindex™ increased between 1929 and 1955 at an average annual rate of a little over 4 percent compared to a rise in the general price level of less than 2½ percent, still an annual appreciation of over 1½ percent in a period which includes the Great Depression and the inflation following World War II.

That the secular rise in the prices of rare books was moderate before the 20th century, both in absolute terms and in relation to changes in the general price level, is indicated by an expert's opinion that "in the last [18th] century the ordinary large and good libraries averaged about £1 per lot, while in the present [19th] century they average at least £2 per lot" (Wheatley 1898, 177). This indicates an average annual rate of increase in book prices of not over 1 percent per year, if the figures are regarded as secular averages, in a period in which the general price level showed no trend. The rate of increase seems, however, to have been considerably higher for the "top" items. Thus the price of a Gutenberg bible appears to have risen during the 19th century at an annual rate of about 4 percent.

(g) National monuments: These items and their appurtenances, represented mainly by religious and civic buildings and royal and aristocratic residences, most of which are many centuries old, have by definition no market value, and their cost of reproduction, even if ascertainable, is of little economic interest. Whatever value could be rather arbitrarily put on them would in modern economies represent only a minute fraction of national assets. Their exclusion from national balance sheets and from all existing estimates of national wealth thus appears justified by both conceptual and practical considerations.

(h) Equity in unincorporated business enterprises: The treatment of the equity in unincorporated business enterprises is the most important example of the influence of alternative methods of sectorization on the value of national assets. If unincorporated business enterprises are treated analogously to corporations as a separate sector, their net worth appears as one of the financial assets of the owners, generally the household sector, but in the case of the German G.m.b.H.—a form of business organization between a partnership and a corporation—also other sectors. In that case national assets, as well as the assets of the household sector, are larger by the net worth of unincorporated enterprises than if such enterprises are treated as an unsegregated part of the household sector. Since most existing systems of national and financial accounts follow the latter course, it has been adopted also in this study, though conceptually the treatment of unincorporated enterprises as a separate sector appears preferable, as it considerably increases the informative and analytical value of sectoral accounts.

A quantitative appraisal of the effect on the national balance sheet of the treatment of unincorporated enterprises since the turn of the century is possible only for the United States. It shows that the share of the net worth of unincorporated enterprises (including agriculture) in national assets and in the assets and net worth of the household sector has declined sharply, and in 1975 amounted to 7 percent of national assets, 17 percent of those of the household sector, and 20 percent of the latter's net worth, compared to 16, 34, and 36 percent in 1900 (Goldsmith 1982, 76, 120; Goldsmith, Lipsey, and Mendelson, 1963, 2:72–73). Hence the differential effect of the alternative treatment of unincorporated enterprises has lost in importance.

Another interesting example of the problem is presented by the German G.m.b.H.'s. The net worth of G.m.b.H.'s, whose ownership is divided among the household, corporate, and foreign sectors, now amounts to nearly 2 percent of national assets and is three-fifths as large as the net worth of corporations (table A6).

(i) Social Insurance: The problems raised by the treatment of social insurance are in part the same as those presented by unincorporated enterprises. Usually the accounts of the social insurance organizations are consolidated with those of the central government, with the result that their claims against the government, if they are accounted for at all, disappear in consolidation. Similarly, no entry is shown in the accounts of the household sector for its social insurance claims. Thus social insurance claims are treated differently from the essentially similar items representing pension claims against local governments and private employers. In this study in contrast, social security organizations have been treated as financial institutions. Consequently their assets, which consist predomi-

nantly, though in some countries not exclusively, of claims against the government, appear in the financial sector; and their liabilities are entered among the assets of the household sector.

There remains, however, one significant and quantitatively very important difference between the treatment of social insurance organizations on the one hand and fully funded pension plans on the other. While the latter's assets correspond to their actuarial liabilities, in the case of social insurance organizations only the actual assets are entered in the national balance sheet, and their liabilities are regarded as equal to their assets rather than to the much larger amounts corresponding to an actuarial evaluation. In this respect, however, social insurance organizations are similar to many local government and some private pension plans, which also have considerable unfunded liabilities, though these generally are considerably smaller relative to their assets than is the case for social security organizations. For the United States unfunded pension claims have been estimated for the late 1970s at about one-third of all other national assets, at approximately four-fifths of all other claims (Goldsmith 1982, tables 24 and 86), and at about equal to all other assets of households.

It is important to realize that inclusion of unfunded insurance claims would not only very substantially increase the amount of financial and national assets but would also sharply raise the financial interrelations ratio and the share of households in national assets; would reduce the financial intermediation ratio; would completely alter the structure of the balance sheet of households; and would, last but not least, sharply change the size distribution of household wealth and its movements. How large that change would be is indicated by an estimate that, in the United States in 1962, allowance for society security claims alone would increase the share in net assets of the bottom half of all families with male heads age 35–64 (excluding insurance and pension claims) from 6 percent to about 12 percent, while it would reduce that of the top 3 percent from 40 to approximately 33 percent (Feldstein 1976, 804). Inclusion of other unfunded pension claims would increase these differences. It is likely also that the differences in the income size distribution resulting from the inclusion of unfunded pension claims are larger now than they were two decades ago.

(j) Accruals: Accruals, i.e., debts or credits for services rendered, or charges due but not yet paid for, exemplified by interest or tax accruals, are recognized by business accounting, and there is no conceptual reason why they should be excluded from financial assets or liabilities in national and sectoral balance sheets. In practice, however, their treatment varies, and it is often uncertain whether and to what extent they have been included in the statistics from which national balance sheets have been

built up. It is likely that they have been covered more completely and consistently in the corporate sector, whose balance sheets are generally based on business type accounts, than for the other sectors, for which balance sheets are put together from heterogeneous sources. In this study accruals are necessarily taken into account only to the extent they appear in the sources, and no attempt has been made to estimate them separately. It is therefore fairly certain that part, and possibly a considerable part, of the accruals that would be called for if the principles of business accounting were consistently followed have been omitted from the balance sheets used in this study. This is not a serious drawback since scattered evidence indicates that accruals consistently applied would account for only a small fraction of financial assets and liabilities. Since they would appear with the same amounts among assets and liabilities, their economic importance is limited.

(k) Intangibles: This is the most difficult, though generally neglected, marginal component of national and sectoral balance sheets for both conceptual and practical reasons. As a result the treatment of intangibles is one of the most unsatisfactory aspects of both business and national accounting theory. By the principle of the measuring rod of money, many intangibles should be included in national and sectoral balance sheets, particularly legally well-defined items like patents and copyrights and, to a lesser extent, goodwill since they can be bought and sold, and the determination of their market value is not intrinsically more difficult than for some other assets.

However, apart from their nonhomogeneous and hence nonstandardized nature and the scarcity of relevant price and quantity data, the valuation of intangibles faces two basic difficulties. The first is the uncertain scope of intangibles. Where is the line to be drawn between goodwill and monopoly or oligopoly profits, or more generally differential rents? How are the capitalized profits and rents already included in the value of other assets, particularly land and corporate shares, to be separated from those which are not? The second difficulty is the near-impossibility of locating the liabilities which correspond to the intangibles treated as assets which then increase the net worth of the owners. Which, if any, units should be debited with the value of the intangibles credited to owners, in order to establish the equivalence between financial assets and liabilities that is a principle of business and national accounting?

These problems appear insoluble, and the only practicable solution is the omission of intangibles from national and sectoral balance sheets. This admittedly somewhat cavalier answer to the problem is facilitated by the fact that the amounts of intangibles that can be identified in published corporate balance sheets or in tax returns appear to be very small compared to national assets. The solution is somewhat more difficult to defend for sectoral balance sheets because to a substantial extent different sectors would have to be credited and debited, so that net credits and debits would arise which would affect sectoral balance sheets, and would do so to a different extent for different sectors. In the only case of an estimate of intangibles in a national balance sheet that has come to attention, they amounted in France in 1976 to 1.0 percent of total and 2.3 percent of financial assets, though to 1.9 percent of total and to 6.4 percent of the financial assets of the household sector, the balance sheet not showing a countervailing debit entry and thus slightly increasing the national and household total assets, financial assets, and net worth (Benedetti, Consolo, and Fouquet 1979, 46–48).

Another type of intangibles, capitalized research and developed expenditures, has been omitted less for conceptual than for statistical reasons. The conceptual argument, that such expenditures are usually not capitalized in the balance sheets of those who undertake them—business and government—is not beyond refutation, since national accounting deviates in several aspects from business accounting, e.g., in the valuation of tangible assets. The absence of estimates of the amounts involved except in a very few cases is thus decisive.

One of the few estimates of the capitalized value of basic and applied research and development expenditures concerns the United States since 1929 (Kendrick 1976, 204–5). According to these estimates, in 1969 capitalized research and development expenditures represented 6 percent of the stock of nonhuman tangible assets compared to 0.4 percent four decades earlier. The ratio to national assets would, of course, be lower in 1969, about 2½ percent. It would be considerably higher—close to 10 percent—if compared to only the equipment and structures of the business and government sectors. While the inclusion of the capitalized value of research and development expenditures would not seriously affect the structure of most national balance sheets, particularly before the 1950s, it might now do so in some sectors in some developed countries.

iii) Foreign Assets and Liabilities

There is no doubt that foreign assets and liabilities belong in a national balance sheet. Indeed, if balance sheets are sectorized the rest of the world constitutes one of the sectors. There are, however, conceptual and statistical problems, some of them quite complex and far from resolved, of how foreign assets and liabilities should be treated. A uniform treatment is as yet out of reach, particularly before the last few years, when the standardized balance of payments schedules of the United Nations and the International Monetary Fund have been implemented by an increasing number of countries. Before World War II foreign assets were often reported or estimated only on a net basis. Even now in some cases only aggregate net foreign assets and liabilities are estimated or reported. In this study as a regrettable compromise gross foreign assets (or, if unknown, net foreign assets if positive) have been added to the value of tangible assets located within the national territory and to that of financial instruments issued by domestic units excluding, where substantial and known, government issues sold abroad. This treatment involves duplication, and hence overstates national assets, to the extent that the statistics of specific financial instruments used include those of foreign issuers. Similarly, the amounts of specific financial instruments held in the country, and hence national assets, are overstated by the proportions owned abroad, which usually will be relatively small for countries or dates where gross foreign assets are large. The overstatement will thus be moderate in cases where gross foreign investments consist mostly of the securities of foreign issuers or direct foreign investments, because these two categories do not appear among the specified financial instruments; and where the share of domestic issues held abroad and of domestic tangible assets owned by foreigners is small. There is hardly any way of determining the extent of the overstatement involved by treating gross foreign investments as a component of national assets, but it seems unlikely that it has ever exceeded a very few percent of national assets. This approach has been adopted because the alternative of omitting an estimate for gross foreign investments is likely to have distorted the structure of national assets and changes in it, which are the primary objectives of this study, more seriously, particularly in countries and periods of relatively large foreign investments, such as in France, Germany, Great Britain, Switzerland, and the United States. In the majority of cases where no estimates of gross foreign investments could be found or net instead of gross foreign units are centered, national assets as used in this study are understated to the extent of foreign investments not included implicitly in the specified financial instruments. These are, with few exceptions, countries and periods in which such foreign investments constituted only a very small fraction of national assets, probably less than 1 percent.

iv) Human Capital

While the standard system of national accounts is rightly limited to nonhuman tangible and financial assets, since human beings belong to a different class than these assets and cannot be regarded as additive to them, a consideration of human capital is of interest for some uses of national balance sheets and has received increasing attention in recent years. A few attempts at estimating the orders of magnitudes involved have been made, even going back to the 17th century, though they have not been presented as an element of a system of national accounts.

In line with the practice adopted for national balance sheets, human capital would have to be defined as the market value or, in its absence, the cost of reproduction, of the labor force. In fact, generally one of two methods have been employed, the capitalization of future earnings net of the cost of maintaining the labor force; or the cost of rearing and educating the labor force. A third method, which is closer to the requirement of using market values, the application of the price of unfree labor to the entire labor force, has hardly ever been used. This is not the place for an intensive discussion of the conceptual and statistical problems of measuring human capital in a way that renders it comparable to the tangible and financial assets that make up national and sectoral balance sheets in their standard definition. All that is intended is to provide a few examples which give an idea of the order of magnitude involved in comparison to tangible assets.

Among the estimates using the method of capitalization of earnings, the earliest serious example is that of Farr for Great Britain, a calculation made in the 1850s of which it was said only a generation ago that it "remains to this day the fundamental standard on which any sound estimate of the value of a man to his decendents must be based" (Dublin and Lotka 1946, 12—notice the qualification "to his decendents"). Farr discounted the expected earnings of an agricultural laborer of 25 years of age at 5 percent—when the risk-free interest rate (consols) was close to 3 percent and obtained a value of £246. Applying this figure to the 1850 occupied British labor force of 9.4 million (Mitchell and Deane 1962, 60) yields a figure of £2.3 billion, which compares with values of about £4.0 billion for tangible assets and of £2.7 billion for financial assets (table A7). This figure would have to be regarded as a lower limit because average earnings of the entire labor force were considerably above those of farm laborers, but it would be too high because the average age of the labor force was well above 25. It is sad to have to report that when Irving Fisher needed a figure for the value of human capital of the United States, he simply multiplied Farr's estimate by the ratio between the earnings of Farr's British farm laborer of 1853 and the average earnings of a member of the American labor force and thus obtained for 1907 a figure of $2900 (1909, 118–19). Application of this figure to the labor force of 47 million yielded an estimate of its value of about $135 billion, approximately equal to 0.7 times national wealth, to 1.5 times financial assets, and to about 10 years of gross labor income. Quite a few other estimates of this type were made before World War I in Great Britain and Germany (Dublin and Lotka 1946, 13 ff.; Meyer 1930, 13 ff.), some of them flawed by starting from gross rather than net earnings; and there were also a few approaches to the problem from the cost side (Meyer 1930, 6 ff.). For the United States a recent estimate from the earnings side, which includes nonmarket earnings and assigns a large capitalized value to leisure, puts human wealth at $22 trillion in 1950 and $109 trillion in 1973 (Jorgenson and Pachon 1980, 52), or at 10 or eight times, respectively, of national assets and, still more astonishing, about 130 years and 120 years of gross labor income.

Proceeding from the retrospective cost side, the value of tangible human capital (rearing cost) and of intangible human capital (mainly cost of education, training, and health maintenance) has been estimated in the United States for the end of the 1960s at $1.15 trillion and $2.55 trillion, respectively (Kendrick 1976, 205). The total of $3.70 trillion—only 5 percent of the estimate from the prospective discounted net earnings approach—would be approximately equal to a little more than the value of national wealth and to one-half of national assets—close to Fisher's ratios of 1909.

The approach to measuring human capital on the basis of the price of unfree labor is statistically feasible only for prerevolutionary and antebellum America. On the basis of the market value of the unfree population (tables A21–A22) and its relation to the total population, the human capital of the United States is then evaluated at about £110 million for 1774, $0.90 billion for 1805, and $5.80 billion for 1850. These figures correspond to ratios to national wealth of about 1¼ in 1774, nearly two-thirds in 1805, and nearly four-fifths in 1850. They are, of course, lower in relation to all national nonhuman assets, namely, about unity in 1774 and about one-half in 1805 and in 1850. All the ratios are probably on the low side, since it may be assumed that the value of a free laborer was above that of a slave, though one must not be too categorical about the relation, as the higher level of education of the free labor force may have been offset, partly, fully, or more than entirely, by the lower ratio of maintenance cost to earnings of the unfree labor force.

Human capital has been excluded from national balance sheets throughout this study because of the absence of unanimity, or even prevalence, of opinion about the methods to be used in evaluating human capital; the immense range of the possible and defensible estimates—much larger than for any other component of tangible nonhuman or financial assets; the dependence of the earnings approach on the almost arbitrary choice of the discount rate and of the allowance for the value of leisure; and, last but not least, the categorical difference between human and nonhuman capital, which raises grave doubts about their additivity. The absence of estimates except for a few scattered cases would, of course, have enforced such a policy even if it had not been regarded as the right one from the conceptual point of view, a conclusion also reached by Lenti after an intensive discussion in his comprehensive treatise on national accounts (1978, 953).

v) Overview

In terms of quantity the two by far most important items that may be considered to be added to those included in the standard scope of the national balance sheet, dwarfing all other debatable items, are unfunded pension and other social insurance claims, and human capital. The first would increase financial assets, and the second would constitute a third major category additional to tangible and financial assets. At the present time unfunded pension claims would, according to the necessarily very rough estimates, increase financial assets by about two-thirds and national assets by about one-third in the United States. The value of human capital (cf. section iv above) has been put at either about one-half of that of national assets under the standard concept and hence at equal to that of all tangible assets (retrospective method); or at eight times total national assets as conventionally defined (prospective method). The addition of these two items would not only change the dimension of the national balance sheet but, what is more important, would radically alter its component structure and the distribution of national assets among sectors, sharply increasing the share of households in assets and of the government in liabilities and the distribution of assets within the household sector, greatly increasing the share of household in the lower income and wealth classes.

b) Classification of Assets and Liabilities

To be useful for economic analysis and to permit comparisons over time and among countries, national and sectoral balance sheets should group the numerous types of tangible assets and financial instruments into a limited number of categories that as far as possible have common economic characteristics and are invariant over time and space. To do this is already very difficult conceptually. It is doubly so in practice, with the result that the conceptual cloak has to be cut to fit the cloth of available statistics.

Table 30 shows the 20 classes of tangible assets and financial instruments which have been distinguished in the national and sectoral balance sheets used in or constructed for this study. The nature of the available data has made it impossible to present separate figures for each of the 20 items for each benchmark data and for each country. In some cases it has been necessary to combine among tangible assets agricultural and other land, or residential and other structures, or nonresidential structures and equipment. Among financial assets it has often been impossible to separate mortgages from loans by financial institutions or from other claims. In a number of cases an item covering all claims against financial institutions (including their equity), and hence equal to their total assets, has had to be used instead of the three items of currency and demand deposits, other deposits and insurance and pension claims, because the more detailed information was not available. Moreover, the content of some of the items has changed over time in a given country or differs among countries. These reservations apply primarily to financial assets, and here particularly to the catchall item of other claims.

The classification of tangible items used here is considerably less detailed than that desired by the statisticians of the United Nations (1977, tables 5.1 and 5.2), though not yet realized in the official statistics of even a single country, as it distinguishes only eight instead of 19 items. Of the 11 items of the United Nations schedule not shown separately in this study, five are breakdowns of inventories and two refer to the conceptually and statistically difficult item of land improvements. In the case of financial assets, the number of items being distinguished is the same—about a dozen—but there are some, though generally minor, differences. The chief ones are the omission, due to the conceptual and statistical difficulties, of the distinction between short- and long-term debt securities and other claims, and the separate entries in this study for government and corporate debt securities and mortgages.

c) Sectorization

Sectorization poses more problems, both conceptual and statistical, than the classification of assets and liabilities. In this case, however, there is a clearer principle of classification: the creation of sectors that are as homogeneous as possible in the structure of their balance sheets and in the management of their portfolios. This principle unfortunately calls for more sectors than can be implemented at the present time, let alone for the past century. Hence compromises are unavoidable. Availability of data has forced limitations to, generally, only five sectors for the countries for which it has been possible to present sectoral balance sheets, namely, households (including nonprofit organizations and unincorporated business enterprises), government, nonfinancial corporations, financial institutions, and the rest of the world. No sectoral balance sheets are shown for countries which do not permit the separation of these five sectors, particularly countries that combine households and nonfinancial corporations in their national wealth estimates or in their national financial accounts.

In contrast to the four to nine domestic sectors in the balance sheets presented in Appendix B and discussed in Chapter 4, the United Nations schedule calls for 15 sectors or subsectors, including five subsectors of the household sector, four of the financial institutions sector, and three of the government sector (1977, 17), none of which is broken down in this study due to the absence of sufficiently detailed data. Indeed, the United Nations schedule cannot be fully implemented for a single country even at the present time, though with substantial additional work it could be done, except for the household sector, for recent years for a few developed countries. On the other hand, a considerably finer breakdown

Table 30 Standard Sectorized National Balance Sheet Form

	All Sectors (1)	Households (2)	Nonprofit Institutions[b] (3)	Unincorporated Business (4)	Nonfinancial Corporations (5)	Government[c] (6)	Financial Institutions (7)	Rest of the World (8)
I. Land	...	...	...	...	...	...	...	...
1. Agricultural	...	...	...	...	...	...	...	...
2. Other	...	...	...	...	...	...	...	...
II. Reproducible tangible assets[a]	...	...	...	...	...	...	...	...
1. Structures	...	...	...	...	...	...	...	...
a) Residential	...	...	...	...	...	...	...	...
b) Other	...	...	...	...	...	...	...	...
2. Equipment	...	...	...	...	...	...	...	...
3. Inventories	...	...	...	...	...	...	...	...
4. Livestock	...	...	...	...	...	...	...	...
5. Consumer durables	...	...	...	...	...	...	...	...
III. Tangible assets	...	...	...	...	...	...	...	...
IV. Monetary metals	...	...	...	...	...	...	...	...

V. Financial assets	...	...	...	...	...	...	...	...
1. Currency and demand deposits	...	...	...	...	...	...	...	...
2. Other deposits	...	...	...	...	...	...	...	...
3. Insurance and pension claims	...	...	...	...	...	...	...	...
4. Loans by financial institutions	...	...	...	...	...	...	...	...
5. Mortgages	...	...	...	...	...	...	...	...
6. Government debt	...	...	...	...	...	...	...	...
7. Corporate bonds	...	...	...	...	...	...	...	...
8. Corporate stock	...	...	...	...	...	...	...	...
9. Trade credit	...	...	...	...	...	...	...	...
10. Other claims	...	...	...	...	...	...	...	...
VI. Foreign assets	...	...	...	...	...	...	...	...
a) Gross	...	...	...	...	...	...	...	...
b) Net	...	...	...	...	...	...	...	...
VII. National assets (III + IV + V + VIa)	...	...	...	...	...	...	...	...
VIII. Liabilities (V1–7, 9, 10)	...	...	...	...	...	...	...	...
IX. Net worth (VII–VIII)	...	...	...	...	...	...	...	...

[a]In principle including military assets.
[b]Often combined with households.
[c]If possible separating central from local governments and government enterprises from general government.

than that called for by the United Nations blueprint is possible, though not without considerable effort, in a number of countries for nonfinancial corporations and for financial institutions, and is already provided by several countries in their financial accounts and in their statistics of corporate balance sheets.

This study deviates in only one significant point from the sectorization suggested by the United Nations as well as from the practice of official financial accounts, namely, the treatment of social security organizations as part of the financial institutions sector rather than of the government sector. This treatment seems to be more in accord with the definition of financial institutions as economic units whose assets are predominantly financial, particularly when they also own financial instruments other than claims against the government. One consequence of this treatment is that the assets of social security organizations are paralleled by liabilities to beneficiaries and thus appear among the financial assets of the household sector, and hence also among national assets. The amounts so entered, however, generally do not correspond to actuarially calculated liabilities but are, as already shown, far below them.

Sectoral balance sheets are in principle the result of the combination of the balance sheets of all units belonging to the sector, i.e., they do not eliminate claims and equity relations among units. The data available, however, sometimes cancel claims among financial institutions by consolidation, and it has not been possible, nor has it even been attempted, to introduce uniformity in this respect. Similarly, intercorporate stockholdings are occasionally eliminated by consolidation, e.g., in the official flow of funds statistics in the United States, and again the data in the basic sources have generally been accepted.

Since the national balance sheet is conceptually the sum of the sectoral balance sheets, the value of national assets depends on the degree of sectorization. The most important case is the treatment of unincorporated business enterprises already discussed in Section ii.(c), of this chapter.

An increase in financial and national assets similar to that resulting from the treatment of unincorporated enterprises as a separate sector occurs if the assets held by households under trust agreements and administered by separate trustee organizations (e.g., the Public Trustee in Great Britain), or by the trust departments of other financial institutions, are treated as a separate subsector of financial institutions, a treatment justified by the fact that these trust assets are legally segregated and their administration is almost completely separated from the portfolio management of the beneficiaries. Because of lack of data this study has adhered to the convential procedure.

An evaluation of the statistical effect of the alternative treatment of trust funds is possible only for the United States. Here, the treatment of personal trust funds as a component of the financial institutions sector rather than as an integral part of the assets of the household sector would have increased the assets of financial institutions in the postwar period by between 6 and 10 percent and raised national assets by 1½ percent, but would not have affected the total assets of the household sector (Goldsmith, 1982, table 49).

d) Valuation

i) Balance Sheets in Current Prices

The problems arising in valuing the components of national and sectoral balance sheets, both conceptual and practical, are numerous and sometimes complex, and they affect the estimations more than most other subjects of controversy except the scope of assets and liabilities covered. Nevertheless discussion will be brief because a substantial literature exists (e.g., Dorrance 1978; United Nations 1968, 1977), and I have dealt elsewhere a little less compactly with some of the problems involved (Goldsmith 1967, 1982).

The basic principle adopted in this study, as in practically all national accounting work, is valuation of all items at market prices; or, where they are not available, at the nearest approximation thereto, i.e., replacement cost for most types of reproducible assets and par value for most claims and liabilities. The principle has four important corollaries.

The first is that market prices are applied for some important items *pars pro toto*, i.e., the prices established for usually only the small part of the stock that is turned over in any one period, usually a year (e.g., corporate shares), or for a sample of the stock (e.g., in the United States agricultural land), is applied to the entire stock in existence.

Second, all identical components enter the sectoral and national balance sheets at the same figure irrespective of their value in the owner's or debtor's balance sheet or in their imagination. This may be called the objectivist view which has been adopted by virtually all theorists of national accounting except Dorrance (most recently 1978); and has been followed in all published aggregative national and sectoral balance sheets, though not in those balance sheets of the household sector or its subsectors which are obtained by blowing up sample inquiries or estate tax returns. The subjectivist approach, which accepts the evaluation of all balance sheet components by the unit which is supposed to make up the balance sheet, if consistently followed in theory and applied in practice, which is impossible, leads to chaos and destroys additivity of the balance sheets of individual economic units.

Third, we do not need to inquire whether and to what extent observed market prices are retrospectively cost-determined or prospectively earnings-determined.

The fourth corollary is based on the going-concern paradigm, i.e., assets are valued as if they were going to serve until their retirement in their present or equivalent position rather than at their second hand sale or scrap value.

In practice the quantitatively largest deviations from the principle of market price or replacement cost occur among tangible assets in the cases of subsoil assets, which are generally evaluated on the basis of expected discounted net earnings, but are not further discussed here because these two categories are not included in the balance sheets with which this study deals; and among financial instruments for medium- and long-term claims. Differences between market prices and replacement cost should not exist, because in principle where market prices can be determined they dominate replacement cost estimates. In practice, however, not only do such differences exist and sometimes are substantial but the estimates used for structures and equipment are generally based on replacement costs derived by the perpetual inventory method. This is partly because of the scarcity and the nature of the available market price data, and partly in order to preserve homogeneity, and hence comparability, among the different types of reproducible tangible assets.

A special problem arises in the valuation of nonfarm dwellings, particularly one-family homes. This is the only type of nonfarm real estate for which a fairly broad market exists, so that market prices can be ascertained regularly or occasionally. This opportunity has, however, only rarely been taken advantage of, so that indices of house prices are available only for a few countries for the postwar period—e.g., Germany, Great Britain, and the United States among the countries covered in this study—and for earlier periods seem to be limited to the United States. These indices demonstrate that the movements of the prices of existing houses, which necessarily include the underlying land, and those of the costs of constructing new homes, which are used in building up the perpetual inventory estimates of the stock of dwellings, are not identical. Indeed the differences between the two indicators of home prices are sometimes substantial and enduring and show a cyclical pattern. In this situation it was decided, in the interest of comparability among countries and over time, not to correct the perpetual inventory method estimates of the replacement cost of dwellings for the difference between market and replacement value even in the few cases where statistics were available for doing so.

The United States is the only country for which the relation between market prices and costs of construction can be determined back to the late 19th century. There was hardly any difference in the trend of the two series between 1890 and 1945, as they increased by 270 and fully 255 percent, respectively (Grebler, Black, and Winnick 1956, 342, 351; U.S. Bureau of the Census, *Historical Statistics*, 1975, 647), which corresponds to average growth rates of 2.40 and 2.34 percent per year. Within this period of over half a century there were, however, several deviations of shorter or longer duration. Thus prices led construction costs between 1890 and World War I, the relation (1929 = 1.00) increasing from 0.92 to 1.14, but fell seriously behind during the inflation following World War I, the ratio dropping to 0.77 in 1920. After catching up in the 1920s, home prices fell much more sharply than costs during the Great Depression but rose more rapidly during the next decade, with the result that in 1945 the ratio between the two indices was quite close to what it had been in 1929 or in 1890. Differences were apparently small until the late 1960s. In the accelerating inflation of the following decade, the available official statistics show an approximate doubling between 1970 and 1978 in home prices (U.S., Bureau of the Census, *Statistical Abstract*, 1979, 79) as well as in the costs of residential construction (U.S., Bureau of the Census, *Economic Report of the President*, 1981, 237). American experience would thus seem to justify the not unexpected conclusion that the long-term movements of the market prices and the costs of construction of dwellings are similar but that there are substantial, and sometimes fairly enduring, differences between the two series. These differences must be kept in mind when benchmark dates having a different position in short or long cycles are being compared.

In Great Britain the difference between the trend in home prices and in homebuilding costs over the three decades ending in 1975 were relatively small. The average annual rise in home prices of 7½ percent was only slightly in excess of that of homebuilding costs of 7¼ percent, both being far above the rise in retail prices of 5¾ percent but well below that of average earnings of 8¼ percent (Nationwide Building Society, *Occasional Bulletin*, var. issues). During the 1950s building costs advanced more rapidly than home prices, with the result that in 1958 the index of building costs on a 1945 basis was about 20 percent above that of home prices. The difference had disappeared by the mid-1960s. The boom of home prices of the early 1970s then lifted their index to about one-third above the index of homebuilding costs. The difference had been reduced to one-tenth at the end of 1975 as building costs advanced by 50 percent within two years. The rise in home prices came to a halt in 1981 after having doubled in 1976–80. Building costs continued to rise through 1982 though at a declining rate. As a result both house prices and building costs were then at slightly more than twice their 1975 level.

Financial claims are conventionally entered in national or sectoral balance sheets at face value. This is unobjectionable from the point of view of the market price principle, both for objectivists and subjectivists, for claims and liabilities due on demand or within a very short period. Claims of this type include practically all deposits with financial institutions and the short-term obligations of households, e.g., consumer credit;

and of business enterprises, such as trade and bank credit; and of governments, like Treasury bills. Currency is usually regarded as equally liquid though in practice it represents a perpetual debt of the central bank or the government. No systematic investigation of the proportion these claims constitute of total financial assets has come to attention. In 1975 they seem to have represented in the United States about one-half of the value of all claims, and two-fifths of all financial assets excluding equity in unincorporated enterprises and personal trust funds (based on Goldsmith 1982). Problems, therefore, are limited to the other half of claims and liabilities. If the market price principle is applied only to instruments which are traded on an exchange or in an active over-the-counter market, differences between market and face value are relatively moderate, because the difference cannot be large for medium-term investments with a maturity of, say, up to five years, unless the likelihood of default has to be taken into account; and the share of long-term securities so traded is now generally small, though it probably was much larger before World War II and particularly in the 19th century. Referring again to the United States, it is unlikely that traded long-term debt securities accounted in 1975 for more than one-tenth of all claims, and their derivation from face value averaged less than 10 percent during the preceding two decades (Eisner 1980, table 66). Hence this deviation generally would be inconspicuous in the national balance sheet. In Germany where the official financial accounts show the difference explicitly, the book value of fixed interest securities at the end of 1977, i.e., a period of sharply rising interest rates, was 4 percent below the market value, and the difference was equal to less than one-half of 1 percent of all claims outstanding, never exceeding 2 percent in the preceding 17 years (Deutsche Bundesbank 1978, 144 ff.). The collapse of bond prices in the United States in the early 1980s is an exception of limited duration.

On the other hand, if the principle of valuing not immediately redeemable claims on the basis of their expected future yield, including repayment of face value at stipulated maturity, is strictly adhered to, and therefore applied to all bonds, notes, and mortgages, and to insurance, pension, and other claims, the differences between the resulting quasi-market values and the face value of these claims, or the values at which they are carried in the balance sheets of holders and issuers or in the national balance sheet, would sometimes be very large, and sufficient to substantially affect basic balance sheet ratios. This is particularly true for recent years in which interest rates have risen in most developed countries at a rate and to levels never before experienced. Thus in the United States a 25-year high-grade bond or mortgage issued in 1965 at 5 or 6 percent would at the end of 1978, when the current rate was in the order of the 9–10 percent, have had a market value of only about two-thirds of its face value. Unfortunately, the maturity distribution for all not immediately redeemable debts is not known, but the average probably was somewhat over ten years. Since the total par value of such not immediately redeemable claims was in the neighborhood of $3000 billion at the end of 1978 (based on Board of Governors of the Federal Reserve System 1979), the difference between discounted and par value might have approached $1 trillion. This would have been equal to nearly 5 percent of national assets. The changes wrought in sectoral balance sheets, particularly those of financial institutions, would, of course, have been substantially larger. The difference between book and discounted value would, e.g., have far exceeded the net worth of all financial institutions. While such a treatment of claims might be in accord with the strict application of the market valuation principle and is not without interest for economic analysis, it has not been applied in this study, partly because the rise of interest rates in the late 1970s was exceptional; partly because of the practical impossibility of implementing it for more than a few other dates and countries; partly because it leads to results very different from actual balance sheets and from holders' and issuers' evaluations; and partly, maybe, for lack of courage.

Valuation is most difficult for insurance and pension claims, for which it is often not clear what the market value or its closest substitute is. Cash surrender value probably comes nearest to it, but it has the drawbacks of not being applicable to private pension or social insurance claims. The actuarial value of liabilities provides the other extreme. Apart from being very difficult to estimate, given the uncertainties of future benefits in social security schemes and future interest rates, it produces enormous entries which have little economic significance. In this study, therefore, the compromise has been adopted of equating insurance and pension claims to the assets of the issuing issurance organizations, i.e., of attributing these assets to the beneficiaries in the household sector, thus ignoring the very small amounts that should be allocated to shareholders of incorporated insurance companies outside that sector. This compromise has at least the advantage that the amounts involved can be determined with reasonable accuracy.

A particular conceptual problem is posed by the valuation of corporate equity. The problem does not arise on the assets side of sectoral or national balance sheets, where holdings of corporate shares are entered at market value for stocks listed on exchanges or traded in an active over-the-counter market, or at values assimilated to them for other stocks. If the same value is used among liabilities, a gap arises in the balance sheet of the corporate sector between the market value of stocks of corporations and the value of their equity, derived as the difference between the market value or the replacement cost of their assets and the face value of their liabilities. This gap will be the larger, among other things, the more the replacement cost of reproducible assets and the market value of nonreproducible assets exceed their original depreciated cost. To avoid this gap, corporate equity has been entered on the right-hand side of the balance sheets of national, corporate, and financial institutions at the value of adjusted net worth. This is admittedly a violation of the second corollary of the market value principle but could be remedied, at least to the extent of permitting users to make the adjustment by the creation of a positive or negative item obtained by subtracting the market value of corporate stock from the net worth of corporations. It was beyond the resources of this study to make the necessary calculations, which would have to be rough. An indication of their order of magnitude is, however, provided by Tobin's *q* or a similar measure (Goldsmith 1982, 167–68). It is evident from the actual values of such ratios that the size of the adjustment is sometimes quite large. Thus in the United States in the post-war period it was as low as a little over one-half in 1975, but sometimes above unity. In 1975 the adjustment would have been in the order of $700 billion, or fully one-tenth of all financial assets or over 5 percent of national assets.

ii) Balance Sheets in Constant Prices

Like all components of a system of national accounts national and sectoral balance sheets can be expressed in addition to their primary denomination in current market prices in a uniform set of prices of a base period. This second form, however, is more problematical for balance sheets than for most other components of the system of national accounts. The concept of national accounting aggregates as bundles of goods or services physically unchanged over time or identical in space is more easily, or rather less uneasily or unrealistically, applied to current product, input-output, and tangible wealth accounts. It is very problematic for current income accounts; and it is hardly applicable to flow-of-funds accounts, which make sense only in terms of current values. The difficulty of their application to national and sectoral balance sheets stems from the fact that these combine tangible and financial assets, and it is very difficult to apply the concept of a bundle of physically identical goods differing in time or location to financial assets. What is the physically unchanged essence of a claim in monetary units? Its purchasing power? Over what commodities and services, and for whom? What is its capitalized yield in monetary or purchasing power terms?

Reduction of national or sectoral balance sheets from current values to base period, or base area, may be desired for one of three purposes, comparison of absolute values over time or space or comparison of structure. In all three cases the main conceptual and practical difficulty is to find deflators for land and for financial assets. The easiest, but least informative, solution is to use a common deflator for all components, tangible as well as financial, of the balance sheet, thus shifting from the current monetary unit as the *numéraire* to a unit of "constant purchasing power," defined as the implicit gross national product deflator, a consumer price index or a similar measure with all their well-known problems. The results are not without interest for intertemporal comparisons, but of course produce structural relations identical with those shown in balance sheets expressed in current prices.

An alternative approach is the hybrid combination of using specific deflators for tangible assets (very difficult to obtain for land) and purchasing power deflators for financial assets and liabilities, deflated net worth emerging as the residual between the so deflated components, and thus having its own hybrid implicit deflator. This approach can be refined by deflating the current values of equities by appropriate price indices, although the meaning of the resulting deflated figures is problematical; and by applying different deflators to financial assets and liabilities held or issued by different sectors, e.g., a consumer price or wage index to that of households and a price index of business product or cost to those of enterprises.

From a practical point of view the importance of deflation depends on the scatter of the various deflators. The smaller the scatter, the less important deflation is for the analysis of differences in space and of changes over time in the structure of national and sectoral balance sheets. It is, therefore, necessary for comparisons over time to look at the implicit deflators of national product, which are the standard measure of purchasing power; and those of fixed capital expenditures, which in the absence of comprehensive and sufficiently detailed price indices must be used to represent the price movements of structures and equipment that constitute the bulk of physical assets.

For the average of 18 countries there was, as table 31 shows, no difference in the rate of increase of the deflators for national product and for fixed capital formation for the period from 1961 through 1975. Similar calculations for earlier periods are not yet easily feasible for most countries. For the entire period the average gross national product and fixed capital formation deflators were almost the same. There were, however, offsetting differences for the two subperiods of 1961–67 and 1968–75. In the first, the deflator for fixed capital formation rose slightly less than that for national product, the difference averaging 0.6 percent per year, and thus was equal to one-eighth of the rate of increase in the general price level. In the second, much more inflationary subperiod, the fixed capital expenditures deflator rose considerably more than the national national product deflator, namely, on the average by 0.7 percent or by one-tenth more than the latter. Differences were, of course, larger for individual countries. For the period as a whole the ratio between the increases in the deflator for fixed capital expenditures and that of gross national product ranged in 11 of the 18 countries between 0.84 and 1.14, with no apparent

Table 31 **Comparison of Increase in National Product and Fixed Capital Formation Deflators in 18 Market Economies, 1961–1975 (% per Year)**

	Gross National Product			Gross Fixed Capital Formation[a]			Difference[b]			Ratio[b]
	1961 to 1967 (1)	1968 to 1975 (2)	1961 to 1975 (3)	1961 to 1967 (4)	1968 to 1975 (5)	1961 to 1975 (6)	1961 to 1967 (7)	1968 to 1975 (8)	1961 to 1975 (9)	1961 to 1975 (10)
1. Australia	2.43	8.71	5.74	2.21	8.71	5.63	−0.22	0	−0.11	0.98
2. Belgium	3.30	6.74	5.11	3.80	7.45	5.73	+0.50	+0.71	+0.62	1.12
3. Canada	2.59	6.62	4.72	1.89	7.84	5.39	−0.70	+1.12	+0.67	1.14
4. Denmark	6.02	9.05	7.63	4.19	9.55	7.02	−1.83	+0.50	−0.61	0.92
5. France	3.95	8.03	5.84	3.35	8.27	5.62	+0.60	+0.24	−0.22	0.96
6. Germany (BRD)	3.32	5.65	4.56	2.77	5.96	4.46	−0.55	+0.31	−0.10	0.98
7. Great Britain	3.50	10.26	7.11	2.61	11.40	7.21	−0.89	+1.14	+0.10	1.01
8. India[c]	6.88	7.75	7.28	5.15	10.66	7.68	−1.73	+2.91	+0.40	1.05
9. Israel	6.75	15.71	11.44	6.85	18.59	12.96	+0.10	+2.88	+1.52	1.13
10. Italy	4.76	10.15	7.60	3.83	11.90	8.06	−0.93	+1.75	+0.46	1.06
11. Japan	5.13	7.94	6.62	2.59	6.59	4.70	−2.54	−1.35	−1.92	0.71
12. Mexico	2.94	9.19	6.23	2.03	11.78	7.12	−0.91	+2.59	+0.89	1.14
13. Norway	2.27	8.07	4.93	2.56	8.83	5.44	+0.29	+0.76	+0.51	1.10
14. South Africa	2.53	8.54	5.69	2.54	9.05	5.97	+0.01	+0.51	+0.28	1.05
15. Sweden	4.20	7.62	5.77	4.31	6.82	5.18	+0.11	−0.80	−0.59	0.90
16. Switzerland	5.05	6.66	5.90	4.06	5.74	4.95	−0.99	−0.92	−0.95	0.84
17. United States	2.03	6.80	4.55	1.30	6.71	4.15	−0.73	−0.09	−0.40	0.91
18. Yugoslavia	12.63	14.49	13.62	12.15	14.60	13.45	−0.48	+0.11	−0.17	0.99

[a]Consumer durables not included.
[b]Capital formation deflator less, or divided by, national product deflator.
[c]Figures in cols. 1, 2, 4, 5, 7, and 8 refer to 1961/68 and 1969/75 respectively.

Source of basic data:
Cols. 1–3 Derived from data in *IFSYB* (1979).
Cols. 4–6 Derived from data in *YNAS* (var. issues).

relation between the width of the difference and the rate of inflation. The difference was by far the largest in Japan, where the deflator of fixed capital expenditure rose at a rate of only 4.7 percent a year compared to a rate of inflation of 6.6 percent as measured by the national product deflator, the difference being much larger absolutely and still more so relatively in the first than in the second subperiod, possibly reflecting a particularly rapid rise of productivity in the capital goods industries.

A comparison of the rate of growth of real fixed reproducible capital, i.e., structures and equipment, used in this study on the basis of deflation by the gross national product deflator and in other studies for five countries, the only ones for which this is possible for the entire last century, is presented in table 32. For the period as a whole the differences are quite small, ranging from 0.1 percent per year in the case of Japan and Norway, or about 2 percent of the growth rate, to 0.4 percent for the United States. Some of the differences for one of the shorter periods of generally three to four decades are, however, considerably larger. This is the case particularly for the interwar period, which is heavily affected in three of the five countries by the destruction during World War II. In evaluating the differences between the rates of growth of this study and those shown by other estimates, it must be kept in mind that some of the latter are also derived by deflation of stock estimates in current prices, though using specific instead of uniform (gross national product) deflators rather than by quantity series. The differences thus reflect in part the differences between general and specific deflators, a problem which has already been discussed for the postwar period. The main result of both comparisons is that in general the use of deflated current price estimates of the reproducible capital stock will not seriously affect the results, i.e., that the margin of error in the real growth rates of the capital stock will not be substantially increased for long periods by using the gross national product deflator rather than specific deflators or quantity series, though use of the latter two measures, if they were available, would certainly be preferable.

Differences of the type shown in tables 31 and 32 cannot be unequivocally regarded as measuring the differences in the prices of current output and of the market prices of tangible assets, and for at least four reasons. First, it is not known whether quality improvements, which are insufficiently taken into account in all price indexes, are more important and by how much, in capital goods than in other goods and services. Second, the deflators differ among the various categories of structures and equipment; these differences, however, can be taken into account, given sufficient resources, to the extent, that these categories are being distinguished in the basic national accounts. Third, the market prices for structures and equipment, to the extent they exist, differ, particularly in the short run, from costs of reproduction which are reflected in the deflators. The direction and extent of these differences, however, are not well known, except in the case discussed above of one-family homes in a few countries and hardly ever, except for the United States, for any

Table 32 **Comparison of Rate of Growth of Reproducible Tangible Assets by Direct and Indirect (Deflation) Methods in Five Countries, 1876–1978 (% per Year)**

Country		Method	
		Direct	Indirect
1. Germany			
a)	1876–1913	3.0	2.7
b)	1914–1948	...[a]	...[a]
c)	1949–1977	...	6.1
d)	1876–1977	...	2.3
2. Great Britain			
a)	1876–1913	1.3	1.3
b)	1914–1948	0.6	1.9
c)	1949–1978	3.8	3.4
d)	1876–1978	1.8	2.0
3. Japan			
a)	1886–1913	2.5	2.0
b)	1914–1955	1.5	2.6
c)	1958–1978	11.1	9.2
d)	1886–1978	4.0	3.9
4. Norway			
a)	1881–1913	2.0	2.4
b)	1914–1953	2.7	2.8
c)	1954–1978	5.6	5.5
d)	1881–1978	3.2	3.3
5. United States			
a)	1881–1912	4.3	4.4
b)	1913–1950	1.7	2.0
c)	1951–1978	3.7	4.5
d)	1881–1978	3.2	3.6

[a]Assumed to be zero.

Source:

Direct method:

Line 1.a	Hoffmann and associates 1965, 253–54.
Lines 2.a, 2.b	Feinstein 1976, T 96–97.
Lines 3.a–3.d	Goldsmith 1983b, 10.
Lines 4.a–4.d	*HSN* 1978, 106–7.
Lines 5.a, 5.b	*HS* 1978, 256.
Line 5.c	U.S. Department of Commerce 1982, 1, 259.

Indirect method:

Table 12 plus rate of population growth (for lines a and b, Mitchell 1975; for line c, *IFSYB* 1981).

period before the 1950s. Fourth, and probably most important, the trends of prices of several types of physical assets may, and often do, even in the long run, differ considerably from those of either structure and equipment or from the national product deflator. The differences are probably not very large for inventories. They may be for livestock, but its share in national wealth is generally small enough that even substantial differences cannot seriously affect the overall picture. It is different for land. Its share in national wealth is usually high before the 20th century, and in less developed countries up to the present; its prices are poorly known; and it is possible, and even likely, that its prices have at times deviated significantly from those of reproducible tangible assets, and have shown a more rapid secular rise. Among financial assets corporate shares have usually fluctuated more in current prices and even in purchasing power than short- or long-term claims or tangible assets, and have not rarely shown different trends.

In view of these serious conceptual and statistical problems I have regarded it as beyond the line of duty to attempt to construct national, let alone sectoral, balance sheets in constant prices; and thus to deal with the rate of growth of individual assets or with changes in the structure of national balance sheets over time in constant as distinct from current prices.

Because all comparisons among countries are made on the basis of relative rather than of absolute figures, i.e., in the form of the shares of individual assets of liabilities in national assets or tangible or financial assets or of measures like the financial interrelations ratios, this study does not have to meet head-on the even more difficult problem of reducing the absolute figures to a common *numéraire*, e.g., dollars of 1970. It thus avoids the necessity of reducing the original balance sheet figures, which are expressed in two dozen national currencies of widely different years, to a common base. How difficult such a translation is has become evident in the recent calculations of purchasing power parities (for market economies see Summers, Kravis, and Heston 1980), which indicate that among the 20 countries purchasing power parities are sometimes over three times as high as exchange rates that thus must be ruled out as a basis of comparison and combination. It is only in tables 1–6 that this problem has been encountered, and here only in the determination of weights for the combination of the structure ratios of individual countries into groups and ultimately a planetary total.

e) Benchmark Dates

Since the construction of annual national balance sheets, let alone sectional ones, for long periods and for a substantial number of countries is out of the question for an individual's effort, it is necessary to select a set of benchmark dates. The choice is limited by the availability of basic data or of outside estimates of important components, particularly the stock of fixed capital and of financial assets. Within these constraints decisions have to be made whether to use uniform dates for all or most countries covered, and whether to improve intertemporal or international comparisons by locating the benchmark dates at years identical or similar in cyclical standing. In this study an attempt has been made to select benchmark dates as simultaneous as possible among individual countries, and as close as possible to turning points in long cycles. On the other hand no attention has been paid to the position of benchmark dates in a country's short cycles.

In line with these principles national balance sheets have been constructed for years as close as possible to 1850, 1875, 1929, 1950, and 1973, which may be viewed as turning points of long cycles. In addition 1913, 1939, and 1965 have been regarded as important benchmark dates because of their position before the distortions caused by World War I, World War II, and the postwar inflation. Estimates also have been made for a year between 1975 and 1978 to bring the information up-to-date as far as was possible when these estimates were made three years ago. The choice of benchmark dates before 1850, which is limited by scarcity of information to Great Britain (1688, 1760, 1800, 1830), the United States (1774, 1805), and France (1815) is determined solely by availability of data. It has been possible to construct or use national balance sheets for all, or nearly all, 10 benchmark dates between 1850 and 1978 for six of the countries (Belgium, Germany, Great Britain, India, Italy, United States), and for eight or nine benchmark dates for five more (Denmark, France, Japan, Norway, and Switzerland). The actual dates corresponding to the standard benchmark dates are identified in table 33. It will be seen that the two coincide, or differ by only one year, for all or almost all countries for 1913, 1929, 1939, and 1973. The variation for the other standard benchmark years are larger, but hardly large enough seriously to impair comparability.

Sectoral balance sheets have been used or constructed, with the exception of the United States, for only one recent year.

3. Statistical Difficulties

Appendix C discusses briefly some of the statistical difficulties encountered in estimating some of the components of national and sectoral balance sheets. The discussion is by no means exhaustive, and does not deal with difficulties specific to individual countries except as illustrations. It may be disregarded by readers not interested in technicalities.

Table 33 **Reconciliation of Actual and Standard Benchmark Dates of National Balance Sheets**

	Standard Benchmark Dates									
Country	1850	1875	1895	1913	1929	1939	1950	1965	1973	1978
	Actual Year									
1. Australia[a]	...	...	...	...	...	...	1956	1965	1973	1977
2. Belgium	1850	1875	1895	1913	1929	1939	1948	1965	1973	1976
3. Canada	...	...	...	...	...	...	1955	1965	1973	1978
4. Denmark	...	1880	1900	1913	1929	1938	1948	1965	1973	1978
5. France[b]	1850	1880	...	1913	1929	...	1950	1960	1972	1976
6. Germany	1850	1875	1895	1913	1929	1938	1950	1960	1972	1977
7. Great Britain[c]	1850	1875	1895	1913	1927	1937	1948	1965	1973	1977
8. Hungary	...	...	...	...	...	...	...	1959	1970	1977
9. India[d]	1860	1875	1895	1913	1929	1939	1950	1960	...	1975
10. Israel[e]	...	...	...	...	...	...	1951	1966	...	1976
11. Italy	1861	1881	1895	1914	1929	1938	1951	1963	1973	1977
12. Japan	...	1885	1900	1913	1930	1940	1955	1965	1970	1977
13. Mexico[f]	...	...	...	...	1930	1940	1948	1965	1973	1978
14. Norway	...	1880	1899	1913	1930	1939	1953	1965	1972	1978
15. Russia/USSR[g]	...	...	...	1913	1928	1937	1950	1969	1972	1977
16. South Africa	...	...	...	1913	1929	1938	1955	1965	1973	1978
17. Sweden[h]	...	...	...	...	...	...	...	1963	1973	1978
18. Switzerland[i]	...	1880	1900	1913	1929	1938	1948	1965	1973	1978
19. United States[j]	1850	1880	1900	1912	1929	1939	1950	1965	1973	1978
20. Yugoslavia	...	...	...	...	...	...	1953	1962	1972	1977

[a]In addition 1947.
[b]In addition 1815.
[c]In addition 1688, 1760, 1800, 1830 and 1957.
[d]In addition 1970.
[e]In addition 1962.
[f]In addition 1960.
[g]In addition 1959.
[h]In addition 1969.
[i]In addition 1960 and 1976.
[j]In addition 1774 and 1805.

4. Sources

At the present stage of development of national and sectoral balance sheets, their construction resembles a puzzle composed of pieces of unequal size that do not always completely fill the assigned space and sometimes overlap or exceed the space, and that originate in various official documents, scholarly studies, and popular publications. The footnotes to the country tables in Appendices A and B will give an idea of the number and variety of the sources used in the construction of the 20 national and the six sets of sectoral balance sheets used in this study, most of which were specifically constructed, modified, or extended in time for it. The range of sources actually involved is, of course, much larger, since the notes do not list the sources of the estimates of national balance sheets I have published elsewhere, i.e., most of the sources underlying the balance sheets for Belgium, Germany, India, Japan, Russia/USSR, Switzerland, the United States, and Yugoslavia.

There are only two types of sources from which substantial parts of the balance sheets of a number of countries could be taken, and these are essentially limited to the postwar period. The first are the estimates of the stock of structures and equipment derived by the perpetual inventory method, which are available for most countries for all or part of the postwar period and for a few of them (Germany, Great Britain, India, Italy, Japan, and Norway) which even go back to the late 19th century. The second are the statements of the stocks of financial assets and liabilities produced as part of their flows-of-funds accounts by an increasing number of countries (now for 13 of the 20)—the exceptions being Denmark, Great Britain, Hungary, Israel, Mexico, Switzerland, and, of course, the Soviet Union—few of which, however, go back as far as the early 1950s. Great Britain (Revell 1967), India and Japan (Goldsmith 1983a, 1983b), and the United States (Goldsmith, Lipsey, and Mendelson 1963; Goldsmith 1982) are the only countries for which statements of this type, though unofficial ones, extend to the turn of the century. International statistical publications, with the outstanding exception of the International Monetary Fund's *International Financial Statistics Yearbook* and its predecessors, which cover the period beginning with 1948, have been found of little help as they generally treat finance very summarily. For many of the entries for the postwar years and for most of those of the preceding period, there is therefore no way of getting around the laborious method of putting the figures together from numerous national sources. The results are thus a function of the time spent on search for data, though the search is likely soon to yield diminishing returns per unit of time. Since I could devote less than two years to the entire study and could consult local libraries in only about half a dozen of the 20 countries, I am afraid that the point of diminishing returns had not yet reached when I had to stop. Thus most of the nearly 3000 figures in the basic country balance sheets could be improved, some substantially, by further search, and particularly by the exploration of source material available only on the spot. By and large, however, these improvements, desirable as they are, would not substantially affect the picture of the changes in the balance sheet structure of the 20 countries over the between 75 and nearly and 300 years covered, or the differences in the balance sheet structure among countries.

Of the nearly 150-odd balance sheets shown in Appendix A, which underlie most of the discussion in Chapters 1 and 3, only very few were obtained, and then only with some changes or additions, from others' published estimates; nearly 50 were taken, again sometimes with some changes, from my own publications, while more than one-half were constructed for this study. On the other hand, most of the sectorized balance sheets of Appendix B on which Chapter 4 is based were derived from published sources.

3
The Structure of National Balance Sheets

This chapter is based on the national balance sheets for each of the 20 countries for between three and 14 dates stretching from 1688 to 1978 shown in Appendix A, in which each of two dozen types of assets is expressed as percentages of total national assets. The tables are preceded by brief remarks on the sources and quality of the estimates and by a few comments on the meaning of the figures. They are followed by notes, which guide the reader to the sources of the estimates, even if it will not in every case enable him to reproduce them as I would have wished.

Because of the differences in the importance of the various countries, the number of benchmark dates for which estimates are presented, the difficulties involved in constructing individual entries, the number of steps between the basic data and the estimates, and, last but not least, the time at which the notes were written, they differ considerably in length and detail. I regret, in particular, that I did not provide a more extensive discussion for Australia, Canada, Israel, South Africa, and Sweden, though the period covered for most of these countries is relatively short. Notes have been omitted or kept very brief for those countries for which I have already published national balance sheets elsewhere, namely, Belgium (Goldsmith 1975b; Goldsmith and Frijdal 1975), Germany (Goldsmith 1976), India (Goldsmith 1983a), Japan (Goldsmith 1983b), Russia/USSR (Goldsmith 1964), Switzerland (Goldsmith 1981), and the United States (Goldsmith, Lipsey, and Mendelson 1963; Goldsmith 1982).

A standard scheme of classification of assets is used, with some minor deviations which are due to limitations of the basic data, but the content of some of the categories of financial instruments is not identical in all countries, again reflecting the nature of the source material. These variations are not serious enough, except in a few cases, to invalidate comparisons among countries or over time. While these difficulties are absent, or much less serious in the case of tangible than of financial assets, it must be kept in mind that the technological character of some of the categories of reproducible tangible assets, particularly of nonresidential structures, of equipment, and of consumer durables has substantially changed over the last century.

The national balance sheets, though not the sectoral balance sheets of Appendix B, fail to show liabilities or net worth, because in national aggregation the share of the various types of liabilities is very close to that of the corresponding financial assets, and the share of net worth is approximately equal to that of tangible assets, since net foreign assets or liabilities generally account for only a small proportion of the totals.

The discussion in Chapters 3 and 4 of the changes in the structure of tangible and financial assets over the last century, which is possible only for one-half of the 20 countries, or for shorter periods, as well as the comparison of balance sheet structure among countries are based on a set of tables each of which deals with one balance sheet ratio, all the entries being taken from the country tables in Appendix A, or are derived from the absolute figures underlying them. The ratios are shown, as far as available, for 10 benchmark dates between 1850 and 1978. The actual dates to which the entries refer generally deviate by one or a few years from the benchmark dates which can be ascertained from table 33.

An adequate discussion of the time trends and intercountry differences evidenced or suggested by these ratios would require much more space and more intensive analysis than was available or possible in this study. The figures, their movements, and their interrelations can be understood only within the framework of the varied economic and financial history of the 20 countries in the 19th and 20th centuries. Such an intensive treatment was obviously out of the question here, even if the author were sufficiently familiar with their histories and if the existing literature made such a venture possible.

In interpreting movements in the ratios or differences among countries, it must be kept in mind that the numerators and denominators of the ratios are expressed in the current prices of the time and place. Movements and differences in the ratios can therefore be regarded as reflecting quantitative changes and differences only to the extent that relative asset prices are constant between dates or among countries being compared. This condition is rarely if ever met, and the deviations from it may be large. This is particularly true when the ratios are based on total national assets, which include items as heterogeneous in their price movements or relations as land, reproducible assets, equities, and claims. The movements of relative asset prices over long periods or their relations among countries are not well known, but there is considerable evidence that secularly the relative prices of equipment and consumer durables (adjusted for efficiency) have tended to fall and those of land and most types of structures to rise, although those differences have varied a great deal over time or among countries. Hence constancy in the current price shares of equipment and consumer durables generally indicates an increase in their share in quantitative terms, while it suggests a decline in the case of structures and land.

1. Overviews for 1880, 1913, 1950, and 1978

Since the structure of the combined balance sheets for groups of countries has been discussed in Chapters 1 and 2, and the share of the various types of assets in total national assets in each of the 20 countries is the subject of the remainder of this chapter, this section will briefly compare the structure of the balance sheets of between 10 and 20 countries at four points of time: around 1880, when the financial system of most countries, except that of Great Britain, was in an early stage of development: on the eve of World War I, when most of the countries had installed their modern financial system; in the middle of the century shortly after the upheavals of World War II and the inflations which accompanied or followed it in most countries; and in the late 1970s, after fully three decades of unprecedented economic growth. Emphasis will be put on some similarities or differences in important structural characteristics of the national balance sheets, disregarding other features that can be followed in tables 38–59 as well as probably the most important single characteristic, the financial interrelations ratio, which has already been discussed in Chapter 1.

Around 1880 most of the 10 countries whose national balance sheets are shown in table 34 were still in the early stages of their modern economic development, though generally already near the end of their railway age. Agriculture was still very important, as evidenced by the fact that the share of agricultural land and livestock in tangible assets—thus ignoring farm residences and equipment—averaged two-fifths, though it ranged from only one-fourth in the United States to one-half in France. The share of dwellings varied considerably, stretching from approximately one-tenth to one-fifth, as did that of nonresidential structures and equipment. No obvious explanation of the differences suggests itself, some of which probably reflect inconsistencies in the underlying estimates. The share of financial (including foreign) assets in national assets was still low in most countries. It averaged a little over one-third, indicating a financial interrelations ratio of fully 0.5, but the range was wide, from less than one-fourth in Japan (or one-eighth in India if the population's hoards of gold and silver are excluded) to close to nearly one-half in Great Britain and, difficult to explain, fully one-half in Denmark.

Table 34 Structure of the National Balance Sheets of 11 Countries at the End of the Third Quarter of the 19th Century

	Belgium 1875 (1)	Denmark 1880 (2)	France 1880 (3)	Germany 1875 (4)	Great Britain 1875 (5)	India 1875 (6)	Italy 1881 (7)	Japan 1885 (8)	Norway 1880 (9)	Switzerland 1880 (10)	United States 1880 (11)
I. Tangible assets	72.4	47.3	64.2	72.6	51.7	67.9	71.8	76.7	73.2	47.5	60.9
1. Land	23.2	17.6	32.6	29.2	20.7	25.7	34.8	35.2	31.0	17.7	18.9
a) Agricultural	...	12.8	28.8	26.5	16.3	...	31.0	25.8	24.9[d]	11.7	11.9
b) Other	...	4.8	3.8	2.7	4.4	...	3.8	9.4	6.1	6.0	7.0
2. Reproducible assets	49.2	29.6	31.6	43.4	31.0	42.2	37.1	41.5	42.2	29.8	42.0
a) Dwellings	...	4.5	11.0	8.7	5.7 }		15.1	14.2	14.6	6.0	7.7
b) Other structures	...	6.6	7.9	17.8	12.6 }	32.1 }	14.3 }	12.5	16.3 }	17.6 }	14.2
c) Equipment	...	4.6	4.7	8.2	5.2 }	}	}	2.6	5.1 }	}	4.7
d) Inventories	...	4.4	3.8	4.5	4.0	5.4	3.5	5.3	2.8	1.9	8.8
e) Livestock	...	7.3	2.8	3.0	1.5	4.6	1.9	6.2	2.0	2.4	2.8
f) Consumer durables	...	2.2	1.4	1.3	2.0	...	2.3	0.8	1.4	1.9	3.8
II. Financial assets	27.6	50.0	30.7	24.7	38.6	32.1	28.2	23.3	26.8	43.2	38.3
1. Monetary metals	...	0.8	2.1	1.3	1.1	20.6	0.2	0.2	0.5	0.5	0.9
2. Claims against financial institutions	5.3	14.1	4.0	6.0	9.5	0.8	4.4	5.9	8.2	9.4	5.3
3. Loans by financial institutions	2.8	4.6	2.0	2.1	3.2	0.2	2.5	2.1	4.1	2.8	2.8
4. Mortgages	2.5	13.8	4.7	6.0	5.8	...	2.7	0.6	2.6	18.9	2.6
5. Government domestic debt	4.3	2.7	7.8	2.1	7.2	1.8	13.6	3.7	2.2	2.2	4.9
6. Corporate bonds	1.5	0.4	4.5	1.0 }	8.1 }	0.4	1.1	0.0	0.0	2.8	4.2
7. Corporate stocks	6.5	9.2	2.7	1.7 }	}		0.9	0.5	1.7	4.7	9.2
8. Trade credit	4.0	4.4	2.8	4.6	3.6	3.0	2.7	5.3	4.3	1.9	5.5
9. Other	0.6	...	...	...	...	5.4[b]	...	5.4[c]	3.1	...	2.8
III. Foreign assets[a]	...	2.6	5.1	2.7	9.7	...	...	...	...	9.2	0.8
IV. National assets	100.0	100.0	100.0	100.0	100.0	100.0	100.0	100.0	100.0	100.0	100.0

[a]Gross or, if positive, net.
[b]Mostly agricultural household debt, chiefly on mortgages.
[c]Agricultural debt.
[d]Including forests (12.0).
Source: Country balance sheets in Appendix A.

The pronounced variations in the share of the main financial instruments reflect basic differences in the countries' financial structure and institutions. India, of course, is a special case, gold and silver hoards representing nearly two-thirds of the country's financial assets and one-fifth of its national assets. But differences remained substantial among the 10 other countries. Thus the share of claims against financial institutions in total financial assets, which averaged one-fifth, ranged from not much over one-tenth in France to over three-tenths in Denmark and Norway. Differences were even greater in the share of mortgages, partly reflecting the importance of specialized mortgage lending institutions, particularly large in Denmark and Switzerland but absent in Great Britain and Italy and the United States. The large differences in the share of government debt—highest in France, Great Britain, and Italy—are easier to explain as the result of the varying weight of past military expenditures or budgetary deficits. The role of the domestic corporate securities in the financial superstructure varied greatly, from about 6 percent in Italy and Norway to a full one-fifth in France and over one-third in the United States. The differences were generally greater in the relation of foreign to domestic securities. While of small importance in most countries, foreign securities were equal to about one-third of domestic securities in France, more than one-half in Germany, nearly two-thirds in Great Britain, and nearly 100 percent in Switzerland. Few of these differences can be explained by the level of real national product per head. Institutional factors appear to be more important.

The range of countries covered in table 35 for the point just before World War I, which ended a century of rapid economic development in a world becoming integrated economically and hardly affected by wars, revolutions, or inflation, extended from two still predominantly agricultural countries (India and Russia) to Great Britain, then the financially most developed and internationally leading country. The share of agricultural land and livestock in tangible assets reflects the contrast: approximately three-fifths in India and Russia, about one-eighth in Great Britain, and between 20 and 30 percent in the other large developed countries.

Considerable differences are also visible in the makeup of the financial superstructure, apart even from the uniquely high share of monetary metals held by the population in India of still nearly one-half of all financial assets and one-eighth of national assets. Thus the share of financial institutions ranged from less than one-tenth in India (one-sixth if monetary metals are excluded from financial assets), to one-fourth to one-third in most other countries, even including Russia. The share of mortgages was far above the average in the central-European countries with a developed mortgage banking system, primarily Denmark, Ger-

Table 35 **Structure of the National Balance Sheets of 13 Countries on the Eve of World War I[a]**

	Belgium (1)	Denmark (2)	France (3)	Germany (4)	Great Britain (5)	India (6)	Italy (7)	Japan (8)	Norway (9)	Russia (10)	South Africa (11)	Switzerland (12)	United States (13)
I. Tangible assets	52.5	41.5	50.6	56.7	33.8	74.7	68.2	61.1	58.3	71.9	65.7	39.9	54.6
1. Land	9.8	10.9	16.8	15.2	7.4	40.2	26.8	25.8	18.3	44.2	18.4	14.4	19.3
a) Agricultural	...	5.5	12.8	11.4	3.4	...	22.7	18.1	13.0	...	13.8	8.7	10.5
b) Other	...	5.5	4.0	3.8	4.0	...	4.1	7.7	5.3	...	4.5	5.7	8.8
2. Reproducible assets	42.7	30.6	33.8	41.5	26.4	34.6	41.5	35.4	39.9	27.7	47.3	25.5	35.3
a) Dwellings	...	12.6	9.5	10.5	5.2		10.3	10.1	11.8	4.3	4.5		8.4
b) Other structures	...		17.7	12.7	11.3	24.3	22.1	9.1	14.8	9.0	25.3	20.9	12.3
c) Equipment	...	6.0		10.8	4.2			5.1	7.7	3.7			4.6
d) Inventories	...	3.0	3.2	4.0	4.3	3.4	4.4	7.2	4.3	4.6	4.9	1.5	3.7
e) Livestock	...	7.2	2.1	2.0		6.8	2.4	3.4		3.6	9.4	1.5	1.9
f) Consumer durables	...	1.8	1.4	1.4	1.5	...	2.2	0.5	1.2	2.4	3.3	1.5	4.5
II. Financial assets	39.8	57.9	40.8	40.3	48.4	25.3	31.7	38.9	41.7	28.1	34.3	48.9	43.7
1. Monetary metals	0.5	0.4	1.5	0.8	1.0	12.0	0.9	0.9	0.4	1.2	0.3	0.5	0.8
2. Claims against financial institutions	10.4	20.0	9.7	13.0	11.4	2.1	10.4	13.0	13.4	9.0	6.9	17.6	9.2
3. Loans by financial institutions	4.7	4.4	4.8	4.2	6.0	0.7	3.5	6.4	...	...[b]	4.5	4.3	4.8
4. Mortgages	2.4	17.7	4.0	9.5	3.1	...	2.0	3.0	4.2	2.1		11.9	4.0
5. Government domestic debt	6.9	3.3	7.8	4.2	5.3	1.7	10.1	3.4	3.4	2.2	1.2	4.5	1.9
6. Corporate bonds	2.2	0.3	5.5	0.6	4.3	1.0	0.6	0.2	0.4	0.2	...	1.1	4.8
7. Corporate stocks	8.3	8.8	5.1	3.9	14.0		0.8	4.7	4.5	2.1	16.4	7.5	12.5
8. Trade credit	3.7	3.0	2.4	4.1	3.4	1.7	3.3	7.2	3.0	11.2	4.9	1.5	2.7
9. Other	0.7	...	...	...	...	6.0	...	...	12.4	...	...	...	3.1
III. Foreign assets[c]	7.7	0.6	8.5	3.1	17.8	...	...	...	...	...	...	11.2	1.7
IV. National assets	100.0	100.0	100.0	100.0	100.0	100.0	100.0	100.0	100.0	100.0	100.0	100.0	100.0

[a]1913, except for Italy (1914) and the United States (1912).
[b]Line 3 included in line 9.
[c]Gross or net if positive.
Source: Country tables in Appendix A.

many, and Switzerland. The importance of domestic government debt varied greatly, in part reflecting past war expenditures or deficit financing being highest, as a generation earlier, in France, Great Britain, and Italy. An important characteristic of the financial superstructure is evidenced in the share of domestic corporate securities. It ranged from less than one-tenth of financial assets in India, Italy, and Russia, to fully one-fourth in Great Britain, nearly two-fifths in the United States, and nearly one-half in South Africa, where it reflected the huge foreign investments in gold mining shares. The importance of foreign investments varied greatly. It was relatively small compared with domestic financial assets or national wealth in most countries, accounting even in the United States for only about 4 and 3 percent, respectively. In contrast, foreign investments amounted to approximately one-fifth of domestic financial assets in Belgium, France, and Switzerland, and to more than one-third in Great Britain. They were equal to about one-sixth of domestic tangible assets in Belgium and France, over one-fourth in Switzerland, and an extraordinary full one-half in Great Britain, a ratio as far as can be ascertained never duplicated elsewhere or at other times. An idea of the relative importance of "security capitalism," finally, is provided by the share of all government and private domestic and foreign securities in total financial assets. This characteristic ratio varied from about one-tenth in India, about one-fifth in Japan, Norway, and Russia, to over one-half in Belgium, France, and South Africa, to reach a peak in Great Britain with approximately three-fifths.

The structure of national balance sheets around 1950, which can be followed in table 36, shows the effects of the inflation and currency reforms in several countries during and immediately after World War II, both in the small size of the financial superstructure compared with national wealth, as in France, Germany, Italy, and Japan; or in the makeup of the superstructure in the low shares of mortgages and corporate bonds and the high proportion of government debt in countries that did not devalue, particularly in Australia, Belgium, Canada, Great Britain, South Africa, and the United States; and in the low shares in countries having experienced currency reform or hyperinflation like Germany and Japan. The share of corporate securities was in most countries substantially below the level of 1913, but that of all securities was in most cases surprisingly similar because of the generally higher share of government debt, except in France, where the share declined sharply.

The differences in the structure of the national balance sheets in the late 1970s, evident in table 37, were still in the same direction as those observed before World War I or in mid-century, but they were generally smaller reflecting a tendency toward regression to the mean. Thus there were still substantial differences in the share of agricultural land and

Table 36 **Structure of the National Balance Sheets of 18 Countries around 1950**

	Developed Countries (Market Economies)							
	European							
	Belgium 1948 (1)	Denmark 1948 (2)	France 1950 (3)	Germany 1950 (4)	Great Britain 1948 (5)	Italy 1951 (6)	Norway 1953 (7)	Switzerland 1948 (8)
I. Tangible assets	54.7	47.3	64.4	71.2	36.1	70.6	55.8	43.6
1. Land	10.2	5.4	14.6	20.1	6.4	19.3	12.1	9.0
a) Agricultural	...	2.3	7.3	13.5	1.7	12.4	7.2	3.3
b) Other	...	3.1	7.3	6.6	4.7	6.9	5.0	5.6
2. Reproducible assets	44.5	41.9	49.8	51.0	29.7	51.3	43.6	34.6
a) Dwellings	13.4	7.9	15.9	12.1	8.4	20.6	12.0	7.2
b) Other structures	21.7 (b+c)	11.4	13.2	18.1	9.3	22.9 (b+c)	13.1	11.6
c) Equipment		14.0	10.4	10.2	4.9		11.5	11.6
d) Inventories	3.9	3.8	6.6	5.2	4.3	4.4	4.5	1.7
e) Livestock	0.9	2.4	0.9	1.8	0.4	0.9	0.7	0.8
f) Consumer durables	4.6	2.4	2.7	3.5	2.5	2.4	1.8	1.8
II. Financial assets	42.8	51.3	35.6	28.5	63.9	29.3	44.2	50.7
1. Monetary metals	1.4	0.1	0.4	0.0	0.4	0.2	0.2	2.7
2. Claims against financial institutions	13.5	21.7	10.1	9.5	19.5	9.7	18.4	19.1
3. Loans by financial institutions	3.4 (3+4)	4.7	6.8	3.3	5.6	3.4	...	2.5
4. Mortgages		9.2	2.2	1.2	1.4	1.2	3.7	9.9
5. Government domestic debt	13.5	6.7	5.5	4.3	20.3	8.8	6.9	5.3
6. Corporate bonds	0.3	0.4	0.5	0.3	0.7	0.2	0.5	0.5
7. Corporate stocks	4.5	4.7	5.1	3.3	12.3	2.5	1.3	8.9
8. Trade credit	6.1	3.7	4.9	5.2	3.6	3.3	3.3	1.7
9. Others	...	...	...	1.4	...	...	10.0	...
III. Foreign assets[a]	2.5	1.3	...	0.2	...	...	...	5.8
IV. National assets	100.0	100.0	100.0	100.0	100.0	100.0	100.0	100.0

[a]Gross or net, if positive.

[b]Includes 2.5 agricultural household debt.

Source: Country balance sheets in Appendix A.

Table 36 (Continued)

	Developed Countries (Market Economies) Non-European						Centrally Planned Economies		Less Developed Countries	
	United States 1950 (9)	Australia 1956 (10)	Canada 1955 (11)	Israel 1951 (12)	South Africa 1955 (13)	Japan 1955 (14)	USSR 1950 (15)	Yugoslavia 1953 (16)	India 1950 (17)	Mexico 1948 (18)
I. Tangible assets	46.0	56.1	45.7	60.1	46.8	64.7	76.0	80.9	67.8	57.6
1. Land	9.0	9.3	8.0	13.2	10.5	42.3	25.6	20.9	32.5	18.3
a) Agricultural	2.4	...	1.7	5.9	6.5	26.0	22.2	18.4	29.0	15.0
b) Other	6.6	...	6.3	7.3	4.0	16.4	3.4	2.4	3.5	3.3
2. Reproducible assets	37.0	46.9	37.6	46.9	36.4	22.5	50.3	60.0	35.3	39.3
a) Dwellings	12.0	9.6	8.5	13.5	5.6	3.5	13.1	12.9	7.6	6.6
b) Other structures	10.7	18.8 }	20.2 }	11.1	14.7 }	10.5 }	20.8 }	35.5 }	14.7 }	9.4
c) Equipment	4.9	6.4 }		8.2	6.0 }					8.4
d) Inventories	3.7	4.6	3.2	7.3	4.6	6.0	11.2	6.9	5.5	6.1
e) Livestock	0.6	2.4	0.7	0.9	2.3	1.0	2.6	2.2	4.8	3.8
f) Consumer durables	5.0	5.1	5.1	5.9	3.3	1.4	2.6	2.4	2.7	5.1
II. Financial assets	51.5	43.2	51.2	39.9	53.2	34.9	24.0	19.1	30.5	42.4
1. Monetary metals	1.2	0.2	0.5	0.0	0.5	0.0	...	0.0	8.6	0.6
2. Claims against financial institutions	15.7	15.0	13.5	15.0	13.9	11.0	7.2	7.5	5.9	11.4
3. Loans by financial institutions	2.5	7.4 }	8.8 }	5.9	4.3	8.5	6.2	7.9	1.2	6.3
4. Mortgages	3.3	... }		...	4.2	...	0.2	...	...	4.7
5. Government domestic debt	12.7	10.9	10.4	5.9	11.9	1.4	5.6	...	3.1	2.0
6. Corporate bonds	1.9	0.5	2.4	0.0	...	1.2	...	...	0.1	0.7
7. Corporate stocks	8.0	6.5	7.9	1.5	13.9	3.9	...	...	1.8	14.1
8. Trade credit	2.4	1.0	2.6	7.3	4.6	4.5 }	4.8 }	3.8	5.2[b]	2.6
9. Others	3.8	1.8	5.0	4.4	...	4.4 }			4.6	...
III. Foreign assets[a]	2.4	0.7	3.2	...	...	0.4	...	...	1.8	...
IV. National assets	100.0	100.0	100.0	100.0	100.0	100.0	100.0	100.0	100.0	100.0

[a]Gross or net, if positive

[b]Includes 2.5 agricultural household debt.

Source: Country balance sheets in Appendix A.

Table 37 **Structure of the National Balance Sheets of 20 Countries in the Late 1970s**

	Developed Countries (Market Economies)								
	European								
	Belgium 1976 (1)	Denmark 1978 (2)	France 1976 (3)	Germany 1977 (4)	Great Britain 1977 (5)	Italy 1977 (6)	Norway 1978 (7)	Sweden 1978 (8)	Switzerland 1978 (9)
I. Tangible assets	54.2	47.6	54.6	53.0	47.3	49.1	53.6	44.0	35.4
1. Land	9.8	6.8	12.8	13.2	7.0	8.2	8.6	6.7	6.1
a) Agricultural	...	1.4	4.3	6.7	1.2	2.5	2.9	1.2	0.9
b) Other	...	5.4	8.5	6.5	5.8	5.7	5.7	5.5	5.2
2. Reproducible assets	44.4	40.9	41.8	39.9	40.3	40.9	45.7	37.2	29.3
a) Dwellings	15.2	11.5	19.3	13.0	10.2	16.6	9.5	11.6	6.6
b) Other structures	22.0 (b and c)	14.0	8.3	14.2	12.2	16.1 (b and c)	18.9	13.2	10.8
c) Equipment		10.5	6.8	5.7	10.5		11.1	6.4	9.0
d) Inventories	2.5	1.6	4.3	2.6	3.6	3.9	3.8	2.7	1.4
e) Livestock	0.4	0.8	0.4	0.3	0.2	0.6	0.1	0.2	0.3
f) Consumer durables	4.2	2.6	2.7	4.1	3.7	3.7	1.8	3.1	1.3
II. Financial assets	40.9	50.4	41.4	44.0	52.7	50.9	46.4	53.6	49.5
1. Monetary metals	0.9	0.1	0.5	0.4	0.2	0.7	0.1	0.2	1.3
2. Claims against financial institutions	20.8	24.7	14.8	18.0	21.5	28.2	17.2	18.7	23.5
3. Loans by financial institutions	8.0 (3 and 4)	4.3	8.7	2.5	9.2	6.8	...	13.9	5.0
4. Mortgages		13.4	3.2	8.4	2.9	0.5	...	...	7.8
5. Government domestic debt	8.4	2.5	1.9	3.2	8.6	10.0	6.8	3.9	2.3
6. Corporate bonds	0.6	0.7	0.8	0.3	0.7	0.7	1.9	1.0	1.1
7. Corporate stocks	2.1	3.1	5.4	4.8	6.0	1.2	2.3	3.4	7.1
8. Trade credit	...	1.6	6.1 (8 and 9)	2.7	3.5	2.9	2.9	3.1	1.4
9. Other	...	...		3.8	...	...	15.3	9.4	...
III. Foreign assets[a]	4.9	2.0	3.9	3.0	9.3[b]	...	...	2.4	15.0
IV. National assets	100.0	100.0	100.0	100.0	100.0	100.0	100.0	100.0	100.0

[a]Gross or net, if positive.

[b]Distributed among II.

Source: Country balance sheets in Appendix A.

Table 37 (Continued)

	Developed Countries (Market Economies)						Centrally Planned Economies			Less Developed Countries	
	Non-European										
	United States 1978 (10)	Australia 1977 (11)	Canada 1978 (12)	Israel 1976 (13)	South Africa 1978 (14)	Japan 1977 (15)	Hungary 1977 (16)	USSR 1977 (17)	Yugoslavia 1977 (18)	India 1975 (19)	Mexico 1978 (20)
I. Tangible assets	50.2	62.1	46.9	47.4	56.7	49.5	73.4	77.6	45.5	65.0	58.4
1. Land	12.5	7.9	11.4	8.8	10.5	25.0	19.9	17.7	8.4	16.3	11.3
a) Agricultural	2.7	...	1.6	1.6	4.8	5.4	12.1	10.9	7.0	12.3	3.4
b) Other	9.8	...	9.6	7.2	5.7	19.6	7.8	6.8	1.4	4.0	8.0
2. Reproducible assets	37.7	54.2	35.5	38.6	46.2	24.4	53.5	59.9	37.1	48.7	47.1
a) Dwellings	11.1	11.8	8.9	12.4	6.5	5.0	9.7	9.7	5.4	8.3	14.4
b) Other structures	11.9	35.6	20.9	11.7	22.0	11.0	17.8	36.1	23.6	31.6	14.4
c) Equipment	5.7			7.0	8.3	4.0	9.1				9.7
d) Inventories	4.2	3.9	2.1	4.2	4.2	2.6	9.2	9.0	5.4	4.2	4.5
e) Livestock	0.3	0.7	0.3	0.3	1.0	0.4	1.1	1.5	1.3	1.3	1.0
f) Consumer durables	4.5	2.2	3.3	3.0	4.3	1.4	6.7	3.7	1.5	3.3	3.0

II. Financial assets	47.4	37.5	50.2	52.6	40.9	50.1	26.6	22.4	52.1	35.0	41.6
1. Monetary metals	0.3	0.2	0.3	0.1	0.6	0.0	0.0	0.3	0.0	5.8	0.1
2. Claims against financial institutions	13.3	15.8	16.9	32.2	16.8	15.1	13.7	12.1	14.7	8.3	13.9
3. Loans by financial institutions	3.6	10.6	5.6	6.2	3.8	11.7	11.1	8.0	17.8	4.0	7.4
4. Mortgages	6.6	...	5.3	...	3.2	...	...	0.2	1.7	...	1.8
5. Government domestic debt	6.2	5.2	6.5	6.7	5.8	2.6	...	...	...	3.7	2.8
6. Corporate bonds	2.4	0.4	1.7	0.0	1.7	2.7	...	...	...	0.1	0.1
7. Corporate stocks	7.3	3.0	4.6	1.1	4.8	4.2	...	...	...	1.4	12.0
8. Trade credit	2.2	0.9	2.5	4.2	4.2	6.9 }	1.8 } (8–9)	1.8 (8–9)	5.9	3.7	3.6
9. Other	5.3	1.3	6.9	2.0	...	6.8 }			12.0	8.1	...
III. Foreign assets[a]	2.5	0.5	3.0	...	2.4	0.4	...	...	2.3	...	...
IV. National assets	100.0	100.0	100.0	100.0	100.0	100.0	100.0	100.0	100.0	100.0	100.0

[a]Gross or net, if positive

[b]Distributed among II.

Source: Country balance sheets in Appendix A.

livestock in tangible assets, but they were in general substantially smaller, ranging from only about 3 percent (Great Britain, Sweden, Switzerland) to the neighborhood of one-sixth (Hungary, India, USSR). Variations were still marked in the case of residential structures, the range extending from about one-eighth of reproducible tangible assets in India, Hungary, South Africa, USSR, and Yugoslavia, over one-third in France, though keeping between one-fourth and one-third in most countries.

One of the most important differences in the structure of domestic financial assets was the share of financial institutions. In many countries they accounted for over two-fifths of all financial instruments, e.g., in Australia, Belgium, Denmark, Great Britain, Israel, and Italy as well as in the USSR and Hungary, while the share was only in the order of one-third in others, e.g., Canada, France, Great Britain, Japan, Mexico, Sweden, and Switzerland, and was as low as one-fourth in the United States and in India. These variations reflect among other things the relative importance of direct and indirect financing, of the financial activities of the government, and of foreign investments. Differences were pronounced in the share of domestic corporate securities, now primarily corporate stock. Among developed countries the ratio, volatile because of often substantial fluctuations in stock prices, was in the late 1970s highest in the United States with one-seventh, but was in the order of one-tenth in many of the other developed countries, e.g., Canada, France, Germany, Great Britain, Japan, South Africa, and Switzerland, and as low as approximately 5 percent in Belgium, Denmark, and Norway, and lowest with 2 percent or less in Israel and Italy. It is not surprising that of the two less developed countries one showed the third lowest ratio—India with about 4 percent of all financial assets while the other, surprisingly, showed the highest ratio—Mexico with nearly 30 percent. The ranking of the ratio of foreign investments to domestic financial assets among the seven countries for which the data are available, including the most important ones, was very similar to what it had been in 1913, but the ratios were in most cases considerably lower than more than half a century earlier. Switzerland now led with about 30 percent of domestic financial assets followed by Great Britain with fully 20 percent, reversing the order of 1913. Belgium and France held third and fourth places, while Germany, the United States, and Denmark occupied the three lowest positions in the same order as before World War I. The absolute value of the ratio was higher only for Switzerland and fractionally for the United States.

2. The Division between Tangible and Financial Assets

Table 38 shows the share of tangible in national assets for the 20 countries at each of the 3–14 benchmark dates for which the information is available, the share of financial (domestic and foreign) assets being its complement. Since the ratio of financial to tangible assets, i.e., the financial interrelations ratio, has already been analyzed in Chapters 1–5, no further discussion is required.

3. The Structure of Tangible Assets

a) The Share of Land

The intercountry differences and the intertemporal trend in the share of land in tangible assets are so pronounced and generally so much in line with what is known from other evidence that the picture shown in table 38 can be accepted with a considerable degree of confidence. Three caveats are, however, in order.

The first is the tenuous character for most of the estimates of nonagricultural land, which are derived as ratios of the value of the overlying structures, ratios which often have little solid backing since census-type estimates, such as are available for many countries in the case of agricultural land, are lacking.

The main problem with the estimates of agricultural land is the uncertainty about whether and to what extent they include the value of forest land and of standing timber. Specific estimates are shown for all or most benchmark dates only for three countries (Norway, the Soviet Union, and Switzerland); they are known to be included in a few others; and they are not covered in most, including the United States. Since the value of forests thus generally escapes being included, the shares of land in tables 39 and 40 must generally be regarded as minima.

The third caveat refers to the difference in the valuation of, or the price information on, land as opposed to reproducible assets. Land prices are much more influenced by rates of capitalization, by differential rents of land reflecting quality and location, and by lack of the limiting influence of cost of reproduction. They may, therefore, be assumed to show trends and cyclical movements different from, and to fluctuate more than, most types of reproducible assets. The land market is also often more affected by legal restrictions and traditional considerations than that for most other types of assets, and land often becomes the object of an open commercial market later than they do.

The share of land, and particularly of agricultural land, in tangible assets is one of the most important and informative national balance sheet ratios, as it can be regarded as a proxy for the degree of industrialization and modernization. Before the industrial revolution the countrywide share of land was undoubtedly well in excess of one-half. Its share in late 17th century England was put by Gregory King at nearly two-

Table 38 **Share of Tangible Assets in National Assets**

Country	Standard Benchmark Year[a]									
	1850 (1)	1875 (2)	1895 (3)	1913 (4)	1929 (5)	1939 (6)	1950 (7)	1965 (8)	1973 (9)	1978 (10)
1. Australia	...	...	...	...	...	...	56.2	58.7	54.6	62.4
2. Belgium	79.4	72.4	64.6	52.5	54.8	50.5	54.7	57.2	50.0	53.9
3. Canada	...	...	...	...	...	...	45.7	45.9	45.5	46.9
4. Denmark	...	48.4	44.2	41.5	39.2	44.2	47.2	48.9	45.3	47.9
5. France[b]	79.7	64.2	...	50.6	55.5	...	64.5	44.6	52.0	54.6
6. Germany	83.2	72.6	58.1	56.7	71.0	63.9	71.2	52.1	54.1	53.0
7. Great Britain[c]	59.6	51.7	33.8	33.8	29.0	27.0	36.1	40.9	43.6	47.3
8. Hungary	...	...	...	...	...	...	...	86.8	82.9	73.4
9. India[d]	61.1	67.9	71.4	74.7	77.1	72.7	69.0	65.1	63.7	65.0
10. Israel	...	...	...	...	...	...	60.1	54.4	...	47.4
11. Italy	82.9	71.8	69.0	68.2	59.7	57.8	70.6	54.2	46.8	49.1
12. Japan	...	76.7	74.5	61.1	45.3	41.5	65.0	55.4	52.4	49.0
13. Mexico	...	...	...	...	73.8	60.6	57.6	59.7	57.1	58.4
14. Norway	...	73.2	64.4	58.3	49.2	57.6	55.8	56.1	53.5	53.4
15. Russia/USSR	...	...	...	70.9	91.4	78.2	76.0	82.3	81.7	77.6
16. South Africa	...	...	...	65.7	59.0	52.0	46.8	46.8	48.9	56.7
17. Sweden	...	...	...	...	...	...	...	49.2	44.7	44.0
18. Switzerland	...	47.4	38.4	40.0	37.8	38.6	43.6	39.7	38.3	35.4
19. United States[e]	68.1	60.9	58.5	54.7	43.7	43.1	46.0	43.8	47.4	50.2
20. Yugoslavia	...	...	...	...	...	...	81.2	57.6	49.8	46.6

Note: In this table, as in tables 39–69, the figures represent percentages.

[a]For actual dates see table 33.

[b]In 1815 83.6.

[c]In 1688 85.3; 1760 71.4; 1800 63.7; 1830 56.9.

[d]If gold and silver are regarded as tangible assets, differing from the treatment in other countries, the ratios are increased to 87.0; 88.5; 88.8; 86.7; 84.0; 81.0; 76.4; 71.4; 71.4; 68.8 and 70.8 percent.

[e]In 1774 78.2; 1805 75.6.

Source of basic data: Country balance sheets in Appendix A. (Also for tables 39–49 and 50–57.)

thirds, and the estimate for 1760 is still close to three-fifths. As late as 1850 the share of land in tangible assets was in the neighborhood of one-half in the other four European countries, for which table 39 provides the information, and probably about nine-tenths of it represented agricultural land. In Russia it stayed at the preindustrial level of over three-fifths beyond the Revolution, probably until the mid-1930s.

From the middle of the 19th century on, the share of land fell rapidly in the more advanced European countries, and at the eve of World War I it had declined to between one-third and one-fifth. In the United States and Italy the share was still close to two-fifths. The trend of the share of land in Western Europe was mixed. In the United States the ratio began to fall substantially, and in the postwar period it has declined to the Western European level of less than one-fifth.

India and Japan deviated from the pattern. In India the share of land nearly doubled from fully one-third in the third quarter of the 19th century to three-fifths in the 1930s. This was the combined result of a sharp rise in the absolute and relative price of agricultural land following the establishment of an open land market (see Goldsmith 1983a, chap. 1) and of the very slow growth of the country's stock of reproducible capital. During the postwar period India showed the customary sharp decline in the share of land that accompanies industrialization. The share of land in the value of all tangible assets in Japan has been extraordinarily high throughout the last century, averaging fully two-fifths for over half a century after the Meiji restoration; it fell below that level only in the 1930s, but exceeded it substantially in the 1950s and 1960s at a level of two-thirds to one-half of all tangible assets. To say that this reflects the extraordinarily high level of relative land prices only reformulates the problem, the very small amounts of usable land per inhabitant providing only a partial answer. The three centrally planned countries, for which only very rough estimates of the share of land are available, and in which that share has a different meaning since most of the land is public property, showed a substantial decline that by now has reduced it to around one-fifth, similar to that in developed market economies other than Japan.

The movements in the share of land are the result of two often diverging tendencies, those of agricultural and nonagricultural land, i.e., to a substantial extent residential land. The picture of the trends of the share of agricultural land that is provided by Table 40 is striking and uniform. In the five developed countries for which the estimates go back to or beyond the middle of the 19th century, the share of agricultural land fell from nearly two-fifths of all tangible assets to an average of not much over one-fifth by 1913, and in the late 1970s averaged about 5 percent for the 10 developed market economies. Substantial differences, however,

Table 39 Share of Land in Tangible Assets

Country	Standard Benchmark Year[a]									
	1850 (1)	1875 (2)	1895 (3)	1913 (4)	1929 (5)	1939 (6)	1950 (7)	1965 (8)	1973 (9)	1978 (10)
1. Australia	...	...	...	...	...	...	16.6	12.8	13.2	12.5
2. Belgium	54.5	32.1	25.2	18.7	16.7	16.1	18.7	29.0	20.9	18.1
3. Canada	...	...	...	...	...	...	17.6	23.7	23.7	24.3
4. Denmark	...	37.2	29.3	26.3	25.4	22.3	11.4	15.3	17.5	14.2
5. France[b]	56.5	50.8	...	33.2	26.5	...	22.7	21.9	23.4	23.4
6. Germany	45.8	40.3	33.2	26.9	20.2	17.1	28.3	23.6	22.0	24.9
7. Great Britain[c]	29.9	40.1	31.4	22.2	17.7	17.5	17.7	15.5	16.3	14.9
8. Hungary	...	...	...	...	...	...	...	29.7	28.5	27.1
9. India[e]	35.3	39.7	43.8	53.7	59.6	62.0	48.0	31.8	33.0	25.1
10. Israel	...	...	...	...	...	...	22.0	20.3	...	18.5
11. Italy	47.2	48.4	49.2	39.2	29.9	31.6	27.4	20.0	19.4	16.8
12. Japan	...	45.9	46.6	42.2	45.9	34.5	65.3	65.6	61.1	50.7
13. Mexico	...	...	...	...	29.9	25.1	31.8	21.9	20.0	19.3
14. Norway	...	42.4	36.8	31.3	27.4	23.4	21.6	19.9	16.9	15.8
15. Russia/USSR	...	...	...	61.5	56.2	38.6	33.7	28.4	34.7	22.8
16. South Africa	...	...	...	28.0	24.7	24.0	22.4	22.4	20.0	18.5
17. Sweden	...	...	...	...	...	...	...	16.7	15.2	15.3
18. Switzerland	...	37.3	32.2	36.0	25.3	20.0	20.6	17.1	17.2	17.2
19. United States[f]	41.3	31.1	35.0	35.3	26.9	23.7	19.6	24.4	24.0	24.9
20. Yugoslavia	...	...	...	...	...	...	25.8	28.3	24.9	18.5

[a]For actual dates see table 33.
[b]In 1815, 55.1.
[c]In 1688, 64.5; 1760, 57.3; 1800, 46.7; 1830, 44.8.
[d]If gold and silver are regarded as tangible assets the shares are reduced to: 24.8; 29.0; 35.2; 46.4; 54.7; 55.7; 42.5; 29.0; 30.5 and 23.0.
[e]In 1774, 52.6; in 1805, 51.9.

Table 40 Share of Agricultural Land[a] in Tangible Assets

Country	Standard Benchmark Year[b]									
	1850 (1)	1875 (2)	1895 (3)	1913 (4)	1929 (5)	1939 (6)	1950 (7)	1965 (8)	1973 (9)	1978 (10)
1. Australia	...	...	...	...	...	...	...	...	...	...
2. Belgium	...	...	...	...	...	...	...	...	...	...
3. Canada	...	...	...	...	...	...	3.7	3.5	3.1	3.4
4. Denmark	...	27.2	16.4	13.3	12.8	10.2	4.9	3.5	3.5	2.9
5. France[c]	49.9	44.9	...	25.4	17.9	...	11.4	12.1	8.7	7.9
6. Germany	43.2	36.4	28.0	20.2	12.8	9.6	19.0	14.0	7.6	12.6
7. Great Britain[d]	19.9	31.5	21.0	9.9	5.3	4.8	4.8	5.1	3.9	2.5
8. Hungary	...	...	...	...	...	...	...	25.0	18.9	16.5
9. India[e]	...	...	...	...	...	...	...	...	...	...
10. Israel	...	...	...	...	...	...	9.8	6.3	...	3.3
11. Italy	41.8	43.1	44.1	33.3	22.8	24.8	17.5	8.8	6.3	5.1
12. Japan	...	33.7	32.8	29.7	33.2	21.5	40.1	19.3	14.3	11.0
13. Mexico	...	...	...	...	23.0	17.8	26.1	12.8	8.5	5.8
14. Norway	...	38.4	28.1	22.4	17.5	13.3	12.8	9.6	6.2	5.3
15. Russia/USSR	...	...	...	...	...	...	...	...	...	...
16. South Africa	...	...	...	21.1	22.0	16.3	13.8	13.5	10.5	8.5
17. Sweden	...	...	...	...	...	...	...	4.0	2.8	2.8
18. Switzerland	...	...	...	21.7	...	7.8	7.6	3.5	2.3	2.5
19. United States[f]	35.8	19.5	16.5	19.2	8.3	6.2	5.3	5.5	5.3	5.4
20. Yugoslavia	...	...	...	...	...	...	22.7	22.6	20.7	15.4

[a]Includes in most countries forests.

[b]For actual dates see table 33.

[c]In 1815, 50.4.

[d]In 1688, 61.1; 1760, 50.7; 1800, 36.2; 1830, 35.7.

[e]Slightly below table 39, line 9.

[f]In 1805, 48.8.

remained among these countries—the range extending from 3 to 13 percent—which are not easy to explain and are probably due in part to differences in the method of valuation. While the share of agricultural land is certain to have fallen substantially in the less developed countries during the postwar period, it is doubtful that the decline has been as pronounced as in India and Mexico, the only representatives of the group in table 40.

The data are insufficient to present a comparison over time or among countries of the value of forest land and of standing timber, though it is known to be substantial in most countries, not only in relation to total land values but also to all tangible assets. For the United States the share has been put for the postwar period at approximately one-tenth of all land and 3 percent of tangible assets (Goldsmith 1982, table 86). In both France and Germany, countries of relatively small forest areas, the value of forests in the 1970s was estimated at approximately 8 percent of all land and 2 percent of all tangible assets (INSEE 1980, 49; Goldsmith 1976, 162). In Norway, the only country for which estimates have been found for a long period, the share has fallen from about two-fifths of all land and one-sixth of tangible assets a century ago to approximately one-sixth and 3 percent, respectively (table A14). In Switzerland the share declined from approximately one-tenth of all land and of less than 5 and about 2 percent of tangible assets in 1913 and 1938 to well below 1 percent in 1978 (table A19). In Japan in 1977 forest land and standing timber accounted in the official estimates for 5 percent of all private land and for somewhat over 2 percent of tangible assets (Economic Planning Agency 1979, 427, 606). In the Soviet Union, finally, the shares have been put in the late 1970s at about one-fourth of all land and fully 5 percent of tangible assets (table A16).

The estimates of the level and movements of the share of nonagricultural land are not sufficiently precise and reliable to justify a separate comparative table. The evidence, however, suffices for three conclusions. First, there has been a definite upward trend in the share of nonagricultural land in tangible assets. As a result the share in developed countries appears to average now about one-eighth of total tangible assets. The trend has been even more pronounced and at a much higher level in Japan, where the share has risen from about one-eighth before World War I to approximately two-fifths since the 1960s. Second, the ratio of the value of nonagricultural to agricultural land has risen sharply over the past century, with the result that at the present time nonagricultural land accounts in most developed market economies on the average for about three fourths of total land value. Third, residential land seems always to have constituted the largest single component of nonagricultural land, though the material is not sufficient to determine the level or the changes in that relation.

b) The Structure of Reproducible Tangible Assets

For the economic analyst, as opposed to the financial economist, the information it provides on the structure of the stock of reproducible tangible assets is probably the most interesting aspect of national balance sheets. It is therefore fortunate that the estimates for this large component of national assets are now in general more reliable and comparable than those for land and for some important financial assets. This, however, is true only for the 20th century and for structures and equipment when most of the estimates used in this study have been derived by the perpetual inventory method, i.e., by the cumulation of expenditures depreciated following generally the straight-line method, and adjusted for changes in replacement cost though not in market values. For the 19th century, in contrast, most of the estimates are heterogeneous and rough, with the exception of those for Denmark, Germany, Great Britain, Italy, Japan, and Norway, which are derived by the same methods as those for most of the present century. The estimates are much less satisfactory for inventories, livestock, and consumer durables, which generally account for only about one-fourth of the stock of all reproducible tangible assets. Even so, the available estimates do not permit intensive analysis because they are usually insufficiently detailed, in some cases distinguishing only dwellings from all other structures and equipment, and sometimes combining livestock with inventories.

i) Residential Structures

The share of residential structures in the total stock of reproducible tangible assets, which fortunately can be calculated for all or most countries, show considerable intercountry differences. At the present time it varies, as table 41 shows, between about 15 percent in South Africa and the Soviet Union and nearly one-half in France. For one-half of the 20 countries, however, it lies between one-fourth and one-third, with an unweighted average of fully one-fourth, virtually the same as a quarter-century earlier. The two lowest ratios reflect in the first case the dual nature of the economy, most of the dwellings of the nonwhite four-fifths of the population being primitive and to a great extent constructed outside the monetarized part of the economy; in the second, the low priority accorded to housing in Soviet planning and the consequent housing conditions, notoriously poor for a country of its income level. The extraordinarily high ratio shown for France, though only in the 1970s when the official national balance sheet is used, is not easy to explain. The low Japanese ratio reflects housing conditions well below what would be expected at the country's level of real income per head.

Among the five countries for which the data go back that far, the present share is now substantially higher than in the mid-19th century in

Table 41 **Share of Residential Structures[a] in Reproducible Assets**

Country	Standard Benchmark Year[b]									
	1850 (1)	1875 (2)	1895 (3)	1913 (4)	1929 (5)	1939 (6)	1950 (7)	1965 (8)	1973 (9)	1978 (10)
1. Australia	...	...	...	...	...	...	20.6	20.7	20.8	22.8
2. Belgium	...	...	...	...	...	...	...	33.1	36.6	34.2
3. Canada	...	...	...	...	...	...	22.6	22.3	24.5	25.2
4. Denmark	...	...	...	...	...	...	18.8	19.0	22.9	28.1
5. France[c]	36.0	34.8	...	28.0	28.0	...	32.0	30.0	45.1	46.7
6. Germany	14.3	20.0	24.7	25.2	27.7	26.9	24.0	25.9	27.4	32.6
7. Great Britain[d]	19.5	18.3	19.0	19.6	21.2	25.7	28.3	24.2	26.1	25.3
8. Hungary	...	...	...	...	...	...	...	21.3	17.2	18.1
9. India	...	...	...	...	...	...	21.6	28.2	18.4	17.1
10. Israel	...	...	...	...	...	...	28.8	29.8	...	32.1
11. Italy	42.7	40.8	34.2	24.9	22.6	20.3	40.2	40.4	40.9	40.6
12. Japan	...	34.1	39.3	28.5	22.4	23.3	15.6	16.3	16.0	20.5
13. Mexico	...	...	...	...	23.8	23.2	16.7	24.0	26.8	30.6
14. Norway	...	34.6	33.8	29.7	26.6	27.2	27.5	22.0	21.4	21.1
15. Russia/USSR	...	...	...	15.5	24.5	19.6	26.0	18.9	18.7	16.2
16. South Africa	...	...	...	9.5	9.2	11.0	15.3	15.1	14.9	14.1
17. Sweden	...	...	...	...	...	...	...	34.6	31.7	31.3
18. Switzerland	...	...	...	...	...	21.3	20.7	20.9	22.4	22.6
19. United States[e]	18.8	18.4	27.3	23.9	29.0	30.2	32.4	29.0	27.9	29.4
20. Yugoslavia	...	...	...	...	...	...	21.5	...	...	...

[a]Generally only nonagricultural residential structures.

[b]For actual dates see table 33.

[c]In 1815, 39.6.

[d]In 1688, 37.4; 1760, 18.8; 1800, 16.1; 1830, 21.3.

[e]In 1805, 15.7.

France (only in the 1970s), Germany, Great Britain, and the United States, while it shows a small decline, though at a very high level, in Italy.

The movements, it must be stressed again, concern essentially the share of nonagricultural residential structures. If figures were available for all dwellings, the upward trend would be less pronounced, and might in some cases even disappear. An idea of the relationships involved may be given by the estimates that in the United States the value of agricultural dwellings in 1850 was of the same order as that of nonagricultural residences, but had fallen to about one-fourth in 1880, to about one-tenth in 1900, and to 5 percent in 1958 (Goldsmith 1952, 306; Goldsmith, Lipsey, and Mendelson 1963, 2:68 ff.). The omission in most cases of agricultural dwellings therefore should not seriously affect the comparisons for the 20th century, but does so progressively for earlier dates.

ii) Nonresidential Structures and Equipment

This dominating component of the stock of capital is extremely heterogeneous, containing, e.g., factories, stores, office and government buildings, railroad tracks, sewage installations and public roads. Its classification varies greatly among countries; and its composition changes substantially over time. The available data unfortunately do not permit an adequate analysis of these changes and differences on an international basis within the framework of this study.

At the present time nonresidential structures and equipment account, as table 42 shows, for between fully one-third and two-thirds of all tangible assets, with an unweighted average of 55 percent, only slightly above the value of 1950. The differences among countries are generally inversely related to that in the shares of dwellings, e.g., being lowest for France and Italy. It is tempting to draw conclusions from the share of nonresidential structures and equipment regarding the relative importance of the "productive" capital stock, but it is doubtful that in the present state of the statistics the figures are able to bear that burden. As it is, no long-term trends are evident in the figures. For the five large developed market economies the average has been close to one-half throughout the period. It was slightly higher for the two interwar benchmarks than for the postwar period, but the significance of the difference is doubtful without much more detailed analysis.

iii) Equipment

Since equipment, i.e., mainly machinery and vehicles, can be regarded as another and preferable proxy of industrialization, one would wish that the available estimates were more numerous, and more comparable in coverage and valuation over time and among countries than they are.

Table 42 **Share of Nonresidential Structures[a] and Equipment in Reproducible Assets**

Country	1850 (1)	1875 (2)	1895 (3)	1913 (4)	1929 (5)	1939 (6)	1950 (7)	1965 (8)	1973 (9)	1978 (10)
	Standard Benchmark Year[a]									
1. Australia	...	...	...	...	...	...	53.8	61.9	62.4	64.7
2. Belgium	...	...	...	...	...	...	50.6	48.6	43.9	49.5
3. Canada	...	...	...	...	...	...	53.7	59.9	58.4	58.9
4. Denmark	...	37.8	...	...	...	...	60.5	59.9	57.0	59.9
5. France[b]	37.3	39.8	...	52.4	51.2	...	47.4	45.8	36.3	36.2
6. Germany	65.8	59.8	55.3	56.6	57.8	59.4	55.6	50.9	50.3	50.2
7. Great Britain[c]	62.1	57.4	56.2	58.5	53.8	50.2	48.2	52.5	55.7	56.3
8. Hungary	...	...	...	...	...	...	...	47.4	50.7	50.3
9. India	...	...	...	...	...	...	41.7	45.1	59.2	64.8
10. Israel	...	...	...	...	...	...	41.3	46.7	...	48.2
11. Italy	35.0	38.5	45.4	53.4	55.4	56.3	44.6	43.3	40.9	39.4
12. Japan	...	36.3	36.4	40.2	49.4	52.7	46.7	55.7	59.0	61.6
13. Mexico	...	...	...	...	49.1	41.9	45.3	48.3	51.1	51.2
14. Norway	...	50.8	51.7	56.5	57.9	56.9	56.4	67.7	67.0	66.7
15. Russia/USSR	...	...	...	45.8	42.3	39.2	41.4	56.5	58.1	60.2
16. South Africa	...	...	...	53.4	53.1	58.2	56.9	57.9	60.7	65.6
17. Sweden	...	...	...	...	...	...	...	50.2	53.6	52.7
18. Switzerland	...	...	...	...	...	67.5	67.0	66.8	66.4	67.6
19. United States[d]	47.9	44.9	44.7	47.9	44.7	47.8	42.2	46.1	48.3	46.7
20. Yugoslavia	...	...	...	...	...	...	62.5	...	...	...

[a]For actual dates see table 33.
[b]In 1815, 28.1.
[c]In 1760, 28.1; 1800, 31.2; 1830, 44.1.
[d]In 1805, 53.0.

Even so, the figures assembled in table 43 are not without interest but must be interpreted very cautiously.

For the 12 countries for which data for the late 1970s are available, the share of equipment in the stock of reproducible assets averaged almost one-fifth, compared to about one-fourth each for residential and other structures, with a range from 15 to 30 percent. There are no obvious explanations for these differences, in particular for the rather unexpected position of Great Britain near the upper and of Germany, and the United States at the lower boundary.

The movements over time of the ratio differ sufficiently among countries to prevent generalization. Thus the British ratio showed a downward tendency between 1850 and 1929 but rose substantially during the postwar period. In Germany the movement was just the opposite, up from 1850 to 1913, down in the postwar period. In the United States no trend is evident from the late 19th century to World War II, while the movement is irregularly and moderately upward in the postwar period. For the few countries for which the data go back well into the 19th century, the unweighted average ratio at current prices increases from nearly 14 percent around 1875 to 18 percent in 1913 and to 20 percent in the postwar period, suggesting a modest upward trend. In evaluating these movements it should be kept in mind that the prices of equipment probably declined secularly compared to those of structures, so that the increase in the share of equipment in tangible assets would be more pronounced in terms of constant prices.

iv) Inventories

Since inventories are a fairly well defined component of the stock of capital, their technological characteristics have not changed substantially, and the estimates are reasonably satisfactory for more recent dates comparisons of their share in reproducible assets over time, and among countries that can be derived from table 44 are less hazardous than in the case of some other components of the national balance sheet.

At the present time the share of inventories averages a little less than one-tenth for the 20 countries, ranging from 4 to 17 percent. The three highest ratios—all close to 15 percent—are shown for the countries with a centrally planned economy in which inventories are known to be relatively large, reflecting inefficiencies of the planning mechanism. Among the non-communist countries the ratios, averaging 8 percent, are not clearly correlated to other characteristics of the economy, except that the relatively high ratio for Japan seems to be connected with the particularly widespread practice of subcontracting in that country.

In most of the 10 countries for which the data go back to the third quarter of the 19th century, a moderate downward trend in the ratio is

Table 43 **Share of Equipment in Reproducible Assets**

	Standard Benchmark Year[a]									
Country	1850 (1)	1875 (2)	1895 (3)	1913 (4)	1929 (5)	1939 (6)	1950 (7)	1965 (8)	1973 (9)	1978 (10)
1. Australia	...	...	...	...	...	...	13.7	...	...	...
2. Belgium	...	...	...	...	...	...	...	23.0	...	...
3. Canada	...	...	...	...	...	...	...	...	...	...
4. Denmark	...	15.5	20.3	19.5	22.3	27.8	33.5	30.4	28.4	25.6
5. France[b]	11.5	14.9	...	...	...	...	21.0	24.7	16.0	16.2
6. Germany	17.2	18.8	20.2	26.0	23.1	24.4	20.0	20.9	17.5	14.3
7. Great Britain	21.3	16.7	12.8	15.8	13.8	16.6	16.5	26.2	24.9	26.1
8. Hungary	...	...	...	...	...	...	...	14.1	15.0	17.0
9. India	...	...	...	...	...	...	...	...	...	...
10. Israel	...	...	...	...	...	...	17.5	17.7	...	18.1
11. Italy	...	...	...	...	...	...	...	...	...	...
12. Japan	...	6.2	8.8	14.4	16.3	19.5	...	...	...	...
13. Mexico	...	...	...	...	...	19.7	21.4	20.0	21.0	20.7
14. Norway	...	12.2	15.2	19.3	16.7	18.0	26.4	24.9	24.3	24.7
15. Russia/USSR	...	...	...	13.5	...	...	...	...	...	...
16. South Africa	...	...	...	...	...	...	16.4	15.6	16.2	17.9
17. Sweden	...	...	...	...	...	...	...	16.6	17.4	17.3
18. Switzerland	...	...	...	...	...	33.2	33.4	32.6	29.9	30.7
19. United States[c]	10.5	11.2	11.3	12.9	12.4	12.0	13.3	16.5	15.0	15.2
20. Yugoslavia	...	...	...	...	...	...	...	...	...	...

[a]For actual dates see table 33.
[b]In 1815, 10.5.
[c]In 1774, 9.9; in 1805, 6.3.

Table 44 **Share of Inventories in Reproducible Assets**

Country	Standard Benchmark Year[a]									
	1850 (1)	1875 (2)	1895 (3)	1913 (4)	1929 (5)	1939 (6)	1950 (7)	1965 (8)	1973 (9)	1978 (10)
1. Australia	...	...	...	...	...	...	9.8	7.3	7.3	7.1
2. Belgium	...	...	...	...	...	...	8.8	6.7	7.0	5.7
3. Canada	...	...	...	...	...	...	8.4	8.0	6.6	6.0
4. Denmark	...	14.9	11.3	9.8	10.5	9.6	9.0	8.0	6.2	3.8
5. France[b]	13.6	11.9	...	9.5	9.3	...	13.2	14.1	10.6	10.2
6. Germany	10.2	10.3	10.0	9.6	5.5	6.5	10.2	10.9	6.3	6.6
7. Great Britain[c]	7.4	...	...	...	12.1	10.3	15.9[d]	12.3[d]	9.9[d]	9.0[d]
8. Hungary	...	...	...	...	...	...	...	17.1	17.2	17.1
9. India	14.8	12.8	9.9	9.9	15.3	7.9	15.7	10.8	11.2	8.5
10. Israel	...	...	...	...	...	...	15.6	12.7	...	10.9
11. Italy	9.3	9.3	9.4	10.6	10.8	14.1	8.5	8.4	9.1	9.5
12. Japan	...	12.8	12.3	20.4	15.7	14.9	31.1	20.6	17.5	12.3
13. Mexico	...	...	...	...	9.8	14.4	15.5	12.4	9.4	9.6
14. Norway	...	11.4[e]	11.3[e]	10.8[e]	12.0[e]	11.6[e]	10.4	6.5	6.7	8.4
15. Russia/USSR	...	...	...	16.6	17.3	21.5	22.3	16.9	15.3	15.0
16. South Africa	...	...	...	10.3	11.4	10.7	12.7	12.4	11.8	9.0
17. Sweden	...	...	...	...	...	...	...	6.8	6.7	7.2
18. Switzerland	...	6.4	6.1	5.9	5.7	4.2	4.9	5.3	5.1	4.7
19. United States[f]	14.0	21.0	11.9	10.4	10.2	8.9	9.6	11.5	10.7	11.1
20. Yugoslavia	...	...	...	...	...	...	11.5	13.2	12.8	14.5

[a]For actual dates see table 33.

[b]In 1815, 14.0.

[c]In 1769, 25.0; 1800, 22.6; 1830, 16.5.

[d]Includes livestock, probably not exceeding 2.0 at any date.

[e]Includes livestock.

[f]In 1774, 13.5; in 1805, 15.7.

indicated by the decline of the average from 11 to 9 percent, approximately the level for 17 countries in the late 1970s.

v) Livestock

This is a rare case in which the content of the component is well defined though there is sometimes some question about the treatment of horses, the estimates are reasonably reliable, great technological changes have been absent, the trend of the share in all reproducible assets is unequivocal and uniform, and the reason for the movement is obvious.

As table 45 shows, the share has declined in all 13 countries for which estimates are available, and the more sharply, the farther back the records go. Thus the share has fallen within the last 130–300 years from over one-sixth of reproducible assets in Great Britain, one-fourth in the United States, and one-seventh in France, to less than 1 percent at the present time. At the eve of World War I, the unweighted share still averaged 11 percent for 10 countries for which information is available, but only 1½ percent in the late 1970s, paralleling the universal secular decline in the importance of agriculture in the economy. The share now exceeds 1 percent in only nine of the 20 countries (Australia, Denmark, Hungary, India, Italy, Mexico, South Africa, the Soviet Union, and Yugoslavia), all countries in which agriculture is still of substantial importance. Even in India the share has come down from an average of 14 percent for the four benchmark dates before World War I to less than 3 percent in the late 1970s.

vi) Consumer Durables

The situation is almost the reverse in the case of consumer durables. The definitions vary among countries; most of the estimates are very rough and not a few are derived by the rule of thumb of four times the rate of expenditures; the character of consumer durables has radically changed since the turn of the century; the movements of the estimated ratios over time are irregular and vary among countries, in part undoubtedly because of the poor quality of many of the estimates; and the reason for some of the movements shown by the estimates are far from clear.

As table 46 stands, it suggests that the share of consumer durables in reproducible assets now averages fully 7 percent with a range from 4 to 12 percent. There is no clear association between the ratio and the countries' real income per head. The fact that the ratios are highest for the United States and Germany is compatible with a positive association, but the relatively high ratios for Great Britain, Hungary, and Italy and the astonishingly low ratios for Australia, Norway, and Switzerland contradict it.

Table 45 **Share of Livestock in Reproducible Assets**

Country	Standard Benchmark Year[a]									
	1850 (1)	1875 (2)	1895 (3)	1913 (4)	1929 (5)	1939 (6)	1950 (7)	1965 (8)	1973 (9)	1978 (10)
1. Australia	...	...	...	...	...	...	5.0	3.6	3.2	1.4
2. Belgium	...	...	...	...	...	...	2.0	1.7	1.5	1.0
3. Canada	...	...	...	...	...	...	1.8	1.3	1.3	0.8
4. Denmark	...	24.8	19.6	23.5	11.3	9.2	5.7	4.1	4.3	2.0
5. France[b]	8.7	9.0	...	6.1	5.6	...	1.8	2.3	1.2	0.9
6. Germany	7.2	6.8	5.8	4.9	3.3	2.9	3.4	1.6	0.8	0.8
7. Great Britain[c]	4.3	...	...	...	2.8	2.2	...	...	...	...
8. Hungary	...	...	...	...	...	...	...	2.8	2.6	2.0
9. India	12.2	11.0	14.4	19.7	8.7	12.6	13.7	5.6	4.0	2.7
10. Israel	...	...	...	...	...	...	1.9	1.4	...	0.9
11. Italy	6.1	5.1	5.8	5.8	4.5	3.2	1.8	1.4	0.9	1.4
12. Japan	...	15.0	10.8	9.5	8.1	6.9	...	...	...	...
13. Mexico	...	...	...	...	9.2	8.5	9.7	5.8	3.9	2.2
14. Norway	...	...	...	...	...	...	1.6	0.7	0.4	0.2
15. Russia/USSR	...	...	...	13.1	8.5	9.6	5.2	2.2	2.2	2.5
16. South Africa	...	...	...	19.8	15.2	10.3	6.4	4.3	3.9	2.1
17. Sweden	...	...	...	...	...	...	...	1.0	0.7	0.6
18. Switzerland	...	8.1	8.8	5.8	4.2	2.8	2.3	1.5	0.9	0.9
19. United States[d]	12.8	6.7	5.4	5.3	2.1	1.8	2.1	1.0	1.1	0.8
20. Yugoslavia	...	...	...	...	...	...	3.6	4.4	4.8	3.5

[a]For actual dates see table 33.

[b]In 1815, 14.0.

[c]In 1688, 17.8; 1760, 21.9; 1800, 23.7; 1830, 11.8.

[d]In 1774, 24.8; 1805, 9.4.

Table 46 **Share of Consumer Durables in Reproducible Assets**

Country	Standard Benchmark Year[a]									
	1850 (1)	1875 (2)	1895 (3)	1913 (4)	1929 (5)	1939 (6)	1950 (7)	1965 (8)	1973 (9)	1978 (10)
1. Australia	...	...	...	...	...	...	10.8	6.4	6.2	4.0
2. Belgium	...	...	...	...	...	...	10.3	10.1	11.0	9.5
3. Canada	...	...	...	...	...	...	13.7	9.7	9.1	9.3
4. Denmark	...	7.5	6.2	5.8	6.4	6.2	5.7	8.9	9.5	6.4
5. France[b]	4.8	4.5	...	4.1	5.6	...	5.5	7.8	6.9	6.5
6. Germany	2.4	3.1	4.1	3.4	5.7	4.1	6.8	7.5	10.4	10.3
7. Great Britain[c]	6.7	6.5	6.7	5.8	10.0	11.1	7.8	10.7	8.4	9.5
8. Hungary	...	...	...	...	...	...	...	11.5	12.1	12.5
9. India	...	...	...	...	...	...	7.6	10.0	7.2	6.8
10. Israel	...	...	...	...	...	...	12.5	9.5	...	7.9
11. Italy	6.9	6.2	6.0	5.3	6.7	6.1	4.6	6.6	8.3	9.1
12. Japan	...	1.8	1.2	1.5	3.3	2.2	6.3	7.4	7.5	5.8
13. Mexico	...	...	...	...	8.0	12.3	12.9	9.6	8.7	6.4
14. Norway	...	3.2	3.2	3.0	3.5	4.3	4.1	3.3	4.5	4.0
15. Russia/USSR	...	...	...	8.7	7.5	10.0	5.2	5.4	5.8	6.1
16. South Africa	...	...	...	6.9	10.9	9.9	9.2	10.3	8.7	9.2
17. Sweden	...	...	...	...	...	...	...	7.5	7.3	8.2
18. Switzerland	...	6.7	6.1	5.9	5.7	4.2	5.1	5.7	4.9	4.4
19. United States[d]	7.0	9.0	10.5	12.8	13.7	11.2	13.5	12.4	11.9	11.9
20. Yugoslavia	...	...	...	...	...	...	3.9	4.4	6.1	3.9

[a]For actual dates see table 33.

[b]In 1815, 4.2.

[c]In 1688, 14.0; 1760, 6.3; 1800, 6.5; 1830, 6.3.

[d]In 1774, 15.9; in 1805, 6.3.

The ratio has generally shown a slight upward movement, but it is fairly continuous and substantial only in Germany, for which the quality of the estimates is relatively good. In the United States, the ratio after nearly doubling between 1850 and 1913 showed no trend for the last half century, where the figures are of fair quality, staying close to one-eighth. For the 11 countries for which data are available, the unweighted average of nearly 8 percent in the late 1970s compares with that of 5.8 percent in 1913, a difference just sufficient, partly because it is positive in all but two countries, to suggest a moderate upward secular trend. In appraising the difference, it must be remembered that the prices of consumer durables have probably risen considerably less than those of structures and inventories, so that the increase in the ratio in terms of constant prices is likely to have been substantial.

4. The Structure of Financial Assets

a) The Financial Intermediation Ratio

As the financial interrelations ratio measures the size of the financial superstructure relative to that of the real infrastructure, so the financial intermediation ratio, i.e., the quotient of the assets of financial institutions and of all domestic and foreign financial assets, measures the importance of financial institutions in terms of resources within the financial superstructure. The ratios shown in table 47 are generally fairly reliable but for two reasons may overstate or understate the correct values. On the one hand, the total for financial assets generally does not include several minor components, such as loans within the household sector and accruals. On the other, the figures used for the assets of all financial institutions may be regarded as overstated to the extent of interfinancial assets included, such as interbank deposits, deposits of other financial institutions with banks, and shares of financial institutions held by other financial institutions, but will be understated when the assets of financial institutions are measured by only their deposit and insurance liabilities. These items vary in relative size among countries and over time, somewhat impeding intertemporal and international comparability of the entries in table 47. These reservations, however, do not seriously distort the picture, but they account for the apparent anomaly of the few ratios above 50 percent.

Since financial institutions started their substantial development, outside of Great Britain only in the third quarter of the 19th century or later while some other financial instruments such as trade credit, mortgages, and government debt are much older, the secular trend of the financial

Table 47 Financial Intermediation Ratio

Country	Standard Benchmark Year[a]									
	1850 (1)	1875 (2)	1895 (3)	1913 (4)	1929 (5)	1939 (6)	1950 (7)	1965 (8)	1973 (9)	1978 (10)
1. Australia	...	...	...	...	...	...	34.0	35.1	38.3	41.8
2. Belgium	10.7	19.1	19.7	21.9	21.4	30.0	29.9	41.6	44.7	45.4
3. Canada	...	...	...	...	...	...	24.8	26.8	30.6	31.9
4. Denmark	...	26.8	33.2	34.2	33.7	38.8	41.1	45.0	44.9	47.1
5. France[b]	3.9	10.1	...	17.0	27.3	...	27.2	25.8	31.8	32.7
6. Germany	20.3	21.9	26.2	30.1	36.7	40.4	33.1	33.2	40.5	38.5
7. Great Britain[c]	14.7	19.7	15.4	17.3	18.4	21.0	30.5	33.0	37.9	40.8
8. Hungary	...	...	...	...	...	...	...	47.0	36.3	42.5
9. India[d]	1.3	2.4	3.9	8.3	11.7	14.3	19.4	21.3	22.3	23.6
10. Israel	...	...	...	...	...	...	37.5	47.6	...	61.2
11. Italy	8.3	15.7	21.9	32.7	34.2	33.6	32.9	40.7	51.2	55.2
12. Japan	...	25.5	30.6	33.4	41.2	39.1	31.7	30.9	28.9	29.9
13. Mexico	...	...	...	...	19.4	23.8	27.0	32.0	38.1	33.4
14. Norway	...	30.6	33.2	32.1	37.4	36.0	41.6	36.1	38.8	37.0
15. Russia/USSR	...	...	...	32.4	21.5	34.3	30.0	52.5	52.6	54.0
16. South Africa	...	...	...	20.2	24.9	23.9	26.1	31.6	34.8	38.8
17. Sweden	...	...	...	...	...	...	...	27.7	27.3	26.1
18. Switzerland	...	17.9	22.9	29.3	32.0	32.7	33.8	35.2	36.0	36.4
19. United States[e]	12.5	13.6	20.0	21.3	16.4	28.8	29.1	24.0	26.1	26.8
20. Yugoslavia	...	...	...	...	...	...	39.3	23.1	21.9	27.0

[a]For actual dates see table 33.

[b]In addition 1815, 3.0.

[c]In addition 1800, 9.1; 1830, 11.5.

[d]If gold and silver hoards are excluded from the denominator the ratios are 3.8; 7.0; 9.8; 15.8; 16.9; 20.5; 27.7; 25.9; 26.0; and 28.4.

[e]In addition 1805: 9.3.

intermediation ratio is necessarily upward. By the middle of the 19th century, the ratio averaged nearly one-eighth for the six developed countries for which the data go back that far. The ratios rapidly increased until World War I, when they averaged nearly one-fourth for the same six countries and slightly above one-fourth for the larger group of 12 developed countries (including Russia). This means that, with some allowance for interfinancial assets, financial institutions appeared as creditor or debtor in nearly one-half of all financial instruments, indicating a substantial degree of institutionalization of the financial process at the eve of World War I. The ratio continued slowly upward in the interwar period. For the 11 countries (now excluding Russia), the average ratio advanced from 27 percent in 1913 to 33 percent in 1939. After a temporary setback in some countries reflecting the inflation during and immediately after World War II, the process of institutionalization resumed, and quite vigorously so, in the postwar period. As a result, the financial intermediation ratio averaged in the late 1970s nearly two-fifths for the 15 non-Communist developed countries. In most countries, including the financially most important ones other than Japan, financial institutions now constitute, again making some allowance for omitted financial and for interfinancial assets, one party in two-thirds or more of all financial instruments. The process of institutionalization thus does not have very much room for enlarging the scope of indirect at the expense of the once dominating direct financing. There is no evident association between the level of the financial intermediation ratio and economic or financial characteristics of a country such as real income per head, size, industrialization, or degree of inflation.

The level of the financial intermediations ratio has almost certainly been considerably lower for less developed countries, though the data are insufficient to quantify the difference before 1929; and the ratio has been rising in the postwar period more rapidly than in the developed countries. In India, possibly the financially largest less developed country, the ratio was extremely low during the 19th century, 4 percent in 1860, even if monetary metals were excluded from financial assets, but rose steadily, reaching fully one-fourth at the end of the interwar period. Contrary to the experience of developed countries, and probably also to that of most other less developed countries, there has been no substantial increase in the ratio during the postwar period, due in part to the very large expansion of the lending activities of the government. Taking these into account, the degree of institutionalization of the financial process is now at least as high in India as in the large developed countries; and the process is probably more completely under actual or potential government control than in any other non-Communist country (see Goldsmith 1983a, chap. 3).

In the Soviet Union, as in most other Communist countries, the financial intermediation ratio is now in the neighborhood of one-half, reflecting the almost complete absence of financial instruments in which a government owned and operated institution is not either the issuer or the holder. This situation has prevailed during most of the postwar period, while the ratio was considerably lower before then when government bonds were of some importance. The Yugoslav ratio of nearly three-tenths is still considerably below the level of non-Communist developed countries, and also considerably below that of the early 1950s before the country abandoned the rigid Soviet-type system of comprehensive planning.

b) Currency and Deposits

Currency and deposits, including money as well as time and saving deposits, are shown as a separate item in only one-half of the country tables of Appendix A, being included for the other countries in total claims against financial institutions. Their tabulation, therefore, would not provide an adequate basis of a discussion of the share of money (which before World War I should include gold and silver coins in circulation) and of nonmonetary deposits in financial assets. In this situation a different approach has been followed. For the postwar period use is made of the statistics of the International Monetary Fund, which provide for all countries covered in this study, with the obvious exception of the Soviet Union where these statistics are regarded as state secrets, and of Hungary, figures for money and quasi-money (lines 34 and 35 in the International Monetary Fund's *International Financial Statistics*), which have the advantage of fairly uniform coverage. No equally satisfactory solution is available for the preceding century. In the absence of internationally comparable monetary statistics, it has been necessary to use long-term series which have been recently developed for Germany, Great Britain, Japan, and the United States, and to rely on rougher estimates for the other countries.

During the postwar period the ratio of money broadly defined showed a slight downward trend, as the unweighted average of 15 countries declined from 15½ percent in the early 1950s to 13 percent in the late 1970s, as can be seen in table 48. The movement was not uniform as the ratio increased in four countries (France, Germany, Italy, South Africa) and substantially so in one (France). The generally downward movement, however, was the result of two opposing tendencies, a decline in the ratio of money narrowly defined (M-1) and an increase in that of quasi-money. On the average the share of M-1 was almost cut in half from 10½ to 5½ percent, 13 of the 15 countries participating in the movement. The share of quasi-money, in contrast, rose from 5 to 7½ percent of

Table 48 **Share of Money in Domestic Financial Assets, 1950, 1965 and 1978**[a]

	Currency			Money (M-1)			Quasi-Money			Money Plus Quasi-Money (M-2)		
	1950 (1)	1965 (2)	1978 (3)	1950 (4)	1965 (5)	1978 (6)	1950 (7)	1965 (8)	1978 (9)	1950 (10)	1965 (11)	1978 (12)
1. Australia	2.5	0.9	0.9	10.3	4.1	2.9	15.4	7.3	6.9	25.7	11.4	9.8
2. Belgium	7.6	5.6	2.9	14.8	10.7	6.7	1.0	2.8	5.4	15.8	13.5	12.1
3. Canada	1.3	1.0	0.8	...	2.1	2.6	...	2.3	2.8	...	4.3	5.4
4. Denmark	1.9	1.6	0.7	8.8	6.4	4.7	6.6	6.3	4.7	15.4	12.7	9.4
5. France	4.4	6.3	2.2	8.5	17.2	8.5	0.2	2.8	7.3	8.7	20.0	15.8
6. Germany	5.1	3.2	1.5	10.1	7.9	4.3	3.4	13.2	12.7	13.5	21.2	17.0
7. Great Britain	2.5	1.5	1.1	7.5	4.4	3.4	3.1	2.9	3.6	10.6	7.3	7.0
8. India	10.1	9.7	4.0	14.7	14.6	7.6	2.5	5.5	5.2	17.2	20.1	12.8
9. Israel	6.1	2.1	0.7	16.2	5.2	2.1	1.6	5.4	7.2	17.8	10.6	9.3
10. Italy	4.8	4.1	2.1	12.7	14.2	12.8	6.0	10.9	10.1	18.7	25.1	22.9
11. Japan	3.2	2.1	1.6	9.6	8.3	6.7	8.2	8.2	10.8	17.8	16.5	17.5
12. Mexico	4.4	3.2	2.5	8.8	7.6	5.7	2.9	2.6	2.3	11.7	10.2	8.0
13. Norway	3.7	3.3	1.9	7.7	5.6	4.4	9.0	8.9	9.3	16.7	14.5	13.7
14. South Africa	1.2	0.9	0.9	5.9	4.2	3.5	1.9	4.2	6.6	7.8	8.4	10.1
15. Sweden	...	2.5	1.4	...	4.1	2.4	...	6.5	6.1	...	10.6	8.5
16. Switzerland	5.5	2.8	2.1	9.5	7.7	6.6	10.1	8.6	10.6	19.6	16.3	17.2
17. United States	2.3	1.4	1.3	10.6	6.5	4.6	3.4	5.6	7.6	14.0	12.1	12.2
18. Yugoslavia	...	2.4	2.6	...	11.7	11.4	...	9.5	13.8	...	21.2	25.2

[a]Standard benchmark years; for actual dates see table 33.

Source: For numerator *IFSYB* (1979); for denominator country tables in Appendix A.

financial assets, 12 countries showing an increase, very pronounced in eight of them. As a result, the share of M-1 in M-2 fell, on the average, from two-thirds to well below one-half. The same basic tendency toward a declining importance of transactions money is evident in the sharp fall of the share of currency in domestic financial assets from, on the average, fully 4 to less than 2 percent, a movement which reduced the share of currency in M-1 from two-fifths to below one-third.

In the late 1970s the share of M-2 in domestic financial assets ranged from 5 percent in Canada to 25 percent in Yugoslavia, but kept for one-half of the 18 countries within the narrower range of 9–14 percent. There is a fairly clear division between the seven English-speaking and Scandinavian countries for which the ratio averaged 9½ percent and did not rise above 14 percent, and the 11 other countries with an average of over 15 percent, and no country with a ratio below 10 percent. This difference reflects in most cases the later and less complete monetization and the lesser financial sophistication in the second group. Similarly, the share of currency in financial assets in the second group with 2.2 percent was almost twice as high as the 1.2 percent average of the first group. On the other hand, the difference in the share of currency in M-2 was small, 13 percent in the first against 15 percent in the second group.

The movements in a characteristic of monetary structure, the currency/deposit ratio, can be followed in table 49, which shows the ratio with both the narrower (M-1) and the broader (M-2) definition of money as the denominator. Both ratios show a downward trend in most countries, but the slope is much steeper for the ratios of currency to M-2, because the volume of quasi-money expanded more rapidly than that of money narrowly defined. In the late 1970s the currency/M-1 ratio averaged 0.33 for the 18 countries, indicating that check deposits were about twice as large as currency with a wide range of 0.16–0.59, while the average of the currency/M-2 ratio was 0.28, and the range was absolutely narrower but relatively wider, extending from 0.06 to 0.31. The intercountry differences in the first set of ratios among developed countries do not seem to be related to putative determinants like real income per head, the financial interrelations or intermediation ratios, or the degree of inflation. The ratios were, however, well above the average in the two less developed countries.

The estimates of the share of money in financial assets for the century before World War II, brought together in table 50, are much more precarious, as they had to be derived from numerous sources which do not use standardized definitions. Thus for some countries gold and silver coins are not included in the estimates of currency in circulation for part of the period (Belgium, Denmark, Italy, Norway, Switzerland), but these are fortunately mostly those in which coins were of small importance before World War I and, as in all countries, almost disappeared from

Table 49 Currency-Deposit Ratio, 1950, 1965 and 1978[a]

	Currency/M-1			Currency/M-2		
	1950 (1)	1965 (2)	1978 (3)	1950 (4)	1965 (5)	1978 (6)
1. Australia	0.24	0.21	0.31	0.10	0.08	0.09
2. Belgium	0.52	0.52	0.44	0.48	0.42	0.18
3. Canada	0.30	0.26	0.32	0.14	0.12	0.10
4. Denmark	0.22	0.24	0.16	0.13	0.12	0.08
5. France	0.51	0.37	0.25	0.50	0.32	0.11
6. Germany	0.51	0.40	0.34	0.38	0.14	0.09
7. Great Britain	0.33	0.34	0.33	0.23	0.20	0.16
8. India	0.69	0.67	0.53	0.59	0.49	0.31
9. Israel	0.38	0.40	0.35	0.34	0.19	0.06
10. Italy	0.38	0.29	0.17	0.26	0.16	0.09
11. Japan	0.33	0.22	0.23	0.18	0.09	0.09
12. Mexico	0.53	0.42	0.48	0.42	0.31	0.17
13. Norway	0.48	0.59	0.43	0.22	0.23	0.14
14. South Africa	0.20	0.22	0.25	0.16	0.11	0.09
15. Sweden	0.64	0.62	0.59	0.28	0.24	0.17
16. Switzerland	0.47	0.36	0.31	0.22	0.17	0.12
17. United States	0.22	0.21	0.27	0.16	0.11	0.10
18. Yugoslavia	...	0.20	0.23	...	0.11	0.10

[a]Standard benchmark years; for actual dates see table 33.
Source: As for table 46.

then on. Differences in coverage are probably of more importance for deposits in commercial banks. As a rule only demand deposits are included, but separate figures for monetary deposits are not always available.

The picture shown in table 50 for 10 countries is nevertheless fairly clear in two respects. First, intercountry differences have been substantial and did not disappear in the century before World War II. Second, the ratios exhibit in most countries definite trends, which generally are in accord with what one would expect in the process of financial development such as the declining role of paper currency and particularly of coin, and the increasing share of check deposits in the stock of money and among all financial assets. In evaluating the ratios it must be kept in mind that they are quotients of two ratios, the ratio of money to national product and the ratio of all financial assets to product. Thus a relatively high share of money in financial assets may be due to a high coefficient of monetization or a low ratio of financial assets to national product or to a combination of both.

Taking the statistics at their face value, the average ratio of money to financial assets showed little change between the 1875 benchmark and 1913, dropped slightly between 1913 and 1929, and hardly changed over

Table 50 **Share of Money in Domestic Financial Assets in 10 Countries, 1880–1939**

Country	Standard Benchmark Years[a] 1875 (1)	1895 (2)	1913 (3)	1929 (4)	1939 (5)
	I. Currency				
1. Belgium[b]	3.8	3.1	2.7	3.6	7.4
2. Denmark[b]	2.4	1.5	1.3	1.1	1.2
3. France	7.2	5.8	5.9	5.5	6.9
4. Germany	7.3	3.2	2.4	3.3	4.2
5. Great Britain	2.6	1.4	1.5	1.3	1.3
6. Italy[b]	6.3	4.5	5.5	3.8	3.5
7. Japan	10.0	6.1	3.5	2.1	2.2
8. Norway[b]	2.5	1.9	1.5	1.5	2.6
9. Switzerland[b]	0.8	1.0	0.8	1.2	1.9
10. United States	2.9	2.4	1.5	0.7	1.3
	II. Demand Deposits with Commercial Banks				
1. Belgium	5.1	4.8	5.8	5.7	7.2
2. Denmark	...	...	...	1.7	1.8
3. France	1.6	2.4	2.3	6.2	5.5
4. Germany	1.1	2.0	3.8	6.5	3.1
5. Great Britain	9.3	7.1	6.9	5.0	5.4
6. Italy	2.0	...	2.6	5.0	4.4
7. Japan	2.0	4.9	3.2	1.9	2.5
8. Norway	5.2	6.6	8.4	7.3	4.5
9. Switzerland	2.9	3.3	4.6	7.7	4.1
10. United States	4.8	7.2	6.7	4.1	6.2

the 1930s. The total decline in the 60 years before World War II from 8.6 to 8.2 percent of financial assets amounts to only 5 percent of its starting value, and would be only slightly larger if coins in circulation were included in 1875 for all countries. The differences among countries were fairly wide throughout the period. The share of money in financial assets ranged both around 1875 and 1939 from 3 or 4 to 12 percent. In four countries (Germany, Italy, Norway, and the United States) the ratio failed to show a long-term trend, the average standing at slightly below 8 percent at the beginning, middle, and end of the period. The share of money increased substantially in Belgium, France, and Switzerland in the interwar period. It had a downward trend throughout most of the period in Great Britain and Japan.

In contrast to these moderate movements in the ratio of total money to financial assets, changes were sharp and diverse for the three components of the money supply, coins, bank notes, and deposits (mainly demand) with commercial banks. Thus the share of currency in the total money supply, shown in table 51, declined between 1875 and 1929, a movement

Table 50 (Continued)

Country	1875 (1)	1895 (2)	1913 (3)	1929 (4)	1939 (5)
	Standard Benchmark Years[a]				
	III. Currency and Deposits				
1. Belgium	8.9	7.9	8.5	9.3	14.6
2. Denmark	. . .	. . .	. . .	2.8	3.0
3. France	8.8	8.2	8.2	11.7	12.4
4. Germany	8.4	5.2	6.2	9.8	7.3
5. Great Britain	11.9	8.5	8.4	6.3	6.7
6. Italy	8.3	. . .	8.1	8.8	7.9
7. Japan	12.0	11.0	6.7	4.0	4.7
8. Norway	7.7	8.5	9.9	8.8	7.1
9. Switzerland	3.7	4.3	5.4	8.9	6.0
10. United States	7.7	9.6	8.1	4.8	7.5

[a]For actual dates cf. table 33.
[b]Bank notes only.
Source of basic data:
For bank notes and deposits:
Lines 1–5, 7–9 — Mitchell 1975, 674 ff. Rough estimates for lines 3 and 7 in col. 1.
Line 7 — Bank of Japan 1966, 166–67, 194–95.
Line 10 — *HS* 1975, 992–93.
For coins:
Line 3 — *ASF* 1966, 515.
Line 4 — Hoffmann 1975, 814–15.
Line 5 — Sheppard 1971, 180.
Lines 7, 10 — As for bank notes and deposits.
Line 9 — Mitchell 1974, 674 ff. for cols. 3 and 4; for cols. 1, 2, and 5 extrapolated on basis of total liabilities of commercial banks.

evidenced in the increase of the ratio of commercial bank deposits to currency rising from about 0.8 to 2.1, most of the increase taking place before World War I. All countries participated in this movement, though the extent of the rise and the level of the ratios were very different among countries. On the other hand, the ratio increased in seven of the 10 countries between 1929 and the late 1930s, the average falling from 2.1 to 1.4 as bank deposits declined and currency in circulation or hoarded increased under the influence of the Great Depression and bank failures.

The changes in the composition of currency as between coins and notes were even more dramatic but are easier to explain. Between around 1880 and the eve of World War I the share of bank notes in currency in circulation—close to zero in mid-19th century in most countries—increased in six countries on the average from 0.21 to 0.27. Mainly as the result of the disappearance of gold coins from circulation by government fiat, the ratio was sharply higher in 1929 at 0.44, and it further increased slightly to 0.46 in the late 1930s, the increases ranging from about 90

Table 51 **Share of Bank Notes and Coins in M-1 in 10 Countries, 1875–1939[a]**

Country	1875 (1)	1895 (2)	1913 (3)	1929 (4)	1939 (5)
1. Belgium[b]	0.43	0.39	0.32	0.39	0.51
2. Denmark[b]	. . .	. . .	. . .	0.39	0.40
3. France	0.81	0.71	0.72	0.47	0.56
4. Germany	0.87	0.62	0.39	0.34	0.58
5. Great Britain	0.22	0.16	0.18	0.21	0.19
6. Italy[b]	0.76	. . .	0.68	0.43	0.44
7. Japan	0.83	0.55	0.61	0.53	0.47
8. Norway[b]	0.32	0.22	0.15	0.17	0.37
9. Switzerland[b]	0.22	0.23	0.15	0.13	0.32
10. United States	0.38	0.25	0.17	0.15	0.17

[a]Standard benchmark years; for actual dates see table 33.
[b]For col. 1 only bank notes.
Source of basic data: Table 50.

percent (Germany) to 300 percent (India). The differences among countries in the relative importance of coin and of bank notes before World War I were very large, as can be seen in table 49, but were radically reduced, mainly between the 1913 and 1939 benchmarks. This decrease in inequality, which is indicated, e.g., by the decline in the ratio of the sum of the absolute deviations from the mean to the mean from 1.5 in 1875 and 2.0 in 1913 to only 0.2 in 1939, may be regarded as a movement toward a more modern monetary system in which bank money becomes dominant.

For the postwar period, additional internationally comparable data on domestic (central and commercial) bank credit to private and public borrowers are available in the International Monetary Fund's *International Financial Statistics Yearbook* which can be related to the estimates of total financial assets underlying the country balance sheets of Appendix A. These data are used in table 52 to show the relation between domestic bank credit and financial assets and national product and in table 53 to measure the share of the government in total domestic bank credit.

It is evident from table 52 that both the importance of domestic bank credit as reflected in its relation to all financial assets and to national product as well as the movements of the two ratios over the postwar period differ greatly among the 18 countries covered. At the end of the period the share of domestic bank credit in total domestic financial assets ranged from 9 to 33 percent, with an (unweighted) average of 17 percent. However, for one-half of the 18 countries the ratio lay between 11 and 16 percent.

Table 52 Domestic Bank Credit, 1950–1978[a]

	% Domestic Financial Assets				% Gross National Product			
	1950 (1)	1965 (2)	1973 (3)	1978 (4)	1950 (5)	1965 (6)	1973 (7)	1978 (8)
1. Australia	17.8	15.5	14.0	16.8	53.4	48.2	42.3	44.6
2. Belgium	...	12.3	13.1	13.5	...	37.5	42.2	43.8
3. Canada	8.1	7.5	9.1	10.6	30.6	30.7	35.9	47.3
4. Denmark	17.6	13.0	11.4	9.7	75.6	47.3	43.9	42.8
5. France	14.3	18.3	14.3	16.7	24.5	18.3	43.5	49.4
6. Germany	21.9	16.8	24.5	24.3	33.1	31.0	76.7	86.4
7. Great Britain	...	11.1	10.8	9.4	...	52.7	53.7	61.9
8. India	11.7	13.6	11.7	13.6	16.0	26.2	25.6	32.0
9. Israel	21.3	9.8	...	11.7	33.0	28.1	37.5	49.6
10. Italy	...	19.9	20.8	21.1	...	65.5	86.4	90.8
11. Japan	26.5	23.3	21.6	20.8	57.4	95.3	98.3	81.9
12. Mexico	10.4	8.6	9.5	16.4	13.7	12.7	15.2	30.2
13. Norway	18.4	13.9	14.3	13.8	68.3	50.7	54.1	58.3
14. South Africa	6.3	8.4	9.4	10.8	27.0	34.6	40.7	33.1
15. Sweden	...	16.1	15.3	15.4	...	57.1	62.2	65.0
16. Switzerland	15.7	18.0	18.4	19.0	88.1	100.5	101.1	131.6
17. United States	12.9	11.2	13.6	13.3	61.1	47.4	53.4	48.9
18. Yugoslavia	...	21.8	36.2	33.2	...	48.1	81.2	75.8

[a]Standard benchmark dates; for actual years see table 33.

Source: For bank credit, *IFS* (1972 Suppl. for col. 1, 1981 for cols. 2–4 for financial assets and gross national product country tables in Appendix A.

The differences in the share of the public sector in total domestic bank credit and their movements over the postwar period, shown in table 53, are probably more significant. At the end of the period the share of the government averaged 26 percent, ranging from 6 to 50 percent. If data were available for Hungary and the Soviet Union for which the ratio is close to unity, the average would be raised to approximately one-third. An analysis of the differences is prevented by the failure of the basic data to show separate figures for general government as well as for government enterprises.

In all countries except Italy, Japan, Mexico, Switzerland, and Yugoslavia the government's share in domestic bank credit declined over the postwar period, the (unweighted) average falling from fully two-fifths to one-fourth. What is more significant is that in about one-half of the countries the decline of the ratio was substantial and fairly regular. The unusually large holdings of central government securities accumulated during World War II at the beginning of the period are only a partial explanation and useful for that purpose only for the first half of the period, during which the average ratio fell from 42 to 30 percent. The

Table 53 Share of Government[a] in Domestic Bank Credit[b]

	1950 (1)	1965 (2)	1973 (3)	1978 (4)
1. Australia	58.6	54.5	38.4	37.1
2. Belgium	75.4	64.6	52.2	49.9
3. Canada	39.9	24.0	18.7	13.0
4. Denmark	45.0	0.7	−9.1	5.9
5. France	50.6	28.4	13.7	10.8
6. Germany	34.0[c]	17.5	14.0	22.5
7. Great Britain	71.4[c]	61.8	38.1	39.7
8. India	66.6	65.7	49.9	44.9
9. Israel	48.3	15.2	27.9	27.4
10. Italy	37.5[d]	25.5	31.4	41.0
11. Japan	11.1	5.1	5.6	11.9
12. Mexico	32.0	40.0	56.5	46.0
13. Norway	45.0	29.9	30.6	26.7
14. South Africa	36.9	23.4	17.2	22.5
15. Sweden	27.7	17.7	18.4	20.6
16. Switzerland	1.7	10.6	11.1	9.7
17. United States	62.4	40.2	31.1	28.9
18. Yugoslavia[e]	9.1[d]	19.3	7.5	11.0

[a]Includes local governments and government entities; net basis.
[b]Standard benchmark dates; for actual years cf. table 33.
[c]1951.
[d]1957.
[e]Apparently does not include public sector enterprises.
Source: *IFS* 1972 suppl., for col. 1; *IFSYB* 1981 for cols. 2–4.

ratios are relatively low for the less developed market economies, but they are distributed throughout the entire range for developed market economies without a clear relation between the level of the ratio and that of economic or financial development. The variations are rather the result of differences in the institutional structure of the various countries, in particular the relation of the size of central and commercial banks to that of all financial institutions.

In 11 of the 18 countries the ratio of domestic bank credit to total financial assets increased over the postwar period and in seven it declined, but the movements were in most cases irregular. There are at most nine countries in which a trend, upward in seven of them, can be detected.

The ratio of domestic bank credit to national product is the product of the ratio of credit to financial assets and that of the latter to national product, and the two are positively though only loosely, correlated. The range of the ratios shown in cols. 5–8 of table 52 is therefore narrower, extending at the end of the period from 0.30 to 1.32 with an unweighted average of 0.64 and an interquartile range of 0.47 to 0.86. Again the two less developed market economies showed relatively low ratios averaging 0.37; and again there was no clear relation among developed market economies between the ratio of domestic bank credit to national product and the level of economic or financial development.

c) Insurance and Pension Claims

Of all types of financial assets, insurance and pension claims, including social security claims to the extent of the assets of the funds rather than to the much larger but vague actuarial liabilities, have in most countries shown the steadiest and most pronounced upward trend in relation both to all financial assets and still more to national assets and incomes. Thus their share in financial assets more than quadrupled in Great Britain and in the United States from about 2 percent in the mid-19th century to 10 and 8 percent in the 1970s. Through the interwar period, most of the increase was accounted for by life insurance companies, while since then private and public pension funds have become dominant.

At the present time there are, as can be seen in table 54, three distinct groups of countries. In the first, which comprises Australia, Great Britain, Israel, South Africa, Sweden, and the United States, the ratio to financial assets is slightly above one-tenth. In the second group, made up of Belgium, Canada, Denmark, Germany, Norway, and Switzerland, insurance and pension funds account for between 5 and 7 percent of all financial assets. Interesting enough, this group now also includes India. The ratio averaged only slightly less than 3 percent in the third heterogeneous group of France, Italy, and Japan. Mexico which with less than 1 percent had the lowest ratio. These differences reflect the relative importance of the social security system and the methods by which it is financed; the scope and age of compulsory private and public pension funds; the popularity of life insurance, which is much higher in English-speaking countries than in most of the rest of the world; and the duration and intensity of inflation. A relatively high rate of inflation would be expected to be negatively related to the share of insurance and pension claims, but its effect is not evident in table 54 in the present ratios, but clearly though temporarily in France, Germany, and Italy immediately after World War II. Nor do differences in real income per head appear to be determinant.

In most developed countries the upward trend of the ratio of insurance and pension claims was more in evidence before the 1960s than since. The average for six developed countries of six percent in the late 1970s was slightly below that of the mid-1960s, but almost twice as high as the averages for 1950 and 1913 and four times as high as the average of 1½ percent around 1875. The decline of the ratio between the benchmarks of 1965 and 1978 reflects the acceleration of inflation.

Table 54 **Share of Insurance and Pension Claims[a] in Financial Assets**

	Standard Benchmark Year[b]									
Country	1850 (1)	1875 (2)	1895 (3)	1913 (4)	1929 (5)	1939 (6)	1950 (7)	1965 (8)	1973 (9)	1978 (10)
1. Australia	...	...	...	...	...	...	7.4	8.0	9.5	9.7
2. Belgium	...	...	...	...	...	...	...	9.1	5.9	5.1
3. Canada	...	...	...	...	...	...	8.8	7.0	6.0	5.6
4. Denmark	...	...	...	...	...	...	6.8	6.8	6.1	6.4
5. France		1.2	...	2.7	1.3	...	1.0	1.2	2.5	2.4
6. Germany	0.5	1.0	2.6	3.9	3.3	6.7	2.8	5.8	6.2	5.8
7. Great Britain[c]	2.2	2.9	2.9	4.4	5.0	6.8	7.8	11.8	10.3	10.1
8. Hungary	...	...	...	...	...	...	...	...	...	...
9. India	...	...	...	0.4	1.3	2.1	2.8	3.7	4.9	5.0
10. Israel	...	...	...	...	...	...	2.9	7.7	...	11.6
11. Italy	...	0.4	1.4	2.8	3.1	4.8	2.0	3.0	2.7	2.6
12. Japan	...	...	...	...	...	...	2.0	2.9	2.9	3.2
13. Mexico	...	...	...	...	1.2	1.2	1.3	1.3	1.1	0.9
14. Norway	...	...	1.5	1.8	2.9	4.8	4.7	8.1	8.0	7.1
15. Russia/USSR	...	...	...	0.4	...	...	...	...	...	...
16. South Africa	...	...	...	3.6	8.9	8.2	...	10.5	11.8	13.6
17. Sweden	...	...	...	...	...	...	...	8.5	10.6	11.2
18. Switzerland	...	...	...	...	...	6.8	7.7	8.5	6.6	6.7
19. United States	1.9	2.5	2.5	3.1	3.6	7.4	9.2	8.1	8.2	8.2
20. Yugoslavia	...	...	...	...	...	...	...	...	...	...

[a]Includes social security claims to the extent of assets of funds.
[b]For actual dates see table 33.
[c]In 1800, 1.0; in 1830, 1.7.

d) Government Debt

Table 55, which shows the ratios of public debt (generally excluding foreign debt) to total financial assets, reflects both the fairly general and steady expansion of government economic activities and ownership and the irregular but pronounced influences of military expenditures. Thus the ratios show in some countries, particularly Great Britain and the United States, war-related peaks, attenuated because the benchmark dates of 1875, 1929, and 1950 are several years behind the conclusion of major wars, but fail to do so in other countries (Germany and Japan) because war debts were wiped out by inflation or currency reform.

Turning to long-term trends, the direction of the ratio was downward in all major developed countries between the middle of the 19th century and 1913, a period without worldwide wars, cutting it in half from nearly one-fifth to less than one-tenth for the four large developed countries (France, Germany, Great Britain, and United States). The ratio almost returned to its 1850 level by the end of the 1930s mainly as a result of, first, the heavy debt incurred in connection with World War I, and then the deficits of the Great Depression. By the late 1970s it was back to less than one-tenth, the 1913 level—after having reached a peak of nearly one-fourth at the end of World War II—as the inflation of the postwar period helped to reduce the burden of the debt of World War II and of the absolutely large new debt issues. At that time the unweighted average share of public debt in all financial assets for the 15 developed market economies was somewhat above one-tenth, as the 11 other countries showed on the average ratios somewhat higher than those of the four large ones.

The movements of the share of government debt in India in all financial assets (including as for other countries monetary metals) differ from the pattern of most developed countries, as probably do those in most other less developed countries. The share of domestic government debt, the only one that directly affects the structure of the national balance sheet, stayed close to 7 percent throughout the half-century before World War I. It jumped to 15 percent in 1929, mainly reflecting the partial substitution of domestic for foreign debt, and has remained somewhat below that level throughout the postwar period. If foreign debt (not shown in table 55) is included, the ratio rose fairly rapidly from one-tenth in 1860 and 1875 to about one-fourth from 1913 to 1939. But during the postwar period it increased from a low of one-tenth in 1950, a result of the retirement of most of the foreign debt during World War II, to nearly one-fifth since the mid-1960s, reflecting large-scale borrowing by the central government to help finance the ambitious five-year plans. The trends are different again if monetary metals are excluded from financial assets to make the ratios more nearly comparable to those of other

Table 55 **Share of Public Debt[a] in Financial Assets**

Country	Standard Benchmark Year[b]									
	1850 (1)	1875 (2)	1895 (3)	1913 (4)	1929 (5)	1939 (6)	1950 (7)	1965 (8)	1973 (9)	1978 (10)
1. Australia	...	...	...	...	...	...	25.0	18.2	13.0	13.6
2. Belgium	25.0	15.7	18.9	14.4	16.7	20.4	29.8	23.7	18.6	18.4
3. Canada	...	...	...	...	...	...	19.1	15.0	12.1	12.3
4. Denmark	...	5.5	4.5	5.7	4.9	5.3	12.6	4.7	2.5	5.0
5. France[c]	21.6	21.8	...	15.8	32.7	...	15.5	8.4	3.8	4.3
6. Germany	13.8	7.7	12.5	9.7	8.6	11.4	14.9	5.6	5.2	7.4
7. Great Britain[d]	31.6	15.0	8.9	8.0	25.8	22.6	31.8	23.5	15.8	16.3
8. Hungary	...	...	...	...	...	...	...	...	...	...
9. India	6.7	5.6	6.7	6.8	14.8	13.7	9.6	15.5	12.1	10.7
10. Israel	...	...	...	...	...	...	14.7	11.5	...	12.7
11. Italy	31.6	48.1	42.4	31.9	29.1	33.4	30.1	14.7	15.9	19.5
12. Japan	...	15.9	9.0	8.9	9.3	13.7	4.0	1.2	2.4	5.2
13. Mexico	...	...	...	...	0.8	2.4	4.8	6.9	8.6	6.7
14. Norway	...	8.3	10.3	8.1	14.6	12.1	15.7	16.1[e]	14.5[e]	18.4[e]
15. Russia/USSR	...	...	...	7.8	7.0	16.1	23.3	...	...	...
16. South Africa	...	...	...	3.6	17.8	15.1	22.3	12.6	11.6	13.4
17. Sweden	...	...	...	...	...	...	...	6.6	5.1	6.9
18. Switzerland	...	4.2	3.7	7.5	9.2	10.7	9.4	3.7	3.2	3.7
19. United States[f]	10.2	12.4	5.2	4.1	6.1	13.5	23.5	11.7	10.9	12.5
20. Yugoslavia	...	...	...	...	...	...	...	10.1	7.4	3.1

[a]Generally only domestic debt.

[b]For actual dates see table 33.

[c]In 1815, 10.4.

[d]In 1760, 26.7; in 1800, 46.5; in 1830, 45.4.

[e]Includes debt of government enterprises (4.5, 1.9, 3.7).

[f]In 1805, 18.6.

[e]Includes debt of government enterprises (4.5, 1.9, 3.7).

countries, where monetary metals play only a secondary role. In that case the share of domestic government debt in financial assets oscillated without definite trend between one-fifth and one-eighth before Independence, and averaged about one-sixth during the postwar period. Inclusion of foreign debt raises considerably the level of the ratio, which now increases from about one-fourth in the third quarter of the 19th century to about one-third from the 1890s to the 1930s, but keeps between one-fifth and one-fourth in the postwar period.

The figures for Mexico may be more representative for less developed countries. Here the ratio of domestic government debt to all financial assets increased steadily from less than 1 percent in 1930 to on the average 7 percent since the mid-1960s.

e) Corporate Securities

Though corporate stocks were of some importance at occasional times in the 18th century in London, Paris, or Amsterdam, it is only since the railway age that they developed into an important component of financial and national assets and that corporate bonds became a major financial instrument and a rival of government bonds in the portfolios of individuals and institutions. It is mainly the large role of corporate stocks and bonds in the financial superstructure which justifies the designation of the near-century from the middle of the 19th century to the Great Depression as the period of "security capitalism" which was characterized by large holdings, large relative to financial assets and to the portfolios of the household sector, of corporate securities by individual investors. This phase of financial development has been on the decline since the 1930s. By the late 1970s corporate securities were in most countries rapidly losing in importance in individuals' portfolios. True, there were still large amounts of corporate bonds and stocks outstanding, but the mass of bonds and a large and increasing proportion of stocks were now held by financial institutions, nonfinancial corporations, and in some countries by the government rather than by individual investors. These trends are reflected in tables 56 and 57, though for the process of institutionalization of holdings of corporate stocks table 66 has to be consulted.

Domestic corporate bonds generally reached the peak of their importance among financial assets in the fourth quarter of the 19th and the first quarter of the current century. At the eve of World War I they constituted fully one-tenth of all financial assets in the United States and France and over 6 percent in Great Britain. The importance of domestic corporate bonds was much less in smaller countries, with the result that their unweighted average share for 11 developed countries was below 4 percent. Initially railroad bonds predominated, but the nationalization of

Table 56 **Share of Domestic Corporate Bonds[a] in Financial Assets**

	Standard Benchmark Year[b]									
Country	1850 (1)	1875 (2)	1895 (3)	1913 (4)	1929 (5)	1939 (6)	1950 (7)	1965 (8)	1973 (9)	1978 (10)
1. Australia	...	...	...	...	...	...	1.0	1.1	1.0	1.1
2. Belgium	...	5.4	4.6	4.7	1.1	2.1	0.7	1.1	1.2	1.2
3. Canada	...	...	...	...	...	...	4.5	4.3	3.7	3.2
4. Denmark	...	0.7	0.5	0.5	0.6	0.5	0.9	1.2	1.3	1.4
5. France	4.4	12.5	...	11.2	3.9	...	1.5	2.7	1.7	1.7
6. Germany	1.3	3.7	0.9	1.3	1.9	1.1	1.2	1.2	0.8	0.6
7. Great Britain[c]	...	...	9.3	6.4	3.7	3.5	1.1	2.1	1.8	1.1
8. Hungary	...	...	...	...	...	...	...	...	...	...
9. India	...	...	...	...	...	...	...	...	...	...
10. Israel	...	...	...	...	...	...	...	...	...	...
11. Italy	9.4	3.9	3.1	2.0	1.1	1.0	0.8	1.9	1.8	1.3
12. Japan	...	...	0.0	0.6	3.1	1.8	3.5	6.0	5.6	5.4
13. Mexico	...	...	...	...	...	...	1.6	1.0	0.5	0.2
14. Norway	...	...	...	0.9	1.3	1.5	1.0	5.2	2.6	4.1
15. Russia/USSR	...	...	...	0.7	...	...	...	...	...	...
16. South Africa	...	...	...	...	...	...	...	2.7	2.9	3.9
17. Sweden	...	...	...	...	...	...	...	1.4	1.5	1.8
18. Switzerland	...	5.4	5.7	1.9	2.3	1.7	0.9	1.9	1.7	1.7
19. United States[c]	8.8	10.7	8.2	10.6	6.9	6.6	3.6	3.8	4.5	4.8
20. Yugoslavia	...	...	...	...	...	...	...	...	...	...

[a]Excluding bonds of mortgages banks.
[b]For actual dates see table 33.
[c]Includes foreign bonds in cols. 7–10.

Table 57 **Share of Domestic Corporate Stock in Financial Assets**

Country	Standard Benchmark Year[a]									
	1850 (1)	1875 (2)	1895 (3)	1913 (4)	1929 (5)	1939 (6)	1950 (7)	1965 (8)	1973 (9)	1978 (10)
1. Australia	...	...	...	...	...	...	14.7	15.1	11.4	8.0
2. Belgium	32.1	23.6	14.5	17.4	17.5	7.1	9.9	7.1	5.5	4.7
3. Canada	...	...	...	...	...	...	14.6	10.5	8.4	8.7
4. Denmark	...	17.5	15.8	15.1	21.4	13.2	9.1	8.6	7.6	6.0
5. France	4.9	7.6	...	10.4	6.1	...	14.4	33.0	18.9	11.8
6. Germany[b]	3.0	6.0	5.7	9.0	13.2	8.5	11.5	24.0	11.3	9.8
7. Great Britain[c]	14.7[d]	16.8[d]	24.3	21.2	22.1	24.1	19.2	17.3	12.9	11.4
8. Hungary	...	...	...	...	...	...	...	...	...	...
9. India	0.7	1.2	2.1	4.0	5.3	6.1	5.9[e]	6.1[e]	5.8[e]	4.3[e]
10. Israel	...	...	...	...	...	...	3.7	2.2	...	2.2
11. Italy	10.4	3.2	3.9	2.6	9.4	7.2	8.4	15.8	6.6	2.4
12. Japan	...	2.0	15.0	12.1	12.5	20.2	11.1	11.2	7.4	8.4
13. Mexico	...	...	...	...	24.4	30.3	33.2	20.1	15.6	28.8
14. Norway	...	6.4	8.8	10.8	9.3	8.3	3.0	8.9[f]	5.8[f]	4.9[f]
15. Russia/USSR	...	...	...	7.5	...	...	...	...	...	...
16. South Africa	...	...	...	47.8	29.3	36.5	26.1	24.9	18.6	11.1
17. Sweden	...	...	...	...	...	...	...	13.7[g]	7.5[g]	6.1[g]
18. Switzerland	...	9.0	10.1	12.5	17.0	15.4	15.8	16.6	12.2	11.0
19. United States	17.2	23.6	22.2	27.5	34.6	20.3	14.9	28.2	20.1	14.6
20. Yugoslavia	...	...	...	...	...	...	...	...	...	...

[a]For actual dates see table 33.

[b]Includes G.m.b.H. parts; without them the ratios are, beginning in 1913: 74, 10.8, 6.9, 8.3, 15.4, 7.4, and 6.4.

[c]In 1760, 6.7; in 1880, 3.0; in 1830, 2.9.

[d]Includes corporate bonds.

[e]Includes small amounts of corporate bonds.

[f]Includes capital of government enterprises (6.3, 3.9, 3.7).

[g]Includes capital of government enterprises (2.2, 1.4, 1.3).

railroads in Germany, Italy, Japan, and Switzerland greatly reduced their importance in these countries. The ratio declined rapidly during the interwar period in most countries covered. At mid-century it averaged less than 2 percent in the 12 countries for which the information is available, now consisting mostly of bonds of public utility and industrial corporations. The ratio was fractionally higher at 2.0 percent in the late 1970s, reflecting increases in Japan and the United States. By that time, however, the holdings of corporate bonds had become progressively concentrated in financial institutions.

The movements of the share of corporate stocks in financial assets, shown in table 57, are more varied but more significant. They show in most countries an upward trend until the 1920s and generally sharp declines during the postwar period, but the levels of the ratios and the details of their movement differ greatly among countries. At the peak, generally the 1929 or 1939 benchmarks, the ratios varied in developed countries from 10 percent in France to nearly one-half in South Africa, a special case, the peak occurring already in 1913 and reflecting the relatively large volume of gold mining stocks, a large part of which was held abroad. For 12 countries the unweighted average was 18 percent in 1929 and still 16 percent a decade later. (A weighted average would be higher and the decline more pronounced because of the higher level and sharper fall of the United States ratio).

During the postwar period the share declined in all countries (except for Norway), falling for 16 countries from 13½ percent at mid-century to 9 percent in the late 1970s. This degradation of the position of corporate stocks in the financial superstructure of most developed countries, and still more in the portfolios of the household sector, has several reasons. One is that in many countries stock prices failed to keep pace with the rate of inflation from the mid-1960s on. A second is the generally low level of new stock issues; a third, connected with it, the declining importance of the private corporate sector in several countries. The levels and movements show, however, considerable differences among countries. Corporate stocks now have been reduced to a very minor position in several countries' financial superstructure, e.g., in India, Israel, Italy, and Norway; while they are still of substantial importance, accounting for between 8 and 15 percent of financial assets, in the leading countries.

Corporate stocks seem to play a minor role in most less developed countries, at least outside the large Latin American countries—the Mexican ration of over one-fourth is the highest among the 18 countries, but probably is not representative, though comprehensive statistical evidence is lacking. This reflects the relatively small importance of the private corporate sector and the preferences of the often closely held corporations for debt financing. In India the share of corporate stock in financial assets after rising substantially and steadily, though at a low level, until Independence, has declined in the postwar period to about 4 percent in the mid-1970s, and a dominating proportion is now held by government-owned financial institutions.

f) Trade Credit

Though trade credit is probably the oldest financial instrument used to a substantial extent, going back at least to the Middle Ages and antedating the two other instruments already in use before the Industrial Revolution—government securities and mortgages—estimates of its size are rare—it is even omitted in most of the modern official flow-of-funds statistics—and hazardous. In the national balance sheets of Appendix A, trade credit has sometimes had to be estimated very roughly on the basis of inventories, to which it is fairly closely related, or of national product, in order to complete the balance sheets rather than in the hope of obtaining estimates that can stand on their own feet. A tabulation, such as table 58, based on these data can therefore be regarded as only a rough basis for an intertemporal or international comparison of the share of trade credit in financial assets.

The material does, however, permit at least two conclusions. The first is that over the long run the share of trade credit in financial assets is likely to have decreased considerably. In Great Britain the share seems to have been in the order of one-fourth in the 18th century, but to have moved irregularly downward from 8 percent of financial assets in the third quarter of the 19th century to 6 percent in the 1970s. In the United States, where the figures may be less deficient, the share seems to have been as high as one-fifth as late as the mid-19th century, but to have declined rapidly to below five percent without further trend, since the 1920s. Second, in the late 1970s when most of the estimates have a somewhat firmer basis, often in the tabulations of corporate balance sheets, the ratio for 15 developed market economies averaged fully 6 percent, one-half of the ratios falling between 5 and 7 percent. The exception is Japan with nearly 15 percent, explained in part by the large extent of subcontracting. The Indian and the Mexican ratios of about one-tenth are somewhat above those of all countries except Japan, but this may not be representative of the averages of their groups.

g) The Role of Foreign Investments

Differences in levels among countries and changes over time are nowhere as great as in the relative importance of foreign investments in the financial superstructure, roughly measured by the ratio of gross foreign investments (or where unavailable, net foreign investments if positive). Before World War I these investments were overwhelmingly in

Table 58 **Share of Trade Credit in Financial Assets**

Country	Standard Benchmark Year[a]									
	1850 (1)	1875 (2)	1895 (3)	1913 (4)	1929 (5)	1939 (6)	1950 (7)	1965 (8)	1973 (9)	1978 (10)
1. Australia[b]	...	...	...	...	...	...	2.4	2.3	2.2	2.4
2. Belgium	14.3	14.6	9.9	8.0	10.0	8.5	13.5	6.4	5.7	5.4
3. Canada	...	...	...	...	...	...	4.9	4.3	4.5	4.7
4. Denmark	...	8.3	6.3	5.1	5.1	6.1	7.0	6.5	4.1	3.0
5. France[c]	16.4	7.9	...	4.8	6.5	...	13.9	6.9	10.0[d]	13.4[d]
6. Germany	20.9	16.8	10.7	9.4	10.8	9.4	18.1	7.7	6.3	5.7
7. Great Britain[d]	7.4	7.6	4.7	5.1	4.4	3.8	5.7	6.5	6.0	6.6
8. Hungary	...	...	...	...	...	...	...	14.4	11.7	6.7
9. India	7.8	9.2	7.0	6.8	10.5	4.1	16.1	12.4	11.7	10.6
10. Israel	...	...	...	...	...	...	18.3	12.1	...	8.0
11. Italy	17.8	9.6	8.1	10.5	8.5	9.9	11.2	5.9	4.8	5.7
12. Japan	...	22.7	19.2	18.5	8.8	9.7	12.8	17.2	18.4	13.7
13. Mexico	...	...	...	...	15.7	10.1	6.2	11.6	8.1	8.7
14. Norway	...	16.0	11.2	7.1	6.3	8.0	7.4	7.9	6.6	6.2
15. Russia/USSR	...	...	...	...	...	...	...	...	...	...
16. South Africa	...	...	...	14.3	12.4	8.8	8.7	8.7	9.2	9.7
17. Sweden	...	...	...	...	...	...	...	8.2	6.9	5.5
18. Switzerland	...	3.6	2.7	2.6	2.6	2.1	3.0	2.9	2.7	2.2
19. United States[e]	20.4	14.1	9.1	5.9	4.8	3.0	4.4	3.9	5.0	4.4
20. Yugoslavia	...	...	...	...	...	...	19.9[d]	17.9[d]	21.1	10.8

[a]For actual dates see table 33.
[b]Corporate inventories only.
[c]In 1815, 24.0.
[d]Includes other financial assets.
[e]In 1760, 26.7; in 1800, 20.2; in 1830, 11.5.

Table 59 **Ratio of Gross Foreign to Domestic Financial Assets**[a]

Country	Standard Benchmark Year[b]									
	1850 (1)	1875 (2)	1895 (3)	1913 (4)	1929 (5)	1939 (6)	1950 (7)	1965 (8)	1973 (9)	1978 (10)
1. Australia	...	...	...	...	...	...	1.5	2.3	2.9	1.3
2. Belgium[c]	...	...	15.6	19.5	15.9	19.0	5.8	8.9	12.6	12.3
3. Canada	...	...	...	...	...	...	6.3	6.0	6.9	6.0
4. Denmark	...	5.3[c]	...	1.0	2.4	2.5	2.5	4.7	4.1	4.0
5. France[d]	10.5	17.8	...	21.6	1.9[c]	...	...	...	7.6	9.5
6. Germany	...	11.5	12.9	7.9	5.8	2.5[c]	0.7	7.1	7.5	7.1
7. Great Britain[e]	8.7	25.9	28.7	37.5	18.0	14.1	1.4	4.0	19.9	21.2
8. Hungary	...	...	...	...	...	...	...	...	...	...
9. India	...	...	...	...	...	...	8.3[c]	...	...	...
10. Israel	...	...	...	...	...	...	...	...	...	...
11. Italy[c]	...	...	...	...	...	...	...	0.7	1.5	0.4
12. Japan[c]	...	...	...	...	1.8	0.5	1.1	...	0.6	0.8
13. Mexico	...	...	...	...	...	...	...	...	...	...
14. Norway	...	...	...	...	...	...	...	...	...	...
15. Russia/USSR	...	...	...	...	...	...	...	...	...	...
16. South Africa	...	...	...	...	...	...	...	4.4	4.6	6.0
17. Sweden	...	...	...	...	...	...	...	5.2	5.0	4.5
18. Switzerland	...	21.5	26.2	23.0	12.8	10.1	12.0	18.3	30.7	31.1
19. United States	1.5	2.1	1.6	3.9	4.2	8.0	3.3	3.8	3.9	5.1
20. Yugoslavia	...	...	...	...	...	...	...	...	...	...

[a]Excluding monetary metals.
[b]For actual dates see table 33.
[c]Net foreign assets, if positive.
[d]In 1815, 11.0.
[e]Net foreign assets through 1939. In addition 1.1 in 1800, 6.9 in 1830.

the form of widely distributed holdings of foreign government and corporate securities, but in recent decades they have come to consist to a large extent of short-term claims of the domestic banking system against foreign financial institutions or of domestic corporations' holdings of shares in their foreign subsidiaries.

For the postwar period, information on gross foreign investments, shown in table 59, is available for 13 of the 20 countries, and they are likely to be relatively small in the other seven countries. The unweighted average for the late 1970s is close to 8 percent of domestic financial assets (approximately 4 percent for all 20 countries if the ratios are assumed to be very low for the nonreporting countries). The ratios range, however, from less than 1 percent in Italy and Japan, and probably also for the seven nonreporting countries, to over one-fifth of domestic financial assets in Great Britain and nearly one-third in Switzerland. The average was undoubtedly considerably lower at the end of World War II—possibly as low as 3 percent—as the ratios have increased in almost all countries, and considerably so in the most important ones. Even now, however, the ratios in the leading capital exporting countries are well below those on the eve of World War I. For the six most important countries, foreign investments then averaged nearly one-fifth of domestic financial assets, considerably above the average of about one-eighth in the late 1970s, which is even slightly less than the average of the 1880 benchmark of about 15 percent. In absolute terms, the four largest holders of foreign investments are the same countries now as they were more than six decades ago: France, Germany, Great Britain, and the Unites States, although the order of rank has changed, the United States moving up from near the bottom of the list and replacing Great Britain at the top. To explain the figures of table 59 would mean restating the history of international economic relations since the mid-19th century.

4
Sectorized National Balance Sheets

The full value of national balance sheets for economic analysis is obtained only if they are sectorized and if balance sheets, comparable with and adding up to the national balance sheet, are available for at least five sectors, households (generally including nonprofit organizations and unincorporated business), enterprises (generally limited to those in corporate form), government, financial institutions, and the rest of the world. Unfortunately, sectorized national balance sheets have been published in only three countries by their statistical offices (France, Great Britain, and Japan), and here only for a few recent years. Four attempts have been made to draw up a sectorized national balance sheet for Great Britain (Morgan 1960; Revell and Roe 1971; Stone and Roe 1971; Mason 1976), and two for India (Joshi 1966; Venkatachalam and Sarma 1976), but they differ greatly in structure and have not been kept up to date, and it proved possible to construct sectorized national balance sheets for another country (Germany). Finally sectorized national balance sheet estimates are available for the United States for a number of benchmark years between 1900 and 1939 and annually from 1945 to 1980 (Goldsmith, Lipsey and Mendelson 1963; Ruggles and Ruggles 1982; Goldsmith 1982). Because of space limitations and time constraints this section is limited to the discussion of the sectorized national balance sheets of five countries for one recent date (France, Germany, Great Britain, India, Japan), and of that of the United States for 1900 and 1975 on the basis of the balance sheets assembled in Appendix B. These provide two tables for each country and date, the first of which shows the structure of assets and liabilities for each of the four to nine sectors being distinguished, while the second distributes the national total of each type of asset and liability among the several sectors.

The discussion in this section deals, first, with the share of the four main domestic sectors in total national assets, in tangible and financial assets, and in liabilities, and hence by implication with their complement, net worth. The second part of the section compares the present portfolio structure of the largest sector, households including nonprofit organization and unincorporated farm and nonfarm enterprises, in the five countries plus Canada, adding some comments on the changes that have occurred in that structure in the United States since 1900 and in France since the middle of the 19th century.

1. The Sectoral Distribution of the Main Aggregates

a) National Assets

In terms of total national assets, the household sector broadly defined as in practically all available estimates is, as table 60 shows, the largest single sector, accounting for between fully one-fourth and three-fifths of the national total, with an average for the six countries of about 45 percent. While there is no basis of judgment for other countries, except for the United States, for dates before World War II, all the scattered evidence points to an even higher share of the household sector, particularly if it is as here broadly defined. Indeed the statement that in many still less developed countries, and even for the now developed countries before the industrial revolution, the share of the broadly defined household sector must be, or have been, close to unity is trivial, the only important exception being the ownership of land by the state or the church. The second obvious exception is the modern centrally planned economies. Thus in the Soviet Union the private sector's share (including cooperative farms) of national assets seems to have been reduced around 1960 to about one-fourth (Goldsmith 1964, 96). Even in the narrower definition, limited to nonfarm households excluding unincorporated business, the household sector is probably in most countries, and most likely in all less developed countries, still the largest single sector, with the possible exception of Great Britain and Japan, where its total assets may now not substantially exceed those of the enterprise sector, if the latter is defined to include government enterprises. In the United States, Germany, and Canada (Davies, 1979, 242), the only countries for which the necessary estimates are available, the share of the narrowly defined nonfarm household sector still exceeds one-third of national assets, substantially more than any other sector.

In the United States the share of the household sector narrowly defined (i.e., excluding unincorporated business) does not seem to have

Table 60 **Sectoral Distribution of National Assets in Six Countries in the 1970s**[a]

	Year	Households (1)	Unincorporated Enterprises (2)	Nonprofit Organizations (3)	Corporate Enterprises (4)	General Government: Central (5)	General Government: Local (6)	Financial Institutions (7)	Rest of the World (8)
1. France	1976		42.3		23.7	11.9		18.2	3.9
2. Germany	1977	38.8		26.6		10.9		20.4	3.3
3. Great Britain	1975		28.3		24.5[b]	6.5	9.3	22.3	9.1
4. India	1970		57.5		6.3	23.7		8.8	3.8
5. Japan	1977		37.7		31.1	9.4		21.7	. . .[c]
6. United States	1900	36.6	24.2	. . .	23.3	1.0	3.6	11.3	. . .[d]
United States	1975	35.7	9.6	1.9	16.9	4.2	9.3	20.8	1.6

[a]Also, as in tables 62–64 and 66–68 in 1900 for United States.
[b]Includes public authorities.
[c]About 1% of assets of domestic sectors (Economic Planning Agency [1979], 457).
[d]About 1% of assets of domestic sectors (*HS* [1975], 869; not segregated in source table.
Source of basic data: Country tables in Appendix B.

shown a trend since the turn of the century—a temporary upward bulge in the late 1920s (Goldsmith, Lipsey, and Mendelson 1963, 2:28) mainly reflecting that period's abnormal rise in stock prices. The stability of the household sector's share in national assets is the result of offsetting downward changes in the share of both unincorporated and corporate business enterprises and increases in those of the government and of financial institutions. Most of these changes, except the decline in the share of corporate business, are common to most other developed as well as less developed countries, This, however, does not justify the conclusion that there have not been significant changes in other countries in the share of the narrowly defined household sector since the 19th century.

The share of unincorporated business enterprises, including agriculture, can be estimated within a reasonable margin of error only for the United States, where it is now below one-tenth. It is likely to be of the same order of magnitude in most developed countries, but is undoubtedly much higher in practically all less developed countries because of the much larger importance of peasant agriculture. In India, for example, it should now still be in the neighborhood of one-half, though considerably lower than in 1950, when it may have been of the order of two-thirds.

Estimates of the share of nonprofit institutions are available for only two countries, the United States and Great Britain, for which the ratio lies between 1¼ and 2 percent. It is almost certain, though evidence is fragmentary, that the share is lower in developed countries outside the English-speaking world and still lower elsewhere; and that it was lower in the preceding century. If church property is included, the share is, however, likely to have been higher in Catholic and Islamic countries, at least through the 19th century and in some of them even today.

Determination of the share of enterprises in national assets is difficult because of differences in the treatment of government enterprises, both those that may be regarded as an integral part of the general government, such as the post office; and those which are in different countries and in the same country at different times similar to private enterprises, such as railroads, airlines, electric and gas utilities, and more recently basic mining and manufacturing industries like coal, oil, and steel. There is no doubt, however, that the share of government enterprises in total enterprise and in national assets has considerably increased since the turn of the century.

In the 1970s corporate enterprises, including public enterprises, except in the United States where they are relatively small, accounted for between one-eighth of national assets in India and Germany (in the latter case because of the omission of the very important G.m.b.H.'s), and between one-sixth and one-third in France, Great Britain, Japan, and the United States. The share of all enterprises seems to have varied less in the 1970s among the six countries ranging, including agriculture, between about one-fourth in Germany and in the United States and possibly about one-third in France, and Great Britain, and Japan, to about two-fifths in India.

Present differences are modest for the six countries covered in table 60 in the case of the share of the general government which at the present time accounts for approximately one-eighth of national assets, except in India where it is close to one-fourth.

Statistical evidence of the increase in the secular share of the general government is limited to the United States, where it rose from about 5 percent in 1900 and 1929 to nearly 15 percent in the postwar period. There is little doubt, however, that a similar trend existed in all the other five countries. In India, probably an extreme case among market economies, the share including government enterprises rose from 7 percent in 1950–51 to 24 percent in 1970, which is close to the present share in Great Britain.

The trend of the division between central and local governments since the turn of the century can be followed only for the United States. Here the share of the central government increased from fully one-fifth in 1900 to nearly one-third in 1975. There is little doubt that the trend was in the same direction in most other non-Communist countries.

In the case of financial institutions, the tables in Appendix A permit the calculation of the approximate share of financial institutions in national assets, for all countries for the benchmark dates for which it has been possible to draw up a national balance sheet, by using the information on total assets of or on claims against financial institutions which slightly understates their total assets. Table 61 shows that the share of financial institutions in national assets has in all 20 countries had an upward trend, which is the more pronounced the longer the period for which the information is available. For six developed countries, including France, Germany, Great Britain, and the United States, the share rose from about 3 percent in 1850 to 10 percent in 1913, 13 percent around 1950, and 19 percent in the late 1970s. At the latter date the (unweighted) average for all 20 countries was only insignificantly lower at 18 percent, but the range extended from less than 10 percent in India to nearly one-third in Israel with an interquartile range of 16–21 percent. While the ratio was somewhat lower for centrally planned economies—13 percent for the USSR, Hungary, and Yugoslavia—there was no clear association among developed market economies between the share of financial institutions and the level of real income per head. Some high income countries, like the United States, Canada, France, Germany, and Sweden had low ratios while some low income countries like Great Britain, Italy, and Israel had high ratios. An explanation of the differences among developed market economies would require taking into consideration the monetary history, methods of financing of the main

Table 61 **Share of Financial Institutions in National Assets**

	Standard Benchmark Year[a]								
Country	1850 (1)	1875 (2)	1895 (3)	1913 (4)	1929 (5)	1939 (6)	1950 (7)	1965 (8)	1978 (9)
1. Australia	...	...	...	...	...	...	15	16	16
2. Belgium	2	5	7	10	10	15	14	18	21
3. Canada	...	...	...	...	...	...	14	15	17
4. Denmark	...	14	19	20	20	22	22	23	25
5. France[b]	1	4	...	10	13	...	10	15	15
6. Germany	3	6	11	13	10	15	10	16	18
7. Great Britain[c]	6	10	10	11	13	15	20	20	22
8. Hungary	...	...	...	...	...	...	...	6	14
9. India	1	1	1	2	3	4	6	7	8
10. Israel	...	...	...	...	...	...	15	22	32
11. Italy	1	4	7	10	14	14	10	19	28
12. Japan	...	6	8	13	23	23	11	14	15
13. Mexico	...	...	...	...	5	9	11	13	14
14. Norway	...	8	12	13	19	15	18	16	17
15. Russia/USSR	...	...	...	9	2	8	7	9	12
16. South Africa	...	...	...	7	10	12	14	17	17
17. Sweden	...	...	...	...	...	...	...	14	15
18. Switzerland	...	9	14	18	20	20	19	21	24
19. United States[d]	4	5	8	9	9	16	16	14	13
20. Yugoslavia	...	...	...	...	...	...	8	10	15

[a]For actual dates see table 33.

[b]1815, 1.

[c]1760, 3; 1800, 3; 1830, 5.

[d]1774, 2; 1805, 2.

Source of basic data: Country tables in Appendix A.

sectors, international financial relations, institutional pecularities, and other factors, a task which cannot be undertaken here.

b) Tangible Assets

It would unduly strain the reader's patience to treat the sectoral distribution of the other main aggregates—besides tangible assets, almost equivalent to national wealth, financial assets, liabilities and their complement, net worth—in as much detail as has just been inflicted on him for national assets as the most comprehensive aggregate. The discussion of the three other aggregates will therefore be brief to the point of barrenness, and reliance will be put on the reader's examination of the relevant tables.

The sectoral distribution of tangible assets, shown in table 62, differs in at least three respects from that of national assets, First, and trivially, the share of financial institutions which account for up to a full fifth of total assets is negligible, never above 3 percent. Second, the share of enterprises is considerably higher, particularly if agriculture is included. Third, the share of households and the general government is generally also higher, but less regularly so and to a lesser extent, the increase varying among countries and over time.

c) Financial Assets

Because of the availability of sectorized flow of funds accounts for recent years in Belgium, Canada, Italy and Norway, it has been possible to extend the coverage of table 63 to 10 countries, including all the most important market economies. For financial assets the characteristic difference, of course, is the high share of financial institutions which reflects the concentration of their portfolios in financial assets. In the late 1970s financial institutions have on the average held two-fifths of all financial assets. This means that, with allowance for interfinancial assets, financial institutions are the creditor or debtor in the case of approximately three-fourths of all financial instruments. The ratios, however, range from less than 30 percent in India, reflecting the extensive lending activities of the central government, to close to one-half in Belgium and Italy. This relation, called the financial intermediation ratio, has been discussed for a larger number of countries and for a fairly long period of the past in Chapter 3.

Households, including unincorporated enterprises and nonprofit organizations, are in all countries other than Japan the second largest holders of financial assets though their share is generally well below that in total assets. In the late 1970s it averaged just below 30 percent for the 10

Table 62 **Sectoral Distribution of Tangible Assets in Six Countries in the 1970s**

	Year	Households (1)	Unincorporated Enterprises (2)	Nonprofit Organizations (3)	Nonfinancial Enterprises (4)	General Government: Central (5)	General Government: Local (6)	Financial Institutions (7)	Rest of the World (8)
1. France	1976		62.0		31.3	14.8		1.9	0.0
2. Germany	1977	49.1		34.2		15.3		1.3	0.0
3. Great Britain	1975		32.5		40.1[a]	5.6	19.0	2.8	0.0
4. India	1970		68.1		7.3	24.4		0.2	0.0
5. Japan	1977		48.9		37.0	12.9	1.2	1.2	0.0
6a. United States	1900	32.9	35.9	[b]	23.8	7.6	5.3	0.6	0.0
6b. United States	1975	32.7	17.4	2.9	24.0	6.3	15.8	1.1	0.0

[a]Includes public corporations.

[b]Included in col. 1.

Source of basic data: Country tables in Appendix B.

Table 63 **Sectoral Distribution of Financial Assets in 10 Countries in the 1970s**

	Year	Households (1)	Unincorporated Enterprises (2)	Nonprofit Organizations (3)	Nonfinancial Corporations (4)	General Government: Central (5)	General Government: Local (6)	Financial Institutions (7)	Rest of the World (8)
1. Belgium	1976		39.6			2.9		47.9	9.6
2. Canada	1978		33.6		11.5	3.8	3.8	36.0	11.3
3. France	1976		27.9		13.1	8.1		41.3	9.6
4. Germany	1977	28.5		15.7		4.7		43.8	7.3
5. Great Britain	1975		24.8		11.3	6.9	1.1	39.0	16.9
6. India	1970		27.3[a]		5.3	26.6		28.4	12.4
7. Italy	1977		23.9		11.4	8.7	1.3	48.6	6.1
8. Japan	1977		26.6		25.1	5.9		42.4	. . .[b]
9. Norway	1978		24.3			18.4	1.9	37.8	17.6
10a. United	1900	42.6	7.7	. . .[c]	23.0	0.2	1.3	25.2	. . .[d]
10b. States	1975	40.4	1.1	0.8	9.1	1.9	2.2	41.3	3.2

[a]If gold and silver are included in financial assets 38.8 with proportional reduction in other columns.

[b]Nearly three percent of financial assets of domestic sectors.

[c]Included in col. 1.

[d]About 2½%.

Source: For lines 3–6, 8, and 10, country tables in Appendix B. For line 1 Banque Nationale de Belgique 1979, 5; for line 2 Bank of Canada, flow-of-funds accounts; for line 7 Banca d'Italia, *Assemblea Generale Ordinaria dei Participanti, Anno 1979*, appendice, 116–17; for line 9 Statistisk Sentralbyrå, *Kreditmarkedstatistikk-Finansielle Sektorbalanser 1973–1978*, 1979.

countries for which the information is available, with a range of about one-fourth (France, Great Britain, India, Italy, Japan) to one-third (Canada) and over two-fifths (United States). Intercountry differences are very large in the share of nonfinancial corporations and presumably in all business enterprises. The former ranged from 5 percent in India to 25 percent in Japan, though most other developed countries kept close to the average for the eight countries of fully one-tenth of total financial assets. The government's share was substantial, averaging fully one-sixth for 10 countries, but varied widely with a peak ratio in India of fully one-fourth. Foreigners held on the average about one-tenth of all domestic financial assets, but the scatter was again wide, from only a few percent in Japan and the United States to one-sixth of the total in Great Britain.

d) Liabilities

The outstanding characteristic of the sectoral distribution of debt, shown in table 64, is again the high share of financial institutions, which is necessarily almost identical with that observed in the case of financial assets because of the low ratios of tangible assets and net worth to the total assets of financial institutions. Among the other sectors, however, the shares in total liabilities often differ, and sometimes substantially so, from those in financial assets, indicating net creditor or debtor positions; and from those in total assets, reflecting different net worth ratios.

Thus the share of the household sector is generally much lower and that of the enterprise and government sectors much higher than it is in total or financial assets. It is on the average below one-eighth (including unincorporated business), for the seven countries for which the information is available, ranging from an (unlikely) 2 percent in Italy to nearly a fifth in Canada and the United States. Nonfinancial corporations account on the average for a full one-fifth of all liabilities, and the share is close to the average in most countries—India with a share of one-eighth and Japan with one of nearly two-fifths being the exceptions, which reflect the small size of the private corporate sector in India and the heavy reliance on external finance of Japanese business. The government accounts on the average for the 10 countries for fully one-sixth of total liabilities, but intercountry differences are pronounced. The share is below one-tenth in three countries (France, Germany, and Japan), but reaches nearly one-half in India, partly because of the central government's role as the largest financial intermediary. Financial institutions have, as in the case of financial assets, the largest share of the national total, again with an average of slightly above two-fifths. Liabilities to foreigners account for on the average well below one-tenth of the total, ranging from a few percent in Japan and the United States to nearly one-fifth in Great

Table 64 Sectoral Distribution of Liabilities in 10 Countries in the 1970s

	Year	Households (1)	Unincorporated Enterprises (2)	Nonprofit Organizations (3)	Nonfinancial Corporations (4)	General Government: Central (5)	General Government: Local (6)	Financial Institutions (7)	Rest of the World (8)
1. Belgium	1976		18.5			20.3		49.5	11.7
2. Canada	1978		17.3		23.4	7.5	7.0	38.7	6.1
3. France	1976		10.9		22.6	9.4		45.8	11.3
4. Germany	1977	12.9		23.3		8.5		45.6	9.7
5. Great Britain	1975		7.7		18.7	9.2	5.6	40.7	18.1
6. India	1970		10.0		13.0	47.7		27.3	1.9
7. Italy	1977		2.1		22.6	16.1	5.4	47.0	6.8
8. Japan	1977		10.9		38.3	7.5		43.2	. . .
9. Norway	1978		42.8			11.7	4.3	35.6	5.6
10a. United States	1900	10.2	17.3	. . .	33.7	2.9	4.5	31.4	. . .
10b. United States	1975	14.7	4.5	0.7	17.5	10.8	4.7	44.2	2.9

Source: As for table 60.

Britain, reflecting its position as a leading international financial intermediary.

e) Sectoral Net Creditor and Debtor Positions

In contrast to the wide variations of the share of the various sectors in total financial assets and liabilities, the direction and size of their net creditor or debtor positions are more regular. Thus in the late 1970s the household sector (even including unincorporated business enterprises) was a net creditor in all 10 countries, while the nonfinancial corporate and government sectors were net debtors. On the average the excess of financial assets over liabilities of the household sector amounted to nearly one-fifth of national assets, which was matched by net liabilities of slightly below one-tenth each of national assets of the nonfinancial corporate and government sectors.

f) A Comparison of India and the United States

Because they may be regarded as representatives of large countries at very different stages of economic and financial development, table 65

Table 65 **Changes in Sectoral Distribution of Assets and Liabilities in India and the United States (% of total)**

	Households[a] (1)	Nonfinancial Private Corporations (2)	Government (3)	Financial Institutions (4)	Rest of the World (5)
	India, 1950-51–1970-71				
Total assets	−24.9	+3.6	+16.3	+2.6	+2.5
Tangible assets	−21.2	+4.8	+16.2	+0.1	. . .
Financial assets[b]	−21.0	+0.3	+18.2	−3.6	+6.0
Liabilities	−7.6	+3.4	+19.8	−1.8	−13.9
	United States, 1900–1975				
Total assets	−13.6	−6.4	+8.9	+9.5	(+1.6)
Tangible assets	−15.6	+0.2	+15.2	+0.5	. . .
Financial assets	−8.2	−13.9	+2.6	+16.1	(+3.2)
Liabilities	−7.6	−16.2	+8.1	+13.0	(+2.7)

[a]Including unincorporated enterprises and nonprofit institutions.
[b]Excluding gold.
Source of basic data: tables B8 (and a corresponding table for 1950-51), B12, and B14.

compares the changes in the sectoral distribution of total, tangible, and financial assets and of liabilities in India in the first two decades after Independence and in the United States during the first three quarters of this century.

The striking fact emerges that the sectoral distribution of these aggregates has changed more in India in 20 years than in the United States in 75 years. Thus the share of households broadly defined has declined in India by 25 percentage points, or by nearly one-third, while it has fallen in the United States by only 14 percentage points, or not much over one-fifth. As a result, the share of households in national assets in India in 1970 with 58 percent was actually slightly below the corresponding share in the United States at the turn of the century of 61 percent, though India's present real income per head or any indicator of economic welfare are, of course, still far below the then level in the United States. Similarly, reflecting much steeper trends though tending in the same direction, the share of the government in national assets had increased much more rapidly in India. It more than tripled in India in two decades, from 7 to 24 percent, while in the United States it took three-quarters of a century to achieve a proportionally similar increase from 5 to 14 percent. (This difference is obviously not extrapolatable.) The difference in the movement of the share of private corporations is even larger, declining by fully 6 percentage points, or over one-fourth in the United States, but increasing in India by 3½ percentage points, involving an increase by over 130 percent. The level of the Indian share of not much over 6 percent in 1970 was, however, still below two-fifths of the contemporary American ratio, and it is a safe prognostication that it is not likely ever to reach it. The story is different, however, for financial institutions. Here the share in national assets increased by nearly 10 percentage points in the United States, or by nearly 85 percent, while it advanced in India by only 2½ percentage points, or not much over 40 percent, though the average annual rates of increase in the shares was more than twice as high in India with 1.8 percent than in the United States with 0.8 percent. The level of the Indian share in 1970 of less than 9 percent was still below one-half of the contemporary level in the United States, though it approached the American level at the turn of the century of 11 percent.

The differences in the changes in the sectoral distribution of tangible assets are very similar to those in national assets. On the other hand, there are considerable differences in the distributional change for financial assets and liabilities, which can be followed in table 65. In particular, the share of financial institutions in both declined slightly in India between 1950 and 1970, while it increased in the United States between 1900 and 1975 by about 15 percent of national assets, or by about over three-fifths and over two-fifths, respectively, of the starting value of the ratio. As already mentioned, this lag in the development of financial institutions in India is connected with the high and increasing share of the central government as a lender, which is also reflected in the sharp increase in the share of the government in financial assets by 18 percent of national assets to over one-fourth of the total, or to more than three times the 1950 level. In the United States, in contrast, the share of the government in financial assets remained very small, hardly exceeding 4 percent even in 1975. The changes in the sectoral distribution of debt are equally pronounced and reflect the same forces. Thus the share of financial institutions increased in the United States by 13 percentage points, or by over two-fifths of the 1900 level, reaching nearly 45 percent in 1975, while it declined slightly in India, falling in 1970 to not much over one-fourth of total debt. Quite differently, the share of domestic public debt in India, mostly owed by the central government, rose by 20 percentage points to nearly one-half of total debt in 1970, 70 percent above the 1950 level; whereas in the United States the increase in public debt of eight percentage points, though more than doubling the 1900 proportion, left it still below one-sixth of total debt.

g) Selected Balance Sheet Components

The tables in Appendix B make it possible to compare intercountry differences in the sectoral distributions of individual assets and liabilities, including corporate equity and net worth, in the 1970s. These comparisons, however, are affected by differences in the classification, definition, and sometimes valuation of the various components. Complete, or even nearly complete, standardization in these respects was beyond the resources of this study and would probably require close collaboration with the authors of the primary flow of funds data used, i.e., generally the central banks' statisticians. For this reason discussion is limited to two important and well-defined types of financial assets, corporate stock and government debt.

i) Corporate Stock

Corporate stock has been selected for discussion because it is of considerable interest for financial analysis, because of its supposed usability as an indicator of economic power, and because it is reasonably consistently defined in different countries. It should be noted, however, that the statistics used refer to the market value for stocks listed on exchanges and to presumably similar estimates for other stocks, but not to their adjusted book value (price-adjusted value of assets less liabilities) which almost always differs from market value, and often to a considerable degree, and to an extent varying among countries and over time.

Before evaluating the sectoral distribution of corporate stock shown in table 66, it is necessary to look at the importance of corporate stocks within a country's financial structure, measured by the relation of their market value to that of all financial assets. Large intercountry differences then appear, the share in the 1970s ranging from 6 percent in Germany (partly explained by omission of G.m.b.H.'s), 7 percent in Japan, 8 percent in India, and 10 percent in Great Britain, and approximately 15 percent in France and the United States. The ratios are considerably lower than they were two to three decades earlier in Great Britain and Germany with one-sixth around 1960, India with 8 percent in 1950, and Japan with 12 percent in 1964, though not in the United States, where the sharp decline in the ratio occurred between the abnormal peak of 1929 of over one-third, one of the highest values of the share of corporate stock in financial assets ever observed, and the end of World War II, the ratio having fallen to 16 percent in 1945, hardly above that for 1975.

Turning to the intercountry differences in the sectoral distribution of corporate stock, variations are even larger. In the late 1970s the share of the household sector broadly defined, which in this case should be almost identical with that of the narrower concept of nonfarm households, ranged from fully one-fifth in France, Germany, and India via one-third in Japan to nearly one-half in Great Britain and the United States. The ratios for Great Britain and the United States, though now by far the highest among the six countries, are substantially below previous levels, the decline in the last two decades amounting to approximately one-fifth of their level in the 1950s. In the United States, the only country where the movements of the ratio can be traced back for another half century, the share of households was near three-fourths in 1900, and it is likely that it was then approximately as high in most developed countries.

The decline in the share of households is offset, and sometimes more than offset, by the increase in that of financial institutions. Here again intercountry variations are wide. In the late 1970s the share of financial institutions was below one-tenth in Belgium and France and in the neighborhood of one-eighth in Germany, but above one-fourth in the United States and around two-fifths in Great Britain, India, and Japan. These ratios do not by themselves provide a measure of the influence of financial institutions over the corporate nonfinancial economy. Many other factors would have to be taken into account such as the types of institutions owning corporate stock; the concentration of the holdings among financial institutions; the types of stock held by them; the legislation and practices regarding the voting by banks of their customers' shares kept with them for safekeeping; the dependence of corporations on external financing; the extent of the institutions' representation on the corporations' boards of directors; the relations between the stockholdings by financial institutions and the credit extended to and the deposits of, and the offering of, securities by the corporations whose stock is held in the institutions' portfolios; and many other institutional features of the

Table 66 Sectoral Distribution of Corporate Stock in 10 Countries in the 1970s

	Year	Share in Financial Assets (1)	Share of: Households (2)	Unincorporated Business (3)	Nonprofit Organizations (4)	Nonfinancial Corporations (5)	Government[a] (6)	Financial Institutions (7)	Rest of the World (8)
1. Belgium	1976	8		85			9	6	...
2. Canada	1978	9		68		2	1	20	9
3. France[b]	1976	16		24		35	20	8	13
4. Germany[b]	1977	6	21		40		10	12	17
5. Great Britain	1975	10		43		11	3	39	4
6. India	1970	8		21		5	22	37	15
7. Italy	1977	5		6		30	30	13	21
8. Japan	1977	7		30		24	1	45	...[d]
9. Norway	1978	3		29			42	14	12
10a. United States	1900	21		73		20	...	7	5[e]
10b. United States	1975	14	47		3	20[c]	...	27	3

Note: Brackets in the original join columns: Belgium 85 covers cols. 2–5; Canada 68 covers cols. 2–4; France 24 covers cols. 2–4 too; Germany 40 covers cols. 3–5; Great Britain through Japan cover cols. 2–4; Norway 29 covers cols. 2–5; 10a 73 covers cols. 2–4; 10b 47 covers cols. 2–3.

[a]Including government enterprises except in Great Britain and in the United States.
[b]Includes corporate bonds.
[c]Eilbott (in Goldsmith 1973, 431) for 1953; rough estimate for 1975.
[d]For listed corporations less than 3%.
[e]Based on data in Lewis 1938.
Source: As for table 60.

situation. Thus it certainly cannot be asserted that German financial institutions have less influence on the corporations of which they own some stock than their British counterparts because statistically their share in all corporate stock is only in the order of one-eighth, while it exceeds one-third in Great Britain or the United States where the share is somewhat above one-fourth. Therefore, changes in the share of corporate shares held by financial institutions cannot, without further research, be interpreted as changes in the influence of the institutions on corporate business policies, though there is a refutable presumption that the two move in the same direction. By this test one would conclude from the figures in table 61 that, for example, the influence of financial institutions has increased in the United States since the turn of the century and in Great Britain and India since the 1950s. This, however, is doubtful in the case of the United States, partly because the statistics do not cover one of the most important sources of financial institutions' influence on large corporations, investment bankers. There can be little doubt that this influence was much more pronounced in 1900, at the peak of the power of the house of Morgan and other leading investment bankers, than in 1975.

Still greater are the intercountry differences in the share of the government in corporate stock outstanding. While the share is negligible or small in four of the 10 countries—Canada, Japan, and the United States, and in Great Britain too outside the nationalized industries—it is substantial in Belgium, Germany, and particularly in France, Italy, India, and Norway. Where a large part of financial institutions are owned by the government, as is the case in France and Italy and to an even larger extent in India, the holdings of these two sectors must be combined to assess the potential, though not necessarily the actual, degree of the government control over private corporate business and particularly over large corporations. When their combined share in all corporate stock nears or exceeds 60 percent, as it has done in India since 1970—compared to a share of not much over 25 percent two decades earlier— and virtually all financial institutions' stock is owned by the government, government control over the sector of large corporations is, at least potentially, almost complete, even disregarding the additional influence exercised by the government through import controls, new issues controls, and allocations of credit. To what extent potential control is actually exercised depends on many factors, among others the relationships between the bureaucracy and business and the political climate (see, for India, Goldsmith 1983a chap. 3).

There are, finally, substantial differences in the share of corporate stock outstanding owned by foreigners, now generally in the form of concentrated direct investment by transnational corporations rather than as before World War I in the form of widely diffused ownership by a multitude of individual investors. The share of foreign owners is now substantial in Canada, France, Germany, India, Italy, and Norway, but low in Great Britain, Japan, and the United States—in Japan as a matter of government policy. It is now, taking the statistics as they stand, in the neighborhood of one-sixth in France, Germany, India, and Italy, the Indian ratio having been cut in half since Independence. For the three European countries, these ratios are very likely considerably higher than they were before World War II, and still more so than before World War I.

The conclusion to be drawn from table 66 and other relevant statistics thus is that over the last half-century, and particularly since World War II, the proportion of all corporate stock outstanding held in the portfolios of individuals has been declining fairly steadily and has by now been reduced to between one-half and one-fifth. Taken together with the reduction of individual's share in corporate bonds outstanding, the epoch of "security capitalism," in its pre–1929 form, is nearing its end in most countries.

ii) Government Debt

The central government debt serves two economic functions apart from its obvious role of financing the government's peacetime or wartime current deficits or its capital expenditures. The first, over a century old, is to provide individual investors and savings and insurance organizations with a standardized risk-free liquid investment. The second, which has increased in importance in the 20th century, is to serve as a tool of monetary policy, a function which finds its primary expression in changes in the holdings of chiefly short- and medium-term government securities by the central bank and the commercial banks issuing check money. The distribution of the government debt among the various sectors, and particularly the share of the monetary institutions, and changes in it, are therefore of great interest for financial analysis. Since this subject is only peripheral to this study it has been treated summarily and superficially. In particular, it has not been attempted to divide the holdings of government securities by financial institutions into those of the banking system and of other financial institutions, nor has it been possible to separate holdings of short-term and other securities. Finally, it has not always been possible to separate the securities of the central government from those of state and local government or even from corporate bonds. This is not too serious a drawback since in most countries the securities of the central government now constitute the majority of all debt securities held by financial institutions.

Table 67 shows, even given the limitations just mentioned, that at the present time financial institutions hold close to or more than half of the

Table 67 **Sectoral Distribution of Central Government Domestic Debt in 10 Countries in the 1970s**

	Year	Share in Financial Assets (1)	Share of: Households (2)	Unincorporated Business (3)	Nonprofit Organizations (4)	Nonfinancial Corporations (5)	Government[a] (6)	Financial Institutions (7)	Rest of the World (8)
1. Belgium	1976	11.5		24			1	73	2
2. Canada	1978	5.6		41		1	1	49	8
3. France[a]	1976	4.7		26		3	6	57	8
4. Germany[a]	1977	7.4	30		6		0	59	5
5. Great Britain	1975	12.5		42		2	0	46	10
6. India	1970	13.7[b]		16		0	23	61	...
7. Italy	1977	15.3		24		6	2	68	...
8. Japan	1977	4.0		10		2	3	85	...
9. Norway	1978	11.4			3		15	53	29
10a. United States	1900	2.1		33		0	0	67	...
10b. United States	1975	9.0		19	0	3	11	55	12

[a]All bonds.

[b]Including gold and silver among financial assets; excluding them the ratios (cf. Goldsmith 1983a, table 3-56) would be 16.3.

Source: As for table 60.

total debt of the central government in all countries. Supplementary evidence indicates that the banking system is the largest holder, followed by insurance and pension organizations (Goldsmith 1969, 162–63). In the United States, for example in 1975, the central bank owned nearly one-third of the total federal debt (including agencies) held by financial institutions, while commercial banks and other financial institutions accounted for fully two-fifths and one-fourth, respectively, disregarding the fully 15 percent held by the Social Security system (Board of Governors 1979, 137; U.S. Bureau of the Census, *Statistical Abstract*, 1978, 337). In Japan in 1977, the commercial banks held nearly one-half and the central bank and nonbank financial institutions fully one-fourth each (Bank of Japan 1978, 79–80). In Great Britain, on the other hand, the holdings of other financial institutions in 1975 with 30 percent of the total outstanding were almost twice as large as those of the banking system (Pettigrew 1980, 91–92). Except in India, most of the remainder is held by the household sector, its share of total central government debt outstanding ranging from about one-tenth in Japan and one-sixth in India to nearly one-third in Germany and over two-fifths in Great Britain. It is only in India that intergovernmental holdings are large, though the holdings by state and local governments exceeded one-tenth of the total federal debt in the United States. The holdings of business enterprises were minor in all countries. The share of foreign holdings varied greatly. It is now quite substantial—with between one-twelfth and one-eighth of the total—in France, Great Britain, and the United States, the countries with reserve currencies, and also in Canada and Norway, but fairly small, for different reasons, in the other five countries.

Changes in the distribution over the postwar period do not seem to have been significant, though at least in the United States they appear to have continued the previous trends of a decrease in the share of the household sector. The exception is Great Britain where, contrary to the experience in most other countries, the share of the household sector in central government debt increased slightly, partly offset by the sharp reduction of the share of foreign holdings.

In evaluating the level and changes in the distribution of central government domestic debt outstanding, it is well to keep in mind differences in the importance of central government securities in the various countries' total financial assets, a proportion which now varies from as little as 4 percent in France and Japan, to one-sixth in Great Britain, India and Italy. This proportion has shown wide variations in the past, in particular increasing sharply, though in part only ephemerally, during wars, accompanying a generally downward trend which can be followed in the country tables in Appendix A and has been discussed briefly in Chapter 3, 4.d.

2. The Structure of Sectoral Balance Sheets

This section is limited to sectoral balance sheets tied in with a national balance sheet, with the exception of Canada for which a recent aggregative balance sheet of the household sector exists that is not paralleled by balance sheets of the other sectors. Thus the numerous balance sheets of the household sector, or of parts of it, which are derived from sample surveys of households but usually do not cover all types of assets and liabilities, are omitted.

a) The Household Sector

Table 68 shows aggregative balance sheets for the household sector in seven countries. Balance sheets are presented, with the exception of the United States, for only one postwar year, though comparable estimates are available for some recent years in France, Great Britain, India, Japan, and the United States, generally from the same sources. Comparable annual balance sheets for earlier periods are available only for the United States, where they go back to the early 1950s (Goldsmith, Lipsey, and Mendelson 1963; Ruggles and Ruggles 1982). The data thus would permit, given space and time, a much more substantial discussion of the changes in the balance sheets of the household sector in the postwar period. In most countries the balance sheets refer to the household sector broadly defined. Balance sheets for non farm households alone exist only for the United States and Canada.

The first characteristic of the balance sheets of the household sector is the low ratio of debt to assets and the correspondingly high net worth ratio. For the six countries liabilities on the average between 1970 and 1977 amounted to only one-eighth of assets, with a range from 5 percent in India to 17 percent in the United States, although the figures include the debt of unincorporated enterprises. In the United States these now account for only fully one-fifth of the debts of the broadly defined household sector, but at the turn of the century their share was close to two-thirds (Goldsmith 1982, 52). As is known from the evidence of sample inquiries of household finances, the countrywide averages are the result of fairly wide differences among individual households, though households with a debt ratio of over one-fourth of assets are rare, except among households with very few assets or debts in excess of assets. In the five countries where the necessary information is available, mortgages, mostly on homes, account for on the average about three-fifths of total debt. Most of the rest consists of consumer credit, in developed countries mostly for the purchase of consumer durables, in India to a considerable extent for noneconomic purposes such as weddings and funerals. In the

Table 68 **Structure of Balance Sheet of Household Sector in Seven Countries in the 1970s[a]**

	Canada 1970 (1)	France 1976 (2)	Germany 1977 (3)	Great Britain 1975 (4)	India 1970 (5)	Japan 1977 (6)	United States 1900 (7)	United States 1975 (8)
I. Tangible assets	46.3	72.8	68.8	58.7	75.6	65.0	66.4	56.2
1. Land	10.0[b]	12.1	27.6	13.0	41.1	44.5	25.3	16.7
2. Dwellings	23.3	45.6	30.4	28.0	16.8	12.0	18.8	18.2
3. Other structures	6.3	3.4	...	2.3		4.0	5.4	8.9
4. Equipment	...	2.8	...	1.6	17.7	...	2.4	2.2
5. Inventories and livestock	...	2.4	...	1.1		0.7	7.9	1.3
6. Consumer durables	6.7	6.4	10.8	12.7		3.8	6.7	9.0
II. Financial assets	53.7	27.2	31.2	41.3	24.4	35.0	33.4	43.8
1. Gold and silver	...	...	...	...	10.0	...	...	...
2. Currency and demand deposits	10.0	6.4	2.7	14.6	6.3	24.7	3.6	3.0
3. Other deposits	5.4	12.9	15.1				3.8	12.7
4. Insurance and pension claims	12.3	2.0	6.6	10.0	3.3	4.1	1.9	9.7
5. Bonds	7.9	1.9	3.4	5.4	2.2	2.9	4.2	3.6
6. Corporate stock	12.4	3.8	1.7	7.4		2.8	11.7	9.2
7. Loans	5.6	0.3	1.6	3.8	2.4	...	7.8	1.6
8. Other		...			0.1	0.4	0.4	3.9
III. Total assets	100.0[c]	100.0	100.0	100.0	100.0	100.0	100.0	100.0
IV. Liabilities	13.0	8.2	13.2	11.4	5.3	13.4	13.4	17.0
1. Consumer credit	5.0	...	0.9	1.7	...	...	0.6	3.3
2. Mortgages	5.9	6.6	11.6	7.3	...	...	6.6	10.2
3. Other	2.1	1.6	0.7	2.4	...	...	6.2	3.5
V. Net worth	87.0	91.8	86.8	88.6	94.7	86.6	86.6	83.0

[a]Includes unincorporated business enterprises except in Germany. [b]One-fourth of value of dwellings and other structures including land.
[c]Equity in unincorporated business (12% of total amounts) eliminated.
Source of basic data: col. 1—Davies (1979), 242; cols. 2–8—country tables in Appendix B.

only country for which the debt ratio can be traced back before World War II, the United States, the ratio has shown only slight and irregular movements since the turn of the century, rising from 13 to 17 percent as part of the increase in consumer debt was offset by a reduction in bank debt incurred largely by unincorporated business.

Probably the most significant relationship on the asset side of the household sector's balance sheet is the division between tangible and financial assets. Here intercountry differences are large. While tangible assets constitute not much over one-half of the total in the United States, though they include the substantial holdings of farmland, and in Great Britain, their share rises to close to or above two-thirds in France, Germany, India, and Japan. The high ratios reflect either, as in India, a high share of agriculture in the economy; or, as in Japan, an extraordinarily high level of nonagricultural land prices; or, as in Great Britain and particularly in France, high values of residential structures. These factors also help to explain the division of tangible assets between land and reproducible assets shown in table 68. The share of land averaged one-fourth of all tangible assets in five of the six developed countries, but is much higher in Japan—a hard to believe full two-thirds. Among reproducible tangible assets, dwellings predominated to the extent of on the average three-fifths with a range from one-half or less in India and the United States to about two-thirds in the other five countries. The ratios for nonresidential structures, equipment, and inventories, three categories attributable mainly to unincorporated enterprises, showed considerable intercountry variations, in particular that for nonresidential structures. Not all of the ratios for the three categories may be significant because of differences in the coverage and errors of estimation in the underlying figures, but they partly reflect the different importance of unincorporated business, particularly agriculture. Variations in the share of consumer durables were wider, ranging from one-eighth in France to one-fourth in the United States. The high American figures are not astounding, but the low value for France is puzzling.

Turning to the structure of the financial assets of the household sector, two fairly distinct groups of countries emerge, and the differences between the broader and the narrower concepts are much less important that that for tangible or total assets. The first group, made up of Canada, Great Britain, and the United States, is characterized by a share of deposits of about one-third of total financial assets, a share of insurance and pension funds in the neighborhood of one-fifth, and a share of corporate stock of also about one-fifth. In the other group of countries, consisting of France, Germany, Italy, India (if financial assets are defined narrowly to exclude gold and silver), and Japan, deposits dominate the portfolio, accounting for between less than one-half (India) and over two-thirds (France, Japan) of the total. In all of these countries the share of corporate stock is very low, averaging less than one-tenth of the portfolio, though ranging from 5 percent in Germany to over 20 percent in the United States and Canada. The share of bonds, mostly government securities, averaged slightly over one-tenth, with a range from 7 to 13 percent. The share of other financial assets, which include mortgages and other loans, varied widely, in part because of different coverage in the seven countries. The relatively high, though declining, ratio in India reflects the importance of loans to farmers made by noninstitutional lenders belonging to the household sector broadly defined. It has been sharply reduced during the 1970s, partly because of legislation freezing or even writing off outstanding loans and partly as a result of a large increase in other financial assets of households. At the present time their share in the total portfolio of households is unlikely to exceed a few percentage points.

The basic contrasts in the structure of the financial assets of the household sector in these two groups of countries reflect long standing differences in at least their saving habits, in the character of their financial institutions, in the structure of yields, and in government policies. An adequate treatment of these differences would require a separate study.

It is interesting to follow trends in the portfolio structure of households in the United States since the turn of the century as they have greatly altered its character (Goldsmith, Lipsey, and Mendelson 1963, 2:72 ff.). The two outstanding movements have been the substantial decline of the share of corporate stock from over one-third to one-sixth of the portfolio, and the practical disappearance of loans, mostly mortgages, which in 1900 accounted for one-fifth of total financial assets. These have been offset by the sharp increases in the share of insurance and pension claims from 5 to 15 percent of the total, and by the near-doubling of that of saving-type deposits from one-eighth to well over one-fifth, contrasting with the decline of the share of money from 12 to fully 4 percent. The share of bonds was cut in half from 14 to 6 percent and its structure changed radically. In 1900 government securities, about evenly divided among federal and state and local issues, represented one-fourth of the bond portfolio, corporate bonds, mainly those of railroads, three-fourths. Three-quarters of a century later, the relations were reversed. Government securities now accounted for seven-eighths of the total, of which two-thirds were federal issues and one-third state and local government securities, prized by wealthy investors because of their exemption of their interest from income tax, while corporate and foreign bonds had been reduced to one-sixth of the total bond portfolio (Goldsmith 1982, 45).

Changes in the portfolio structure during the postwar period showed the same tendencies in Germany, Great Britain, India, and Japan as in the United States, namely, increases in the shares of saving-type deposits and particularly of insurance and pension claims.

What we see here at work is the institutionalization of the saving process and of the portfolios of individual investors, which has been in progress since World War I and has been accelerated since the 1930s, continuously reducing the sphere of direct financing, where the issuers of securities sell them directly through the investment banking machinery or through the open market to individual investors rather than placing them with financial institutions, as is becoming more and more common. The process has gone so far in most countries that direct financing is limited to small proportions of all new issues of corporate and foreign securities, and to still somewhat larger but generally minor shares of those of the government. Indeed there is in many countries not much room left for a further reduction of the share of net direct security investment by the household sector.

France is the only country in which changes in the structure of the balance sheet of the household sector can be followed for well over a century. However, the available balance sheets, shown in table 69, are incomplete, not covering equipment, inventories, livestock, and consumer durables—four categories that in 1976 were equal to less than one-sixth of the included components, though two of them (livestock and inventories) were considerably more important at earlier dates. There is a clear break in trend between the period running from the middle of the 19th century to World War II and the postwar period. Between the middle of the 19th century and World War I the share of real estate declined sharply from three-fifths to two-fifths. That of rural real estate alone fell from nearly one-half to one-fifth of the total, while the share of urban real estate increased from one-eighth to nearly one-fifth, almost to parity with the rural component. Among financial assets, whose share increased from two-fifths to over three-fifths, the proportion of securities rose sharply—not unexpectedly in a period which has been characterized as security capitalism—from one-eighth to over two-thirds. At the same time, and this is a specific characteristic of the French system, foreign securities came to constitute at the eve of World War I one-third of the entire portfolio. After relatively small changes in the interwar period—except for the shrinkage in the share of foreign securities—the downward drag on fixed face value claims exercised by almost continuous inflation and the rise in the relative prices of real estate combined to lift the share of real estate, now predominantly urban, to well above the level prevailing in the interwar period; and to increase it during the postwar period from fully one-half to over two-thirds, almost 10 percentage points above what it had been in the mid-19th century. The changes among financial assets were even more spectacular. The share of securities fell sharply

Table 69 Structure of Household Wealth[a] in France, 1851–1976

	1851 to 1855 (1)	1878 to 1885 (2)	1892 to 1895 (3)	1913 (4)	1928 (5)	1946 to 1950 (6)	1963 (7)	1975 (8)	1976 (9)
I. Real Estate	59.2	53.2	52.2	38.7	39.4	53.0	58.0	72.3	68.4
1. Rural	46.4	38.2	32.2	20.2	. . .	25.3	. . .	11.8	15.0[c]
2. Urban	12.8	15.0	20.0	18.5	. . .	27.7	. . .	60.5	53.4
II. Financial assets	40.8	46.8	47.8	61.3	60.6	47.0	42.0	27.7	31.6
1. French securities	4.9	8.6	23.1	28.1	33.4	18.5[b]	16.5[b]	6.2	6.6[b]
2. Foreign securities			8.0	14.1		3.6	0.5		
3. Other	35.9	38.2	16.7	19.1	27.2	24.9	25.0	21.5	25.0
III. Total assets %[a]	100.0	100.0	100.0	100.0	100.0	100.0	100.0	100.0	100.0
Total assets bill. fr.[a]	72.2	146.0	206.6	233.0	. . .	. . .	. . .	3000[d]	4637[d]

[a]Does not include equipment, inventories, livestock, and consumer durables.
[b]Of which stocks 10.7 in col. 6, 12.8 in col. 7, 4.5 in col. 9.
[c]Rough estimate based on data in INSEE, *Le Patrimoine National* (1979), 25.
[d]New francs.

Sources:

Cols. 1, 2 Théry (cited in Michalet [1968], 96–97); line I divided on basis of estimates of Pupin (1916) for 1853 and 1878;
Cols. 3, 4 Théry (col. 3) and Lescure (col. 4) cited in Michalet (1968);
Cols. 5–7 Michalet (1968), 232; split of lines I and lines II-1 + 2 based on data for 1949 and 1962-63, *op. cit*, 237, 242.
Col. 8 Babeau and Strauss-Kahn (1977), 67, based on sample enquiries rather than as the other columns on aggregative macroeconomic statistics;
Col. 9 Benedetti et al. (1979), 48.

from nearly one-half in the late 1940s to one-fifth in the mid-1970s; foreign securities almost disappeared from the portfolio; and the share of corporate stocks in all securities rose from less than one-half to over two-thirds, though they lost in importance in relation to all financial assets (declining from well over one-fifth to one-seventh), and still more so compared to total covered household assets, namely, from fully one-tenth to less than 5 percent.

b) Nonfinancial Corporate Business

After some experimentation, it was concluded that the balance sheets of the nonfinancial corporate sector assembled in Appendix B were not sufficiently detailed or homogeneous to provide the basis for an international comparison. There exist, of course, in all the six countries for all or much of the postwar period, fairly detailed aggregations of balance sheets of corporations in a usually substantial number of industries, derived from either the corporations' tax returns or from their reports to regulatory agencies or stockholders. All of them, however, suffer from being based on book values and hence understating, to a degree increasing with the inflation starting in the mid-1960s but differing from country to country, the share of land, structures, and equipment as well as of net worth in total assets. While it is not impossible to adjust for this bias, and this has occasionally been undertaken, to do this for the six countries was beyond the resources available for this study.

c) The Government Sector

The scope and structure of the government sector in the seven countries covered in this section, as it is reflected in their balance sheets, varies so much among them, particularly with respect to the coverage and valuation of government enterprises and of the stock of military assets, that an adequate intercountry comparison would have required an unfeasible degree of detailed analysis of the sources and methods of the available figures, and a degree of familiarity with the peculiarities of the individual countries' government accounting and budgetary practices not possessed by the author. The omission of the sector from this section's discussion is, of course, regrettable in view of its increasing and now in most countries large share in both tangible and financial assets. As these limitations do not apply to government debt, or only to a lesser degree, a brief discussion of the importance of government debt among the various countries' financial instruments (and in this case for all 20 countries covered by this study and not only for the postwar period) has already been presented in Chapter 3, 4.d, while Section g.ii of this chapter has reviewed the sectoral distribution of the government debt in 10 market economies.

d) Financial Institutions

In the case of financial institutions, it has again proven possible to go beyond the countries for which sectorized national balance sheets are available, and to present in table 70 a comparison of the structure of all financial institutions, excluding only Social Security funds, in 13 of the 20 countries for one year between 1971 and 1977, omitting, beyond the Soviet Union and Hungary, Denmark, Israel, Mexico, South Africa, and Switzerland, for which no comprehensive figures are readily available. The balance sheets used for eight of the 13 countries included in table 70 are in the standardized form published by the Organization of Economic Cooperation and Development, though the standardization is in some instances formal rather than substantive. These figures are in most cases superior for international comparisons to the data available in national sources and used in the national balance sheets in Appendix B. While the entries for Australia, Canada, France, Germany, and India had to be taken from national sources, they should be of about the same quality as for the eight countries, although there were some problems in adapting the data to the OECD classification, and it was not easily possible except in Canada to determine the share of government securities held. Since the OECD statistics are limited to financial assets and liabilities, the tangible assets owned by financial institutions were omitted for all 13 countries, though the footnotes indicate their relative size where that information is available from other sources. While the omission of tangible assets is not serious for an analysis of balance sheet structure, since they do not seem to account for more than 7 percent of financial assets in any country, it affects net worth by absolutely the same amount, but relatively in much larger proportion. Indeed, the relation of net worth to liabilities that can be derived from lines II and III of table 70 has no economic meaning without adjustment for the omission of tangible assets.

The structure ratios shown in table 70 are, of course, weighted averages of similar ratios for the various types of financial institutions that make up the total. They are thus determined by the balance sheet structures of the different types of institutions that vary substantially and systematically, central and commercial banks having high ratios of short-term assets and liabilities while long-term assets and obligations predominate among saving and insurance organizations. It is not possible nor essential here to present structure ratios for the different types of financial institutions, but they can be derived in virtually all cases from the sources identified in the notes to table 70.

One of the main differences among countries in the portfolio structure of financial assets of financial institutions, and a significant one, is the share of funds made available to the government, except in Canada and the United States predominantly the central government, and in some countries to its enterprises. This share ranged among the 11 countries for which its value is shown in table 70, from about one-eighth in Canada, Great Britain, and Sweden, to about one-forth in Australia, Belgium, and Japan, and to over one-third in India, with an average of fully one-fifth, disregarding the extremely low share in Yugoslavia which is due to the fact that most of the other funds are made available to government or collective enterprises.

The ratio of cash and deposits, which is an indication though not an exhaustive measure, of interfinancial relations, varies widely, partly because of differences in netting practices in the statistics. It exceeds one-tenth in Belgium, Canada, France, Great Britain (two-thirds of the extremely high ratio of nearly one-third representing deposits with foreign financial institutions), and Italy, but keeps below 5 percent in Germany, India, Japan, and the United States.

The share of assets in the form of corporate stock (apparently excluding the shares of government enterprises) also shows a wide scatter around the average of only 4 percent. The share ranges from not much over 1 percent in Belgium, Italy, and Norway, to 6–7 percent in Australia, Canada, and the United States, and to 11 percent in Great Britain, reflecting the relatively high share in the assets of all financial institutions of insurance organizations, which keep a substantial part of their funds in stocks. It has already been pointed out that ratios such as this one cannot be used without considerable additional evidence to assess the influence of financial institutions on the companies whose shares they hold in their portfolio, and hence on the private corporate sector.

In all countries loans to nongovernment borrowers, including in some cases government enterprises, constitute the largest single asset. Their share in total assets ranges from fully one-third in Great Britain and Italy to three-fourths in Germany, averaging slightly above one-half for the 13 countries. The share is generally below the average in countries where government debt makes up a large proportion of the portfolio (e.g., Australia, Belgium, India, and Italy) or where international short-term assets are very large (Great Britain).

The crucial distinction between short-term and long-term uses of funds cannot be made for all countries, even apart from the fact that formally long-term instruments like bonds and, to a much lesser extent, mortgages need not actually be held until maturity, while some formally short-term loans may actually remain for long periods on the books of the lenders. The relationship between short-term and long-term engagements, including all nongovernment bonds in the latter category, but excluding all

Table 70 **Structure of Financial Assets and Liabilities of Financial Institutions in 13 Countries in the 1970s (Total Financial Assets = 100.0)**

	Australia 1973 (1)	Belgium 1976 (2)	Canada 1978 (3)	France 1976 (4)	Germany 1977 (5)
I. Financial assets[a]	100.0	100.0	100.0	100.0	100.0
1. Gold and IMF claims		2.7	1.4	5.2	5.0[g]
2. Cash and monetary transferable deposits	5.4 (lines 1–2)	14.1	8.0 (lines 2–3)	2.4	0.2
3. Other deposits	. . .	1.2		8.6	3.4
4. Short-term loans (excluding 7)	45.4 (lines 4–5)	21.9	31.5	23.3	15.5
5. Long-term loans excluding 7		20.0	24.9	47.8[d]	60.0
6. Bonds	5.5	8.6	5.4	9.5	13.7[d]
7. Government debt	25.5	24.6	14.3	. . .[e]	. . .[e]
8. Shares	6.2	0.7	5.8	3.2	2.2
9. Other claims	11.9	6.1	8.8	. . .	. . .
II. Liabilities[a]	103.0	98.6	93.4	92.0	97.2
1. Cash and transferable deposits	47.0 (lines 1–2)	35.1	55.3 (lines 1–2)	20.7	14.8
2. Other deposits		28.1		44.5	53.3
3. Short-term borrowing	5.6	3.1	4.4	4.9	0.3
4. Long-term borrowing	. . .	. . .	0.1	7.2	0.2
5. Bonds	19.4	15.7	3.0	8.0	16.8
6. Insurance and pension liabilities[a]	24.9	8.6	17.6	5.6	11.0
7. Other liabilities	6.0	8.0	13.1	1.1	0.8
III. Net worth[b]	−3.0[c]	1.4	6.5	8.0[f]	2.8

[a]Does not include social security funds assets and liabilities.
[b]Excludes tangible assets.
[c]Tangible assets 5.9%.
[d]Includes claims against government.
[e]Included in lines I.4–I.6.
[f]Tangible assets 6.8%.
[g]All international assets of central bank.
[h]Assumed equal to assets of insurance and pension organizations.
[i]All corporate securities.
[j]Included in line I.6.
[k]All borrowing.
[l]Included in line II.3.
[m]Tangible assets 1.1.
[n]Mostly borrowing from government.
[o]Tangible assets about 1%.
[p]Mostly claims against and liabilities to financial institutions.

Great Britain 1977 (6)	India 1971 to 1972 (7)	Italy 1977 (8)	Japan 1977 (9)	Norway 1977 (10)	Sweden 1976 (11)	United States 1977 (12)	Yugoslavia 1976 (13)
100.0	100.0	100.0	100.0	100.0	100.0	100.0	100.0
...	...	2.6	...	0.8	0.6	0.4	0.1
4.1	4.6	10.1	2.1	8.1	4.8	2.2	5.7
32.3		6.6	0.6		3.0	0.6	18.8
24.0	46.9	22.6	61.8	55.6	9.5	23.2	
12.8		13.1			51.3	30.3	38.0
2.1	10.5[i]	13.6	4.5	13.8	12.0	13.9	0.5
14.0	35.3	29.4	23.3	17.7	12.7	15.2	7.5
10.8	...[j]	1.2	2.8	1.0	3.2	7.4	...
...	2.7	0.8	4.9	3.0	2.9	6.8	29.4[p]
94.8	96.8	96.3	99.5	92.6	90.2	93.7	95.2
14.1	54.1	35.4	20.3	48.6	12.0	12.4	28.6
56.4		31.2	47.2		35.5	37.0	23.0
6.3	11.6[k]	6.8	11.4	19.1[n]	0.6	4.0	0.2
0.3	...[l]	3.3			6.1	0.4	9.0
0.5	8.1[i]	13.6	6.1	11.5	21.9	7.0	0.5
15.1[h]	16.5	1.7	7.9	10.1	10.5	19.5	...
2.1	6.4	4.3	6.6	3.3	3.6	13.5	33.9[p]
5.2	3.2[m]	3.7	0.5	7.4	9.8	6.3[o]	4.8

Source of basic data:

Col. 1	Supplied by Research Department of Reserve Bank of Australia.
Cols. 2, 6, 8–13	*OECD Financial Statistics*, 11, 1 (1977) for Yugoslavia and 12, 1 (1978) for the other countries.
Col. 3	Reserve Bank of Canada for credit institutions; *IFSYB* 1979, for life insurance companies; pension funds not included.
Col. 4	Benedetti et al. 1979, 48.
Col. 5	Deutsche Bundesbank 1978, 161.
Col. 7	Venkatachalam and Sarma 1976, table 1.

funds made available to the government, averages fully two-thirds for the seven countries for which table 70 provides the necessary data, but ranges from one-seventh in Sweden and about one-fifth in Germany to over 1½ in Great Britain, partly because of the large international short-term business of British banks. Bonds account on the average for fully one-fourth of all long-term loans in the six countries which provide the information, the share fluctuating between less than 15 percent in Great Britain and one-half in Italy. Since in most countries only a small proportion of nongovernment bonds outstanding is held by noninstitutional investors, the intracountry differences in this ratio, as well as in the share of nongovernment bonds in the total assets of financial institutions, are essentially determined by the size of the supply of such bonds. This, in turn, depends on the relative importance of privately owned public utilities (railroads now being government owned in most countries) and of mortgage banks, in most countries the two most important groups of issuers of nongovernment bonds.

The equally significant relations between short-term and long-term liabilities is generally similar to that between short- and long-term assets for the average ratio for seven countries—about one-to-two—but sometimes quite different for individual countries.

Appendices

Appendix A brings together the national balance sheets of the 20 countries covered by this study, which I have been able to construct on the basis of existing estimates of components of tangible national wealth and of financial assets and liabilities or from my own estimates. The tables are preceded by a short discussion of the character of sources, limitation of the estimates, and distinctive features of the balance sheets. They are followed by source notes the length of which depends on the ease or difficulty of constructing the balance sheets from the basic data, the number of balance sheet dates covered, the importance of the country, and the time the notes were written, the more recent write-ups being more detailed than the earlier ones. The source notes have been omitted and the comments sharply reduced for the countries on which I have published articles or books dealing with their financial development or their national balance sheets, i.e., for Belgium (Goldsmith 1975a; Goldsmith and Frijdal 1975), Germany (Goldsmith 1976), India (Goldsmith 1983a), Japan (Goldsmith 1983b), Russia/USSR (Goldsmith 1964), United States (Goldsmith 1952, 1954, 1982; Goldsmith, Lipsey, and Mendelson 1963), and Yugoslavia (Goldsmith 1975a).

In order to provide as much comparability as possible over time and among countries, the national balance sheets are shown in the form of percentages of total national assets (tangible, financial, and foreign assets) rather than as the original absolute figures expressed in different currencies and at widely varying price levels. The absolute figures for total national assets, however, are shown in every case in order to enable the user, who so desires, to approximate the original estimates.

For the same reason the classification of assets is not the same as that used in the original estimates, where they range in number from less than a dozen to half a hundred. Instead, the original estimates have been rearranged into a standardized classification, which distinguishes eight types of tangible assets and 12 types of financial instruments. In some cases, several components of the standard classification had to be combined because the original estimates did not provide the necessary detail. In others, two or more components in the original more detailed estimates had to be allocated to one item of the standard classification. The content of any one of the components of the standard classification is thus not entirely uniform among countries, and sometimes not even between the estimates of one country at different benchmark dates. These differences are not likely to be large enough to interfere seriously with international or intertemporal comparisons. In some cases warning notes have been added.

The tables of Appendix B that deal with sectoral balance sheets are generally limited to the main economic sectors, namely, households (usually including nonprofit institutions), central government, state and local governments, farm and nonfarm unincorporated enterprises (often combined with households), nonfinancial corporations, and the rest-of-the-world sector. The often significant government enterprises are unfortunately but rarely separated from either the government or the nonfinancial corporate sector, a deficiency which interferes with international and sometimes also with intertemporal comparability. The breakdown of financial institutions into up to two dozen subsectors, which is available for several countries in the postwar period, has been omitted as requiring too much space, having interest mainly to specialists, and being easily accessible. Had data and space permitted, I would have liked to show separately the figures for the three subsectors most interesting for economic and financial analysis, monetary authorities, the banking system, and other financial institutions.

In a few countries and for a few benchmark dates, "notional" values for one to three components of tangible assets (land, inventories, consumer durables) and for one important financial asset (trade credit) have been entered usually by analogy with available figures for similar countries or other benchmark dates. These figures have no independent existence. They are used primarily to permit the derivation of an estimate of total tangible and financial assets, and hence of national assets, which is required as the denominator of the balance sheet structure ratios, that form the core of the analysis. Notional values are never used for fixed reproducible assets, which generally contribute the largest and for economic analysis one of the most important components of the national balance sheet, or for the assets of financial institutions, government debt, or corporate securities.

I regret that for most countries I have had to use estimates of my own making which I have prepared over the last quarter of a century, as no others were available. The increasing recent interest in national balance sheets leads me to hope that if such a review of the field is repeated in a decade or two the estimates of a solitary worker will be replaced by more detailed and better founded calculations by statistical organizations or individual scholars in the different countries; and will be available for a larger number of countries, not only as one aggregate for the entire nation but also for the main economic sectors, as an integral part of their system of national accounts.

Since neither this appendix nor this study are intended as a catalogue raisonné of all existing estimates of national balance sheets, I have not regarded it as necessary to reproduce or discuss the few other national balance sheets which have come to attention—and some of whose components have occasionally been used—all except one of which refer to one or a few dates in the postwar period, such as several ones for Great Britain (Mason 1976; Morgan 1960; Pettigrew 1980; Revell 1967; Rothman 1974; Stone and Roe 1971), one for India (Joshi 1966), and three for the United States (Dickinson and Eakin for 1929; Board of Governors of the Federal Reserve System 1979, excluding government sector, annually since 1945; Ruggles and Ruggles 1982, annually from 1947 to 1981.

Abbreviations

The following abbreviations will be used in source notes for text tables and in Appendices A and B:

AEM	Secretaria de Presupuestos y Programacion (Mexico), *Anuario Estadistico de los Estados Unidos Mexicanos*
ASF	Institut National de la Statistique et des Etudes Economiques (France), *Annuaire Statistique de la France*
ASI	Istituto Centrale di Statistica (Italy), *Annuario Statistico Italiano*
HS	U.S. Bureau of the Census, *Historical Statistics of the United States*
HSN	Statistisk Sentralbyrå (Norway), *Historisk Statistikk*, 1978
IFS	International Monetary Fund, *International Financial Statistics*, monthly
IFSYB	International Monetary Fund, *International Financial Statistics Yearbook*
LN	League of Nations, *Statistical Yearbook*
NK	Tsentralnoie Statisticheskie Upravleunie (USSR), *Narodnoie Khosiaistvo SSSR*, annually
SA	U.S. Bureau of the Census, *Statistical Abstract of the United States*, annually

SAB	Central Statistical Office (Great Britain), *Annual Abstract of Statistics*
SAD	Det Statistiske Department (Denmark), *Statistik Årbog* (annually)
SAI	Central Statistical Office (Israel), *Statistical Abstract of Israel* (annually)
SAN	Statistisk Sentralbyrå (Norway), *Statistisk Årbok*
SAS	Statistika Centralbyrån (Sweden), *Statistisk Årborg för Sverige*
SJD	Statistisches Bundesamt (West Germany), *Statistisches Jahrbuch für die Bundesrepublik Deutschland* (monthly)
SÖ	Statistisk Sentralbyrå (Norway), *Statistiske Översikter* (monthly)
SYBUN	United Nations, *Statistical Yearbook*
YNAS	United Nations, *Yearbook of National Accounts, Statistics*

Appendix A National Balance Sheets for 20 Countries

1. Australia

As Australia does not have the benefit of an official capital stock estimate for even recent years, and the Reserve Bank's calculations of the stock of financial assets and liabilities are of a fairly recent date, the construction of a national balance sheet is more difficult and precarious than for most other countries at a comparable state of economic and financial development. It has therefore not been possible to present national balance sheets for any date before World War II, mainly because of the absence of the necessary data for financial assets and liabilities of the business sector and for the value of land.

Changes in the structure of the national balance sheet over the past three decades were, as table A1 shows, substantial. The financial interrelations ratio has decreased sharply from nearly 1.30 in 1947, when it still reflected the effects of wartime inflation, to not much over 0.60 in 1977, a low value for a developed country. Among financial assets, the share of financial institutions has advanced substantially from one-third to fully two-fifths. On the other hand the share of government domestic debt has been cut in half from well over one-fourth to not much over one-eighth, while that of corporate stock has shrunk from 14 to 8 percent. The changes in the structure of tangible assets are characterized by the declines in the share of land from fully one-fifth to one-eighth, and of inventories and livestock from 13 to 8 percent, both reflecting primarily the declining importance of agriculture. On the other hand, the share of nonresidential structures and equipment has increased from a little over two-fifths to nearly three-fifths.

Table A1 National Balance Sheet of Australia, 1947–1977 (National Assets = 100.0)

	1947 (1)	1956 (2)	1965 (3)	1973 (4)	1977 (5)
I. Land	9.6	9.3	7.5[c]	7.2	7.8
1. Agricultural	...	...	...	...	...
2. Other	...	...	...	...	...
II. Reproducible tangible assets	34.0	46.9	51.2	47.4	54.6
1. Structures	21.8	28.5	...	...	...
a) Residential	8.1	9.7	10.6	9.9	12.4
b) Other	13.7	18.8 }	31.7	29.6	35.3
2. Equipment	4.4	6.4 }			
3. Inventories	3.8	4.6	3.7	3.4	3.9
4. Livestock	1.8	2.4	1.9	1.5	0.8
5. Consumer durables	2.3	5.0	3.3	3.0	2.2
III. Tangible assets	43.6	56.2	58.7	54.6	62.4
IV. Monetary Metals	0.2	0.2	0.1	0.1	0.2
V. Financial assets[a]	54.7	43.0	40.2	44.0	37.0
1. Claims[b] against financial institutions excluding 2	15.1	11.6	11.2	13.1	12.1
2. Insurance and pension claims	3.3	3.3	3.3	4.3	3.6
3. Loans by financial institutions	9.3	7.4	9.0	11.4	10.6
4. Government domestic debt	15.6	10.9	7.5	5.9	5.1
5. Corporate bonds	0.5	0.5	0.4	0.5	0.4
6. Corporate stock[a]	7.8	6.5	6.2	6.5	3.0
7. Trade credit[a]	0.9	1.0	0.9	1.0	0.9
8. Other financial assets	2.2	1.8	1.6	1.3	1.3
VI. Foreign assets gross	1.5	0.7	0.9	1.3	0.5
Foreign assets net	−3.5	−2.7	−2.6	−1.7	−1.6
VII. National assets %	100.0	100.0	100.0	100.0	100.0
National assets $A bill	32.2	77.4	160.6	348.0	643.0
VIII. Gross national product; $A bill.[d]	4.1	10.8	20.8	51.3	90.0

[a]Excludes noncorporate trade credit and stocks not traded on Sydney stock exchange.
[b]Including equity.
[c]Private land only.
[d]Year-end rate.

Source of basic data:

Lines I and II	1947, 1956	Garland and Goldsmith 1959, 345.
Line I	1965	Helliwell and Boxall 1978, table 3.
	1973, 1977	Rough estimates, assuming land/reproducible tangible wealth ratio to decline slightly.
Lines II.1.a and 5	1965, 1973	Helliwell and Boxall 1978, table 3.
	1977	Rough estimate assuming ratio to structures and equipment to be same as in 1973.
Lines II.1.b and 2	1965–77	Obtained by adding to 1956 figures net expenditures on structures and equipment (from national accounts; see *YNAS*, var. issues) in constant prices reflated to current prices and subtracting lines II.1.a.
Line II.3	1965–77	Derived as lines II.1.b. and 2, using gross national product deflator.

Line II.4	1965–77	Extrapolated on basis of 1956 value and change in numbers and average slaughter value of cattle and sheep (Australian Bureau of Statistics, *Yearbook Australia* 1977–78, 321, 327, 329 and 735).
Line II.5	1965, 1973	Helliwell and Boxall 1978, table 3.
	1977	Rough estimate assuming same relation to reproducible tangible assets as in 1973.
Line III	1947–77	*IFSYB* 1979, 92–93.
Lines V.1 and 2	1947, 1956	Estimated on basis of figures for 1948 and 1960 (Goldsmith 1969, 504).
	1965–77	Reserve Bank of Australia 1979.
Line V.3	1947, 1956	Assumed equal to 60% of lines V.1 and 2, slightly below the 1965 ratio.
	1965–77	Reserve Bank of Australia 1979.
Line V.4	1947	*IFS* (January 1960), 46.
	1956–77	*IFSY* 1979, 92–93. Figures for local and other government debt in 1973 and 1977 estimated to move in line with those of commonwealth and states; figures for 1965–77 include small amounts of foreign debt of local and other governments.
Lines V.5 and 6	1947, 1956	Rough estimates.
	1965–77	Reserve Bank of Australia 1978, 8; adding increase in trade credit after 1965 to estimated stock in 1965.
Line V.7	1947–65	Rough estimates assuming same relation to national product as in 1973.
	1973, 1977	Reserve Bank of Australia 1978, 8.
Line V.8	1947–77	Rough estimates putting "other" financial assets in 1947, 1956, and 1965, at 4% of identified financial assets, the ratio derived from flow-of-funds accounts for 1966/67 to 1970/71 (Reserve Bank of Australia 1979, ii ff.).
Line VI	1947	Rough estimate.
	1956–77	Communication from Reserve Bank of Australia. Figures cover only direct investments, foreign holdings of Australian government securities, and Australian holdings of foreign exchange.
Line VIII	1947	*SYBUN* 1957, 2–3; estimate of national income increased by 17%, the ratio in the early 1950s.
	1956–77	*IFSYB* 1982, 96–97.

2. Belgium

For the financial analyst and historian interest in Belgium centers on the 19th century, when Belgium was one of the first countries, and the first small country, to industrialize and to develop a modern financial superstructure, particularly of investment banking institutions. The statistical data for the 19th century, though more abundant than for some other European countries, leave unfortunately much to be desired once the sphere of financial institutions is left. At the time of writing, the volumes of the large-scale quantitative economic history of Belgium from Independence to World War I edited by Professor Lebrun were not yet available; once they are, some revisions in some of the estimates will have to be made. (For a less compressed discussion, see Goldsmith 1975a and Goldsmith and Frijdal 1975.)

The balance sheet of table A2 shows, as is to be expected, a sharp decline between 1850, when the modern age in the Belgium economy and its financial superstructure may be said to have already been well under way, and 1913 in the share of tangibles in national assets from four-fifths to not much over one-half; in the share of land in tangible assets from over one-half to less than one-fifth; and a sharp gain in the importance of financial institutions evidenced by the increase in their share in national assets from as little as 2 percent to 10 percent, and possibly even more significantly from one-tenth to one-fourth of total financial assets outstanding. Also noteworthy is the high proportion of net foreign investment, amounting in 1913 to 8 percent of national assets, about one-seventh of national wealth and nearly one-fifth of financial assets, reflecting the position of Belgium as one of the earliest exporters of capital on a substantial scale, and only to a minor extent to its Congo colony.

Compared to the changes in the national balance sheet structure in the half-century before World War I, those occurring in the following period of approximately equal length are less striking. The share of financial in national assets was not higher in 1976 than it had been more than 60 years earlier, and the share of land in tangible assets was the same. Within financial assets, however, the share of financial institutions continued its upward trend, though at a somewhat slower pace, doubling from one-fourth in 1913 to about one-half since the late 1960s, due mostly to the expansion of the banking system. Foreign assets held their own through the 1930s in relation to domestic assets. After having almost been wiped out by World War II and the loss of the Congo, they regained the reasonably high share of 5 percent in the 1970s.

Table A2 **National Balance Sheet of Belgium, 1850–1976 (National Assets = 100.0)**

	1850 (1)	1875 (2)	1895 (3)	1913 (4)	1929 (5)	1939 (6)	1948 (7)	1965 (8)	1973 (9)	1976 (10)
I. Land	43.5	23.2	16.3	9.8	9.1	8.1	10.2	16.6	10.5	9.8
II. Reproducible tangible assets	36.2	49.2	48.3	42.7	45.7	42.4	44.5	40.5	39.9	44.4
1. Structures	...	...	...	...	...	...	...	23.7	...	...
a. Residential	...	...	...	...	...	...	13.4	13.4	14.6	15.2
b. Other	...	...	...	...	...	... }	22.5	10.4 }	17.5	22.0
2. Equipment	...	...	...	...	...	... }		9.3 }		
3. Inventories	...	...	...	...	...	...	3.0	2.7	2.8	2.5
4. Livestock	...	...	...	...	...	...	0.9	0.7	0.6	0.4
5. Consumer durables	...	...	...	...	...	...	4.6	4.1	4.4	4.2
III. Tangible assets	79.7	72.4	64.6	52.5	54.8	50.5	54.7	57.2	50.3	54.2
IV. Monetary metals	...	...	0.5	0.5	0.7	2.7	1.4	1.1	1.3	0.9
V. Financial assets	20.3	27.6	30.2	39.4	38.4	39.3	41.4	38.6	42.9	40.0
1. Claims against[a] financial institutions	2.2	5.3	7.0	10.4	9.7	14.7	13.5	17.8	22.2	20.8
2. Loans by financial institutions	1.4	2.8	3.0	4.7	4.9	3.9 }	3.4	7.1[b]	8.2[b]	8.0[b]
3. Mortgages	2.2	2.5	2.8	2.4	2.4	1.8 }				
4. Government debt	5.1	4.3	6.7	6.9	7.6	10.1	13.5	10.1	9.2	8.4
5. Corporate bonds	0.0	1.5	1.6	2.2	0.5	1.0	0.3	0.5	0.6	0.6
6. Corporate shares	6.5	6.5	5.1	8.3	7.9	3.5	4.5	3.0	2.7	2.1
7. Trade credit	2.9	4.0	3.5	3.8	4.5	4.2	6.1	[c]	[c]	[c]
8. Other	0.0	0.6	0.5	0.7	0.9	...	...	[c]	[c]	[c]
VI. Foreign assets, net	...	...	4.7	7.7	6.1	7.5	2.5	3.1	5.4	4.9
VII. National assets %	100.0	100.0	100.0	100.0	100.0	100.0	100.0	100.0	100.0	100.0
National assets bill. fr.	13.8	32.3	43.0	84.6	821	764	2447	6925	14625	22365
VIII. Gross national product; bill. fr.[c]	1.3	3.3	3.8	8.0	94	80	343	881	1947	2748

[a]Includes equity.

[b]Lines V.2 and 3 include lines V.7 and 8.

[c]Year-end rate except in cols. 1–6.

(Source of basic data on following page)

Source of basic data:

Cols. 1–7:

Lines I–VIII:	Goldsmith 1975, 221, 225, 229; for col. 7 lines I.1–5 Goldsmith and Frijdal, 1975, 193.

Cols. 8–10:

Line I	Extrapolated on basis of estimates for 1964 and 1971 (Goldsmith and Frijdal 194, and indices of prices of agricultural and residential land (Institut National de Statistique *Statistiques des Mutations Immobilières* 1975, var. issues).

Col. 8:

Lines II.1–3	Goldsmith and Frijdal, 193; cols. 9 and 10 extrapolated from 1971 value (ibid.) on basis of gross capital expenditures in current and 1970 prices and depreciation allowances in current prices (*YNAS* 1977).

Cols. 8–10:

Line II.4	Estimates of Institut d'Economie Agricole *Cahiers de l'IEA*, var. issues.
Line II.5	Institut National de Statistique *Bulletin Statistique* (October 1979).
Line IV	Derived from data on quantity of gold holdings of monetary authorities, gold prices, and exchange rates in *IFSYB* 1979, 40 ff.
Lines V, VI	Banque Nationale de Belgique, *Bulletin d'Information et de Statistique*, table XII-1B, var. issues.
Line VIII	*IFSY* 1981, 112–13.

3. Canada

For the last two decades the outside constructor of national balance sheets for Canada needs to estimate only the value of nonagricultural land and, for some dates, that of consumer durables since Statistics Canada provides annual estimates of the stock of reproducible tangible assets other than consumer durables, of the value of agricultural land, and of the financial assets and liabilities of about two dozen sectors and subsectors.

The situation was quite different before 1961 when the flow-of-funds statistics started. While an annual calculation of the assets of financial institutions goes back to 1870 (Neufeld 1972), there is very little information on other financial instruments. Unofficial estimates of the stock of reproducible assets other than consumer durables are available back to the mid-1920s (Hood and Scott 1957), but there are no data for the value of land except census figures for a few benchmark years. It should therefore be possible without prohibitive labor, though with a substantial margin of error, to construct an unsectorized balance sheet for Canada back to 1926, but the task was beyond the resources of this study except for the one year 1955, chosen because it is the only date for which an estimate for all reproducible assets is available. (Hood and Scott 1957, 196). Table A3 is, therefore, regretfully limited to such a balance sheet for four benchmark dates between 1955 and 1978. It is thus possible to follow changes in Canada's tangible and financial wealth only for the last quarter-century, i.e., a period throughout which Canada was economically and financially fully developed.

The changes in the structure of Canada's national balance that can be observed in table A3 are moderate. Thus the financial interrelations ratio remained near 1.20 at the four benchmark dates, fairly high ratios for developed countries, attesting to the existence of a complex and comprehensive financial superstructure. Within tangible assets the share of land stayed close to fully one-fifth, though it showed a tendency to rise, reflecting advances in land prices exceeding those of the general price level. Among reproducible assets the share of dwellings advanced slightly to about one-fourth, while that of consumer durables stayed from the mid-1960s on close to one-tenth.

Changes in the structure of financial assets, on the other hand, were not negligible. Thus the share of claims against financial institutions rose from fully one-fourth to one-third. This was due mainly to the rapid expansion of nonbank institutions, while the share of insurance organizations in the assets of financial institutions was halved from well over one-third to not much over one-sixth. The same tendency is reflected in the increase of the share of loans made by financial institutions, particularly mortgages. In contrast, the importance of government and of corporate securities declined sharply. The share in total financial assets fell from nearly one-fifth to less than one-eighth for government securities and from nearly 15 to 9 percent for corporate stock. At the same time Canada's foreign investment position improved considerably as net liabilities declined from over 10 to less than 6 percent of tangible assets.

Table A3 National Balance Sheet of Canada, 1955–1978 (National Assets = 100.0)

	1955 (1)	1965 (2)	1973 (3)	1978 (4)
I. Land	8.0	10.9	10.8	11.4
1. Agricultural	1.7	1.6	1.4	1.6
2. Other	6.3	9.3	9.5	9.8
II. Reproducible tangible assets	37.6	35.0	34.6	35.5
1. Structures and equipment	28.7	28.4	28.7	29.8
a) Residential	8.5	7.8	8.5	8.9
b) Other	20.2	20.7	20.2	20.9
2. Inventories[a]	3.2	2.8	2.3	2.1
3. Livestock	0.7	0.5	0.5	0.3
4. Consumer durables	5.1	3.4	3.2	3.3
III. Tangible assets	45.7	45.9	45.4	46.9
IV. Monetary metals	0.5	0.3	0.2	0.3
V. Financial assets	50.7	50.8	51.0	50.0
1. Claims against financial institutions[b]	13.5	14.5	16.7	17.0
a) Banks	6.3	5.7	7.1	7.5
b) Insurance organizations	4.8	3.8	3.3	3.0
c) Other	2.4	4.9	6.4	6.5
2. Loans by financial institutions	}	3.7	3.1	3.9
3. Consumer credit	} 8.8	1.6	1.6	1.7
4. Mortgages	}	4.1	4.8	5.3
5. Government securities	10.4	8.1	6.6	6.5
6. Corporate bonds	2.4	2.3	2.0	1.7
7. Corporate stock	7.9	5.7	4.6	4.6
8. Trade credit	2.6	2.3	2.4	2.5
9. Other financial assets[c]	5.0	8.5	9.1	6.9
VI. Foreign assets gross	3.2	3.1	3.5	3.0
Foreign assets net	−5.0	−4.9	−3.1	−2.8
VII. National assets %	100.0	100.0	100.0	100.0
National assets $C bill.	227	472	1055	2185
VIII. Gross national product; $C bill.[d]	30.3	58.6	136	245

[a]Excluding grain stocks (0.4 in 1973).
[b]Including equity but excluding tangible assets.
[c]Residual; mostly claims against associated enterprises.
[d]Year-end rate.

Source of basic data:

Line I.1	1955–78	Estimates of Agriculture Division of Statistics Canada.
Line I.2	1955–78	Assumed to bear same proportion to nonagricultural structures and equipment as in United States (Goldsmith 1982).
Line II.1	1955	Hood and Scott 1957, 196.
	1965–78	Estimates of Statistics Canada; figures refer to midyear.
Lines II.2 and 3	1955	Hood and Scott, 196.
	1965–78	Estimates of Statistics Canada; inventories do not cover grain stocks, which in 1973 amounted to one-sixth of inventories included.
Line II.4	1955	Hood and Scott, 196.
	1965–73	Estimates of Bank of Canada.
	1978	Estimated at four times year-end rate of expenditures on consumer durables.
Line IV	1955–78	Derived from *IFSYB* 1979, 40–43, 128–29.
Line V.1	1955	Assumed equal to assets of financial institutions (Neufeld 1972, 529).
	1965–78	Flow-of-funds statistics of var. issues; Bank of Canada.
Lines V.2–4	1955	Estimated on basis of 1965 ratio of lines V.2–4 to line V.1 and ratio of claims on private sector to total assets of chartered banks and life insurance as shown in *IFSYB* 1979, 128–29.
	1965–78	As for line V.1 (also applies to lines V.6–9 and VII).
Line V.5	1955	Urquhart and Buckley 1965, 203–4.
Line V.6	1955	Assumed to bear same relation to national product as in 1965.
Line V.7	1955	Moved in line with industrial stock price index (*IFSBY* 1979, 128–29), with some additions to allow for new capital issues.
Line V.8	1955	Assumed to bear same relation to inventories as in 1965.
Line V.9	1955	Assumed to bear same relation to sum of lines V.1–8 as in 1965.
Line VI	1955	Urquhart and Buckley, 169.
Line VIII	1955–78	*IFSYB* 1981, 136–37.

4. Denmark

While no national balance sheet has ever been published for Denmark, the country's official statistics and one outside study (Bjerke and Ussing 1958) provide more material for the construction of national balance sheets over the last century than is the case in many other countries. Thus the stock of structures can be estimated on the basis of both the perpetual inventory method back for the entire period—which can be applied also to the stock of equipment and to inventories—and for its second half on the basis of comprehensive statistics of assessed valuations, which also cover land values. Financial statistics permit fair estimates of the assets of and loans by financial institutions and of government securities and somewhat less satisfactory ones for mortgages. This leaves land for the first half of the period for rough estimation with substantial margins of error among major components, livestock, consumer durables, trade credit, and the market value of corporate stock, though it includes comprehensive statistics of nominal capital for almost the entire period. Occasional information on book values and stock price indexes permit fairly satisfactory though synthetic estimates.

Because of their large size and their importance in establishing growth trends and crucial balance sheet relations, the estimates of the value of the stock of structures deserve a more detailed discussion. The study of Bjerke and Ussing (1958) provides annual estimates of gross capital expenditures on structures and on equipment in current and constant prices from 1870 to 1952, which can be continued to the present from the official national accounts. The main problem is the reduction of these figures from a gross to a net basis. In view of the irregularity of the

1. After the estimates of table A-4 were completed, my attention was drawn to estimates of tangible assets published on an annual basis for the period starting in 1950 by *Finanstidende*. They have not been used because the methods of estimation are not known; they do not separate land from structure values; they do not provide separate figures for equipment, inventories, and livestock; and because they may not be comparable with the estimates of table A4 for 1948 and earlier benchmarks. While the level of the estimates of *Finanstidende* for total tangible assets are reasonably close to those of table A4 (they exceed them for the average of the four common benchmark dates of 1960, 1965, 1973, and 1978 by 3½ percent), they differ in trend, increasing between 1960 and 1978 at an annual rate of nearly 14 percent against a rise by less than 13 percent for the estimates of table A4. Moreover, there are substantial differences between most of the components for which figures are provided in both sets of estimates. Thus the level of the estimates of *Finanstidende* are considerably higher for all land and structures together, and since the middle 1960s for consumer durables, but are substantially lower for the total of equipment, inventories, and livestock.

depreciation allowances in Bjerke and Ussing's study and of the fact that depreciation allowances in the national accounts are published only in current prices and probably are based on original costs, it has seemed preferable to reduce gross to net stock by applying the ratios that correspond to the rates of growth in constant prices and to the assumptions of an average life of 20 years for equipment and of 50 years for structures (see Goldsmith 1962, 19), namely, 0.55 for equipment and 0.60 for structures. This approach has the additional advantage that it is not subject to short-term fluctuations, except in the implicit deflators, and is closer to producing figures of the value of the capital stock at full utilization.

The figures derived by the perpetual inventory method can be compared in the case of structures from the 1920s on with the comprehensive statistics of assessed valuations. It is then found that for the benchmark dates 1929 and 1938 the perpetual inventory estimates are a little less than 10 percent below the assessed valuations. In 1948, in contrast, the perpetual inventory estimate is about 60 percent above assessed values, mainly because of the apparent failure of assessed values to reflect the sharp increase in prices during and in the first years after World War II, and partly because the assessed variations refer to March 31 while the perpetual inventory estimates are calculated for the end of the year, a lag which may account for a difference of as much as 5 percent. In the middle sixties the two estimates almost coincide. For the end of the period (for which the assessed value must be estimated on the basis of the figures for March 31, 1977) the perpetual inventory estimate is 12 percent above the assessed value. Part of the difference is probably due to the fact that assessed values are slightly below market values. Thus in 1973 one-family homes sold on the average at 16 percent above their assessed value (SAD 1975, 85). It may also be that the ratio of net to gross value of 0.6, which has been used in the perpetual inventory calculation, is somewhat above the ratio implied in assessed values. The correspondence between the two sets of figures is, however, not quite as satisfactory in the 1970s if the two main types of structures are separated. In that case the perpetual inventory estimate in 1978 is close to assessed values for dwellings, but is fully one-fourth above them for other structures.

In table A4 the estimates of the value of structures derived from the apparently reliable figures on capital expenditures since 1870 have been used, partly because they are at least comparable over the entire period and with the estimates of the stock of equipment for which no assessed values are available. The assessed values for structures, available only since 1920 and not exactly for the benchmark dates, are show below (in bill. kr.) to enable the user who prefers them to substitute them for the perpetual inventories estimates of table A4.

	All Structures	Dwellings[a]
March 31:		
1927	8.1	...
1936	10.1	...
1950	20.2	...
1960	51.2	...
1965	109.0	52.4
1973	294.2	147.2
1977	275.2	304.1

[a]Include one-half of combined residential and business properties
Source: *SAD* 1973, table 55; 1979, tables 59 and 60.

The limitations of the estimates of some, or most, of the other components of the national balance sheet will be evident from the compressed description of their derivation and sources in the notes to table A4. They are most serious, to repeat, among quantitatively important items, for land before 1929; consumer durables, inventories, and trade credit for the entire period; and corporate stock until 1929.

The national balance sheet of Denmark tells no dramatic story but rather reflects the development of a fairly typical Western European country over the past century.

Thus the financial interrelations ratio has been high in international comparison throughout the period, averaging for the nine benchmark dates between 1880 and 1978 fully 1.20. What is unusual is not the increase in the ratio over the first half of the period but the extraordinarily high level reached in 1913 (1.41) and 1929 (1.55) and the sharp decline in the following 30 years (1.12 in 1948). During the postwar period, when the statistics are more reliable, the ratio has shown no trend, keeping fairly close to slightly above unity, with an average of 1.13 for the four benchmark dates between 1948 and 1978.

The main change in the structure of tangible assets has been, as in all countries, a pronounced decline in the share of land from over one-third of the total in 1880 to one-seventh a century later, all of the decline occurring before 1948. This movement was due exclusively to the precipitous fall of the share of agricultural land from over 25 to 3 percent, mostly again before 1948. The share of nonagricultural land was practically the same—about one-tenth of total tangible assets—in 1978 as it had been a century earlier, though there were some deviations in both directions, particularly the reduction of the share to 7 percent in 1948 and 1960 and its higher level in 1973, which may in part reflect shortcomings of the statistics used.

Among reproducible tangible assets structures accounted for an increasing share of the total, rising fairly steadily from fully two-fifths early in the 20th century, to nearly one-half from the 1929 to 1948 benchmarks, to over three-fifths in 1978. Of the postwar rise by 16 percentage points, dwellings accounted for over one-half and by 1978 came to account for well over one-fourth of all reproducible tangible assets—against probably not more than one-eighth a century earlier—and about 45 percent of all structures. The share of equipment showed relatively almost as large an increase as structures—from about one-sixth in 1880 to one-third in 1948. The decline to a share of one-fourth during the postwar period can be explained by the much less rapid rise in the price of equipment, as reflected in the increase in the implicit deflator of the national accounts, between 1948 and 1978 by an annual average of 3.9 percent compared to one of 7.1 percent for construction and one of 6.2 percent for national product. In terms of constant prices the stock of equipment increased in the postwar period considerably more rapidly (at a rate of 5.3 percent per year) than that of either dwellings or other structures (3.9 percent).

All other components of reproducible tangible assets lost in relative importance except consumer durables, whose share, difficult to measure, showed no trend. The decline was particularly pronounced in the case of livestock, which fell from nearly one-fourth before World War I to about one-tenth in the interwar period and by the late 1970s was down to 2 percent, having moved until World War II at a relatively high level in international comparison, which reflected the important role of animal husbandry in the Danish economy. Most of the decline in the share of inventories—from about 10 percent from 1900 to 1960, to 4 percent in 1978—occurred in the 1970s.

The capital-output ratio has shown considerable decadal variations, which are partly explained by the different degrees of capacity utilization at the various benchmark dates, but no secular trend. It averaged 3.7 for the 10 benchmark dates between 1880 and 1978, rising substantially between 1880 and 1913, staying close to the average from 1929 to 1965, and moving erratically in the 1970s. The relatively high value in 1978 is due in part to the below-average rate of capacity utilization; roughly adjusted for it the value is very close to the secular average. The ratio of reproducible tangible assets to national product, on the other hand, has shown a definite upward trend, particularly between 1880 and 1913, averaging 3.0 for the century and between 1913 and 1965, and reaching 3.7 (about 3.1 roughly adjusted for low capacity utilization) in 1978.

Financial instruments have increased much more rapidly than national product—from a ratio of 3.4 in 1880 to one of 4.7 a century later—but the increase culminated in 1913 and 1929, when the ratio exceeded six, and has kept in the neighborhood of four since the late 1940s. The ratio of financial instruments to tangible assets, in contrast, failed to show a definite secular trend, but exhibited an upward bulge from 1900 to World War II.

The changes in the financial superstructure have been dominated, as in all countries, by the increasing importance of financial institutions. The share of their assets in all financial instruments rose from about one-third from 1900 to 1929 to over approximately two-fifths in the 1950s and by 1978 was close to one-half, indicating that allowing for duplications among financial institutions they were either lenders or borrowers in over four-fifths of all financial instruments. The share of the banking system in the assets of financial institutions showed a continuous and pronounced decline from over two-thirds in 1880 to two-fifths a century later, interrupted only as in many countries in the 1940s. The gainers were primarily mortgage lending and insurance and pension institutions.

Mortgages have always constituted a relatively large proportion of all financial instruments. They averaged one-fourth of all financial instruments for the 10 benchmark dates, reached their peak with nearly one-third early in the 20th century, fell below one-fifth from World War II to 1960, and recovered to over one-fourth in the late 1970s. The share of government debt has been moderate throughout the period without secular trend, exceeding one-tenth only for a brief period after World War II. Trade credit, which has been estimated to follow the movements of inventories, has declined sharply in importance since the 1960s, but before World War II kept fairly close to 6 percent of all financial instruments. The share of corporate stock, after averaging nearly one-fifth of all financial instruments between 1880 and 1929 and one-tenth in the following three decades, has fallen to 6 percent in 1978, one-third of the share one century and less than one-half of that of 40 years earlier, a movement found in many other countries.

Table A4 National Balance Sheet of Denmark, 1880–1978 (National Assets = 100.0)

	1880 (1)	1900 (2)	1913 (3)	1929 (4)	1938 (5)	1948 (6)	1960 (7)	1965 (8)	1973 (9)	1978 (10)
I. Land	17.6	12.9	10.9	10.0	9.9	5.4	5.5	7.5	7.8	6.8
1. Agricultural[a]	12.8	7.2	5.5	5.0	4.5	2.3	1.9	1.7	1.6	1.4
2. Other	4.8	5.7	5.5	5.0	5.4	3.1	3.6	5.8	6.2	5.4
II. Reproducible tangible assets	29.6	31.1	30.6	29.2	34.6	41.8	45.2	41.3	36.7	40.9
1. Structures	11.0	13.2	12.6	14.4	16.3	19.2	19.5	20.0	18.9	25.5
a) Residential	...	...	...	...	...	7.9	7.8	7.8	8.4	11.5
b) Other	...	...	...	...	...	11.3	11.7	12.2	10.5	14.0
2. Equipment	4.6	6.3	6.0	6.5	9.6	14.0	13.8	12.5	10.4	10.5
3. Inventories	4.4	3.5	3.0	3.1	3.3	3.8	4.7	3.3	2.3	1.6
4. Livestock	7.3	6.1	7.2	3.3	3.2	2.4	2.5	1.7	1.6	0.8
5. Consumer durables	2.2	1.9	1.8	1.9	2.2	2.4	4.8	3.7	3.5	2.6
III. Tangible assets	47.3	43.9	41.5	39.2	44.2	47.2	50.7	48.9	44.5	47.6
IV. Monetary metals	0.8	0.5	0.4	0.3	0.2	0.1	0.2	0.1	0.2	0.1
V. Financial assets	49.3	55.5	57.5	59.0	54.2	51.3	46.7	48.9	53.2	50.3
1. Claims against financial institutions[b]	14.1	18.6	20.0	20.4	21.7	21.7	19.7	23.0	24.9	24.7
a) Banks	9.7	10.7	10.3	10.4	10.1	12.7	10.7	10.3	10.5	9.9
b) Insurance	} 4.4	7.9	9.8	10.0	11.6	3.6	3.7	3.5	3.4	3.3
c) Other						5.4	5.3	9.2	11.1	11.5

Table A4 (Continued)

	1880 (1)	1900 (2)	1913 (3)	1929 (4)	1938 (5)	1948 (6)	1960 (7)	1965 (8)	1973 (9)	1978 (10)
2. Loans by financial institutions[c]	4.6	4.4	4.4	4.1	3.9	4.8	4.8	5.0	5.4	4.3
3. Mortgages	13.8	17.5	17.7	14.9	14.7	9.2	8.0	10.1	14.3	13.4
4. Domestic government debt	2.7	2.5	3.3	3.0	3.0	6.7	3.9	2.4	1.4	2.5
a) Central government	...	1.3	1.6	1.2	1.2	5.7	2.7	1.3	0.2	1.8
b) Other	...	1.1	1.7	1.8	1.8	1.0	1.2	1.2	1.2	0.7
5. Corporate bonds	0.4	0.3	0.3	0.4	0.3	0.4	0.5	0.6	0.8	0.7
6. Corporate stock	9.2	8.8	8.8	13.0	7.3	4.8	5.1	4.4	4.2	3.1
7. Trade credit	4.4	3.5	3.0	3.1	3.4	3.7	4.7	3.3	2.3	1.6
VI. Foreign assets gross	...	...	0.6	1.5	1.4	1.3	2.4	2.3	2.2	2.0
Foreign assets net	2.6	−2.3	−3.3	−0.4	−1.8	−1.5	−0.1	−0.9	−1.7	−2.2
VII. National assets %	100.0	100.0	100.0	100.0	100.0	100.0	100.0	100.0	100.0	100.0
National assets bill. kr.	5.45	11.40	22.66	53.69	68.08	146.5	312.6	544.0	1328	2857
VIII. Gross national product; bill. kr.[d]	0.79	1.36	2.27	5.56	7.58	18.0	43.0	73.2	184	325

[a]Including forests.
[b]Includes equity, i.e., equal to total assets.
[c]Nonmortgage loans to private sector.
[d]Year-end rate.

(Source of basic data on following pages)

Source of basic data:

Line I.1:	
Cols. 1–3	Rough estimates assuming ratio to national product to have declined from 90 to 55%, compared with the 1920 ratio of about 45% in line with the decline of the share of agriculture in national income (Bjerke and Ussing 1958, 144–45).
Cols. 4–10	*SAD* 1979, table 59, interpolated or extrapolated on basis of values for adjacent reporting dates.
Line I.2:	
Cols. 1–3	Estimated at 43% of line II.1, the ratio of the 1920s for nonagricultural structures.
Cols. 4–10	As for line I.1.
Lines II.1 and 2	
Cols. 1–6	Derived by perpetual inventory method on basis of Bjerke and Ussing's estimates of gross capital expenditures in constant prices (150–51) and implicit deflators, assuming net gross ratios of 0.55 for equipment and of 0.60 for structures and net capital stock in 1870 of 1.50 and 0.35 bill. D. kr. for structures and equipment, respectively.
Cols. 7–10	As for cols. 1–6 using figures for capital expenditures from national accounts (*YNAS*, var. issues).
Line II.3:	
Cols. 1–6	Estimated at 30 percent of national product, approximately the U.S. ratio for 1900–1948.
Cols. 7–10	Derived by cumulation and adjustment for price changes of figures of investment in inventories and implicit deflators from national accounts (as for lines II.1 and 2).
Line II.4:	
Cols. 1–5 and 7	Moved on 1948 basis approximately in line with changes in number of livestock (*SAD*, var. issues) and their prices (Det Statitiske Departement 1958).
Col. 6	Rough estimate, based on livestock numbers and U.S. prices per head (Goldsmith 1954, 2:815).
Cols. 8–10	Moved in accordance with implicit deflator of livestock inventories in national accounts, since changes in constant price were very small.
Line II.5:	
Cols. 1–6	As for cols. 7–10, but expenditures on consumer durables assumed to increase from 6 to 9 percent of total private consumption (Bjerke and Ussing, 148–49).
Cols. 7–10	Estimated at four times year-end rates of expenditures on consumer durables as shown in national accounts (*SAD*, var. issues).
Line IV:	
Cols. 1–3	*Statesman's Yearbook*, var. issues.
Cols. 4 and 5	*SYBUN*, var. issues.
Cols. 6–10	Derived from data on gold holdings of monetary authorities, and gold price (*IFSYB* 1981, 44–47).
Line V.1:	
Cols. 1–7	Goldsmith (1969), table D-6.
Cols. 8–10	Sum of assets of different types of financial institutions (*SAD*, var. issues).

Line V.2:
- Cols. 1–5: Estimated at about 40% of line V.1, the 1948 ratio.
- Cols. 6–10: Nonmortgage loans by banks, derived from *IFSYB* 1979, 156–57; and *SA*, var. issues.

Line V.3:
- Cols. 1–10: Based on all mortgages outstanding in 1909 of kr. 3.3 bill. and in 1926 of kr. 7.1 bill. (*SAD* 1914, 114; 1930, 106), movement of mortgage loans held by financial institutions, and assumption that share of noninstitutional mortgages declined over the period from 60% to 20% (the observed ratios are approximately 45% in 1909 and 37% in 1926).

Line V.4.a:
- Cols. 1–3: *SAD*, var. issues.
- Cols. 4 and 5: *SYBUN*, var. issues.
- Cols. 6–9: *IFSYB* 1979, 156–57; figure in col. 6 refers to 1949.
- Col. 10: Figure in col. 9 plus net domestic borrowing.

Line V.4.b:
- Cols. 1–8: *SAD*, var. issues.
- Cols. 9–10: Danmarks Nationalbank (February 1980).

Line V.5:
- Cols. 1–8: Assumed to rise from 2% to 5% of national product, the 1973 ratio.
- Cols. 9 and 10: Estimated at slightly below a total that includes some bonds of financial institutions (Danmarks Nationalbank (February 1980).

Line V.6:
- Cols. 1–7: Nominal value (*SAD*, var. issues, except for rough estimate for 1880), multiplied by ratio of book to nominal value assumed to be between 2 and 3 on basis of ratios for a few years (*SAD* 1961).
- Cols. 8–10: Book value (capital plus reserves) of corporations (OECD, var. issues; for 1978 estimated on 1976 basis).

Line V.7:
- Cols. 1–10: Assumed to be equal to inventories.

Line VI:
- Cols. 1 and 2: Rough estimates extrapolating from 1907 figure (*SA* 1930, 96), on basis of balance on current account (Bjerke and Ussing, table VI).
- Cols. 3–9: *SAD* various issues, e.g., 1930, 96; 1961, 221; 1979, 248; figure in col. 3 refers to 1912.
- Col. 10: Figure for 1976 plus deficit on current account in 1977 and 1978. (*IFSYB* 1979).

Line VIII:
- Cols. 1–6: Mitchell 1975, 781 ff.
- Cols. 7–10: *IFSYB* 1979, 160–61.

5. France

Of all leading countries none probably presents the same difficulties to the constructor of a national balance sheet as France except for the 1970s, for three years of which an almost complete official national balance sheet has recently been published (Benedetti et al. 1979; INSEE 1979). This reflects the absence until very recently of official, or for most of the period even unofficial but generally accepted, estimates of the value of reproducible tangible assets and of land, as well as of official or other estimates of the stock of financial assets. There is almost an oversupply of estimates of some components for the period before World War I (Michalet 1968, 94–95, tabulates 31 of them for dates between 1851 and 1913), estimates that often differ widely and rarely are adequately explained, but the supply dries up so much for the interwar period that it has not been possible to draw up a balance sheet for a benchmark year around 1939 as well as for a year around the turn of the century, and that the estimates for 1950 are very precarious. In this situation the construction of a national balance sheet for any date before the 1970s is like putting together a puzzle from heterogeneous pieces. (The estimates of structures and equipment in the 19th century by the perpetual inventory method being developed by M. Lévy-Leboyer, which will fill this important gap, are not yet published.) As a result the margins of uncertainty in the national balance sheet presented in table A5 are larger before 1972 than in those for most other countries. The relations and their movements shown are nevertheless not likely to misrepresent major trends and are generally in reasonable agreement with what is known from less systematic and comprehensive sources.

The relative growth of France's financial superstructure is reflected in the increase in the financial interrelation ratio from about 20 percent in 1815, when the country's modern part of the superstructure was almost limited to the Banque de France, to nearly unity in 1913, a ratio substantially higher than that of about 80 percent registered after several ups and downs in the mid-1970s. These variations, as well as changes in the structure of financial assets, are strongly influenced by the inflation during and after the two world wars. Within financial assets the share of financial institutions has increased, as in all other countries, sharply and fairly steadily from about 3 percent in 1815 to one-fifth in 1913 and to about one-third in the 1970s. The share of the government debt reflects, of course, the effects of the Franco-German War and of World War I, rising from about one-tenth of all financial assets in 1815 to over one-fifth in 1880 and about one-third in 1929 (and probably considerably more in 1871 and in 1919). The inflation during and following World War II, in which France participated to only a limited extent, on the other hand, reduced the share of government debt to below one-sixth in 1950, and was followed by a further decline to about 4 percent in the mid-1970s.

The movements of the share of domestic corporate securities are interesting, though the precarious nature of their estimation suggests caution in interpretation. The share increased sharply with the development of security capitalism from about one-tenth of all financial assets in 1850 to over one-fifth in 1913; fell sharply in the interwar period, partly because of the effect of inflation on corporate bond holdings; reached a peak of about one-third for corporate stock in 1960, the near-disappearance of corporate bonds again reflecting the effects of inflation on fixed interest claims; and declined steadily as the financial structure renormalized and the role of private corporations in the economy diminished, falling to below one-seventh in the mid-1970s for stocks, with 12 percent approximately the share of 1913, but for corporate bonds with less than 2 percent far below the nearly 5 percent of 1850. Foreign securities, and certainly foreign government bonds, played a larger role in the portfolio of French investors from the third quarter of the 19th century to World War I than in most other countries. They accounted for as much as one-sixth of total financial assets; and exceeded in the early 20th century the holdings of French government securities, mortgages, corporate bonds, or corporate stocks.

The changes in the structure of tangible assets are dominated, as in all countries, by the declining share of agricultural land, whose share was cut in half from one-half in 1815 to one-fourth in 1913 and to about one-tenth in the postwar period. Among reproducible assets the shares of residential structures seem to have declined from about two-fifths in 1815 to fully one-fourth in 1913 and 1929, but to have recovered sharply in the 1960s and 1970s to nearly one-half in the 1970s, though part of the increase may reflect the improved nature of the recent estimates. Other changes are less pronounced, except for the near-disappearance of livestock, which accounted for about one-seventh of all reproducible assets in 1815 and even as recently as 1929 for more than one-twentieth.

Table A5 does not include private gold hoards, since there obviously are no regular statistics. These hoards are, however, undoubtedly not negligible in the national balance sheet, as they have been estimated for 1954 at 18 billion francs (Divisia, Pupin, and Roy 1954, 3:45), or about 2 percent of national wealth, fully 5 percent of financial assets and 3 percent of national assets; and for the end of 1976 at nearly fr. 100 billion (derived from *Pick's Currency Yearbook* 1977/79, 742), equal to more than about 1¼ times the official gold stock, about 1.4 percent of national wealth, 1.7 percent of financial assets, 0.8 percent of national assets, and 2 percent of the assets of the household sector, and hence considerably more of the assets of the upper wealth groups. The ratio may well have been of the same order of magnitude throughout the postwar and interwar periods.

Changes in the structure of the national balance sheet between 1976 and 1979, the latest year for which an official estimate has been published (Milot 1982), have been fairly small. The share of financial units in national assets increased from 44½ to 47½ percent. Among them the share of money declined from nearly 11 to 9 percent and that of long-term credits from nearly 25 to 23 percent while the share of corporate stock increased from 16½ to 19¼ percent. Among tangible amounts the share of structures rose slightly from 64 to 66 percent while that of agricultural and raw urban land fell from 13 to 11¾ percent.

Table A5 **National Balance Sheet of France, 1815–1976 (National Assets = 100.0)**

	1815 (1)	1850 (2)	1880 (3)	1913 (4)	1929 (5)	1950 (6)	1960 (7)	1972 (8)	1976 (9)
I. Land	47.5	45.0	32.6	16.8	14.7	14.7	9.8	12.2	12.8
1. Agricultural	43.4	39.8	28.8	12.8	9.9	7.4	5.4	4.5	4.3
2. Other	4.1	4.2	3.8	4.0	4.8	7.4	4.4	7.6	8.5
II. Reproducible tangible assets	37.3	34.6	31.6	33.8	40.6	49.7	34.9	39.8	41.8
1. Structures	22.1	21.3	18.9	. . .	. . .	29.1	17.8	26.0	27.7
a) Residential	15.3	12.5	11.0	9.5	11.4	15.9	10.5	18.0	19.5
b) Other[a]	6.8	8.9	7.9	17.7	20.8	13.2	7.4	8.1	8.3
2. Equipment	4.1	4.0	4.7			10.4	8.6	6.4	6.8
3. Inventories	5.4	4.7	3.8	3.2	3.8	6.6	4.9	4.2	4.3
4. Livestock	4.1	3.0	2.8	2.1	2.3	0.9	0.8	0.5	0.4
5. Consumer durables	1.6	1.7	1.4	1.4	2.3	2.7	2.7	2.7	2.7
III. Tangible assets[a]	84.8	79.7	64.2	50.6	55.3	64.4	44.6	52.0	54.6
IV. Monetary metals[b]	2.0	2.5	2.1	1.5	1.6	0.4	0.4	0.5	0.5
V. Financial assets[c]	11.8	16.2	28.6	39.3	43.1	35.2	54.9	44.2	40.9
1. Currency and demand deposits	0.5	0.8	3.6	8.4	12.2	9.7	14.3	5.8	4.4
2. Other deposits								8.3	9.3
3. Insurance and pension claims			0.4	1.3	0.6	0.4	0.7	1.2	1.1
4. Loans by financial institutions		0.4	2.0	4.8	6.5	6.8	9.8	9.7	8.7

5. Mortgages	5.4	5.3	4.7	4.0	1.9	2.2	1.5	2.7	3.2
6. Government debt	1.8	4.4	7.8	7.8	14.6	5.5	4.6	1.8	1.9
7. Corporate bonds	...	0.9	4.5	5.5	1.7	0.5	1.5	0.8	0.8
8. Corporate stock	...	1.0	2.7	5.1	2.7	5.1	18.8	9.1	5.4
9. Trade credit	4.1	3.3	2.8	2.4	2.9	4.9	3.8	4.8[g]	6.1[g]
VI. Foreign assets gross	1.3	1.7	5.1	8.5	...	...	...	3.3	3.9
Foreign assets net	0.5	0.5	4.9	7.6	0.8	...	...	−0.7	−0.4
VII. National assets %	100.0	100.0	100.0	100.0	100.0	100.0	100.0	100.0	100.0
National assets[d] bill. fr.[e]	73.7	150.1	317.9	506.0	2631	546	1835	7270	12935
VIII. Gross national product; bill. fr.[e,f]	10.0	12.1	22.4	39.6	310	113	312	1055	1787

[a]Does not include roads which in 1976 are estimated to have represented, without allowance for depreciation assumed to be offset by maintenance, 9% of all tangible assets, and 5% of national assets.

[b]Does not include private gold hoards, but includes silver in cols. 2–4.

[c]Does not include foreign securities, which should be added, proportionately reducing all other percentages.

[d]III + IV + V + VII gross.

[e]Old francs for cols. 1–5, new francs (= 0.01 old francs) for cols. 6–9.

[f]Year-end rate except for cols. 1–4.

[g]Includes other financial assets.

Note: The estimates of cols. 8 and 9 were made before publication of INSEE 1980, but its figures differ only occasionally and slightly from Benedetti, Consolo, and Fouquet and INSEE (1979), which are used in table A5.

(Source of basic data on following pages)

Source of basic data:

Col. 1:

Line I.1	Perroux 1955, 63; close to Mulhall's estimate (1899, 589) of 30 bill. fr., and to Chaptal's (1819, 217 ff.) of also 30 bill. fr. for 1812, including 2.8 bill. fr. for forests.
Line I.2	Rough estimate in line with 1850 relation between lines I.1 and I.2.
Line II.1.a	Mulhall 1899, 589.
Lines II.1.b, 2, 3, 5	Rough estimates based on relationship between national product in 1815 and 1850 of nearly 60% (see estimates INSEE, *ASF* 1966, 359). The resulting figures are for lines 3 and 4 somewhat and for line 5 sharply below Mulhall's estimates.
Line II.4	Extrapolated from col. 3 on basis of livestock number and prices (INSEE, *ASF* 1951, 119* ff., 207* ff.).
Lines IV, VI	Very rough estimates.
Line V	Compares with an estimate of Block (cited in Levasseur 1892, 3:84) of 15 bill. fr. for 1820 for "capital mobilier."
Lines V.1–4	Very rough estimates.
Line V.5	Estimated at 8% of land and structures as in 1850.
Line V.6	INSEE, *ASF* 1966, 494.
Line V.9	Estimated at three-fourth of inventories.
Line VI	Based on Lévy-Leboyer 1977, 15.
Line VIII	Based on figure for 1820 (Lévy-Leboyer, unpublished estimates).

Col. 2:

Line I.1	Official inquiries cited in Dument 1962, 186; figure refers to 1851–53.
Line I.2	Estimated at one-fifth of value of structures.
Line II.1	Estimate for private structures, slightly increased for government structures.
Line II.1.a	INSEE, *ASF* 1914–15, 97; figure refers to 1851–53.
Line II.1.b	Line II.1 less line II.1.a.
Lines II.2 and 5	Rough estimates based on later relationships.
Line II.3	Estimated at about one-half of national product.
Line II.4	As for col. 1.
Line IV	Estimate of Pupin 1916, 110, for 1853.
Lines V.1–3	Assets of financial institutions as estimated by Cameron 1967, iii.
Line V.4	Estimated at one-half of lines V.1–3.
Line V.5	Estimate of Chégarey (cited Vliebergh 1899, 108).
Line V.6	INSEE, *ASF* 1966, 494, for central government. Rough estimate for local government somewhat below ratio of debt to national product in 1885.
Lines V.7 and 8	Based on estimates of Théry 1911, 183–84.
Line V.9	Estimated at about three-fourth of inventories.
Line VI	As for col. 1.
Line VIII	As for col. 1.

Col. 3:

Lines I, II.2, 3, 5, V.4–6.a and 7–9	As for col. 2.
Line II.1.a	Based on Mulhall's estimates for 1873 and 1885. The estimate is compatible with one derived from nonagricultural population and house prices.

Line II.1.b	Rough estimate based on relation between lines I.1.a and I.1.b in other years.
Line IV	Pupin's estimates for 1878 (1916, 110).
Lines V.1–3	Goldsmith 1969, table II-3.
Line V.4	Based on lines V.1–3.
Line V.5	Based on estimate for 1876 of 14.4 bill. (Ministère des Finances, 1878, 101).
Line V.6	Based on data for 1885 (INSEE, *ASF* 1966, 315).
Lines VI and VIII	As for col. 1.
Col. 4:	
Lines I, II.3 and 5, V.1–4, 7, 9	As for col. 3, except that ratio of inventories to national product (line II.3) is reduced to two-fifths.
Lines II.1 and 2	Colson's estimates (cited Carré, Dubois, and Malinvaud 1975, 151).
Line II.4	As for col. 2.
Line IV	Colson 1927, 3, 36a.
Line V.5	Based on Miche'l (*Journal de la Société Statistique de Paris*, 1933, 327, ff) estimate for 1905.
Lines V.7 and 8	Estimate for 1900 (Faure cited by Neymarck 1903, 24), plus (*ASF* 1966, 532), adjusted for change in security prices.
Lines VI and VIII	As for col. 1.
Col. 5:	
Line I.1	Dument 1962, 194.
Line I.2	Estimated at 20% of value of structures.
Lines II.1 and 2	Estimated at 100% of national product for line 1.a and at 180% for lines 1.b and 2, somewhat below the 1913 ratios but still considerably above the 1950 ratios.
Line II.3	Estimated at one-third of national product, approximately the average of 1913 and 1950 ratios.
Line II.4	As for col. 2.
Line II.5	Estimated at 20% of national product, slightly above the 1913 ratio.
Line IV	*SYBUN* 1931–32, 263.
Lines V.1–4, 6, 9	As for col. 3.
Lines V.5, 7, 8	As for col. 4.
Lines VI and VIII	As for col. 1.
Cols. 6 and 7:	
Line I.1	Dument 1962, 185, 187; 1953 figure reduced in line with national produce deflator to yield estimate for 1950.
Line I.2	Estimated at 25% of structures, slightly below the 1972 ratio.
Line II.1.a	Estimate of Carré, Dubois, and Malinvaud 1975, 140 in 1956 prices shifted to current prices on basis of Mairesse's implicit deflator for structures and equipment.
Lines II.1.b	Mairesse, unpublished estimates in current prices. (For estimates in 1959 prices see Mairesse 1972, 201.)
Line II.3	Average of 30% of nonfarm structures and equipment and of national product, the 1972 and 1976 ratios.
Line II.4	As for col. 5.
Line II.5	Four times year-end rate of purchases of consumer durables estimated at 7% (1950) or 9% (1960) of private consumption (*IFSYB* 1979, 184), compared to 10%–12% in 1965–76.

Line IV	Derived from *IFSYB* 1979, 40, 42, 182. Does not include presumably substantial private holdings, estimated by Divisia, Pupin, and Roy (1954, 3, 45) at 18 bill. fr. in 1954.
Line V.1 and 2	Assets of financial institutions except insurance (Goldsmith 1969, table D-8). Figure for 1950 increased by 26% over 1948 figures in source on basis of data on assets of financial institutions *IFSYB* 1979, 182.
Line V.3	Assets of insurance organizations (Goldsmith 1969, table D-8).
Line V.4	Estimated at two-thirds of assets on basis of relations in 1950 and 1960 (*IFSYB* 1979, 182) and 1972 (Benedetti, Consolo, and Fouquet 1979, 47).
Line V.5	Estimated at 14% of value of residential structures (line II.1.a), the average of the 1972 and 1976 ratios, hence excluding all nonresidential mortgages.
Line V.6.a	INSEE, *ASF* 1966, 494, 504 for col. 6; *IFSY* 1979, 184, for col. 7.
Line V.6.b	As for line V.6.a for col. 6; INSEE, *ASF* 1974, for col. 7.
Lines V.7 and 8	Rough estimate for col. 6; U.S. Congress, Joint Economic Committee 1964, 16, for col. 7.
Line V.9	Estimated at 75% of inventories, midway within the range for other developed countries.
Line VIII	*IFSYB* 1981, 186–87; *ASF* 1966, 548.
Col. 8:	
Line I.1	INSEE, *Le Patrimoine national*, 1979, 25.
Line I.2	Derived from Benedetti, Consolo, and Fouquet 1979, 17, 18, 47–48, applying land/structure ratios to value of structures including land.
Lines II.1 and 2	Benedetti, Consolo, and Fouquet, 47–48, less for line II.1 estimates for land derived as for line I.2.
Line II.3	Estimate for 1976 reduced in line with year-end rate of expenditures on consumer goods *YNASB* 1979).
Lines II.4 and 5	Benedetti, Consolo, and Fouquet, 47.
Line IV	As for cols. 6 and 7.
Lines V.1–11	Benedetti, Consolo, and Fouquet, 47. Consumer credit has been equated with short-term household debt and mortgages with long-term debt of households, so that mortgage debt of other sectors is not included. Government debt excludes monetary liabilities of government financial institutions. The item "dotations et participations de l'etat" is included in "other financial assets" rather than, as in the source, in corporate stocks.
Line VI	Benedetti, Consolo, and Fouquet, 47.
Line VIII	*IFSYB* 1981, 1861–87.
Col. 9:	
Lines I, II.1–4, VI	As for col. 8.
Line II.5	Estimate for 1975 (INSEE 1979, 78) increased in line with year-end rate of expenditures on consumer durables.
Line IV	As for cols. 6 and 7.
Lines V.1–10	As for col. 8.
Line VI	*ISFY* 1981, 186–87.

6. Germany

The construction of a national balance sheet for Germany back to the middle of the 19th century is greatly aided, and indeed made possible, by the existence of the estimates of most components of tangible and financial assets for the period before World War I by Hoffman and associates (1965), and by the official statistics of the value of reproducible assets by the Statistische Bundesamt (SJD, various issues, e.g., for 1978) and the flow-of-funds statistics of the Deutsche Bundesbank. This leaves essentially the estimates for part of land and of consumer durables and among financial assets for G.m.b.H. parts and trade credit for the outside constructor of national balance sheets, and even some of these estimates can be based on scattered official figures. The errors made in estimating these items cannot be large enough seriously to affect the picture derived from the existing estimates, particularly for the current century. To preserve consistency with estimates for earlier dates and improve comparability with other countries, the flow-of-funds statistics of the Deutsche Bundesbank have been modified to include the liabilities of the Social Security system, assumed equal to its assets; and to add in table A6 a rough estimate of the value of G.m.b.H. parts (a legal form of business organization with limited liability between corporations and partnerships), although the flow-of-funds accounts include some allowance for their nominal capital under other items, thus involving some duplication, and of trade credits among domestic enterprises. A less compressed discussion of the national balance sheet of Germany is available in Goldsmith 1976.

The change in the territory covered by the estimates of table A6 is larger than for any other country except the United States before 1850. Although the territory covered for the period between 1850 and 1913 was somewhat less industrialized and had a lower per head wealth than that to which the 1929 and 1938, and particularly the 1950–77, estimates refer, the differences do not appear to be large enough to invalidate or even seriously to impede structural comparisons over the entire span of the one-and-one-quarter century of Germany's modern economic development.

All long-term comparisons are basically affected in the financial sphere by two inflations, the open hyperinflation of 1919–23 and the repressed inflation of the first half of the 1940s and by the currency reform and debt-writedown which followed it; and in the case of reproducible tangible assets by the large-scale destruction during World War II. Thus comparisons between dates bridging these two interruptions of normal economic and financial development are of limited value, and significant trends must generally be deduced from comparisons of changes in the structure of the national balance sheets between 1850 and 1913, and between 1950 and 1977, the interval between the 1929 and 1938 benchmarks being too short for trend analysis.

As everywhere, the relative size of the financial superstructure has increased in both "normal" periods. Thus the financial interrelations ratio rose from only one-fifth in 1850 to three-fourths in 1913, almost all of the increases taking place before the end of 19th century. The hyperinflation of 1919–23 reduced the ratio to a very low value, and even by 1938 it had not risen much above five-ninths, notwithstanding a rapid expansion of the financial superstructure after the currency reform of 1923 and the rearmament boom of the years of national socialism. The currency reform following World War II, which involved the cancellation of the government's huge war debt and sharp reductions of most other outstanding claims, for a second time radically reduced the financial interrelations ratio, though as early as by 1950 it had recovered to two-fifths, somewhat above the level of 1875. The rebuilding and expansion during the 1950s war so rapid and so much in excess of the very substantial increase in national product and wealth that the ratio by 1960 exceeded nine-tenths, well above its 1913 value, a level from which it declined moderately during the following two decades, standing in 1977 at slightly above seven-eighths.

The share of financial institutions in all financial assets doubled from about one-fifth in 1850 to nearly one-third in 1913, during the formative period for most types of modern financial institutions. It was close to two-fifths in 1929 and 1938 as the liabilities and assets of financial institutions recovered more rapidly from the hyperinflation than most other financial instruments. During the postwar period the ratio increased moderately from one-third to nearly two-fifths, the level of the 1930s. Within financial institutions time and savings deposits gained at the expense of currency and demand deposit, particularly during "normal" periods. Thus in 1977 they accounted for nearly four-fifths of all deposits of financial institutions (including currency) compared to probably not much over one-fourth in 1950. The upward trend and the temporary setbacks during inflations are even more clearly evident in the case of insurance and pension claims. Insignificant in 1850, they accounted in 1913 for about one-eighth of the liabilities of financial institutions and for 4 percent of all financial instruments. Thrown back by two inflations to a share of less than one-tenth of total liabilities of financial institutions and 3 percent of all financial assets in 1950, they had a quarter of a century later climbed back to approximately 15 percent of the former and nearly 6 percent of the latter, well above the 1913 ratios.

Mortgages, largely on residential properties, have in Germany always played a very important role, aided by a well developed system of private and public mortgage banks. Their share in all financial instruments kept close to one-fourth from the mid-19th century to World War I. After having been reduced sharply by the two inflations, their share of fully one-sixth in 1977 was still well below the 1913 level.

The vagaries of the share of the government debt in financial assets are only inadequately reflected in table A6 since the benchmark years do not include those in which that share was particularly high, such as the years of both world wars, nor those in which it was particularly low, as in the late 1940s following their write-off. Among the benchmark years, the peak of 1895 with one-eighth of all financial assets reflects the financing of the acquisition by the government of most of the country's railroad system. Since 1960, government debt has represented about 6 percent of all financial assets, considerably less than at any benchmark date since the mid-19th century.

Corporate securities increased their share in financial assets and experienced their most rapid relative expansion between 1850 and 1913 from 3 to 9 percent. As stocks (and G.m.b.H. parts) were less affected by inflation than claims, their share was considerably higher at about one-eighth of financial assets in 1929 and 1950. During the postwar period, the share first rose sharply to nearly one-fourth of financial assets in 1960 and than fell back equally sharply to one-tenth in 1977, approximately the level of 1913.

Among tangible assets, the share of farm and forest land, agricultural structures and equipment, and livestock has as in all countries reflected the declining importance of agriculture and has fallen sharply, in the case of land from well over two-fifths in 1850 to one-eighth in 1977, most of the decrease occuring before World War I. The share of other land, however, for which the estimates are precarious, seems to have increased from approximately 3 percent of tangible assets in 1850 to 7 percent in 1913 and to 12 percent in 1977. Residential structures have advanced their share in reproducible tangible assets in connection with urbanization and improved living conditions, from one-seventh in the mid-19th century to one-fourth on the eve of World War I and after war destruction have risen during the postwar period from nearly one-fourth in 1950 to one-third in the late 1970s. The share of other nonagricultural structures declined between 1850 and 1913 from nearly one-half to close to one-fifth of all reproducible assets and has remained close to that level in the postwar period. The share of equipment rose from one-sixth of reproducible assets in the mid-19th century to nearly one-fourth in 1929, which is in accord with its role as a rough indicator of modernization; but in the postwar period it fell from one-fifth to one-seventh partly because of the decline in prices of equipment compared to those of structures. The share of inventories, finally, declined from about one-tenth of reproducible assets to about 6 percent from 1929 on, with the exception of a bulge back to one-tenth in 1950 and 1960.

During most of the half-century before World War I, Germany was a capital exporting country, its gross foreign investment rising to one-eighth of domestic financial assets and to 8 percent of national wealth in 1895, though falling back to 8 and 5 percents, respectively, just before World War I. In the interwar period, Germany became a net international debtor and reverted to that position in the 1950s, in both cases reflecting substantial capital imports needed to overcome the effects of war and inflation. In the 1970s, substantial investments abroad and foreign investments in Germany resulted in a small net credit balance keeping well below 1 percent of national wealth, though gross foreign investments rose to 7 percent of domestic financial assets.

Table A6 National Balance Sheet of Germany, 1850–1977[a] (National Assets = 100.0)

	1850 (1)	1875 (2)	1895 (3)	1913 (4)	1929 (5)	1938 (6)	1950 (7)	1960 (8)	1972 (9)	1977 (10)
I. Land	38.1	29.2	19.3	15.2	14.2	10.9	20.1	12.3	11.9	13.2
1. Agricultural[b]	36.0	26.5	16.3	11.4	9.1	6.1	13.5	7.3	4.1	6.7
2. Other	2.1	2.7	3.0	3.8	5.1	4.8	6.6	5.0	7.8	6.5
II. Reproducible tangible assets	45.1	43.4	38.8	41.5	56.8	53.0	51.0	39.8	42.2	39.9
1. Structures	28.4	26.5	23.3	23.2	35.4	32.9	30.4	23.9	27.3	27.3
a) Residential	6.5	8.7	9.6	10.5	15.7	14.3	12.2	10.3	11.6	13.0
b) Other	21.9	17.8	13.7	12.7	19.7	18.6	18.2	12.6	15.7	14.3
2. Equipment	7.8	8.2	7.8	10.8	13.1	12.9	10.2	8.3	7.4	5.7
3. Inventories	4.6	4.5	3.9	4.0	3.1	3.4	5.2	3.9	2.7	2.6
4. Livestock	3.3	3.0	2.2	2.0	1.9	1.5	1.8	0.6	0.3	0.3
5. Consumer durables	1.1	1.3	1.6	1.4	3.2	2.2	3.5	3.0	4.4	4.1
III. Tangible assets	83.2	72.6	58.1	56.7	71.0	63.9	71.2	52.1	54.1	53.0
IV. Monetary metals	1.6	1.3	1.1	0.8	0.3	0.0	0.0	0.6	0.2	0.4
V. Financial assets[c]	15.2	23.5	36.5	39.5	27.1	36.1	28.5	44.2	42.5	42.6
1. Claims against financial institutions[d]	3.4	6.0	11.0	13.0	10.1	14.6	9.5	15.9	18.6	18.1
a) Currency and demand deposits } b) Other deposits (combined)	2.7	4.3	6.8	8.2	6.3	8.1				
a) Currency and demand deposits							5.5	3.2	3.0	2.6
b) Other deposits							2.0	6.9	9.0	9.2
c) Insurance and pension claims[e]	0.1	0.3	1.1	1.7	0.9	2.4	0.8	2.8	2.9	2.7
d) Other[e]	0.6	1.4	3.1	3.1	2.9	3.9	1.2	3.0	3.7	3.6
2. Loans by financial institutions	0.5	2.1	3.7	4.2	4.0	4.9	3.3	2.3	2.9	2.5
3. Mortgages[f]	4.8	6.0	9.0	9.5	3.5	5.6	1.2	6.4	8.7	8.4
4. Government debt	2.3	2.1	5.2	4.2	2.4	4.1	4.3	2.7	2.4	3.2
5. Corporate bonds[g]	0.9	1.0	0.4	0.6	0.5	0.4	0.3	0.5	0.4	0.3
6. Corporate stock	0.5	1.7	2.7	3.2	3.0	2.5	2.4	7.4	3.4	3.0
7. G.m.b.H. parts	...	...	0.0	0.7	0.5	0.6	0.9	4.1	1.8	1.9
8. Trade credit	3.5	4.6	4.5	4.1	3.0	3.4	5.2	3.7	2.9	2.7
9. Other financial assets	...	...	...	...	...	...	1.4	1.2	1.8	2.8

	(1)	(2)	(3)	(4)	(5)	(6)	(7)	(8)	(9)	(10)
VI. Foreign assets gross	...	2.7	4.7	3.1	1.6	...	0.2	3.4	3.2	3.9
Foreign assets net	...	...	...	...	−1.3	0.9	−2.6	1.2	0.5	1.0
VII. National assets %	100.0	100.0	100.0	100.0	100.0	100.0	100.0	100.0	100.0	100.0
National assets M (DM) bill.	73.7	186.4	267.8	639.3	773.0	734.8	576.6	1970	6995	10172
VIII. Gross national product; bill. M(DM)[h,i]	6.6	19.0	27.4	55.1	79.5	108.0	108.7	473	874	1248

[a]Territory of German empire for cols. 1–4, Weimar Republic for cols. 5 and 6, and Federal Republic (BRD) for cols. 7–10.

[b]Includes forests.

[c]Including gross foreign assets.

[d]Including equity.

[e]Includes claims against social security system assumed equal to system's assets.

[f]In cols. 7–10, all long-term credits.

[g]In cols. 7–10, includes mortgage bonds.

[h]Year-end rate except in col. (4).

[i]Mark (cols. 1–4), Reichsmark (cols. 5–8), or Deutsche Mark (cols. 7–10).

Source of basic data:

Cols. 1–7 Goldsmith 1976, 159 ff., except for line VI, cols. 5 and 6, which are from Deutsche Bundesbank, 1976, 331, and line VIII, which are Hoffmann and associates estimates 1965, 253–54, of net national product increased by 5% for cols. 1–6, and *IFSYB* 1981, 194, for col. 7.

Cols. 8–10:

Line I As for cols. 1–7 for cols. 8 and 9; rough estimates based for line I.1 on movements of agricultural land prices for col. 10.

Line II.1–4 *SJD* 1978, 527, and earlier issues.

Line II.5 For cols. 8 and 9 Goldsmith 1976, 163; rough estimate for col. 10.

Line IV Derived from data in *IFSYB* 1979, 41–43, 190–91.

Line V.1–6 Deutsche Bundesbank 1978, 144, 156, 161. Assets of social security organizations included in line V.3.

Line V.7 Rough estimates based on nominal capital of G.m.b.H's *SJD*, var. issues, and ratio of market to nominal value of corporate stock derived from Deutsche Bundesbank 1978.

Line V.8 Goldsmith 1976, 162, for cols. 8 and 9; rough estimate for col. 10.

Line V.9 Residual between line V (Deutsche Bundesbank 1978) plus lines V.7 and V.8 and sum of lines V.1–6.

Line VI Goldsmith 1976, 162, for cols. 8 and 9; Deutsche Bundesbank, May 1979, 56, for col. 10.

Line VIII *IFSY* 1981, 194–95.

7. Great Britain

As the home of the industrial revolution, the first country to develop a modern financial system, and the originator of many, if not most, of the financial instruments and financial institutions, which still dominate the financial scene in most of the world, Great Britain is probably the most interesting country for long-term economic and financial history and analysis, and thus presents a particular challenge to the constructor of national balance sheets. The statistical material available, unfortunately, is hardly up to that challenge before the 20th century. While we now have adequate statistics of the balance sheets of financial institutions from 1880 on (Sheppard 1971), the information is deficient for earlier dates and is inadequate for other financial instruments except for government securities. Great Britain has only recently acquired a comprehensive official regular statement of the stocks of financial assets and liabilities. Great Britain, however, has at least as good estimates of its tangible assets, due to the long labors of Feinstein (1972, 1976, 1978), as any other country going back to the middle of the 18th century. For the 20th century, and particularly for the postwar period, more numerous attempts to construct national and sectoral balance sheets for one or more benchmark dates have been made (Mason, 1976; Morgan 1960; Pettigrew 1980; Revell 1967; Revell and Roe 1971; Rothman 1974; Stone and Roe 1971) than for any other country. Data from some of these estimates have been used in table A7, but they had to be supplemented from other sources.

The story of the economic and financial development of Great Britain over the last three centuries that is listed in table A7 is, notwithstanding all the uncertainties and limitations of the estimates, dramatic and instructive, at least for the financial historian and analyst. Only some of the highlights can be touched upon here, and their treatment is necessarily sketchy.

One of its outstanding features is the movement of the financial interrelations ratio. The figures of table A7 show it at not much above one-sixth in 1688, though because of the substantial margin of error and the probable incompleteness of the estimates of financial assets it may well have been of the order of one-fifth, a ratio now found in the least developed countries. There is no doubt about its rapid rise during the 18th and 19th centuries, reaching in 1875 the level of fully nine-tenths if foreign investments as well as gold are included among financial assets at a time when the country's financial superstructure had acquired a recognizably modern shape. The rise was due until the end of the Napoleonic wars primarily to the expansion of the public debt, which reflected military expenditures; but in the following 60 years it was due to the rapid development of modern financial institutions and instruments and to the accumulation of a large stock of foreign securities. The extremely rapid doubling of the ratio between 1875 and 1895, to nearly the same as in 1913, was the result of a continued expansion of the financial superstructure at a rate well ahead of that of national product, and a substantial decline in the first two decades of the period of the current value of tangible assets in line with the long downward swing in the price level. The inflation accompanying World War I, reflected in a sharp expansion of the assets of financial institutions as well as of government debt, lifted the financial interrelation ratio to about 2½ in the 1920s. The further small increase in the 1930s is mainly due to the decline in the prices of tangible assets during the Great Depression. These are the highest levels of the ratio observed anytime or anywhere. The sharp decline of the ratio from 2.7 in 1937 to 1.4 two decades later is ascribable mainly to the rise in the price level of tangible assets set off when the repressed inflation of World War II broke into the open, a movement which more than compensated for the large increase in government debt and the assets of financial institutions, and then to a reduction of foreign investments. No trend in the ratio is evident from the late 1950s to the early 1970s. The decline between 1973 and 1977 to 1.2 reflects the acceleration of inflation and the sharp rise in tangible asset prices which forms part of it.

Turning first to tangible assets, if only because the statistical data are much less in doubt and new estimates were required only for the value of nonagricultural land and for some dates for consumer durables, we find the usual story, only here documented for a longer period, of the sharply and continuously declining share of agriculture in national wealth. It is evidenced primarily in the downward trend of the share of agricultural land from three-fifths in 1688 and still fully one-third in 1800, to not much over one-fifth near the end of the 19th century, to 5 percent in the late 1920s, and to less than 3 percent half a century later.

Among reproducible assets, the share of residential structures shows no definite secular trend, keeping in the range of one-fifth to one-fourth throughout most of the 150 years from 1830 on; the effects of urbanization that would be expected to raise the ratio apparently were offset by other factors. The share of equipment, which can be followed only since the mid-19th century and is a proxy for industrialization, fails to show a trend, keeping above one-fifth from 1875 to 1948 in a period in which the prices of equipment declined relative to those structures, but is somewhat higher at about one-fourth in the 1960s and 1970s, a movement which merits closer investigation. The shrinkage of the share of livestock from nearly one-fifth of all reproducible assets in Gregory King's estimate for 1688 and still over one-tenth in 1830, to 3 percent in the 1920s and to probably less than 1 percent in the 1970s is self-explanatory. The share of inventories declined slowly though significantly from one-fourth in the 18th century to one-tenth in the 1930s, a ratio maintained until the present. Consumer durables, whose character has changed sharply from handicraft to industrial origin and for which the estimates are probably less reliable than for any other component of tangible assets except nonagricultural land, has fluctuated erratically, if the figures of table A7 are believed, around 6 percent of reproducible assets between 1790 and 1913, and since 1927, when the figures are better, at the higher level of between 9 and 13 percent. (The much higher ratio in King's estimate for 1688 probably reflects mainly the much larger importance of plate and other articles of silver in the 17th century.)

Notwithstanding the extreme difficulty of constructing a reasonably reliable series for the amounts of the different types of financial instruments outstanding in Great Britain before the 20th century, the results of an attempt to do so are shown in the lower half of table A7, but the following comments will indicate how precarious most of the figures are. Indeed, the only firm series is that relating to government debt. The figures for the outstanding issues of financial institutions, which are regarded as equal to these institutions' assets, is also fairly reliable with respect to level and movements from the late 19th century on. The estimate for British company securities understate the correct figures because they are essentially limited to those listed on the London Stock Exchange. The series for bank loans is probably also slightly on the low side as it does not include the loans made by some smaller groups of banks. That for foreign securities, apart from an undoubtedly substantial margin of error, has the disadvantage of being on a net basis and therefore understating the amount of foreign issues held in Great Britain by foreign investments in the country, which must have become fairly substantial after the turn of the century.

The two weakest series are those for mortgages and for trade credit. Indeed, they can be regarded only as rough conjectures since no trustworthy benchmark figure exists for either of them for any date. In this situation, Revell's (1967) rough estimates have been accepted for mortgages starting in 1900 and have been carried back to the 19th and 18th century benchmarks on the basis of the movements in the value of real estate to produce figures that are compatible with Revell's estimate for 1900. Similarly, but even more conjecturally, the volume of trade credit has been estimated on the basis of the movements of inventories and national product in a way to be compatible with the figures for the 1950s on the one end and the other end with Newmarch's estimate of bills in circulation (1851, 169). Taking these limitations into account, it is more likely that the estimates for all financial instruments outstanding during the 19th century shown in table A7 slightly understate than that they exaggerate the correct figures.

The estimates for the late 17th and 18th centuries merit an additional comment. Virtually no comprehensive quantitative estimates have been found for any type of financial instrument for this period, except of course for the national debt; for the stock of gold and silver (Feinstein 1978); for some figures on the nominal capital of companies before 1720 (W. R. Scott 1910–12) and for an unpublished estimate by Petty of the volume of mortgages for the end of the 17th century (communication from Sir John Habbakuk). There is no doubt that the volume of mortgage debt was substantial; that annuities and probably other forms of impecunious consumers' debts were common beginning with the second half of the 18th century (Campbell 1928); that the volume of trade credit was significant; and that near the end of the period the banking system began to acquire importance. But statistics there are none. For this period, and to a good extent for the first half of the 19th century, almost everything remains to be done. It is thus evident that the figures now available permit only very guarded and preliminary statements about the level and movements of financial assets until the mid-20th century and about their relations to national wealth and product, though the main trends are not likely to be misrepresented.

There is thus no doubt that the financial intermediation ratio rose significantly through most of the last three centuries. It must have been close to zero in 1688 before the formation of the Bank of England. In the second quarter of the 19th century it appears to have been not much in excess of one-eighth. During the next half-century the ratio increased substantially to nearly one-fifth, a level near which it remained until the late 1930s. The inflation during and after World War II, which centered in the banking system, as well as the sharp decline in the share of foreign investments raised the ratio to three-tenths in 1948 and to fully one-third in the late 1970s, due primarily to the extraordinary expansion of the assets of the banking system reflecting London's role as an international financial intermediary.

Among financial institutions the share of the banking system was predominant, though to a declining degree until World War I, keeping above two-thirds until the 1870s. By 1913 the share had declined to about one-half, and by the late 1930s it had fallen further to not much over two-fifths. After a temporary recovery due to the inflation of World War II, it declined to one-third in the mid-1960s but rose sharply in the 1970s, reflecting mainly the immense accumulation of Eurocurrency deposits and credits, to reach 55 percent in 1977, the highest ratio of this century. The share of saving banks and building societies in the assets of all financial organizations has risen irregularly from one-eighth to one-sixth over the past century. That of insurance and pension organizations (including the assets of Social Security funds, but not their unfunded actuarial liabilities), however, has risen from about one-sixth in the middle of the 19th century to a peak of over one-third in the mid-1960s, to decline to one-fourth in the late 1970s under the influence of inflation and of the extraordinary expansion of the international activities of the banking system.

The financial superstructure of Great Britain was until the mid-19th century dominated by its large public debt, reflecting almost entirely military expenditures, which constituted the largest financial instrument and the main financial asset of the public. Thus in 1800 the central government's debt was almost equal to all other financial assets; to one-fourth of national wealth, and to two years' national product, ratios rarely if ever observed elsewhere. (The ratio probably was close to three years' income at the end of the Napoleonic wars.) Even in 1850 the share in all financial assets was still close to one-third. As the absolute amount of the central government's debt increased but slowly until World War I, the share of government debt, now including local government debt to a substantial proportion, fell to well below one-tenth in 1913. The sharp increase in Treasury debt, mainly for military expenditures, lifted the ratio to about one-fourth in the 1920s and 1930s, the highest since 1875. World War II debt raised the ratio further to nearly one-third in 1948, already down from the 1945 peak, a level maintained through the 1950s. Though the absolute amount of the public debt more than tripled in the following two decades, and local government debts, raised mostly for productive purposes, came to account for over one-fourth of the total, its ratio had by 1977 fallen to one-sixth, the lowest since before World War I.

Domestic corporate securities became important in the financial structure after a brief flurry in the early 18th century culminating in the South Sea bubble, from the railway era on. In 1850 they represented about one-seventh of all financial assets. Their share had doubled by the time of World War I to about one-fourth, a ratio maintained to the late 1930s, stocks accounting from the 1920s on for over four-fifths of the total. The importance of corporate securities was much lower in the postwar period, declining from one-fifth to not much over one-tenth as share prices failed to keep up with inflation. The reduction was even sharper for corporate bonds, whose share was reduced to about one-tenth of corporate securities and not much over 1 percent of all financial assets compared with 3½ percent in 1937.

The share of trade credit, difficult to determine in view of the wide margin of error of the figures, seems to have been in the order of 5 to 6 percent from the late 19th century on.

During the 19th century Great Britain became the largest international creditor, and the share of its net foreign balance, which was not much smaller than its gross foreign investments, rose from about 7 percent of all domestic financial assets and 5 percent of tangible assets in 1830 to over one-third and fully one-half in 1913, respectively, probably the highest ratios ever observed. Notwithstanding considerable liquidation during World War I, net foreign investments still were equal to about one-sixth of all domestic financial assets in the 1920s and 1930s, and to about one-third of tangible assets. During the early part of the postwar period foreign investments were small, partly reflecting the large liquida-

Table A7 **National Balance Sheet of Great Britain, 1688–1977 (National Assets = 100.0)**

	1688 (1)	1760 (2)	1800 (3)	1830 (4)	1850 (5)
I. Land	55.0	41.0	29.7	25.5	17.8
1. Agricultural	52.1	36.2	23.1	20.3	11.9
2. Other	2.9	4.8	6.7	5.2	5.9
II. Reproducible tangible assets	30.3	30.5	34.0	31.4	41.8
1. Structures	...	...	...	...	25.2
a) Residential	11.3	5.7	5.6	6.7	8.2
b) Other	...	8.6	10.6	13.9	17.0
2. Equipment	9.3				8.9
3. Inventories		7.6	7.7	5.2	3.1
4. Livestock	5.4	6.7	8.0	3.7	1.8
5. Consumer durables	4.2	1.9	2.2	2.0	2.8
III. Tangible assets	85.3	71.4	63.7	56.9	59.6
IV. Monetary metals	3.7	1.9	1.1	1.5	1.5
V. Financial assets	11.0	26.7	34.8	38.9	35.8
1. Claims against financial institutions[a]	...	2.9	3.3	5.0	5.9
a) Banks	...	2.9	2.9	3.5	4.3
b) Savings institutions	...	...	0.0	0.5	0.4
c) Insurance organizations	...	...	0.0	0.7	0.9
d) Others	...	...	0.4	0.2	0.3
2. Loans by financial institutions	...	...	0.7	2.5	2.2
3. Mortgages	5.7	6.7	5.5	5.7	5.9
4. Government debt	...	7.6	16.8	19.6	12.8
5. Corporate bonds	...	...	...	...	5.9
6. Corporate stock	1.1	1.9	1.1	1.2	
7. Trade credit	4.2	7.6	7.4	5.0	3.0
VI. Foreign assets gross[b]	...	...	...	...	...
Foreign assets net[b]	...	−2.0	0.4	2.7	3.1
VII. National assets %	100.0	100.0	100.0	100.0	100.0
National assets £ bill.	0.35	1.05	2.73	4.04	6.74
VIII. Gross national product; £bill.[c]	0.05	0.09	0.23	0.34	0.55

[a]Including equity, i.e., equal to total assets.
[b]In cols. 11–15, distributed among relevant assets.
[c]Year-end rate except in cols. 1–4.

tions during World War II. In the late 1970s the balance became slightly negative, in 1977 to the extent of about 2 percent of financial and of tangible assets, mainly as the result of very large foreign borrowing and lending of the banking system, indicated by the share of foreign assets of approximately one-sixth of all domestic financial assets.

1875 (6)	1895 (7)	1913 (8)	1927 (9)	1937 (10)	1948 (11)	1957 (12)	1965 (13)	1973 (14)	1977 (15)
20.7	10.6	7.4	5.1	4.7	6.4	6.0	6.2	7.1	7.0
16.3	7.1	3.4	1.5	1.3	1.7	1.3	2.0	1.7	1.2
4.4	3.5	4.0	3.6	3.4	4.7	4.7	4.2	5.4	5.8
31.0	23.2	26.4	23.9	22.3	29.7	34.9	33.8	36.5	40.3
18.3	14.5	16.5	14.6	13.2	17.8	17.7	17.1	20.7	22.4
5.7	4.4	5.2	5.1	5.7	8.4	9.2	8.2	9.5	10.2
12.6	10.1	11.3	9.5	7.5	9.4	8.5	8.9	11.2	12.2
5.2	3.0	4.2	3.3	3.7	4.9	8.5	8.9	9.1	10.5
4.0}	4.1	4.3	2.9	2.3}	4.7	5.0	4.3	3.6	3.6
1.5}			0.7	0.5}					
2.0	1.5	1.5	2.4	2.5	2.3	3.7	3.6	3.1	3.8
51.7	33.8	33.8	29.0	27.0	36.1	40.9	40.0	43.6	47.3
1.1	0.8	1.0	0.3	0.6	0.4	0.3	0.3	0.2	0.2
37.5	50.9	47.4	59.9	63.4	63.5	58.8	59.7	56.1	52.5
9.5	10.2	11.4	13.1	15.3	19.5	17.5	19.8	22.4	21.5
6.5	6.2	5.9	6.3	6.4	9.3	6.6	6.8	11.6	11.9
1.1	1.3	1.4	1.7	3.1	3.8	3.1	3.3	3.3	3.2
1.4	1.9	2.9	3.6	5.0	5.0	6.2	7.1	5.8	5.3
0.6	0.8	1.3	1.6	0.8	1.4	1.5	2.6	1.6	1.2
3.2	5.4	6.0	5.3	6.3	5.6	5.7	8.0	10.3	9.2
5.8	4.0	3.1	1.9	2.5	1.4	2.4	2.3	2.8	2.9
7.2	5.9	5.3	18.3	16.5	20.3	18.7	14.1	8.9	8.6
8.1	6.2	4.3	2.6	2.5	0.7	0.8	1.3	1.0	0.7
	16.1	14.0	15.7	17.6	12.3	9.4	10.4	7.3	6.0
3.6	3.1	3.4	3.1	2.8	3.6	4.2	3.9	3.4	3.5
...	...	...	...	...	...	0.8	2.3	9.3	9.2
9.7	14.6	17.8	10.8	9.0	...	0.1	2.0	0.6	−1.0
100.0	100.0	100.0	100.0	100.0	100.0	100.0	100.0	100.0	100.0
12.36	16.18	23.52	47.82	58.17	110.0	177.8	295.6	702.5	1327.6
1.36	1.67	2.73	4.88	5.63	12.3	21.6	37.2	79.3	105.4

(Source of basic data on following pages)

Source of basic data:

Line I.1:	
Col. 1	King 1936, 32.
Cols. 2–5	Feinstein's estimates, 1978, 68, adjusted by price index of agricultural products (Rousseau, cited Mitchell and Deane 1962, 471–72). These estimates differ considerably from the contemporary estimates for total land (Beeke for 1800, Pebrer for 1833, and Giffen for 1865 as cited in Giffen 1970, 43, 95, and 103).
Col. 6	Giffen, 43.
Col. 7	Interpolated between Giffen's estimate for 1885 and two estimates of Craigie 1902, 595, for 1900.
Cols. 8, 9	Campion 1939, 65; figures refer to 1911–13 and 1926–28.
Cols. 10, 11	Value for 1937 assumed approximately equal to 1927, and that for 1948 at 2.6 times 1937 in line with Revell's estimates of total land values (1967, 64).
Cols. 12, 13	Revell and Roe 1971, 57, 65.
Cols. 14, 15	Rough estimates based on changes in agricultural land prices.
Lines 1–2:	
Col. 1	King 1936, *loc. cit.*
Cols. 2–15	Estimated at one-third (cols. 4–8) of or between 30% and 25% (cols. 9–15) of structure value of dwellings plus 20% of value of other structures. The resulting figures are close for cols. 2–5 to those of Feinstein 1978, 68, adjusted for changes in Rousseau's index of industrial prices (cited Mitchell and Deane 1962, 471–72).
Lines II.1, 2:	
Col. 1	King 1936.
Cols. 2–4	Feinstein's estimates in 1851–60 prices (1978, 83) adjusted by prices of structures and machinery (op. cit., 38).
Col. 5	Estimated at slightly below Feinstein's figures for 1855 (1976, T-103).
Cols. 6–13	Feinstein 1976, T-103–05.
Cols. 14, 15	Central Statistical Office (1978, table 11.11).
Lines II.3, 4	
Col. 1	King 1936, loc. cit.
Cols. 2–4	Feinstein (1976, 68) adjusted by wholesale price index (op. cit., 38).
Col. 5	Slightly below Feinstein's estimate for 1860, (1978, 68).
Cols. 6, 7	Estimated at 50 and 40 percent respectively of national product (Feinstein, 1976, T-10) compared to 1913 ratio of 37%.
Cols. 7, 8, 11	Revell 1967, 64.
Cols. 9, 10	Based on Feinstein (1972, T110).
Cols. 12, 13	Revell and Roe 1971, XIX.
Cols. 14, 15	Hibbert et al.'s estimates in 1975 prices (1979, 9), adjusted for changes in inventories in 1975 prices (Central Statistical Office, *Annual Abstract of Statistics*, 1979, 355), and in gross national product deflator.
Line II.5:	
Col. 1	King's estimate (loc. cit.) for household goods, including gold and silver other than coin and bullion.
Cols. 2–6	Rough estimates putting the stock of consumer durables at approximately one-third the value of residential structures the average of the 1900 and 1913 ratios.

Cols. 7–12	Estimated at approximately 4½ times expenditures on consumer durables (Feinstein 1972, table 61 ff.), the 1963 and 1973 ratio.
Cols. 13–15	Based on Calder's estimates (1978, 119), using his medium life length and reducing balance variant.
Line IV:	
Col. 1	King, loc. cit.
Cols. 2–5	Feinstein 1978, 68; 1850 figure interpolated between 1830 and 1860.
Cols. 6–9	Sheppard 1971, 136–37, 180–81; 1875 assumed equal to 1880.
Col. 10	*SYBUN* 1939.
Cols. 11–15	Derived from data quantity and price data in *IFSYB* 1979, 40–43, 422–23; 1948 assumed equal to 1949.
Line V:	Sum of lines V.1–7.
Line V.1:	
Cols. 2–4	Rough estimates (see text).
Col. 5	Based on Newmarch's figure for bank assets (1851, 161 ff.).
Cols. 6–13	Goldsmith 1969, table D-10, interpolated, except for cols. 8 and 11, or extrapolated, for col. 6, on basis of data on assets of financial institutions in Sheppard 1971, 166 ff.
Cols. 14, 15	Derived from data in *SAB* 1979, 418 ff; 1974, 377 ff.
Line V.2:	
Cols. 3–5	Rough estimates based on line V.1 and later relationships between lines V.1 and 2.
Cols. 6–13	Sheppard, 184–85; "gross private credit" by financial institutions.
Cols. 14, 15	Estimated at 41% of asset of financial institutions (line V.1), the 1965 ratio.
Line V.3:	
Cols. 2–6	Estimated to have increased from 20% to 30% (the 1895 ratio is 31%) of value of agricultural and residential and one-half of other land and structures (lines I.1 and II.1).
Cols. 7–11	Revell 1967, 94; 1895 estimated at slightly below Revell's figure for 1900.
Cols. 12–15	Estimated to rise from 25% to 30% of value of agricultural and residential land and structures (ratio for cols. 7–10 averages 28%). In 1978 ratio of home mortgage debt (Mason 1976, 160) was 22% of value of residential real estate.
Line V.4:	
Cols. 1–4	Debt of central government (Mitchell and Deane 1962, 401 ff.); 1688 entry refers to 1691.
Cols. 5–11	Debt of central government (as for cols. 1–4) plus debt of local governments in England and Wales (Biddell 1904, 342; roughly extrapolated for 1850) for cols. 5–7, and Revell 1967, 94, for cols. 8–11. Figures refer to March 31 of following year.
Cols. 12–15	*SAB* 1979, 390, 406, and earlier issues; figures refer to March 31 of following year.
Lines V.5, 6:	
Col. 4	English (1827); figure refers to market value of companies existing in 1827.
Cols. 5–6	Based on relationship of domestic corporate securities listed on London Stock Exchange in 1852 and 1872 (Morgan and Thomas 1969, 132).
Col. 13	Revell and Roe, XVI.
Col. 14	Mason 1976, 160, for lines 5 plus 6; ratio of 1973–1965 market

	value of listed corporate debentures (*SAB* 1974, 374, for line 5). Figures include foreign corporate securities.
Lines V.5, 6:	
Col. 15	Extrapolated on basis of 1965–73 trend for line 5; and on basis of stock price movements and new issues for line 6.
Line V.7:	
Cols. 2–15	Average of (1) one-third of gross national product (Deane and Cole 1967 for cols. 2–4; Feinstein 1976 for cols. 5–10; *IFSYB* 1979, 422–23 for cols. 11 to 15); (2) inventories (lines II.3 and 4).
Line VI:	
Cols. 2, 3	Feinstein 1978, 68.
Cols. 4, 5	Imlah 1958, 70 ff.
Cols. 6–11	Feinstein 1972, tables 37–39, 110.
Cols. 12–15	*Bank of England Quarterly*, var. issues.
Line VIII:	
Cols. 1, 3–5	Mitchell and Deane 1962, 366; cols. 3–5 refer to years 1801, 1831, and 1951, respectively.
Col. 2	Rough estimate based on Feinstein 1978, 84.

8. Hungary

Official estimates of all types of tangible assets, even including subsoil assets, and the balance sheet of the National Bank and of savings banks provide a sufficient basis for constructing a national balance sheet for 1970 and 1977, though rough estimates are needed for trade credit. The balance sheet for 1959 shown in table A8 is more precarious as financial assets have to be very roughly estimated. As it stands, the balance sheets for the 1970s are probably as reliable as those for most other countries, if the necessarily problematical nature of the estimates of land values in a country where most of it is owned by the government or by cooperatives and no land market exists is taken into account.

For the last two decades the structure of the national balance sheet of Hungary shows the changes expected in a rapidly industrializing country. Thus the share of agricultural land in tangible assets declined between 1959 and 1977 from nearly one-fourth to less than one-fifth while that of equipment rose from about one-twelfth to one-eighth.

Financial assets increased more rapidly than tangible assets in the 1970s, though not so much in the 1960s, raising the financial interrelations ratio from approximately one-fifth in 1959 to nearly two-fifths in 1977, a relatively high level for a Communist economy. The dominating role of the monobank within the financial superstructure is equally characteristic of these countries.

The table below compares the balance sheet structure in the late 1970s with that of the dominating and exemplary communist country, the Soviet Union; a halfway house country, Yugoslavia; and a typical free market country, the United States. With respect to the relative size of the financial superstructure and the dominating position of the monobank in it, reflected in the financial interrelations and intermediation ratios, Hungary is close to the Soviet Union and far from either Yugoslavia or the United States, but nevertheless closer to the two countries than the Soviet Union is.

	Financial Ratio		Agricultural Land in Tangible Assets	Share in Reproducible Assets			
	Interrelations (1)	Intermediation (2)	(3)	Residential Structures (4)	Other Structures and Equipment (5)	Inventories (6)	Consumer Durables (7)
Hungary (1977)	0.39	0.36	0.19	0.18	0.52	0.18	0.12
Soviet Union (1977)	0.29	0.54	0.10	0.16	0.60	0.15	0.06
Yugoslavia (1977)	1.15	0.28	0.15	0.78		0.15	0.04
United States (1978)	0.99	0.27	0.05	0.29	0.47	0.11	0.12

On the other hand, the share of agricultural land in Hungary is much closer to that of Yugoslavia, another still half-industrialized country, than it is in either the Soviet Union or the United States. The share of residential structures in the stock of reproducible capital is much lower in Hungary, as well as in the Soviet Union, and presumably in Yugoslavia, than in the United States, evidence of poor housing conditions and the result of the low position of housing in the planners' utility function. The share of inventories in reproducible assets in Hungary is slightly higher than in the Soviet Union or in Yugoslavia, but in all three countries it is well above the ratio in the United States, a well-known characteristic of centrally planned economies.

Taking all these characteristics together it appears that Hungary's national balance sheet structure is between that of the Soviet Union and of non-communist developed countries, though still much closer to the former than to the latter.

Table A8 **National Balance Sheet of Hungary, 1959, 1970, and 1977 (National Assets = 100.0)**

	1959 (1)	1970 (2)	1977 (3)
I. Land[a]	25.8	23.7	19.9
1. Agricultural[a]	21.7	15.7	12.1
2. Other	4.1	8.0	7.8
II. Reproducible assets	61.0	59.3	53.6
1. Residential	13.0	10.2	9.7
2. Other	20.3	21.2	17.8
3. Equipment	8.6	8.9	9.1
4. Livestock	1.7	1.6	1.1
5. Inventories	10.4	10.2	9.2
6. Consumer durables	7.0	7.2	6.7
III. Tangible assets	86.8	82.9	73.4
IV. Financial assets	13.2	17.1	26.6
1. National bank money	}	1.0	1.3
2. National bank deposits	}6.2	4.8	9.4
3. National bank other liabilities[b]	}	0.4	0.6
4. Savings deposits	0.4	1.8	2.4
5. Loans by financial institutions[c]	4.8	7.0	11.1
6. Government debt[d]	...	0.2	...
7. Trade credit	1.9	2.0	1.8
V. National assets %	100.0	100.0	100.0
National assets, bill. forint	1050	2300	4500
VI. Gross national product; bill. forint[e]	175	345	595

[a]Includes timber (5 in 1959, 35 in 1977). Subsoil assets (170 in 1959, 500 in 1977) not included.

[b]Includes capital (5 in 1970; 10 in 1977).

[c]Only loans by National Bank.

[d]Holdings by households only.

[e]Year-end rate.

Source:

Lines I and II — Communication from Hungarian Central Statistical Office (May 21, 1980). Figures similar to those in Office's *A nemzeti vagyon és az allóeszközallomány*, 1960–73, 1970–78, and 1980.

Lines IV.1.3 — For cols. 2 and 3 from balance sheet of National Bank of Hungary as shown in *Information Memorandum for International Loans*, May 1971, p. 8, and May 1979, p. 15. Rough estimates for col. 1 based on movements of net material product (Mitchell 1975, 792).

Line IV.4 — Hungarian Central Statistical Office 1976, 23.

Line IV.5 — Loans of National Bank (as for lines IV.1–3) plus amount slightly below savings deposits to reflect the loans of saving institutions.

Line IV.6 — Information from Hungarian Statistical Office.

Line IV.7 — Assumed equal to about one-fifth of inventories and livestock.

Line VI — Estimates of net material product (*YNAS*, var. issues) plus 20%.

9. India

India presents a particular challenge and opportunity to the constructor of national balance sheets and to the financial historian as it is the only economically, and to a lesser degree financially, still underdeveloped country—and by its size, population, and economic weight the second most important of them—for which a national balance sheet can be constructed, even with some reservations, back to the middle of the 19th century. A less compressed discussion may be found in Goldsmith 1983a.

Table A9 is derived from the balance sheets for 12 benchmark dates, spaced at an average distance of 10 years, though ranging from five to 20 years, presented and discussed in Goldsmith (1983a) where the multifarious sources and the limitations of the estimates are indicated. Their construction for the period of the British Raj, when they cover Undivided India, is best described as a puzzle of unrelated statistics scattered over a multitude of official and other sources, since for the first four decades no systematic statistics of national wealth exist nor are there available until the 1950s comprehensive estimates of the volume of financial assets and liabilities. The margins of error are, therefore, substantial, and the balance sheets less detailed than one would wish. Since, however, a great deal of statistical and institutional material is available against which the structural relations indicated by the balance sheets can be checked, there is no reason to suspect that the picture of the development of India's national wealth and its financial superstructure, which can be derived from the balance sheets, is seriously flawed.

The national balance sheet of India, like so many aspects of its economic development, is characterized by the contrast between the sluggish growth and limited change until Independence, and the greatly accelerated growth and rate of change in the following three decades, though less sharply in the financial sphere than in the infrastructure. Thus the share of financial in national assets (excluding gold and silver from the former) rose from over one-eighth to fully one-fifth between 1860 and 1950 at an average annual rate of 0.6 percent, while it advanced to nearly 30 percent, an average increase by 1.1 percent a year, between 1950 and 1975. Both the financial interrelations and intermediation ratios were still very low in international comparison in the mid-1970s, standing at 0.24 (if gold and silver are treated as financial assets) compared to 0.19 in 1950, and at 0.64 and 0.01 in 1860 respectively. Because of the large hoards of gold and silver, the financial interrelations ratio was, however, abnormally high for a very poor country. In contrast to the common experience it declined over the century, falling from over two-fifths in 1860 to approximately one-half both in 1950 and in 1975. The movements of the two ratios over more than a century can be followed in the table below under alternative treatments of gold and silver hoards.

Variants of Financial Interrelations and Intermediation Ratios
1860–1975

	Financial Interrelations Ratio		Financial Intermediation Ratio	
	1/4 (1)	2/3 (2)	5/1 (3)	5/2 (4)
1860	.64	.15	.01	.04
1875	.47	.13	.02	.07
1895	.40	.13	.04	.10
1913	.34	.15	.08	.16
1929	.30	.19	.12	.17
1939	.38	.23	.14	.21
1950	.47	.31	.19	.27
1960	.54	.40	.21	.26
1970	.57	.45	.22	.26
1975	.54	.41	.24	.28

Note: Col. 1 = financial assets including gold and silver hoards, col. 2 = financial assets excluding gold and silver hoards, col. 3 = tangible assets including gold and silver hoards, col. 4 = tangible assets excluding gold and silver hoards, col. 5 = assets of financial institutions.

Among financial instruments issued by nonfinancial sectors, loans at high interest rates to farmers by local money lenders and other noninstitutional sources remained prominant until World War II, their share falling only from nearly one-half in 1860 to two-fifths in 1939. Their importance declined drastically after Independence, and by 1975 their share had been reduced to about 2 percent, the result of the declining importance of agriculture and the increasing share of financial institutions in financing agriculture. Government domestic debt has always constituted a substantial fraction of financial instruments, but its share declined from one-fifth in 1860 to one-eighth in 1913, reached a peak with about one-third in 1946, but by 1975 had fallen back to one-eighth notwithstanding a very large expansion of its absolute volume. Loans and advances by financial institutions, most of which are now owned by the government, and by the government itself have sharply increased since Independence. In 1975 they constituted the largest single financial instrument representing nearly one-third of total financial assets. The importance of corporate securities has remained small. They never accounted for as much as one-tenth of all financial assets and declined after Independence to only 5 percent in 1975.

The crucial relation in the structure of tangible assets, the share of land, predominantly agricultural, shows at first sight an unexpected movement, rising from not much over one-third in 1860 to between one-half and three-fifths from 1913 to 1950, but then declining sharply to one-fourth in 1975. The factor behind these two opposing movements are, however, quite different. In the first period agricultural land prices rose substantially as for the first time an open fairly broad land market developed, while the rate of growth of the stock of reproducible assets was low. The halving of the share of land in national wealth in the three decades after Independence, on the other hand, is not due to a decline in relative land prices, but is the result of a rapid rise in the volume of the stock of structures and equipment.

The high share of gold and silver hoards has been an idiosyncratic feature of the national balance sheet of India. These hoards declined sharply from one-fourth of national assets in 1860 to below one-tenth from the 1920s on, partly because until the mid-1970s the prices of precious metals rose less than the general price level. In 1975 their share in national assets of 6 percent was only slightly lower than it had been 50 years earlier, as the volume of these stocks increased but slowly, imports being limited to smuggling, and prices were, at least for gold, internationally controlled. The sharp rise in the price of precious metals, which started in the early 1970s, considerably increased that share in national assets. In the late 1970s, with gold at $500 per ounce and silver at $10.00, the market value of the precious metal hoards of the Indian population, mainly in the form of jewelry, should have been in the order of R1000 billion or about one-eighth of the value of all other tangible and financial assets, i.e., back to the share of just before World War I when preindustrial India was the world's main gold and silver sink.

Table A9 **National Balance Sheet of India, 1860–1975[a]**
(National Assets = 100.0)

	1860 (1)	1875 (2)	1895 (3)	1913 (4)	1929 (5)	1939 (6)	1950 (7)	1960 (8)	1970 (9)	1975 (10)
I. Land	21.6	25.7	31.3	40.2	46.0	45.1	32.5	20.7	21.0	16.3
1. Agricultural	. . .	. . .	. . .	. . .	. . .	. . .	. . .	. . .	. . .	. . .
2. Other	. . .	. . .	. . .	. . .	. . .	. . .	. . .	. . .	. . .	. . .
II. Reproducible tangible assets	39.5	42.2	40.2	34.6	31.2	27.6	35.3	44.4	42.7	48.7
1. Structures							. . .	. . .	. . .	. . .
a) Residential	28.9	32.1	30.4	24.3	23.7	21.9	7.6	12.5	7.9	8.3
b) Other							14.7	20.0	25.3	31.6
2. Equipment										
3. Inventories	5.8	5.4	4.0	3.4	4.8	2.2	5.5	4.8	4.8	4.2
4. Livestock	4.8	4.6	5.8	6.8	2.7	3.5	4.8	2.5	1.7	1.3
5. Consumer durables	. . .	. . .	. . .	. . .	. . .	. . .	2.7	4.4	3.1	3.3
III. Tangible assets	61.1	67.9	71.4	74.7	77.1	72.7	67.7	65.1	63.7	65.0
IV. Gold and silver	25.9	20.6	17.4	12.0	6.9	8.3	8.6	6.3	5.1	5.8
V. Financial assets	13.0	11.5	11.2	13.3	16.0	19.0	21.8	28.6	31.2	29.2
1. Claims against financial institutions[b]	0.5	0.8	1.1	2.1	2.7	3.9	5.9	7.4	8.1	8.3
a) Banks	0.4	0.5	0.7	1.1	1.4	3.0	4.8	5.4	5.6	5.8
b) Insurance institutions				0.1	0.3	0.6	0.9	1.3	1.8	1.7
c) Other institutions	0.2[d]	0.3[d]	0.4[d]	0.9[e]	1.0[e]	0.3	0.2	0.7	0.7	0.7

2. Loans by financial institutions	0.2	0.2	0.4	0.7	0.6	0.7	1.2	2.4	3.7	4.0
3. Loans by government	...	...	...	...	...	...	0.5	3.3	4.6	5.0
4. Household debt[c]	6.5	5.4	5.2	6.0	5.7	7.9	2.5	1.5	0.9	0.6
5. Domestic government securities	2.6	1.8	1.9	1.7	3.4	3.7	3.1	5.4	4.4	3.7
6. Corporate stock[f]	0.3	0.4	0.6	1.0	1.2	1.7	1.9[f]	2.1[f]	2.1[f]	1.5[f]
7. Trade credit	3.0	3.0	2.0	1.7	2.4	1.1	5.2	4.3	4.3	3.7
8. Other financial assets	...	...	...	...	...	...	1.6	2.1	3.1	2.5
VI. Foreign assets gross	...	...	...	...	...	...	...	...	...	...
Foreign assets net	−2.2	−5.1	−6.1	−7.0	−4.1	−5.1	1.8	−1.7	−2.8	−1.5
VII. National assets %	100.0	100.0	100.0	100.0	100.0	100.0	100.0	100.0	100.0	100.0
National assets R. bill.	23.2	38.9	57.6	99.6	233	242	578	1038	2929	6018
VIII. Gross national product, bill. R[g]	6.1	10.0	12.6	21.4	30.6	28.4	91	154	417	748

[a]Undivided India for cols. 1–6; Indian Union for cols. 7–10.
[b]Including equity, i.e., equal to total assets.
[c]Mostly, and in cols. 7–10 exclusively, agricultural.
[d]Currency notes of Treasury.
[e]Includes 0.5 currency notes in col. 4, 0.8 in col. 5.
[f]Includes small amounts of corporate bonds.
[g]Year-end rate.
Source: Goldsmith 1983a, tables 1-3, 1-28, 2-1, 2-22, 2-40, 3-3, and 3-56.

10. Israel

The national balance sheet of Israel, shown in table A-10, is of particular interest because it permits us to follow the creation of a fairly modern structure of financial as well as reproducible tangible assets, from a very low starting level in less than a generation on the basis of statistics almost as good as those of any other country. The most serious drawback is the absence of estimates of the value of agricultural land, which is rendered particularly precarious by the ownership of a large proportion of it by the public sector or by cooperatives, and hence is not subject to direct evaluation by the market. The complexity of the financial superstructure involves numerous duplications among financial institutions and the Treasury and presents additional difficulties.

As a result of the rapid increase in population after the creation of the State of Israel in 1947 and massive capital imports, mostly unrequited, the infrastructure of reproducible tangible wealth increased at a spectacular rate, more than tripling (in constant prices) between 1950 and 1962 and again quadrupling between 1962 and 1976, and rose from a very low ratio to a national product of less than 2 in 1957 to 2½ in 1962 to over 3 in 1976. The structure of tangible assets, however, did not change substantially, though the share of inventories and consumer durables and particularly that of agricultural land and livestock seems to have declined.

The financial interrelations and financial intermediation ratios have been quite high in international comparison, particularly in the early part of the period when the country's level of real per head income was still relatively low. Thus the financial interrelations ratio was 0.67 in 1951, only four years after statehood and increased over the following 15 years moderately to 0.83. By 1976 it had risen to about 1.10, a fairly high ratio in international comparison, which reflects the existence of an elaborate financial superstructure involving considerable duplication of assets among financial institutions and between them and the Treasury. These duplications are partly responsible for the high and rising level of the financial intermediation ratio which has been well above 0.4 since the 1960s indicating a relatively small amount of direct financing in the form of holdings of government bonds, other claims, and equity securities by domestic nonfinancial sectors. This is not astonishing in view of the almost continuous inflation, averaging over 12 percent a year for the quarter-century between 1951 and 1976, and 17½ percent between 1966 and 1976.

The accelerating inflation of the later decade is also reflected in the sharp increase in the share of the banking system in the assets of all financial institutions from not much over one-half in 1966 to fully two-thirds 10 years later, still considerably below the share of three-fourths in the early 1950s. That the share of insurance institutions has increased even during the accelerating inflation is due, at least in part, to the indexing of practically all long-term claims. The share of the government's domestic debt, which has during most of the period represented less than half of its total liabilities, in total financial assets has fluctuated without trend between one-ninth and one-seventh. The share of corporate stock has been very small throughout the period, probably between 3 and 5 percent if allowance is made for stocks not listed on exchanges.

The ratio of foreign debt to national wealth rose from about 6 percent in 1951 to about 15 percent in 1962 and to 23 percent in 1976, one of the highest in the world, particularly in view of the large amounts of unrequited transfers to Israel, but explainable by the very rapid rate of growth of the country—aggregate real national product rose at a rate of 8½ percent between 1951 and 1976—the very small absolute and relative capital stock in 1947, and the extraordinary high level of its defense expenditures.

Table A10 National Balance Sheet of Israel, 1951–1976 (National Assets = 100.0)

	1951 (1)	1962 (2)	1966 (3)	1976 (4)
I. Land	13.2	13.0	11.0	8.8
1. Agricultural	5.9	5.2	3.5	1.6
2. Other	7.3	7.9	7.5	7.2
II. Reproducible tangible assets	46.9	44.5	43.4	38.6
1. Dwellings	13.5	13.2	12.9	12.4
2. Other structures	11.1	13.0	12.5	11.6
3. Equipment	8.2	7.5	7.7	7.0
4. Inventories	7.3	6.5	5.5	4.2
5. Livestock	0.9	0.9	0.6	0.3
6. Consumer durables	5.9	3.4	4.1	3.0
III. Tangible assets	60.1	57.5	54.4	47.4
IV. Monetary metals	0.0	0.0	0.2	0.1
V. Financial assets	39.9	42.5	45.4	52.5
1. Claims against financial institutions[a]	15.0	20.2	21.7	32.2
a) Banking system	12.0	12.5	11.6	21.9
b) Insurance	1.2	2.7	3.5	6.1
c) Other	1.8	5.0	6.5	4.2
2. Loans by financial institutions	5.9	6.0	8.0	6.2
3. Loans by government	4.4	3.9	4.0	2.0
4. Government domestic debt	5.9	4.8	5.3	6.7
5. Corporate stock[b]	1.5	1.0	1.0	1.1
6. Trade credit	7.3	6.5	5.5	4.2
VI. National assets %	100.0	100.0	100.0	100.0
National assets £I bill.	3.4	38.6	72.4	52.0
VII. Foreign debt	3.5	8.8	7.7	11.1
VIII. Gross national product; £I bill.[c]	0.9	6.9	11.5	118.0

[a]Including equity.
[b]Only securities listed on exchanges.
[c]Year-end rate.

(Source of basic data on following page)

Source of basic data:

Line I.1	Very rough estimates guided by expansion of cultivated land and agricultural prices.
Line I.2	Estimated at 30% of value of structures based on information on residential structures from Central Statistical Office (Israel).
Lines II.1–3	Derived for 1951–66 from Gaathon's estimates in 1955 prices (242) and for 1976 on a communication from him, shifted to current prices by gross fixed capital formation deflators derived from national accounts (*YNAS* var. issues).
Line II.4	Estimated at about one-third of year-end rates of gross national product (*IFSYB* 1979, 238–39).
Line II.5	Estimated on basis of data on value of livestock at a few benchmark dates (*SAI* 1978, 428–29), and number and prices of livestock (loc. cit., and Gaathon 1971, 22).
Line II.6	Estimated at four times year-end rate of expenditures on consumer durables in national accounts (Central Statistical Office, *Monthly Statistical Bulletin of Statistics*, var. issues e.g., September 1979, 17 ff.).
Line IV	Derived from data in *IFSYB* 1979, 41–93, 238–39.
Line V.1	For cols. 1–3 Heth 1970, 205, increasing 1950 figures by one-fourth in line with growth of assets of banking system; for col. 4 *SAI* 1980, 506 ff., 653.
Line V.2	*SAI* 1980, 224, and 1972, 225, for cols. 3 and 4; rough estimates, based on claims on private sector of deposit banks (*IFSYB* 1979, 236–37) for cols. 1 and 2.
Line V.3	*SAI* 1980, 537; 1973, 582 for cols. 3 and 4; rough estimates for cols. 1 and 2.
Line V.4	*SAI*, var. issues, e.g., 1980, 539; refers to March 31 of following year. Foreign debt about 0.20 in 1951; 1.70 in 1962; 3.80 in 1966; 70.0 in 1976 (loc. cit.).
Line V.5	Only stocks listed on exchanges (Bank of Israel, *Annual Report*, var. issues, e.g., 1979, 312).
Line V.6	Assumed equal to inventories.
Line VII	Based on Central Statistical Office, *Monthly Statistical Bulletin*, December 1978, 28 for cols. 2–4, rough estimates for col. 1, using official exchange rates.
Line VIII	*IFSYB* 1981, 242–43.

11. Italy

Table A11 is taken from a report written in 1975 in collaboration with Salvatore Zecchini of the Servizio Studi of the Banca d'Italia, with only a few changes and estimates for 1977 added by Mr. Zecchini.[1]

The quality and coverage of the basic data used in constructing the national balance sheet for Italy back to 1861 is probably as good as in the case of France and Belgium, though inferior to that for Germany or the United States. The entries depend primarily on fairly recent estimates of the capital stock by the perpetual inventory method (Vitali 1968; Esposito 1973), on an exhaustive tabulation of the balance sheets of credit institutions by de Mattia (1967) and for recent years on the flow-of-funds statistics of the Banca d'Italia published in its annual reports. As in most countries, the estimates for land, inventories, consumer durables, mortgages, and trade credit have a wide margin of error, as do those for private securities outstanding before World War II. The quality of the data is, of course, considerably less unsatisfactory for the last three benchmark dates than for the seven earlier ones, particularly those before World War I.

Notwithstanding the shortcomings of the data from which table A11 has been constructured, it reflects reasonably correctly the significant changes which have occurred in the structure of Italy's real infrastructure and financial superstructure in the full century between unification, when Italy was still a mainly agricultural country, far behind Western Europe and North America and its economic development to a modern industrialized nation, which has not yet fully caught up with the leaders. The transformation is particularly evident in the increase between 1861 and 1977 in the share of financial assets from one-sixth to one-half of national assets; the decline of the share of agricultural land from over two-fifths to 5 percent of tangible assets; the increase of nonresidential structures and equipment from fully one-third to two-fifths of reproducible assets; in the increase in the share of financial institutions in the financial superstructure from less than one-tenth to over one-half, a high ratio in international comparison; the decline in the share of the public debt from nearly one-third to one-fifth, and that of corporate securities from 20 to 4 percent of the value of all financial instruments outstanding; and the elimination of the net foreign investment in Italy that was relatively substantial until World War I.

Many of the secular changes, however, have not followed a straight line trend. Thus the increase in the financial interrelations ratio from 0.21

1. The only published estimate of a national balance sheet for Italy (Siesto 1973, 474) is limited to the year 1970. Its structure of assets is very similar to that shown in table A11 for 1973 and its absolute total is compatible to the total of table A11 for 1970.

to 1.04, evidencing the increasing importance of the superstructure, has been concentrated in the 1862–81, 1915–29, and 1951–73 periods, while it showed no or only little increase between 1881 and 1915 and between 1929 and 1938, fell sharply between 1938 and 1951 as a result of inflation, and declined moderately, as in most other countries, between 1973 and 1977. Similarly the sharp upward movement in the financial intermediation ratio was interrupted between 1914 and 1951. The movements of the share of government debt in financial assets are very irregular. Starting in 1961 from nearly one-third, an internationally very high ratio, it rose to nearly one-half in 1881, reflecting almost continuous budget deficits, but at the eve of Italy's participation in World War I had been brought back to one-third, where it stayed for the three following benchmark dates, i.e., until 1951, the burden of the large war debts being sharply reduced by inflation. In the following decades of rapid economic growth, the share of the government debt in all financial assets was cut in half, staying at nearly one-sixth in 1963 and in 1973, but increasing moderately in the late 1970s.

Table A11 **National Balance Sheet of Italy, 1861–1977 (National Assets = 100.0)**

	1861 (1)	1881 (2)	1895 (3)	1914 (4)	1929 (5)	1938 (6)	1951 (7)	1963 (8)	1973 (10)	1977 (11)
I. Land	39.1	34.8	33.9	26.8	17.9	18.3	19.3	10.8	9.0	8.2
1. Agricultural	34.7	31.0	30.5	22.7	13.7	14.3	12.4	4.8	3.0	2.5
2. Other	4.4	3.8	3.5	4.1	4.2	4.0	6.9	6.0	6.0	5.7
II. Reproducible assets	43.8	37.1	35.1	41.5	41.8	39.6	51.3	43.3	37.4	40.9
1. Structures and equipment	34.0	29.4	27.9	32.5	32.6	30.3	43.6	36.2	30.6	32.7
a) Dwellings	18.7	15.1	12.0	10.3	9.5	8.0	20.6	17.5	15.3	16.6
b) Other private	8.5	7.4	8.6	15.8	16.9	16.5	15.4	13.4	11.4	11.6
c) Public	6.8	6.9	7.3	6.3	6.3	5.8	7.5	5.3	3.9	4.5
2. Inventories	4.1	3.5	3.3	4.4	4.5	5.6	4.4	3.6	3.4	3.9
3. Livestock	2.7	1.9	1.7	2.4	1.9	1.3	0.9	0.6	0.3	0.6
4. Consumer durables	3.0	2.3	2.1	2.2	2.8	2.4	2.4	2.9	3.1	3.7
III. Tangible assets	82.9	71.8	69.0	68.2	59.7	57.8	70.6	54.	46.4	49.1
IV. Monetary metals	0.2	0.2	0.7	0.9	0.5	0.1	0.2	0.6	1.2	0.7

Table A11 (Continued)

	1861 (1)	1881 (2)	1895 (3)	1914 (4)	1929 (5)	1938 (6)	1951 (7)	1963 (8)	1973 (10)	1977 (11)
V. Financial assets	16.9	28.0	30.3	30.8	39.9	42.0	29.1	45.	51.6	50.2
1. Claims against financial institutions[a]	1.4	4.4	6.8	10.4	13.8	14.2	9.7	18.	27.6	28.2
a) Banks	0.9	2.5	2.7	3.8	6.9	5.3	5.7	8.9	13.5	14.6
b) Savings institutions	0.5	1.5	2.8	5.2	4.9	5.3	2.7	5.2	6.4	7.6
c) Insurance organizations	0.0	0.1	0.4	0.9	1.3	2.0	0.6	1.4	1.5	1.3
d) Other	0.0	0.3	0.9	0.5	0.8	1.7	0.7	3.3	6.2	4.7
2. Loans by financial institutions[b]	0.7	2.5	3.1	3.5	5.7	5.2	3.4	8.0	8.1	6.8
3. Private mortgages	3.0	2.7	2.5	2.0	1.0	0.8	1.2	0.7	0.5	0.5
4. Government debt	5.4	13.6	13.1	10.1	11.7	14.1	8.8	6.8	8.3	10.0
a) Central	5.0	12.6	11.9	9.2	10.5	11.9	6.8	4.7	5.0	6.4
b) Other	0.4	1.0	1.2	1.0	1.2	2.2	2.0	2.1	3.3	3.6
5. Corporate bonds	1.6	1.1	1.0	0.6	0.5	0.4	0.2	0.9	0.9	0.7
6. Corporate stock	1.8	0.9	1.2	0.8	3.8	3.0	2.5	7.3	3.5	1.2
7. Trade credit	3.0	2.7	2.5	3.3	3.4	4.2	3.3	2.7	2.6	2.9
VI. Net foreign assets	−0.5	−2.4	−2.6	−1.0	...	...	...	0.3	0.8	0.2
National assets %	100.0	100.0	100.0	100.0	100.0	100.0	100.0	100.0	100.0	100.0
VII. National assets; lire[c]	56.2	95.2	114.9	204.0	110.9	141.8	84.8	239.8	801.6	1766.2
VIII. Gross national product; lire[c,d]	8.8	11.9	12.5	26.1	154.0	174.0	11.2	30.6	100.2	205.9

[a]Includes equity, i.e., equal to assets.
[b]Includes consumer loans.
[c]Bill. lire in cols. 1–6, trill. lire in cols. 7–10.
[d]Year-end rate.

Source of basic data:

Line I.1:

Col. 1	Average of estimates of Mulhall, 1896, 192, for 1840 and 1882 at .25 lire per £.
Col. 2	Mulhall's estimate for 1882 (loc. cit.).
Col. 3	Mulhall (1892), 589.
Cols. 5, 6	Retti-Marsani in *La vita economica italiana* 10, no. 4 (1936), 24.
Col. 6	Vitali in Fuá 1969, 3:421. Includes land improvements of 20.8 bill. lire.
Col. 7	Estimate of Istituto Nazionale Economia Agraria for 1956 reduced by 15% in line with index of agricultural prices.
Cols. 8, 9	*ASI* vols. 25 (1971) and 28 (1974); averages of mid-year values.
Col. 10	*ASI* estimate for 1976 (vol. 30, 1976, 176) increased in line with implicit price index of value added in agriculture.

Line I.2:

Cols. 1–10	Sum of (1) a proportion of the value of dwellings (line II.1.a) increasing from 15% in cols. 1 and 2 to 25% in cols. 9 and 10, and (2) one-tenth of the value of other structures (lines II.1.b and 1.c).

Line II.1:

Cols. 1–6	Derived from Vitali's estimates in constant prices and his indices of investment goods (Fuá 1969, 3:419–21 and 436–38).
Cols. 7, 8	Derived from Esposito's estimates in constant prices (De Meo 1973, 190) and implicit price indices of investment goods of *ASI* 1974.
Cols. 9, 10	Obtained by adding to estimates for 1971 (Esposito, loc. cit.) estimates of net capital formation in constant prices and reflating results by implicit price indices for appropriate category of capital expenditures. Istituto Centrale di Statistica, *Annuario Statistico Italiano*, (var. issues).

Line II.2:

Cols. 1–5	Estimated at one-third of lines II.1.b and 1.c, the 1938 ratio.
Col. 6	Estimate of Giannone, 1964, 97, which is described as "certainly underestimated," less estimate for livestock.
Cols. 7–10	Average of four estimates, namely, (1) value for 1938 plus net changes in constant prices (*ASI*, var. issues), reflating result by index of wholesale prices; (2) one-third of gross national product; (3) one-third of fixed capital of enterprises (lines I.2 + II.1.b); and (4) one-tenth of structures and equipment (line II.1).

Line II.3:

Col. 1	Rough estimates.
Col. 2	Estimate of Ministry of Agriculture.
Cols. 3–6	Estimates of Retti-Marsani (1936, 27). The figure in col. 3 is based on estimate for 1901, that in col. 6 on estimate for 1934.
Cols. 7–10	Assumed to decline from 20% to 15% of inventories (line II.2), compared to ratio of 23% in 1938.

Line II.4:

Cols. 1–5	Roughly estimated at one-fifth of gross national product, the ratio in the 1950s.
Cols. 6–9	Based on estimates of Manfroni 1976, for 1973 expenditures on consumer durables and their implicit prices (*ASI* 1977), and depreciation rates of Manfroni.
Col. 10	Estimates for 1973 plus household net expenditures in constant prices reflated by appropriate price indices.

Line IV:

Cols. 1–3	*Statesman's Yearbook*, var. issues.

Cols. 4–6	*SYBUN*, var. issues.
Cols. 7–10	Derived from data in *IFSYB* 1980, 41–42.
Line V.1:	
Cols. 1–5	Assets of financial institutions from De Mattia 1967, 857 ff., except for line V.1.c (Goldsmith 1969, table D-14) and for Cassa Depositi e Prestiti. Figures for cols. 1–3 are approximate.
Cols. 6, 7	*ASI*, var. issues.
Cols. 8–10	Banca d'Italia, *Relazione Annuale*, var. issues; *Bolletino* 1971, 864–65.
Line V.2:	
Cols. 1–6	Credits to private sectors by financial institutions except insurance organizations (De Mattia); figure in col. 6 estimated on basis of 1936 value. Includes consumer credit.
Col. 7	Banca d'Italia, *Bolletino*, 1971, 910.
Cols. 8–10	As for line V.1.
Line V.3:	
Cols. 1–4	Estimate of 4 bill. lire for 1914, based on Princivalle's figure of 3 bill. lire for 1903 (cited Gini 1962, 182–82) moved in line with value of agricultural land and dwellings (lines I.1 and II.1.a). The estimate for 1914 is compatible with a census of mortgage debts in 1910 (*ASI* 1914).
Cols. 5–10	Assumed to decline from 4% to 2% of value of agricultural land and dwellings; covers only private (noninstitutional) mortgages.
Line V.4:	
Cols. 1–3	Necco 1915, 92.
Cols. 4–7	*ASI*, var. issues.
Cols. 8–10	As for line V.1.
Line V.5:	
Col. 1	Rough estimates.
Cols. 2–4	*ASI*, var. issues.
Cols. 5, 6	Rough estimates.
Col. 7	Value for 1963 reduced by increase in net indebtedness in 1951–63 (*ASI* 1974, 122).
Cols. 8–10	As for line V.1.
Line V.6:	
Cols. 1–6	Nominal capital of nonfinancial corporations (*ASI*, var. issues). It is assumed that excess of nominal over paid-in and of market over paid-in capital offset each other.
Col. 7	Banca d'Italia, *Bolletino*, 1978, 910.
Cols. 8–10	As for line V.1.
Line V.7:	
Cols. 1–10	Estimated at three-fourths of inventories.
Line VI:	
Col. 1	Assumed to be zero.
Cols. 2, 3	Decennial balance of payments *saldi* (Tagliacarne 1961, 355) cumulated from 1861 on. The figure in col. 3 is the average of the values for 1890 and 1900.
Col. 4	Based on Feis 1961, chap. 10.
Col. 8	Cotula and Caron in Banca d'Italia, *Bolletino*, 1971, 6.
Cols. 9, 10	From appendix of Banca d'Italia, *Relazione Annuale*, var. issues.
Line VIII:	
Cols. 1–6	Mitchell 1975, 781, 787.
Cols. 7–10	*IFSYB* 1981, 246–47.

12. Japan

The national balance sheet of Japan for the postwar period essentially can be put together from two official sources: the estimates of tangible assets of the Economic Planning Agency (e.g., 1979), and the flow-of-funds accounts of the Bank of Japan (e.g., 1978). The situation is not quite as comfortable for the prewar period, but thanks to a compendium of financial historial statistics published by the Bank of Japan (1966), and to a series of volumes on the main fields of economic statistics back to the late 19th century sponsored by Hitotsubashi University (Ohkawa 1965) the task is much easier than for many other countries. Table A12 is derived from the national balance sheets in Goldsmith (1983b), where the sources are identified and some of the features of the balance sheets are discussed. A sectorized balance sheet for 1977, derived from the same sources, appears in tables B9 and B10. It would have been fairly easy to produce comparable annual balance sheets since the mid-1950s, but there was no need for them in this study. A more detailed discussion of the national balance sheet of Japan together with a description of sources may be found in Goldsmith (1983).

The structure of Japan's national balance sheet and the changes in it differ considerably between the period extending from the Meiji restoration in 1868 and World War II, when Japan developed from a peripheral preindustrial nation to a major modern power economically approaching, though still substantially behind, the level of the then-leading countries; and—the period after the destruction of a substantial part of its wealth, the loss of its overseas empire and a few years of hyperinflation—the last three decades of extraordinarily rapid economic growth.

The national balance sheets of the first period from 1885 to 1940 reflect the transition from a traditional agricultural to a semi-industrialized westernized country, in the decline of the share of agricultural land in tangible assets from nearly one-half to one-third, while the share of equipment quadrupled from 3 to 13 percent. Simultaneously the financial interrelations ratio (financial: tangible assets) advanced sharply from 0.30, a level characteristic of now-underdeveloped countries, to over 0.60 in 1913 and to 1.40 in 1940, one of the highest values among developed countries, reflecting the existence of a complex comprehensive partly duplicative system of financial instruments and institutions, originally organized following Western models. Within the financial superstructure, the share of financial institutions increased from one-fourth to two-fifths, again a high ratio in international comparison. Other signs of financial modernization are the sharp increase in the share of corporate securities from almost nothing to over one-fifth of all financial assets, and the declines in the shares of agricultural debt from over 20 to 3 percent and of trade credit from also over one-fifth to one-tenth. The sharp increase in the importance of government debt, from 6 percent of all financial assets in 1920 to 14 percent in 1940, reflects partly heavy loan-financed military expenditures. The disappearance of the initially substantial net foreign indebtedness is another indication of financial maturity.

The changes in the structure of the national balance sheet in the postwar period are in many respects similar to those observed during the 65 years before World War II, but, because they start from a balance sheet structure radically changed by war and inflation, they result in a balance sheet that in 1977 closely resembles in its structure that of 1930 before the distortions introduced by the inflationary 1930s and 1940s. Thus the financial interrelations ratio nearly doubled, from not much over one-half in 1955 to unity two decades later, compared to a value of about 1.20 in 1930. Within tangible assets the share of land declined, notwithstanding rapid rises in land prices, from nearly two-thirds to one-half, now mostly represented by urban land, still a ratio very high in international comparison and evidence of the extraordinarily high levels of land prices in Japan. The share of nonresidential structures and equipment rose from less than one-half of reproducible tangible assets to over three-fifths, reflecting the extraordinary expansion of the stock of industrial capital.

The changes are much less pronounced among financial assets. Thus the share of financial institutions remained in the neighborhood of 30 percent throughout the postwar period, the level of 1900, but substantially below that of the 1920s and 1930s. The share of corporate securities fluctuated between one-eighth and one-sixth without definite trend, substantially the same range as between 1900 and 1930. The government debt, while increasing its share substantially, particularly in the 1970s, remained small—about 5 percent even in 1977—well below the level during the prewar period.

Table A12 **National Balance Sheet of Japan, 1885–1977 (National Assets = 100.0)**

	1885 (1)	1900 (2)	1913 (3)	1930 (4)	1940 (5)	1955 (6)	1965 (7)	1970 (8)	1977 (9)
I. Land	35.2	34.7	25.8	20.6	14.3	42.3	36.4	30.9	25.0
1. Agricultural	25.8	24.4	18.1	14.7	8.9	26.0	10.7	7.5	5.4
2. Other	9.4	10.3	7.7	5.9	5.4	16.4	25.7	23.4	19.6
II. Reproducible tangible assets	41.5	39.8	35.4	24.3	27.1	22.5	19.0	21.2	24.4
1. Structures	26.6	26.6	19.2	13.7	15.2	. . .	. . .	. . .	. . .
a) Residential	14.2	15.6	10.1	5.5	6.3	3.5	3.1	3.4	5.0
b) Other	12.5	11.0	9.1	8.2	9.0	10.5	10.6	12.5	15.0
2. Equipment	2.6	3.5	5.1	4.0	5.3				
3. Inventories	5.3	4.9	7.2	3.9	4.0	7.0	3.9	3.7	3.0
4. Livestock	6.2	4.3	3.4	2.0	1.9				
5. Consumer durables	0.8	0.5	0.5	0.8	0.6	1.4	1.4	1.6	1.4
III. Tangible assets	76.7	74.5	61.1	44.9	41.4	64.7	55.4	52.2	49.5
IV. Monetary metals	0.2	0.4	0.9	0.6	0.1	0.0	0.0	0.0	0.0

Table A12 (Continued)

	1885 (1)	1900 (2)	1913 (3)	1930 (4)	1940 (5)	1955 (6)	1965 (7)	1970 (8)	1977 (9)
V. Financial assets	23.1	25.1	38.0	53.5	58.2	34.9	44.6	47.5	50.1
1. Currency and demand deposits						3.1	3.7	3.5	3.4
2. Other deposits	5.9	7.8	13.0	22.7	22.9	7.2	8.8	8.9	10.2
3. Insurance claims						0.7	1.3	1.4	1.6
4. Loans by financial institutions	2.1	3.3	6.4	8.6	6.1	8.5	12.1	12.0	11.7
5. Loans by government	...	...	...	...	...	2.6	2.2	2.6	3.5
6. Agricultural debt	5.0	2.1	2.1	2.8	1.9	...	...	...	...
7. Mortgages	0.6	1.0	0.9	1.2	0.7	...	...	...	...
8. Government debt	3.7	2.3	3.4	5.0	8.1	1.4	0.5	1.2	2.6
9. Corporate and foreign bonds	...	0.0	0.2	1.7	1.0	1.2	2.7	2.7	2.7
10. Corporate stock	0.5	3.8	4.7	6.8	11.8	3.9	5.0	3.6	4.2
11. Trade credit	5.3	4.9	7.2	4.8	5.7	4.5	7.7	8.8	6.9
12. Other financial assets	...	...	...	...	...	1.9	0.7	2.8	3.3
VI. Foreign assets gross	...	...	...	...	...	...	...	...	...
Foreign assets net	−3.7	−1.2	−2.5	1.0	0.3	0.4	−0.1	0.3	0.4
VII. National assets %	100.0	100.0	100.0	100.0	100.0	100.0	100.0	100.0	100.0
National assets ¥[a]	6.60	20.45	42.70	153.7	420.6	56.85	277.9	611.5	1792
VIII. Gross national product; ¥[a,b]	0.81	2.45	4.88	14.0	42.2	9.17	30.3	76.8	193.5

[a]Bill. for cols. 1–5; trill. for cols. 6–9.

[b]Year-end rate.

Source of basic data: Goldsmith 1983b, tables 3-17, 4-19, 7-40.

13. Mexico

Mexico lacks the two main building blocks of a national balance sheet, a national wealth estimate and flow-of-funds statistics. However, its good statistics of financial institutions, the recent as yet unpublished estimates of the stocks of structures and equipment and of inventories, and the census values of agricultural land and of livestock permit the construction of national balance sheets for the postwar period that are probably better, with the exception of the value of corporate stock and of mortgages, than those for most less-developed countries, and probably are not inferior to those for some developed ones. The estimates for the prewar period, which have been made only for the benchmark dates of 1930 and 1940, are admittedly more precarious. There is no point as yet of even attempting estimates for the period of the revolution and its aftermath, i.e., the 1910s and 1920s. It would be very interesting to have as a historical background an estimate for the end of the Porfiriato, but its derivation, if possible at all, would, in the absence of most relevant aggregative statistics, require greater familiarity with Mexican primary data of over a half-century ago and much more intensive work than was possible within the confines of this investigation. The results are shown in table A13.

For the benchmark dates 1948, 1960, 1965, 1973, and 1978, the unpublished estimates of the national accounts section of the Banco de Mexico have been used for structures, equipment, inventories, and livestock, the only existing up-to-date data and presumably the best available set. It was, however, necessary to add estimates for dams, dikes, and roads for which only gross expenditure figures exist; and to split the estimates for structures between residential and other structures, which can be done only with a substantial margin of error, of course not affecting the broader totals. The estimates for the 1930 and 1940 benchmark dates, particularly the former, are subject to larger errors, though for the 1940s figures for gross capital expenditures are provided in the national accounts. Since the Mexican national accounts are in the process of reexamination in connection with their transfer from the Banco de Mexico to the Secretaria de Programacion y Presupuestos, all the estimates of the stock of reproducible tangible assets may have to be revised. The only component of reproducible assets that had to be estimated independently throughout the period are consumer durables, and this could be done only very roughly since the Mexican national accounts do not break down aggregate private consumption and thus do not provide data on the expenditures on consumer durables.

The estimates of the value of agricultural land, which includes forests, could be based for the 1960 and 1970 benchmarks on the data from the census of the same years, which are presumed to reflect market values and include by analogy imputed values for communally owned land (ejidos), although this is not marketable (Departamento de Agricultura 1975, 341). The estimates for 1948, 1965, 1973, and 1978 had to use interpolation or extrapolation, guided mainly by the trend of agricultural prices, the result being particularly hazardous for 1978. The figures for 1930 and particularly for 1940, taken from an unofficial estimate, appear to be on the low side compared to the Census figures for 1950, but no basis was found for a possible adjustment. The estimates for other land had to be derived independently. Those for land underlying residential structures were obtained by applying to structure values ratios based on scattered evidence. The estimates for nonresidential land were made by the same method, but in this case the ratio of 15 percent was fairly arbitrary and maintained throughout the period. As a result the estimates of nonresidential nonagricultural land are, as in most countries, the wealth component subject to the largest relative error.

As Mexico has had good and comprehensive statistics of financial institutions for the postwar period, the series for their assets and loans should be quite reliable, as are the statistics of fixed interest securities outstanding. While comprehensive statistics of trade credit are lacking, there are enough data on large corporations to establish with some confidence the ratio of trade credits to inventories. Among financial assets, therefore, the two most problematic components are the estimates for mortgages and for corporate stock.

In the absence of comprehensive data of mortgages outstanding, their volume had to be estimated on the basis of the relation between new mortgages (net of cancellations) to national product in recent years, a procedure which may involve substantial errors for the earlier part of the period.

The estimate of the market value of corporate stock carries by far the largest absolute and one of the largest relative margins of uncertainty. In 1978 the 166 companies listed on the Mexico Stock Exchange, for which the Exchange tabulated balance sheets had a paid-in capital of about $81 billion ($ = peso) and a book value of $122 billion (communication from Exchange). The relative size of the capitalization of the rest of the approximate 150, supposedly much smaller, companies listed on the Exchange is not known. At about 20 percent of the 166 companies, we obtain a paid-in capital of approximately $100 billion with a book value of about $150 billion. For 28 companies with a paid-in capital of $400 million or over, and a total of $30 billion, the market value at the end of 1978 was about $84 billion, or 2.8 times their paid-in capital. Assuming that the ratio was somewhat lower for the smaller companies and adding the market value of two companies with very large capitalization (Altos Hornos and Telefonos Mexicanos) which, for different reasons, had unusually low market prices, the market value of all shares listed on the Mexico Stock Exchange at the end of 1978 should have been in the order of $250 billion.

This leaves the much more difficult second step of estimating the value of the over 100,000 corporations whose shares are not listed on a stock exchange, a task made precarious by the lack of aggregate statistics of the corporate universe—such as paid-in capital, profits, or dividends—except the income taxes paid by them. These taxes amounted in 1978 to $66 billion, and it is estimated that the average ratio of taxes to profits was slightly below 40 percent (information from Ministry of Finance), pointing to aggregate net corporate profits of the order of $170 billion. A similar though slightly lower figure is obtained by starting from the net profits of over 5000 larger corporate taxpayers of $59 billion in 1977, or of those showing profits of $68 billion (Ministerio de Hacienda 1977) which in 1978, to judge by tax receipts, should have been about 40 percent higher, or $84 and $97 billion, respectively. Since these taxpayers are estimated to account for about 60 percent of the profits of all corporations, the latter's profits in 1978 would have to be put at $140 or $160 billion, respectively. The price-earnings ratio to be applied to these figures undoubtedly must be below the median value of about 13 for 76 large companies listed on the Mexico Stock Exchange. But by how much? It seems unlikely that it could be much below 10, which would indicate a value in the order of $1300 to $1700 billion, the lower end of the range being used in table A14.

Four tests may be applied to these figures. First, the estimated corporate profits of $140 or $170 billion are equal to 7 or 8 percent of the gross national product of 1978. This seems high since in the United States in the same year corporate profits (before inventory and capital consumption adjustments) constituted 9 percent of national product. Second, the estimated value of all stock of $1300 billion is equal to 55 percent of gross national product against 48 percent in the United States at the end of 1978 (Federal Reserve flow-of-funds data), though the ratio was as high as 115 percent 10 years earlier. Third, the market value of the stock of the 166 corporations listed on the stock exchange is of the same order of magnitude as the replacement cost of their fixed assets or of the adjusted book value of their equity. In the United States the ratio of the market value to the current value of fixed assets of all nonfinancial corporations was 0.71 in 1978, though it averaged 0.99 for the last decade and 1.05 for the 30 years 1949–78 (Holland and Myers 1980, 322). Fourth, the value of stocks listed on the Mexico Stock Exchange is less than one-fifth that of all corporate stock outstanding in the country. This is an extraordinarily low ratio in international comparison, but may be explained by the as yet underdeveloped character of the stock market in Mexico, in particular the large share of government corporations, of the subsidiaries of foreign companies and of corporations closely held by a family or a small group of investors. Inconclusive as these considerations are, they do not seem to rule out at least the order of magnitude of an estimate of $1300 billion for the end of 1978.

Estimation is even more precarious for other benchmark dates. The aggregative statistics used to derive the estimate for 1978 are not available before the early 1970s. One is therefore forced to base extrapolation on an index of industrial stock prices of unknown quality and, in the absence of statistics of the outstanding nominal capital of all corporations, on very rough estimates of the nominal value of new issues of corporate stock by new and existing corporations. The margin of error in these extrapolations, of course, increases the farther the benchmark date is from 1978. There is no doubt, however, that the value of corporate stock has increased rapidly, particularly in the 1970s. At the end of 1978 the price index compiled by the Mexico City Stock Exchange was six times as high as it had been eight years earlier, and the nominal value outstanding at that date may have been more than twice as large as it had been in 1970. In the 1950s and 1960s, however, stock prices seem to have lagged considerably behind the rate of inflation, hardly rising at all between 1951 and 1970 in the face of an increase in the price level, measured by the gross national product deflator, of 150 percent, though the nominal value of corporate stock outstanding increased rapidly.

The estimates of the value of all corporate stock for the benchmark dates before 1978, which obviously have a wide margin of error, have been derived by assuming that their prices rose somewhat less rapidly, particularly in the 1970s, than the index of prices of stocks listed on the Mexico Stock Exchange; and that the nominal capital of all corporations, that was in the order of $100 billion in 1968, the only year for which an estimate can be made (based on the capital of the 525 highest capitalized corporations shown in Caso Brecht 1971, 314 ff.), increased approximately in line with national product. This would mean that in 1960,, e.g., the value of corporate stock was in the order of only 3 percent of that of 1978.

Turning from the discussion of methods of estimation and sources of data to that of the resulting figures, it is necessary to keep in mind the current unavoidable substantial margins of errors in the estimates, particularly for the earlier part of the period, and to be correspondingly careful in their interpretation.

It may be astonishing, and does not seem to be attributable to errors in the statistics, that Mexico's financial interrelations ratio has not shown a pronounced trend during the postwar period, standing slightly above 0.70 in 1948 as well as in the 1970s after having fallen to 0.60 at the end of the inflationary 1950s. The ratio, however, had risen sharply between 1930 and 1940 from 0.35 to 0.65, reflecting the fact that the 1930s were the period in which the country's financial superstructure, and particularly its banking system, was rapidly rebuilt after the ravages of the revolution and its immediate aftermath. It is not yet possible to be confident of the level of the ratio before the revolution. The fact that the assets of financial institutions in 1911 were somewhat higher than in 1930 (Goldsmith 1969, 527), while nominal national product was two-thirds below the 1930 level (ibid., 553) and national wealth presumably was below it, though to a lesser extent, point to a ratio well in excess of that of 1930, though below that of 1940.

The capital-output ratio has shown a substantial but irregular increase during the postwar period, rising from 1.8 in 1948 to 2.6 in 1978. The ratio of reproducible assets alone to national product went up more rapidly from about 1¼ to slightly above two. Both ratios had already reached or exceeded the present level in 1930 and showed a sharp decline over the 1930s and 1940s, possibly reflecting in part an overestimation of the earlier estimates of the capital stock.

Within tangible assets, the share of land fell during the postwar period from about one-third to one-fifth. This was due entirely to the sharp decline in the share of agricultural land from over one-fourth in 1948 to not much above 5 percent 30 years later. The share of nonagricultural land, on the other hand, appears to have more than doubled from 6 to 14 percent. Changes in the structure of the stock of reproducible assets were characterized by increases in the share of dwellings—from 17 to 31 percent of the total—and other structures, and the sharp decline of that of livestock from about 10 to 2 percent. The share of inventories declined substantially from approximately one-sixth to one-tenth. That of equipment showed no trend, remaining close to one-fifth of reproducible assets. Its failure to show the increase that might be expected, in view of the progress of industrialization, is due in part to the smaller rise in the price of equipment compared to construction costs. The apparent decline in the share of consumer durables is probably attributable in part to the indirect and unsatisfactory method of estimation, but also is influenced by the decline in their relative prices. Some of these movements were reserved in the 1930s and 1940s.

Financial assets have grown more rapidly than either tangible assets or national product, in the latter case rising from slightly above unity in 1930 and 1.3 in 1948 to over 1.8 in 1978, most of the increase occurring in the last five years and reflecting primarily the quintupling of stock prices. In the long run, however, the main contributor to the increasing role of financial assets has been the rapid rise of the assets of financial institutions, from 20 percent of national product and 7 percent of tangible assets in 1930, to 36 percent and 20 percent, respectively, in 1948; and to over 60 percent of national product and nearly 25 percent of tangible assets in 1978. As a result, the share of the assets of financial institutions in the financial superstructure has increased from one-fifth in the 1930s to over one-fourth in 1948 and to nearly two-fifths in 1973, declining to one-third in 1978 because of the extraordinary rise in stock prices during the 1970s. This means that at the present time financial institutions (eliminating relations among them) are either the lender or the issuer of approximately three-fifths of all financial instruments.

The assets of financial institutions have always been highly concentrated in the central bank; a few large government financial institutions, primarily Nacional Financiera; and institutions belonging to a few private groups headed until recently by a large commercial bank, all the institutions in the group now being consolidated into one multibank (banco multiple). (The situation changed radically with the nationalization of all banks in late 1982.)

Private insurance companies have remained relatively small, as might be expected in a situation of pronounced long-term inflation, their share in the assets of all financial institutions falling from 6 percent in 1930 to less than 3 percent in 1978. Social security organizations, though large, have invested only a small part of their funds in financial assets and therefore have not been regarded as financial institutions. The share of the government's domestic debt in all financial assets has been increasing but has remained relatively low, reaching 7 percent in 1978 compared to 5 percent in 1948 and less than 1 percent in 1930. The share of mortgage debt, which is very imperfectly known, seems to have fallen from nearly three-tenths in 1930 to less than 5 percent in 1978. Trade credit appears to have fluctuated around one-tenth of all financial instruments throughout the period. Uncertainty is greatest about the share of corporate stock. In 1978 it is estimated at nearly three-tenths of all financial assets, and the share appears to have been of the same order of magnitude throughout most of the period, though substantially lower from the mid-1960s on.

The estimates of the national wealth and assets discussed so far omit, as is usual in most such calculations, the value of subsoil assets. This is becoming misleading in the case of Mexico. At the end of 1978 the proven reserves of oil and gas were officially estimated at 46 billion barrels. (Petroleos Mexicanos, 1979, 67). At a world market price at wellhead of $20 per barrel, this was equal to $920 billion, or about $21,000 billion. This figure must first be reduced by the cost/price ratio, which is not known. It must further be reduced because these reserves will become available only in the future. Assuming an average life of reserves of about 60 years, corresponding to the 1978 ratio between reserves and production, and a discount rate of only 5 percent as oil prices at least may be presumed to keep step with inflation, this means a reduction by fully 75 percent. If this is combined with the assumption of a cost price ratio of one-half the present value of Mexico's oil and gas, reserves at the end of 1978 would be in the order of $2500 billion. This would be equal to two-fifths of the value of all other tangible assets, and to over one-fifth of national assets. Even if allowance is made for the fact that a price well below the world market is charged for domestic consumption and the price of gas is still below its thermal oil equivalent, the present value of Mexico's oil and gas reserves is now so large that it cannot be left out of the picture without distorting it. It would, for instance, reduce the financial interrelations ratio for 1978 from 0.71 to about 0.50, and increase the share of land in national wealth from about one-fifth to over two-fifths. The ratios before the sharp rise in the relative prices of oil and gas and before the discovery of the large new oil fields in the mid-1970s would, of course, be much smaller.

Table A13 **National Balance Sheet of Mexico, 1930–1978 (National Assets = 100.0)**

	1930 (1)	1940 (2)	1948 (3)	1960 (4)	1965 (5)	1973 (6)	1978 (7)
I. Land	22.1	15.2	18.3	16.1	13.1	11.4	11.3
1. Agricultural	17.0	10.8	15.0	10.9	7.6	4.8	3.4
2. Residential	} 5.1	2.9	1.9	3.4	3.5	4.5	5.8
3. Other		1.5	1.4	1.9	2.0	2.0	2.2
II. Reproducible tangible assets	51.7	45.4	39.3	46.2	46.6	45.7	47.1
1. Structures	...	20.5	16.0	23.1	24.4	26.0	28.8
a) Residential	12.3	10.5	6.6	10.3	11.2	12.3	14.4
b) Other	} 25.4	10.0	9.4	12.9	13.2	13.7	14.4
2. Equipment		9.0	8.4	10.4	9.3	9.6	9.7
3. Inventories	5.1	6.6	6.1	5.0	5.8	4.3	4.5
4. Livestock	4.8	3.9	3.8	3.1	2.7	1.8	1.0
5. Consumer durables	4.1	5.6	5.1	4.6	4.5	4.0	3.0
III. Tangible assets	73.8	60.6	57.6	62.4	59.7	57.1	58.4
IV. Monetary metals	0.0	0.0	0.6	0.3	0.2	0.2	0.1

V. Financial assets	26.2	39.4	41.8	37.3	40.1	42.6	41.5
1. Claims against financial institutions[a]	5.1	9.4	11.4	11.5	12.9	16.3	13.9
a) Banks[b]	4.2	7.4	6.7	5.1	5.2	15.9[f]	13.5[f]
b) Insurance	0.3	0.5	0.5	0.6	0.5	0.5	0.4
c) Other	0.6	1.5	4.2	5.9	7.2	...[f]	...[f]
2. Loans by financial institutions[c]	2.9	5.2	6.3	6.3	7.6	9.3	7.4
3. Mortgages	7.6	8.0	4.7	3.4	3.6	3.0	1.8
4. Domestic government debt	0.2	1.0	2.0	1.2	2.8	3.7	2.8
5. Domestic corporate bonds[d]	0.0	0.0	0.7	0.6	0.4	0.2	0.1
6. Corporate stock	6.4	11.9	14.1	10.3	8.1	6.7	12.0
7. Trade credit	4.1	4.0	2.6	3.9	4.7	3.5	3.6
VI. National assets %	100.0	100.0	100.0	100.0	100.0	100.0	100.0
National assets $bill.[e]	15.7	25.1	106.6	583.4	983.7	2691	10844
VII. Gross national product; $bill.	4.0	6.4	33.9	161	267	717	2445

[a]Including equity, i.e., equal to total assets.
[b]Central, commercial and savings banks.
[c]Excluding mortgage and loans to government.
[d]Excluding those issued by financial institutions.
[e]Year-end rate.
[f]"Other" included with banks.

(Source of basic data on following pages)

Source of basic data:

Line I.1:
- Cols. 1, 2 — Patiño 1955.
- Cols. 3–7 — Estimated on basis of census data for 1950, 1960, and 1970 (Departamento de Agricultura 1975, 313 ff.) in line with movements of agricultural prices.

Lines I.2, 3:
- Cols. 1–7 — Sum of land underlying dwellings, estimated to rise from 25% to 40% of line II.1; and other land, estimated at 15% of line II.2.

Line II.1:
- Cols. 1, 2 — Patiño, loc. cit. ("edificios particulares"); may include underlying land.
- Cols. 3–7 — Estimated to rise from 40% to 50% of all structures.

Lines II.2, 3:
- Col. 1 — Based on estimate of Reynolds (1970) that real capital stock showed "no significant trend" between 1925 and 1950, and movements of construction costs (Banco de Mexico 1978).
- Col. 2 — Interpolated between 1930 and 1948 values on basis of capital expenditures and price movements (Banco de Mexico, *Informe Annual*, 1978.

Lines II.2, 3
- Cols. 3–7 — Banco de Mexico, 1978, adding 30% to estimates of the stock of depreciable construction to take account of dams, dikes, and roads, based on the average ratio for 1950–78 of gross expenditures on these items (loc. cit). Figures for 1948 and 1978 extrapolated from 1950 and 1977 on basis of capital expenditures and prices.

Line II.4:
- Cols. 1–3 — Estimated at 20% of national product, the average ratio for cols. 5–8.
- Cols. 4–7 — Nonagricultural inventories (Banco de Mexico 1979) plus agricultural inventories of Conasupo and in warehouses (op. cit.), hence slightly understated.

Line II.5:
- Cols. 1, 2 — Patiño, loc. cit.
- Col. 3 — Estimated at 12% of national product, the 1940 and 1960 ratios.

Line II.5:
- Cols. 4–7 — As for line II.4.

Line II.6:
- Cols. 1–2 — Patiño, loc. cit. ("menajes domesticos").
- Cols. 3–7 — Estimated at four times year-end rate of expenditures on consumer durables, which, in the absence of the relevant figures in the national accounts, have been estimated to rise from 4% to 6% of total consumption, the 1970 ratio shown in the input-output table of Secretaria de Programacion y Presupuestos.

Line V.1:
- Cols. 1–4 — Goldsmith, 1969, 527.
- Cols. 5–7 — Banco de Mexico, *Informe Annual*, var. issues.

Line V.2:
- Cols. 1–7 — Estimated at about 55% of line V.1, the 1948 and 1978 ratios dervied from Banco de Mexico, *Informe Annual*, var. issues, and *IFSYB*, 1979, 294–95.

Line V.3: — Net additions to mortgage debt estimated at 1½% of national product, the 1968–76 ratio (*AEM*, various issues, e.g., 1975–76, 971); this may well be an underestimate.

Line V.4:

Cols. 1–4	*LN* and *SYBUN*, var. issues; 1930 entry refer to 1932 and that for 1940 to 1939.

Line V.4:

Cols. 5, 6	*IFSYB* 1979, 297.
Col. 7	Banco de Mexico, *Informe Annual*; may not include debt not in form of government securities.

Line V.5:

Cols. 1, 2	Estimated to be negligibly small.
Cols. 3–5	Basch 1968; probably includes foreign issues.
Cols. 4–7	Banco de Mexico, *Informe Annual*, var. issues.

Line V.6:

Cols. 1–6	Extrapolated from 1978 value on basis of issues of corporate stock, and of stock price index (League of Nations, *Statistical Yearbook*, var. issues; *IFSYB*, 1979, 294–95; Bolsa de Valores, 1979).
Col. 7	See text.

Line V.7:

Cols. 1–7	Estimated as equal to about 80% of inventories, approximately the ratio for large corporations in 1975–78 (Secretaria de Programacion y Presupuestos, 1979) and in 1962 and 1951 (Goldsmith, 1966, tables 52–54).

Line VII:

Cols. 1–3	Goldsmith (1966), table 4.
Cols. 4–7	*IFSYB* 1981, 300–301.

14. Norway

Since Norway has one of the best and oldest statistical systems, particularly in the fields of national accounts, it is not overly difficult to construct national balance sheets essentially from official sources back to the late 19th century, the main gaps referring to some types of land and to the assets of some financial institutions in the prewar period. The quality of the national balance sheet of Norway shown in table A14 is, therefore, higher than for most other countries.

In the last century Norway has experienced, like all other countries, a substantial increase in the financial interrelations ratio from fully one-third to seven-eighths. The share of financial institutions in all financial instruments outstanding, however, has risen only moderately from 31 to 37 percent, indicating the absence of radical changes in the financial superstructure. Among financial institutions growth has been much more rapid, as usual, for insurance and other organizations than for the banking system. Government debt, which kept in the neighborhood of one-tenth of financial instruments until World War II, has since risen to about one-seventh partly to help finance government enterprises. In contrast the share of corporate securities, predominantly corporate stock, has collapsed from a level of nearly one-tenth of financial assets in the prewar period to not much over 1 percent in 1978, the result of the declining importance of the corporate sector in the economy and the lag in stock prices.

Among tangible assets the share of agricultural and forest land has fallen sharply from fully one-third to only one-twentieth, most of the decline taking place in the prewar period. Within reproducible assets, the share of residential structures was sharply reduced, falling from one-third to one-fifth, while that of equipment, which may be regarded as a proxy for industrialization and includes a high proportion in international comparison of ships and recently oil drilling equipment, doubled from one-eighth to one-fourth. That of nonresidential structures stayed close to two-fifths. Allowance for the value of subsoil Northsea oil would somewhat reduce the share of all other assets.

Table A14 **National Balance Sheet of Norway, 1880–1978 (National Assets = 100.0)**

	1880 (1)	1899 (2)	1913 (3)	1930 (4)	1939 (5)	1953 (6)	1965 (7)	1972 (8)	1978 (9)
I. Land	31.0	23.7	18.3	13.5	13.5	12.1	11.2	9.0	8.5
1. Agricultural	12.9	9.5	7.1	5.7	4.6	1.7	1.7	1.8	1.5
2. Forest	12.0	8.6	5.9	3.0	3.0	5.5	3.7	1.6	1.4
3. Other	6.1	5.7	5.3	4.8	5.8	5.0	5.8	5.7	5.7
II. Reproducible tangible assets	42.2	40.7	39.9	35.7	44.1	43.6	44.9	44.5	45.0
1. Structures	30.9	28.6	26.6	24.2	29.2	25.1	29.1	28.5	28.3
a) Residential	14.6	13.7	11.8	9.5	12.0	12.0	9.9	9.5	9.5
b) Other	16.3	14.8	14.8	14.7	17.2	13.1	19.2	19.0	18.9
2. Equipment	5.1	6.2	7.7	6.0	7.9	11.5	11.2	10.8	11.1
3. Inventories	2.8 }	4.6	4.3	4.3	5.1	4.5	2.9	3.0	3.8
4. Livestock	2.0 }					0.7	0.3	0.2	0.1
5. Consumer durables	1.4	1.3	1.2	1.2	1.9	1.8	1.5	2.0	1.8
III. Tangible assets	73.2	64.4	58.3	49.2	57.6	55.8	56.1	53.5	53.5
IV. Monetary metals	0.5	0.4	0.4	0.4	0.3	0.2	0.1	0.1	0.1

Table A14 (Continued)

	1880 (1)	1899 (2)	1913 (3)	1930 (4)	1939 (5)	1953 (6)	1965 (7)	1972 (8)	1978 (9)
V. Financial assets	26.3	35.1	41.3	50.4	42.1	44.0	43.8	46.4	46.4
1. Claims against financial institutions[a]	8.2	11.8	13.4	19.0	15.3	18.4	15.9	18.0	17.2
a) Currency and deposits	4.6	5.9	7.9	8.1	6.1	7.3	8.6	9.2	8.4
b) Insurance	0.3	0.5	0.8	1.5	2.0	2.1	3.5[d]	3.7[d]	3.3[d]
c) Other[a]	3.3	5.4	4.7	9.4	7.1	9.0	3.7	5.0	5.5
2. Loans by financial institutions[b]	...	...	...	...	...	...	...	...	...
3. Mortgages	2.6	4.0	4.2	4.7	5.1	3.7	...[c]	...[c]	...[c]
4. Government debt[c]	2.2	3.7	3.4	7.4	5.1	6.9	5.1	5.8	6.8
5. Corporate bonds	0.0	0.0	0.4	0.6	0.6	0.5	2.3	1.2	1.9
6. Corporate stock	1.7	3.1	4.5	4.7	3.5	1.3	1.1	0.9	0.6
7. Government enterprise capital	...	...	...	...	...	...	2.8	1.8	1.7
8. Trade credit	4.3	4.0	3.0	3.2	3.4	3.3	3.5	3.1	2.9
9. Other financial assets	7.2	8.6	12.4	10.7	9.1	10.0	13.2[e]	15.6[e]	15.3[e]
VI. Foreign assets gross	...	...	...	...	...	...	...	...	...
Foreign assets net	...	...	...	...	...	...	...	...	...
VII. National assets %	100.0	100.0	100.0	100.0	100.0	100.0	100.0	100.0	100.0
National assets bill. kr.	5.83	9.31	16.90	40.45	52.82	183.2	434.2	850.3	1980.2
VIII. Gross national product; bill. kr.[f]	0.73	1.09	1.89	4.11	6.60	21.7	52.0	104	217

[a]Including equity.
[b]Included in V.9.
[c]Including government enterprise debt 1.2 in col. 7; 0.9 in col. 8; 1.7 in col. 9.
[d]Includes social security funds.
[e]Mortgages (line V.3) included in line V.9.
[f]Year-end rate.

Source of basic data:

Line I.1:

Cols. 1–3	*SÖ* 1914. Entry for 1880 refers to 1876–85 average; that for 1900 to 1896–1905 average; that for 1913 is extrapolated from 1906–10 average on basis of average price of rural properties. (*HSN* 1978, 153).
Cols. 4, 5, 7, 8	Extrapolated on basis of 1953 value and average price of rural properties (*HSN* 1978, 153).
Col. 6	Aukrust and Bjerke 1959, 118.
Col. 9	Extrapolated on basis of 1972 value and price increase in 1972–75 (11½% per year).

Line I.2:

Cols. 1–4	Very rough estimates.
Cols. 5, 7–9	Extrapolated from 1953 value on basis of timber prices (*SÖ* 1958, 47; *HSN* 1978, 528) and 0.8% annual increase in productive forest area (*HSN* 1978, 157–58). This implicitly assumes no changes in cost/price ratios and in capitalization rate of earnings.
Col. 6	Aukrust and Bjerke, 118.

Line I.3: Estimated at 20% of structures, a low ratio in international comparison.

Lines II.1, 2:

Col. 1	Estimated on basis of 1899 values and change in capital stock in fixed prices (*HSN* 1978, 106).
Cols. 2, 5	*HSN* 1978, 107.
Cols. 3, 4	Aukrust and Bjerke, 117. Dwellings estimated on basis of shares in total structures in 1899 and 1939. Figures for 1913 slightly reduced below 1915 estimates of Aukrust and Bjerke.
Col. 6	Aukrust and Bjerke, 117.
Cols. 7, 8	*SAN* 1978, 71.
Col. 9	1976 figures increased in line with average rate of increase in capital stock in fixed prices (*SAN* 1978, 70) and national product deflator.

Lines II.3, 4

Cols. 1–5	Estimated at average of 41% of national product and 21% of nonresidential structures and equipment, the 1953 ratios, hence probably progressively understated.
Col. 6	Aukrust and Bjerke, 117.
Cols. 7–9	As for lines II.1, 2.

Line II.5:

Cols. 1, 2	Rough estimate.
Cols. 3–9	Estimated at four times year-end rate of expenditures on consumer durables (*HSN* 1978, 98–99. The recent ratio is 4½ on the basis of an estimate by a public committee for the "most valuable" consumer durables (information from Statistisk Sentralbyrå).

Line IV:

Cols. 1–5	*HSN* 1978, 483 ff.; figures in cols. 1–3 include silver.
Cols. 6–9	Derived from *IFSYB* 1979, 40–43, 322–23.

Line V:

Col. 1	Rough estimate based on Skånland, 1967, 43.
Cols. 2–6	Skånland, 39; total claims of domestic nonfinancial and foreign sectors; entry in col. 3 refers to 1914 and that in col. 6 is interpolated between 1951 and 1956 values.
Cols. 7–9	Statistisk Sentralbyrå *Kreditmarkedstatistikk* 1965, 26 ff.; 1973–78, 40 ff.

Line V.1:

Cols. 1–5	Goldsmith 1969, 533. Entries in col. 2 refer to 1900, those in col. 4 to 1929, and those in col. 5 to 1938.

Line V.1:

Col. 6	Skånland 1967, 43, 46–47; estimates for col. 6 interpolated between Skånland's figures for 1951 and 1956.
Cols. 7–9	As for line V.

Lines V.1, 1.a, 1.b:

Cols. 1–6	Skånland 1967, 43, 46–47; estimates for col. 6 interpolated between Skånland's figures for 1951 and 1956.
Cols. 7–9	As for line V.1.

Line V.2:

Cols. 1–6	Skånland 1967, 39; entry for col. 1 is based on Skånland 1967, 43; that for col. 3 refers to 1914 and that for col. 6 is interpolated between values for 1951 and 1956.
Cols. 7–9	Statistisk Sentralbyrå, *Kreditmarkedstatistikk* 1965, 26–29; 1972–74, 32–35; 1973–78, 38–41; social security claims added.

Line V.4:

Cols. 1–6	*HSN* 1978, 453, 459. Debt of municipalities estimated for col. 1.
Cols. 7–9	As for line V.2.

Lines V.5–7

Col. 1	Rough estimate.
Cols. 2–5	Skånland 1967, 100–01; entry for col. 3 refers to 1914.
Col. 6	*HSN* 1978, 456, extrapolated from 1952 value.
Cols. 7–9	As for line V.2.

Line V.8: Estimated as declining from fully one-third to one-fourth of national product, which puts it at a ratio of inventories falling from about unity to three-fourths.

Line V.9:

Cols. 1–9	Difference between lines V.2 and sum of lines V.2a–2g; consists mainly of debt of households and business, chiefly to financial institutions.

Line VI:

Cols. 2, 3	Skånland 1967, 39.
Cols. 4–6	*HSN* 1978, 509.
Cols. 7–9	As for line V.2.

Line VII:

Cols. 1–5	Mitchell 1975, 782, 788.
Cols. 6–9	*IFSYB* 1981, 326–27.

15. Russia/USSR

The USSR presents a particular challenge to the estimator and analyst of national balance sheets because of the interest in comparing the structure of the balance sheet of the largest centrally planned economy, in which most assets are owned by the government, with those of large capitalist countries. Technically the estimation of the national balance sheet of the USSR is not more difficult than, and the results are probably as reliable or unreliable as, for most other countries. In fact, the statistics available on the value of reproducible tangible assets are at least as extensive and cover on an annual basis at least as long a period as for most countries, including two comprehensive censuses of a type not available for any market economy. Information on financial assets is much weaker and less detailed, but still permits an estimation of the main components, though with a substantial margin of error. Recently one-time semi-official estimates have become available for the value of land, forests, and subsoil assets, particularly controversial in a country without a market for assets, figures which are still missing in most other countries.

For the years 1928, 1937, 1950, and 1959, as well as for Tsarist Russia in 1913, I have, in table A16, not without misgivings as some improvements are possible, used estimates made 20 years ago. Those for 1969, 1972, and 1977 are based directly or indirectly on official or semi-official Soviet statistics, and are therefore subject to the usual reservations, which, however, in this case do not seem to be too serious. 1969 and 1972 have been used as benchmark years because of the availability of estimates by specialists (Garvy 1977 for financial assets for 1969; Powell 1979 for reproducible assets in 1972).

It should be pointed out that the figures shown for two items (consumer durables and nonagricultural land) for most of the benchmark dates are "nominal," i.e., they are not based on official statistics or estimates of other students but are very rough estimates based on analogy with other countries, entered only to obtain a figure for total tangible and national assets. In the case of consumer durables, the estimate underlying table A16 is considerably smaller, indeed only half as large, as an estimate of Bogachev (1979, 5) for "household property," which probably is a more comprehensive concept.

The main differences in the structure of the national balance sheets of 1913 and 1928 is the sharp reduction of the share of the financial interrelations ratio from 0.49—at that time a ratio well below that of developed countries—to 0.09 which reflects the elimination of most of the financial superstructure of Tsarist Russia, particularly the cancellation of old government and private debt and the disappearance of corporate securities. The structure of reproducible tangible assets, on the other hand, did not change substantially as the figures do not reflect the shift of most of them from private to public ownership.

By the late 1930s, the banking and credit system of the Soviet Union had been sufficiently rebuilt, including the creation of a new government debt, to raise the financial interrelations ratio to 0.28. Indeed the share of bank deposits, bank and trade credit, and government bonds in 1937 with 22 percent of national assets was slightly higher than it had been in 1913, though the character of financial institutions and instruments had changed radically.

During the following four decades, the relative size of the financial superstructure changed but little, the financial interrelations ratio keeping close to 0.30 except for a dip around 1970. As a result of the elimination of government bonds and other organizational changes, credits of the monobank and deposits with it and the affiliated savings banks came to dominate the financial superstructure almost completely.

The changes in the structure of tangible assets reflect the rapid industrialization of the country. Thus the share of land, mostly agricultural, is estimated to have declined from nearly two-fifths to not much over one-fifth, still a high ratio in international comparison which reflects the continued substantial importance of agriculture in the Soviet economy. The decline in the share of livestock from approximately 5 to 2 percent was even sharper. The increase of nonresidential structures and of equipment from two-fifths to three-fifths of reproducible tangible assets is the most obvious evidence of industrialization, while the decline of the share of residential structures from one-fifth to one-sixth reflects the low priority accorded to housing in government plans. Although the share of inventories declined from over one-fifth to less than one-sixth of reproducible assets—the same as in 1913—it remained high in international comparison, a reflection as in other Communist countries of inefficiencies in economic administration.

Table A15 compares the present structure of the national balance sheet in the Soviet Union with that of the United States. The financial interrelations ratio is, of course, much higher in the United States—about unity against 0.30—and the financial structure differs greatly, the share of financial institution's assets and liabilities to all financial assets being much higher. The differences in the structure of tangible assets, while less radical, are still substantial. The share of land in the Soviet Union, with less than one-fifth, is slightly below that of the United States with one-fourth, and the relation between agricultural and other land probably is reversed. Among reproducible tangible assets, the shares of nonresidential structures and equipment and of inventories are much higher in the Soviet Union, while that of residential structures is much lower—one-sixth against nearly one-third—differences which reflect the policies of the Soviet government. The share of forests and of subsoil assets, which are not included in table A15, appear to be somewhat higher in the Soviet Union—about one-tenth of tangible assets (Silaev and Shimov 1977, 20), against about 6 percent in the United States in 1975 (Goldsmith 1982, table 86). This difference is not large enough to affect the comparisons substantially.

Table A15 **Structure of National, Tangible, and Financial Assets in USSR and U.S.A, 1977–1978 (%)**

	National Assets		Tangible or Financial Assets	
	USSR (1977) (1)	U.S.A. (1978) (2)	USSR (1977) (3)	U.S.A. (1978) (4)
I. Tangible assets	76.5	50.2	100.0	100.0
1. Reproducible tangible assets	62.7	37.7	82.0	75.1
a) Residential structures	10.1	11.1	13.3	22.1
b) Other structures	25.3	11.9	33.1	23.7
c) Equipment	12.5	5.7	16.3	11.4
d) Inventories	9.4	4.2	12.3	8.4
e) Livestock	1.5	0.3	2.0	0.6
f) Consumer durables	3.8	4.5	5.0	9.0
2. Nonreproducible assets	13.7	12.5	18.0	24.9
a) Agricultural land	11.0	2.7	14.4	5.4
b) Other land	2.8	9.8	3.6	19.5
II. Financial assets	23.5	47.3	100.0	100.0
1. Gold	0.3	0.3	1.3	0.6
2. Claims against financial institutions	12.7	13.3	54.0	28.1
3. Other	10.5	33.7	44.7	71.3
a) Claims	10.5	26.4	44.7	55.9
b) Corporate stock	...	7.3	...	15.4
III. Foreign assets	...	2.5	...	...
IV. National assets %	100.0	100.0	100.0	100.0
National assets amount; $bill.	4400[a]	17887	...	...

[a]R.1 = $1.44 (official rate).
Source: Tables A-16 and A-22.

Table A16 National Balance Sheet of Russia/USSR, 1913–1977 (National Assets = 100.0)

	1913 (1)	1928 (2)	1937 (3)	1950 (4)	1959 (5)	1969 (6)	1972 (7)	1977 (8)
I. Land	44.2	51.4	30.2	25.6	19.7	28.3	23.4	17.7
1. Land	44.2	51.4	30.2	25.6	19.7	21.0	17.4	13.1
2. Forests						7.3	6.0	4.5
II. Reproducible tangible assets	27.7	40.0	47.9	50.3	54.1	54.0	58.2	59.9
1. Residential structures	4.3	9.8	9.4	13.1	11.8	10.2	10.9	9.7
2. Other structures	9.0	16.9	18.8	20.8	16.7	30.5	33.8	36.1
3. Equipment	3.7				7.4			
4. Inventories	4.6	6.9	10.3	11.2	12.8	9.1	8.9	9.0
5. Livestock	3.6	3.4	4.6	2.6	2.1	1.2	1.3	1.5
6. Consumer durables	2.4	3.0	4.8	2.6	3.3	2.9	3.4	3.7
III. Tangible assets	71.9	91.4	78.2	76.0	74.6	82.3	81.7	77.6
IV. Monetary metals	1.2	...	...	...	...	0.1	0.2	0.3
V. Financial assets	26.9	8.6	21.8	24.0	26.2	17.6	18.2	22.1
1. Claims against financial institutions	9.1	1.8	7.5	7.2	9.8	9.3	9.6	12.1
a) Banks (excluding *b*)	4.5	1.8	7.0	6.6	8.1	7.2	7.0	8.5
b) Savings banks	0.8	0.1	0.5	0.6	1.7	2.1	2.7	3.6
c) Mortgage banks	2.1	...	...	...	...	...	...	...
d) Insurance	0.1	...	...	...	0.2	...	...	...
e) Other	1.6	...	...	...	...	...	...	...
2. Domestic government bonds	2.2	0.6	3.5	5.6	6.3	...	...	...
3. Corporate bonds	0.2	...	...	...	...	...	...	...
4. Corporate stock	2.1	...	...	...	...	...	...	...
5. Mortgages	2.1	...	0.1	0.2	0.2	0.2	0.2	0.2
6. Bank Credit	11.2	6.2	5.8	6.2	7.2	6.3	6.6	8.0
7. Other credit			4.9	4.8	2.7	1.8	1.8	1.8
VI. Foreign assets gross	...	...	...	...	...	...	...	...
Foreign assets net	−2.5	...	...	...	...	...	...	...
VII. National assets %	100.0	100.0	100.0	100.0	100.0	100.0	100.0	100.0
National assets bill. (new) rubles	20.7	23.4	82.6	312	615	1850	2297	3090
VIII. Gross national product; bill. (new) rubles	2.2	3.2	28.1	91.2	171	330	390	500

Source of basic data:

Cols. 1–5	Goldsmith 1964, 98 except for line VIII, col. 5 (Becker 1969, 25).
Col. 6:	
Line I	Estimate for 1972 reduced by 5%.
Lines II.1–3	*NK* 1978, 40 (in 1973 prices), reduced by about 5% to take account of increase in prices.
Line II.4	*NK* 1973, 768.
Line II.5	Obtained by assuming that value of livestock bore same relation to total fixed capital in agriculture (*NK* 1977, 40) as in 1972, i.e., about 24%, and reducing resulting figure by 5% for price change.
Line II.6	Estimated at 7% of sum of lines II.1–5, somewhat below Eastern European relation.
Lines IV–VI	Garvy 1977, 108, 147.
Col. 7:	
Line I.1	Sum of estimates for (*a*) agricultural land (320 bill. R. cited by Loiter 1976, 30, and Silaev and Shimov 1977, 20); for method of estimation see Silaev and Shimov, 22–23; neither source indicates date to which estimates refer, but it seems to be close to 1972; and (*b*) other land, roughly put at about 20% of value of buildings (*NK* 1973, 60).
Line I.2	Midpoint of range of estimates cited by Loiter and by Silaev and Shimov, loc. cit.
Line II.1–5	Powell 1979, 69. Line II.1 assumed to bear same relation to sum of lines II.1–5 as in 1970 (*NK* 1977, 49).
Line II.5	*NK* 1973, 768.
Line II.6	Estimated at 7½% of lines I.1.a–1.e.
Line IV	Garvy 1977, 147, increased in accordance with market price of gold (*IFSY* 1979, 43).
Line V.1.a	Estimated at slightly above line V.6.
Line V.1.b	*NK* 1973, 634.
Line V.5	Rough estimate based on value for 1969.
Line V.6	*NK* 1973, 782.
Line V.7	Estimated at same relation to inventories as in 1969 (20%).
Line VI	United States, National Foreign Assessment Center, 1980, 7.
Col. 8:	
Line I	Estimate for 1972 increased by about 10%.
Lines II.1–3	*NK* 1978, 40 (1973 prices), increased by about 5% to take account of rise in prices between 1973 and 1977. The increase in prices between 1972 and 1977, and between 1969 and 1972 as well, apparently was small as the replacement cost of fixed capital covered by the 1972 census was only 12% above original cost (*NK* 1973, 60).
Line II.4	Derived from *NK* 1978, 547–48.
Line II.5	Obtained by assuming that value of livestock in 1973 prices bore same relation to total fixed capital in agriculture (*NK* 1977, 40) as in 1972, i.e., 24%, and increasing by 5% for price change.
Line II.6	Estimated at 8% of lines II.1–5.
Line IV	Quantity assumed same as in 1972. Use of another estimate (*Pick's Currency Yearbook*, 1977–79, 742), leads to a considerably higher ratio, namely, approximately 1%.
Line V.1.a	Estimated at slightly above line V.6.
Line V.1.b	*NK* 1977, 634, extrapolated on basis of trends in preceding years.

Line V.5	Rough estimate based on 1969 level.
Line V.6	Figure for 1976 (*NK* 1978, 659) extrapolated on basis of trend of preceding years.
Line V.7	As for 1972.
Line VI	As for col. 7.

16. South Africa

There are no official estimates of the stock of financial assets and liabilities, and those for the stock of reproducible assets start only in the 1970s. An unofficial estimate for all components of national wealth is limited to 1955 and 1945, though available annually back to 1909 for fixed assets and inventories (Franzsen and Willers 1959). In the cases of financial assets, comprehensive estimates are limited to the assets of financial institutions for a few benchmark dates ending with 1963. In this situation the construction of a national balance sheet, necessarily from heterogenous sources in the fashion of a puzzle, is hazardous for both the prewar and postwar periods. The results of the attempt, shown in table A17 must therefore be used with caution, particularly for the prewar period for which the estimates for corporate stocks are subject to a wide margin of error. Nevertheless the picture shown is reasonable and is not contradicted by other quantitative and institutional information available.

In evaluating the national balance sheet of the Union of South Africa, it must be kept in mind that the country has a dual economy, indicated by the fact, or rather conjecture, that the nonwhite population, which accounts for four-fifths of the total, probably owns less than one-fifth, and possibly not more than one-tenth, of national assets, assuming their share to be substantially below that in national income, which for 1946–47 was put at less than 30 percent (Reynders 1963, 246). This nature of the economy is reflected in the very low share of residential structures of only about one-seventh of total reproducible assets, since the value of the dwellings of the nonwhite majority, particularly outside of large urban centers, is very small.

The changes in the national balance sheet of South Africa between 1913, only a few years after the Union was formed, and 1978, visible in table A17 correspond to what one would expect of a country shifting rapidly from a mainly agricultural to a fairly industrialized economy, and from a rudimentary to a modern financial superstructure. The financial interrelations ratio (financial: tangible assets) rose in these 65 years from a little over one-half, fairly high for an underdeveloped country, to over 1.10 in the 1950s and 1960s, the level of developed countries, but in the late 1970s declined sharply to about 0.75, partly as the result of the failure of stock prices to rise in line with national product, national wealth, or the volume of claims. Within tangible assets the share of land declined from over one-fourth, then mainly agricultural, to less than one-fifth, now mostly urban. The decline in the share of livestock was even steeper, from one-fifth of all reproducible assets to a mere 2 percent. The share of residential structures in contrast advanced from one-tenth to one-seventh, and that of other structures and equipment from fully one-half to nearly two-thirds.

Among changes in the financial superstructure, the increase in the share of financial institutions in total financial assets was pronounced, rising from one-fifth to two-fifths. It occured mostly in the postwar period, and has concentrated in nonbanking organizations whose share in total financial assets doubled from one-sixth to three-tenths. The importance of government domestic debt rose sharply as a result of wartime borrowing of the Union government, but between 1955 and 1978 it declined from nearly one-fourth to one-seventh of all financial instruments outstanding. The high share of corporate stock is a characteristic feature of South Africa's financial superstructure, reflecting the existence of the highly capitalized gold mining industry, a large part of whose equity is owned abroad. The share of corporate stock in total financial assets has, however, declined from possibly as much as one-half before World War I to about one-third in the 1930s and to approximately one-eighth in the late 1970s, partly because the gold mining industry lost in importance in the rapidly growing economy.

Table A17 **National Balance Sheet of South Africa, 1913–1978 (National Assets = 100.0)**

	1913 (1)	1929 (2)	1938 (3)	1955 (4)	1965 (5)	1973 (6)	1978 (7)
I. Land	18.4	14.5	12.5	10.5	10.5	9.8	10.5
1. Agricultural	13.8	10.0	8.5	6.5	6.3	5.1	4.8
2. Other	4.5	4.5	4.0	4.0	4.2	4.6	5.7
II. Reproducible tangible assets	47.3	44.6	39.5	36.4	36.3	39.1	46.2
1. Structures	...	...	...	20.3	20.8	23.2	28.5
a) Residential	4.5	4.1	4.4	5.6	5.5	5.8	6.5
b) Other	} 25.3	23.7	23.0	14.7	15.3	17.4	22.0
2. Equipment				6.0	5.7	6.3	8.3
3. Inventories	4.9	5.1	4.2	4.6	4.5	4.6	4.2
4. Livestock	9.4	6.8	4.1	2.3	1.6	1.5	1.0
5. Consumer durables	3.3	4.9	3.9	3.3	3.7	3.4	4.3
III. Tangible assets	65.7	59.0	52.0	46.8	46.8	48.9	56.7
IV. Gold	0.3	0.4	0.4	0.5	0.5	0.9	0.6

V. Financial assets	34.0	40.6	47.6	52.7	50.5	48.0	40.3
1. Claims against financial institutions[a]	6.9	10.2	11.5	13.9	16.8	17.8	16.8
a) Banks	3.7	4.1	4.5	4.8	4.5	4.8	4.7
b) Savings institutions	0.8	1.7	2.5		3.1	3.1	2.8
c) Insurance organizations	1.2	3.6	3.9	9.1	5.6	6.0	5.9
d) Other	1.2	0.7	0.6		3.7	4.0	3.4
2. Loans by financial institutions	4.5	6.1	7.2	8.5	3.7	4.5	3.8
3. Mortgages					4.0	4.1	3.2
4. Domestic government debt	1.2	7.3	7.2	11.9	6.7	5.9	5.8
5. Corporate bonds	...	...	...	...	1.4	1.5	1.7
6. Corporate stock	16.4	12.0	17.5	13.9	13.3	9.5	4.8
7. Trade credit	4.9	5.1	4.2	4.6	4.6	4.7	4.2
VI. Foreign assets gross	...	...	...	...	2.2	2.2	2.4
Foreign assets net	...	...	...	...	...	−4.5	−4.7
VII. National assets %	100.0	100.0	100.0	100.0	100.0	100.0	100.0
National assets bill. Rand	2.45	4.13	6.89	32.5	65.0	156.5	321.6
VIII. Gross national product; bill. Rand[b]	0.31	0.58	0.87	4.0	8.0	17.4	42.2

[a]Including equities, i.e., equal to total assets.

[b]Year-end rate.

(Source of basic data on following page)

Source of basic data:

Cols. 1–4:	
Line I.1	For cols. 3 and 4, Franzsen and Willers 1959, 322; very rough estimates for cols. 1 and 2.
Line II	Franzsen and Willers, 314. Estimate in line I.1.e for 1913 based on Franzsen and Willers, 296; those for 1929 and 1939 derived by interpolation of ratio of livestock to inventories plus livestock for 1913 and 1955.
Line II.5	Assumed equal to four times consumers' expenditures on durable goods, which are assumed at 10% of total consumers' expenditures (Franzsen and Willers, 317).
Line IV	Franzsen and Willers, loc. cit. for 1955.
Lines V.1.a, 1.b	Goldsmith 1969, 539, for cols. 1–3; *IFSY* 1979, for col. 4.
Lines V.1.c–1.d	Goldsmith 1969 for cols. 1 to 3. Col. 4 interpolated between 1948 (Goldsmith 1969) and 1965 values.
Lines V.2, 3	Estimated at two-thirds of assets of financial institutions excluding Reserve Bank, slightly below the 1965–78 ratio for deposit banks, building societies and life insurance companies. (For these institutions' claims on private sector see *IFSYB* 1979, 371.) Hence noninstitutional mortgages are ignored.
Cols. 1–4:	
Line V.4	Bureau of Census and Statistics, 1960, Q-9, Q-19, for union and local governments, for cols. 1–3; col. 4 as for cols. 5–7.
Line V.6	Based on 1965 value and movements of stock prices (*IFSYB* 1979, 372–73; *SYBUN*, var. issues.
Line V.7	Assumed approximately equal to inventories, the 1973 ratio.
Line VIII	Mitchell 1982, 717, 724.
Cols. 5–7:	
Line I.1	Division of Agricultural Marketing Research 1980, 89.
Line I.2	Roughly estimated at approximately one-fifth of line II.1.
Lines II.1–3	Swanepoel and Van Dyk 1978, 49; for col. 7 unpublished estimate of Economics Department of South African Reserve Bank.
Line II.4	As for line I.1.
Line II.5	Estimates of Economics Department of South African Reserve Bank.
Line IV	Derived from *IFSYB* 1979, 41, 371.
Lines V.1–5	Supplied by Capital Markets Section of Economics Department of South African Reserve Bank.
Cols. 5–7:	
Line V.6	Market value of shares listed on the Johannesburg stock exchange (*South African Reserve Bank*, June 1979), average of end of June values; for col. 7 extrapolated on basis of stock price index.
Line V.7	Assumed approximately equal to inventories on basis of corporate inventories in 1973 (South African Reserve Bank, Economics Department), hence probably somewhat understated.
Line VI	*South African Reserve Bank*, December 1970, SS8H; March 1979, S-64; for col. 7 supplied by Economics Department of South African Reserve Bank.
Line VII	*IFSYB* 1981, 382–83.

17. Sweden

Although Sweden has had for a long time one of the best developed statistical systems, with important series going back to the 18th century, the available data, whether from official publications or other sources, are insufficient to construct a national balance sheet before the1960s, due primarily to the absence of estimates of either the capital stock or the stock of financial assets and liabilities. Even for the last decade, official statistics are limited in the case of tangibles to the gross stock in constant prices of reproducible tangible assets other than consumer durables. The deficiency in the field of financial assets and liabilities, however, has now been remedied by official sectorized flow-of-funds accounts which include information on stocks. Table A18 combines these data with estimates of tangible assets, which for several items leave much to be desired. The situation is less unsatisfactory for the household sector, for which balance sheets based on sample surveys, and hence not fitted into a system of national accounts, and unfortunately not covering insurance and pension claims and consumer durables, exist for seven benchmark dates between 1935 and 1975 (Spånt 1979, 87 ff.).

Table A18, limited to the last 15 years, shows not unexpectedly only moderate changes in balance sheet structure. The financial interrelations ratio, however, has increased substantially from 1.03 to 1.27 a quarter of a century later. The share of deposit and insurance claims in financial assets has stayed slightly above one-fourth since the late 1960s. The importance of government securities is fairly small, ranging between 5 and 7 percent of all financial instruments. The share of corporate securities is low in international comparison and has declined in the last 15 years from 15 to 8 percent of all financial assets. A distinctive feature is the high share of social security funds, which has risen from 2 percent of all financial assets in 1963 to 8 percent in 1978.

The share of land in tangible assets appears to have been declining slightly, but in view of the roughness of the estimates of land values the movement shown in the ratio derived from table A18 may not be significant. Among reproducible assets, the share of residential structures has been falling from 35 to 31 percent, while that of equipment stayed close to 17 percent.

The structure of the national balance sheet was undoubtedly quite different a century ago. Combining estimates of tangible assets for the late 1880s (Mulhall 1899, 589, for Sweden and Norway) with fragmentary data for the main types of financial instruments (for financial institutions Goldsmith 1969, 543), the financial interrelations ratio would seem to have been slightly below one-half, i.e., less than half as high as in the postwar period. Agriculture accounted for over two-fifths of all tangible assets, mostly in the form of land, while the present share of agricultural land is below 3 percent. At that time real income per head of the occupied population in Sweden has been put at less than one-half of the British and not much over two-fifths of the United States level (Clark 1951, 47, 63, 108), while real per head gross domestic product in 1976 was fully one-third higher than in Great Britain and less than 15 percent below that of the United States (Summers, Kravis, and Heston, 1980).

Table A18 National Balance Sheet of Sweden, 1963–1978 (National Assets = 100.0)

	1963 (1)	1969 (2)	1973 (3)	1978 (4)
I. Land	8.2	7.3	6.8	6.7
1. Agricultural[a]	1.9	1.4	1.3	1.2
2. Other	6.3	5.9	5.5	5.5
II. Reproducible tangible assets	41.0	38.7	37.9	37.2
1. Structures	28.0	26.7	25.7	24.8
a) Residential	14.2	13.1	12.0	11.6
b) Other	13.8	13.6	13.7	13.2
2. Equipment	6.8	6.1	6.6	6.4
3. Inventories	2.8	2.7	2.5	2.7
4. Livestock	0.4	0.3	0.3	0.2
5. Consumer durables	3.1	2.9	2.8	3.1
III. Tangible assets	49.2	46.0	44.7	44.0
IV. Monetary metals	0.1	0.1	0.2	0.2
V. Financial assets	48.1	52.0	52.5	53.4
1. Currency and deposits	9.7	9.4	9.2	8.4
2. Insurance[b]	4.3	5.0	5.9	6.2
3. Loans by financial institutions	9.0	12.0	11.8	13.9
4. Other loans	3.5	4.9	5.5	6.3
5. Government securities	3.4	2.8	2.8	3.9
6. Corporate bonds	0.7	0.7	0.8	1.0
7. Mortgage bonds	2.8	3.5	4.0	4.1
8. Corporate shares	5.8	4.5	3.4	2.7
9. Capital of government enterprises	1.1	0.8	0.7	0.7
10. Trade credit	4.2	3.9	3.8	3.1
11. Other financial assets	3.6	4.4	4.5	3.1
VI. Foreign assets gross	2.5	1.9	2.6	2.4
Foreign assets net[c]	1.1	0.6	0.9	−0.3
VII. National assets %	100.0	100.0	100.0	100.0
National assets bill. skr.	719	1190	1816	3262
VIII. Gross national product; bill. skr.[a]	98	162	234	411

[a]Includes forests.
[b]Includes social insurance.
[c]Does not include direct investments.
[d]Year-end rate.

Source of basic data:

Line I.1 — Farm land estimated as 1⅓ times assessed value according to information from Central Statistical Office) plus forest land and standing timber, the latter estimated on basis of statistics for 1965,

1970, and 1975 and prices of wood (*SAS*, var. issues, e.g., 1979, 115).

Line I.2 — Estimated at approximately 30% of residential and 15% of other structures (line II.1), a method which in 1973 yields estimates close to 1⅓ times assessed value.

Lines II.1, 2 — Obtained from official estimates of gross stock in 1975 (Statistiska Centralbyrån, *Statistiska Meddelanden*, N 1978:8.4, appendix 2, vol. 44, no. 5, and later issues) by shifting to current prices on basis of implicit deflators of the relevant types of capital formation derived from the national accounts (*YNAS* 1977, 1114–15), and using net/gross ratios of 0.62 for residential structures, 0.65 for other structures, and 0.55 for equipment which are based on rates of growth of real capital stock between 1963 and 1977 and assumed length of life (see Goldsmith 1962, 19). Estimates of deflator for col. 4 based on deflators for national product.

Line II.3 — For 1978 communication from Statistiska Centralbyrån. For other years extrapolated on basis of changes in inventories as reported in national accounts.

Line II.4 — Estimate for col. 1 based on Norwegian ratios to national product and reproducible tangible assets, moved for cols. 2–4 roughly in line with food prices (Statistiska Centralbyrån, *Allman Manadstatistik*, var. issues), since number of livestock changed little over the period (*SAS* 1978, 109).

Line II.5 — Estimated at four times year-end rate of expenditures on durable goods (*YNAS* 1977, 1113 for cols. 1–3; extrapolated for col. 4).

Line IV — Derived from data on quantities of gold held and gold prices (*IFSYB* 1979, 41 ff.).

Col. 1:

Line V.1 — Obtained by extrapolation from col. 2 on basis of data on money and quasi-money (*IFSYB*, loc. cit.).

Line V.2 — Goldsmith 1969, 543.

Lines V.3, 4 — Based on 1969 relation of loans to assets of financial institutions (Goldsmith, loc. cit.).

Line V.5 — For central government debt *IFSYB*, loc. cit.; rough estimates for local government debt.

Line V.6 — Rough estimate.

Line V.8 — Based on change in stock prices and new issues between 1963 and 1969, (*IFSYB* 1979, 388–89; *SAS*, var. issues).

Line V.9 — Rough estimate.

Line V.10 — Extrapolated from 1969 figures on basis of movement of inventories.

Line V.11 — Estimated at 9% of other financial assets, the 1969 ratio.

Cols. 2–4:

Lines V1–11 — Table A of flow-of-funds statistics (Statistiska Centralbyrån, *Statistiska Meddelanden*, 1978, N. 11, appendix 2B) for cols. 2 and 3, and N. 1979:12 for col. 4 except that holdings of stocks by households have been increased in all years by 43% of basis of 1975 holdings of unquoted to quoted stocks (Spånt 1979, 49).

Line VI — Very rough estimates extrapolated from col. 2 on basis of foreign exchange holdings of banks for gross and balance of payments in current account for net foreign assets.

Line VIII — *IFSYB* 1981, 402–3.

18. Switzerland

Switzerland is of such interest for the financial historian and analyst that an attempt has been made to construct its national balance sheet over the past century, although the basic statistical data on which such an attempt must be based are much poorer in the case of the infrastructure of national wealth than for most other developed countries. No reasonably detailed estimate of national wealth, official or academic, has been made for nearly 40 years, and estimates for earlier benchmark dates are rare and far from consistent. For financial assets, on the other hand, the basic data are not inferior to those available for many other developed countries, though they have never been brought together, and Switzerland still lacks the sectorized statements of financial assets and liabilities which most other developed countries have put together for a greater or smaller fraction of the postwar period as part of their flow-of-funds statistics.

This section is an abbreviated version of Goldsmith (1981), omitting description of methods of estimation and part of discussion of results.

While the margin of uncertainty thus is substantial in many of the estimates, particularly those for 1880, 1900, and 1929, the figures brought together in table A19 should reflect correctly the main changes in the national balance sheet of Switzerland over the past century, and provide a reasonably solid base for an analysis of trends in the infrastructure and the financial superstructure.

There is, for example, little doubt that the financial interrelations ratio (domestic financial plus gross foreign assets divided by tangible assets) has increased sharply over the century, and is now, and indeed has been throughout the 20th century, one of the highest among developed countries. In 1880 the ratio was already slightly above unity, then a high level in international comparison. In 1900 and 1913 it appears to have been in excess of 1.50, again relatively very high values. There seems to have been no further increase between 1913 and 1939, a period during which the ratio rose considerably in several large developed countries, e.g., Great Britain and the United States (Goldsmith 1969, chap. 7). From 1938 on, when the estimates of national wealth are less hazardous, the financial interrelations ratio has not shown a pronounced long-time trend, standing at about 1.60 at the beginning and at 1.80 at the end of the 40-year period. The main exception is the benchmark year 1948, when the ratio fell to nearly 1.30, as the value of financial assets, particularly foreign assets, expanded less than needed to meet the effect of war inflation on the value of tangible assets. The ratios were thus at most benchmark dates higher than those for any country except Great Britain in the first part of the period.

The main change in the structure of tangible assets, which can be followed in table A19 only since 1913, has been the sharp decline in the share of agricultural and forest land, according to the estimates from 22 to 2½ percent of the total, most of the decline apparently occurring between 1913 and 1938. This has been partly offset during the last 40 years by the increase in the share of other, largely residential, land. The changes among reproducible assets have been small, and show no definite long-term trends over the last 40 years except for the sharp decline in the always small share of livestock. Residential structures have accounted at all benchmark dates for between 20 and 23 percent of the total, while the share of nonresidential structures has risen from 34 to 37 percent and that of equipment has declined from 33 to 31 percent. Variations in the shares of inventories and consumer durables are more pronounced, but they must be interpreted cautiously because of the much weaker statistical basis of the estimates. As they stand, they suggest an increase in the share of these two components between 1938 and 1960, from 8 to 11 percent, and a decline after 1965 resulting in only a very small net increase over the entire period.

Changes in the structure of domestic financial assets over the century have been substantial and generally in line with those observed in other developed countries. The outstanding movement is the doubling of the share of financial institutions from fully one-fifth to nearly one-half. This means that, making a rough allowance for interfinancial assets, at the present time financial institutions are involved as either lender or borrower in over four-fifths of all domestic financial instruments against a ratio of less than two-fifths a century ago. Most of the increase in the share of financial institutions occurred between 1880 and 1913 and, to a lesser extent, between 1948 and 1973, while the share was fairly stable at close to two-fifths between 1913 and 1938. Although the banking system always remained dominant among financial institutions, insurance and pension organizations grew more rapidly, increasing their share in total domestic financial assets from 1 to 9 percent and that in the assets of financial institutions from about 5 to 18 percent. Most of these gains were made during the first half of the century, and their share reached its peak in 1960. The share of mortgages, which had been the most important financial instrument in 1880, was cut in half from nearly 45 to below 20 percent, mostly in the first three decades of the period. Throughout the century, assets of financial institutions and mortgages together have accounted for between three-fifths and two-thirds of all domestic financial assets, leaving the remainder to the various other financial instruments.

Among those instruments, the share of the debt of the Confederation has shown wide fluctuations, reflecting between 1900 and 1913 the nationalization of most of the railroads, and between 1913 and 1929 military expenditures during World War I. Since the Confederacy borrowed little for other purposes except in the 1930s and mid-1970s and at times retired debt, its share in total domestic financial instruments outstanding was at most dates very low in international comparison—in the 1970s well below 2 percent. The share of the debt of local governments, mostly for investment, has not shown a definite trend, remaining in the neighborhood of 3 to 4 percent of total domestic financial assets from 1913 on. Corporate bonds have accounted without trend for about 2 percent of the total since 1913, after the retirement of private railroad bonds soon after the turn of the century, when most of the companies were nationalized. The share of corporate stock increased substantially between 1880 and 1929; remained close to one-fifth during the following 35 years; and declined to one-seventh by the late 1970s, the level of 1913, thus sharing, though to a smaller extent, a movement observed in most countries.

The financial structure of Switzerland has always been characterized by a high share of foreign investments. It seems to have reached a first peak around the turn of the century. In 1913, when the first reasonably trustworthy estimate is available, the share was close to one-fifth of all financial assets and over one-fifth of tangible assets. The share declined considerably in the interwar period, falling in 1938 and 1948 to about one-tenth of financial assets and not much over one-eighth of tangible assets. It increased rapidly during the postwar period, reaching in 1978 nearly one-fourth of all financial and over two-fifths of tangible assets with net foreign assets equal to one-fifth of national wealth. It thus appears that the position of foreign investments in the financial structure of Switzerland and in relation to its national wealth in now not much different, though probably a little larger, than it was at the eve of World War I.

Table A19 **National Balance Sheet of Switzerland, 1880–1978 (National Assets = 100.0)**

	1880 (1)	1900 (2)	1913 (3)	1929 (4)	1938 (5)	1948 (6)	1960 (7)	1965 (8)	1973 (9)	1978 (10)
I. Land	17.7	12.4	14.4	9.6	7.7	9.0	7.0	6.8	6.6	6.1
1. Agricultural	11.7	...	6.9	...	2.2	2.4	1.4	1.0	0.7	0.7
2. Forest		...	1.8	...	0.8	0.9	0.6	0.4	0.2	0.2
3. Other	6.0	...	5.7	...	4.8	5.6	5.0	5.4	5.6	5.2
II. Reproducible tangible assets	29.7	26.1	25.5	28.3	30.9	34.6	31.4	32.8	31.8	29.3
1. Structures					17.2	18.8	16.8	18.1	18.7	17.4
a) Residential	23.6	20.5	20.9	23.9	6.6	7.2	6.4	6.9	7.1	6.6
b) Other					10.6	11.6	10.4	11.2	11.6	10.8
2. Equipment					10.3	11.6	10.5	10.7	9.5	9.0
3. Inventories	1.9	1.6	1.5	1.6	1.3	1.7	1.7	1.7	1.6	1.4
4. Livestock	2.4	2.3	1.5	1.2	0.9	0.8	0.6	0.5	0.3	0.3
5. Consumer durables	1.9	1.6	1.5	1.6	1.3	1.8	1.8	1.9	1.6	1.3
III. Tangible assets	47.4	38.4	40.0	37.8	38.6	43.6	38.6	39.7	38.3	35.4
IV. Monetary metals[a]	0.5	0.6	0.5	0.6	2.4	2.7	2.0	1.8	1.7	1.3
V. Financial assets	42.7	48.3	48.4	54.5	53.6	48.0	50.9	49.5	45.9	48.2
1. Claims against financial institutions[b]	9.4	14.1	17.6	19.9	20.1	19.1	20.4	21.2	22.2	23.5
a) Banks	8.8	12.7	14.5	15.5	15.1	13.9	13.9	15.0	16.7	18.3
b) Insurance	0.6	1.4	3.1	4.4	4.2	4.4	5.5	5.1	4.1	4.2
c) Other					0.8	0.9	1.0	1.1	1.4	1.0
2. Loans by financial institutions[c]	2.8	3.8	4.3	5.1	3.0	2.5	3.2	3.9	4.4	5.0

Table A19 (Continued)

	1880 (1)	1900 (2)	1913 (3)	1929 (4)	1938 (5)	1948 (6)	1960 (7)	1965 (8)	1973 (9)	1978 (10)
3. Mortgages	18.9	16.9	11.9	10.3	12.0	9.9	10.0	9.3	7.2	7.8
4. Government debt	2.2	2.3	4.5	5.7	6.6	5.3	2.9	2.2	2.0	2.3
a) Confederacy[d]	0.2	0.2	2.6	3.7	4.1	3.5	1.4	0.8	0.5	0.7
b) Other	2.0	2.1	1.9	2.0	2.5	1.8	1.5	1.4	1.5	1.6
5. Domestic corporate bonds	2.8	3.5	1.1	1.4	1.1	0.5	1.0	1.1	1.0	1.1
6. Domestic corporate stock	4.7	6.2	7.5	10.6	9.5	8.9	11.7	10.0	7.5	7.1
7. Trade credit	1.9	1.6	1.5	1.6	1.3	1.7	1.7	1.7	1.6	1.4
VI. Foreign assets gross	9.2	12.7	11.2	7.0	5.4	5.8	8.7	9.1	14.1	15.0
Foreign assets net	4.7	8.4	8.5	4.0	2.0	1.8	4.3	4.2	8.5	9.0
VII. National	100.0	100.0	100.0	100.0	100.0	100.0	100.0	100.0	100.0	100.0
National assets bill. sfr.	22.0	35.5	67.1	135.9	147.7	225.0	475.4	747.9	1737.0	2312.0
VIII. Gross national product; bill. sfr.[e]	1.3	2.7	4.1	10.5	9.4	18.7	40.7	64.6	141	161

[a]Only holdings of monetary authorities in cols. 4–10.

[b]Includes equity, i.e., equal to assets.

[c]Excludes mortgages and loans to governments.

[d]Includes Swiss Federal Railways.

[e]Year-end rate.

Source of basic data: Goldsmith 1981 except for line VIII:

Cols. 1–3 Goldsmith 1969, 554.

Cols. 4–6 Mitchell 1975, 789 + 5% to shift from net to gross national product.

Cols. 7–10 *IFSYB* 1981, 406–7.

19. United States

Since I have dealt with the statistical problems involved in the construction of sectorized balance sheets for the United States, and less intensively with their interpretation in three earlier publications (Goldsmith 1952; 1954, vol. 3, pt. 1; Goldsmith, Lipsey, and Mendelson 1963; Goldsmith 1982), no further comments or apologies for the almost inevitable limitations of the estimates shown in tables A20–A22 and B11–B14 are required here. The sources of the national, unsectorized, balance sheet for 1774, taken from a recent study by Jones (1980), and those for 1805 and 1850 mostly constructed for this study in the case of financial assets and liabilities but derived for tangible assets chiefly from previous publications (Goldsmith, 1952) are indicated in the notes to table A23 and A24. It is hardly necessary to add that their margin of error is substantially larger than for the current century, particularly since, surprisingly as the method originated in the United States (Goldsmith, 1950), there is no estimate of the reproducible capital by the perpetual inventory method, for the 19th century. Nevertheless, even in their present imperfect form, the figures should present a reasonably trustworthy framework for an analysis of the main changes in the structure of tangible and financial wealth of the United States since Independence.

There is a break in the estimates in the mid-1950s, which becomes apparent when the figures of the overlapping year 1953 in the two sources (Goldsmith, Lipsey, and Mendelson 1963; Goldsmith 1982) are compared. This break is due to the use of newer and supposedly superior data in the more recent source as well as to differences in the coverage and methods of estimation of some components of the balance sheet. It must be taken into account in comparing the distribution of assets and liabilities in the years before and after 1953. For the same period since 1947 or 1945 there recently have become available annual balance sheets for all sectors (Ruggles and Ruggles 1982), and for all private sectors (Board of Governors, 1983), estimates that are close to those for 1950, 1965, 1973, and 1978 in table A22.

An economic, and even more easily a financial, history of the United States could be written by using table A22, but this will not be done here and the task, as well as the spotting of occasional anomalies, will be left to the reader's attention and imagination. It seems worthwhile to point, without the elaborations and qualifications necessary to an adequate understanding by readers not familiar with the subject, to a number of characteristics of the economic and financial development of the United States in the two centuries since Independence—some so much to be expected and so well known as to border on the commonplace—that can be read off from table A22:

1. The abolition of slavery has eliminated a component which in the first half of the 19th century accounted for nearly one-tenth of private wealth.

2. The modernization of the United States has reduced the share of agricultural land from about one-half of tangible assets until the early 19th century to a mere 5 percent, most of the decline occurring before 1880, i.e., before industrialization started in earnest. The accompanying decline in the share of livestock is even more spectacular: from over one-tenth of tangible assets in 1774 and still nearly 5 percent in 1880 to less than 1 percent in the postwar period.

3. Among reproducible assets the share of nonfarm residential structures has risen from one-sixth in 1805 to over one-fourth in 1900 reflecting urbanization, but increased only slightly and irregularly in the 20th century.

4. The share of equipment in reproducible assets, which may be regarded as a proxy for modernization, has doubled between the early 19th century and the postwar period when it approached one-sixth, but most of the increase took place before World War I. The probable decline in relative prices, measured in terms of efficiency, compared to that of structures and inventories accentuates the trend.

5. In view of the precariousness of the estimates for earlier dates, it is inadvisable to interpret the decline in the share of inventories from about 15 percent of reproducible assets in 1774 and 1805 to a little over 10 percent in the postwar period as the measure of a significant trend, though some decline is to be expected as a result of sharply reduced times of transportation, a lesser role of seasonal movements, and improved inventory management techniques.

6. These reservations apply with even more force to the share of consumer durables. Their share apparently increased from 6 to 7 percent of all reproducible assets in the first half of the 19th century to one-eighth at the eve of World War I, but failed to show a definited trend since, held down by the decline in the relative prices of consumer durables in the 20th century.

7. The size of the financial superstructure relative to that of national wealth increased sharply from not much over one-fourth in 1774 to fully four-fifths before World War I, most of the increase occurring during the second half of the 19th century, when the set of modern financial instruments and institutions became fully developed. The ratio then showed two peaks: the first of nearly 1.30 in 1929, reflecting the extraordinary increase of stock prices in the late 1920s; the second in 1945 with over 1.60 due to the repressed inflation of World War II. For the four benchmark dates of the postwar period, the ratio has averaged approximately 1.10, declining from 1.28 in 1965 to unity in 1978, thus showing no distinct trend since the mid-1920s.

8. Within the financial superstructure, probably the most interesting ratio, the share of financial institutions in total financial assets, doubled from about one-tenth early in the 19th century to one-fifth before World War I. Differing from the financial interrelations ratio, the financial intermediation ratio continued its upward trend, though much more slowly, to reach fully one-fourth in 1978.

9. Most of the increase in the 20th century was due to savings deposits and insurance and pension claims rather than to money. The share of the former in the claims against financial institutions advanced from about three-tenths in 1900 to fully one-half in 1978, while that of the latter rose from one-eighth to nearly three-tenths.

10. The share of mortgages, mostly to households, and of consumer credit, increased from less than one-tenth of financial instruments until late in the 19th century to nearly one-fifth in the 1970s.

11. The importance of federal government securities in the financial superstructure has been essentially determined by the requirements of war financing and more recently by the peacetime deficits of the federal government. It was thus relatively high at the benchmark dates of 1805, 1880, and 1939 as well as in 1945. It decreased during the postwar period from the abnormal 1945 level of well over one-fourth of all financial instruments to nearly one-tenth in 1978, still far above the share of 1 percent in 1912 and of fully 2 percent in 1850 though not much above the 7 percent of 1913. The share of state and local government debt, which reflects capital expenditures rather than deficits, has not shown a distinct secular trend since the late 19th century, remaining close to 4 percent of all financial assets.

12. Corporate securities, which were practically nonexistent until the early 19th century, reached the peak of their importance in 1929, when they represented over two-fifths of all financial instruments compared to nearly one-fourth in 1850. In the postwar period, in contrast, their share first increased from less than one-fifth to nearly one-third in the mid-1960s, but then fell back to one-fifth in 1978. The movements are determined by the shares of corporate stock, which in turn is strongly influenced by the fluctuations of stock prices. Thus the value of corporate stock was equal to over one-third of that of all financial instruments in 1929 against an average ratio of about one-fourth at the three benchmark dates of 1880, 1900, and 1912. In the postwar period the share of corporate stock has declined, after a temporary recovery up to the early 1960s, to one-seventh in 1978, the lowest since the mid-19th century, as stock prices failed since the mid-1960s to keep up with inflation. Corporate bonds, in contrast, reached their peak before World War I when, then mostly issued by railroads, they accounted for over one-tenth of all financial instruments. In the postwar period their share has been consistently somewhat below 5 percent.

13. Though the earlier estimates are precarious and may exaggerate the decline in the share of trade credit in all financial assets from nearly one-third early in the 19th century to 5 percent or slightly less since the 1920s, the movement is in the expected direction, reflecting both the declining share of inventories in reproducible assets and the increasing importance of financial institutions and open-market paper in financing inventories.

14. During the 19th century the United States was one of the largest users of foreign capital, mainly to assist in developing its railroad system, and its foreign liabilities exceeded its foreign investments, the balance reaching 4 percent of national wealth in 1880, disregarding the previous peak of nearly 6 percent in 1805. During the 20th century the opposite relation prevailed as the country first repaid most of its international debts and then became the largest exporter of capital. Gross foreign assets were close to 4 percent of domestic financial assets as early as 1912. During the postwar period they kept slightly below 5 percent. Net international claims peaked in relation to national wealth in 1939 with over 5 percent. From the 1950s on, when the ratio stood at 3 percent, the trend reversed, partly as a result of the accumulation of large dollar balances of foreign banks and monetary authorities, with the result that in the 1970s the net balance kept below 1 percent of national wealth. (The figures are somewhat understated because direct investments which constitute a larger part of American foreign claims than of liabilities are entered at book value.)

Table A20 **National Balance Sheet of the 13 American Colonies, 1774 (Total Assets = 100.0)**

	Slaves and Servants					
	Including			Excluding		
	13 Colonies (1)	New England and Middle Colonies (2)	South (3)	13 Colonies (4)	New England and Middle Colonies (5)	South (6)
I. Tangible assets	65.4	74.2	57.3	78.2	75.6	81.4
1. Land[a]	34.4	38.9	30.3	41.1	39.6	43.0
2. Reproducible tangible assets	31.0	35.3	27.0	37.1	35.9	38.4
a) Structures	11.5	13.0	10.1	13.8	13.2	14.3
b) Equipment	2.8	3.3	2.4	3.3	3.4	3.4
c) Crop inventories	2.4	2.3	2.4	2.9	2.3	3.4
d) Livestock	7.7	7.6	7.8	9.2	7.7	11.1
e) Business inventories	1.3	2.5	0.3	1.6	2.5	0.4
f) Materials in households[b]	0.4	0.7	0.2	0.5	0.7	0.3
g) Durable consumer goods	4.9	6.0	3.8	5.9	6.1	5.4

Table A20 (Continued)

	Slaves and Servants					
	Including			Excluding		
	13 Colonies (1)	New England and Middle Colonies (2)	South (3)	13 Colonies (4)	New England and Middle Colonies (5)	South (6)
II. Financial assets	18.3	24.0	13.1	21.8	24.4	18.6
1. Cash[c]	1.9	2.3	1.7	2.3	2.3	2.4
2. Claims	11.5	19.0	4.6	13.8	19.3	6.5
3. Adjustment[d]	4.8	2.7	6.8	5.7	2.7	9.7
III. Non-human assets	83.6	98.2	70.4	100.0	100.0	100.0
IV. Slaves and servants[e]	16.4	1.8	29.6	...	...	...
V. Total assets %	100.0	100.0	100.0	...	...	...
Total assets £mill.[f]	131.3	62.5	68.7	109.8	61.4	48.4
VI. Liabilities	16.3	21.7	11.4	19.5	21.7	16.2

[a]Estimated at three-fourths of "real estate," i.e., the 1805 ratio of land and structures at 64%, on the basis of estimates in 1929 prices (Goldsmith 1952, 306, 310).

[b]Does not include apparel and perishables, which equaled 1.2% and 0.5% of line V for the 13 colonies; 1.9% and 0.5% for New England and the Middle Colonies; and 0.6% and 0.5% for the South.

[c]Includes small amounts of gold and silver coins.

[d]Difference between liabilities (line VI) and claims (line II.2), since apart from relatively small net foreign claims both must be equal.

[e]According to Jones 1980, tables 4-9 and 4-10, slaves constituted 99% and indentured servants 1% of unfree persons covered by the sample. In New England and the Middle Colonies the share of servants was 17% compared to 0.4% in the South.

[f]The British pound used in the estimations was at an agio of 70% (unweighted median of 10 states; Jones 1980, table 1-1) above the colonial pound. In current prices national assets therefore were of the order of £220 mill. including and £190 mill. excluding slaves and servants.

Source of basic data: Jones (1980), tables 4-1 and 6-1.

Table A21 **National Balance Sheet of the United States, 1805, 1850, and 1880 ($bill.)**

	1805 (1)	1850 (2)	1880 (3)
I. Land	0.69	3.02	12.05
1. Agricultural	0.65	2.62	7.55
2. Other	0.04	0.40	4.50
II. Reproducible tangible assets	0.64	4.30	26.70
1. Structures	0.39	2.41	13.90
a) Residential	0.10	0.80	4.90
b) Other	0.29	1.61	9.00
2. Equipment	0.05	0.45	3.00
3. Inventories	0.10	0.60	5.60
4. Livestock	0.06	0.54	1.80
5. Consumer durables	0.04	0.30	2.40
III. Tangible assets	1.33	7.32	38.75
IV. Gold and silver	0.02	0.15	0.60
V. Financial assets	0.41	3.23	23.76
1. Currency and demand deposits 2. Other deposits	0.04	0.37	2.75
3. Insurance	...	0.06	0.62
4. Bank loans	0.07	0.39	1.78
5. Farm mortgages	0.02	0.12	0.55
6. Other mortgages	0.01	0.10	1.10
7. Government debt	0.08	0.35	3.09
a) Federal	0.08	0.07	2.06
b) Other	0.00	0.28	1.03
8. Corporate bonds	...	0.89	2.70
9. Corporate stock	0.04		5.87
10. Trade credit	0.13	0.70	3.50
11. Other financial assets	0.02	0.25	1.80
VI. Foreign assets gross	...	0.05	0.50
Foreign assets net	−0.08	−0.22	−1.58
VII. Unfree persons	0.15	0.80	...
VIII. National assets	1.91	11.55	63.61
IX. Gross national product	0.60	2.63	10.89

(Source of basic data on following pages)

Source of basic data:

Line I:

Col. 1	Estimated at 175 percent of structures, the ratio in 1929 prices (Goldsmith 1952, 306, 310).
Col. 2	Goldsmith 1952, 317.
Col. 3	Sum of lines I.1 and I.2.

Line I.1:

Col. 1	Line I less line I.2.
Col. 2	Goldsmith 1952, 317.
Col. 3	Tostlebe 1957, 54.

Line I.2:

Cols. 1, 3	Estimated at 20% of nonfarm structures. Goldsmith 1952, 306.
Col. 2	Goldsmith 1952, 317.

Lines II.2–5:

Cols. 1–3	Goldsmith 1952, 306; except for line II.4, col. 3 (Tostlebe, 54), and substituting Tostlebe's estimates for agricultural, structures, and inventories in lines I.1, II.1, and II.3 of col. 3 for source.

Line IV:

Cols. 1–3	Goldsmith 1952, 306.

Lines V.1–2

Col. 1	Notes and deposits (roughly estimated) of banks in 1810 (*HS* 1975, 1018).
Cols. 2, 3	*HS* 1975, 1020, plus in 1880 small allowance for building and loan associations; average for June of year and year following.

Line V.4:

Col. 1	Sum of notes, deposits (estimated), and capital less specie in 1810 (*HS* 1975, 1018).

Line V.4:

Cols. 2, 3	*HS* 1975, 1020; average of values for June of year and year following.

Line V.5:

Cols. 1–3	Estimated at 5% of physical assets of agriculture (Goldsmith 1952, 306), in 1805, 7½% in 1850, and 10% in 1880 (the 1900 ratio; Goldsmith, Lipsey, and Mendelson 1963, 2:72).

Line V.6:

Cols. 1–3	Estimated at 5% of nonfarm structures, (Goldsmith 1952, 306), in 1805, 7½% in 1850, and 10% in 1880. (The 1900 ratio was about 13%.)

Line V.7.a:

Cols. 1–3	*HS* 1975, 1118; average of figure for year and year following.

Line V.7.b:

Col. 1	Negligible.
Cols. 2, 3	Local debt for 1850 estimated on basis of 1859 figure (Studenski and Krooss 1952, 7).

Line V.8:

Cols. 2, 3	Rough estimate for railroad bonds, based for col. 3 on 1890 figure (*HS* 1975, 735).

Line V.9:

Col. 1	Bank stocks in 1810 (*HS* 1975, 1018).
Col. 2	Based on figure for railroad stocks and bonds in Hunt 1863, 354, plus bank stocks ("capital accounts"); in *HS* 1975, 1020.

Line V.9:
Col. 3 For railroad stocks based on 1890 figure (*HS*, 735); plus one-half the value of capital assets of public utilities (Ulmer 1960, 242) and manufacturing and mining (Creamer et al. 1960, 241, 304), the 1900 ratio; plus bank stocks (*HS*, 1020).

Line V.10:
Cols. 1–3 Estimated at average of 28% of gross national product (Berry 1968, 32) and 58% of inventories and livestock (lines II.4 and 5), the 1900 ratios (Goldsmith, Lipsey, and Mendelson 1963, 2:73).

Line V.11:
Cols. 1–3 Estimated to rise from 7% to 9% of national product (Berry 1968) on the basis of the 1900 ratio of 10% (Goldsmith, Lipsey, and Mendelson 1963, 2:73).

Line VI:
Cols. 1, 2 Based on Goldsmith 1952, 317–18, assuming average price per slave of $150 in 1805 and $205 in 1850, and slave population of 1.0 million in 1805 and 3.2 million in 1850 (*HS*, 18, 1168). A recent estimate (Sutch 1983, table S1) is much higher, namely, $0.29 bill. for 1805, and $1.29 bill. for 1850. If it is accepted the share of unfree persons in national assets would be increased to 14% in 1805 and to 11% in 1850 compared to 9% and 7% in table A22.

Line VIII: For net balance *HS*, 869; gross foreign investments roughly estimated on basis of figures for 1843, 1869, and 1897 (ibid).

Line IX: Berry 1968, 32.

Table A22 National Balance Sheet of the United States, 1774–1978 (National Assets = 100.0)

	1774 (1)	1805 (2)	1850 (3)	1880 (4)
I. Land	41.1	39.2	28.1	18.9
1. Agricultural	...	36.9	24.3	11.9
2. Other	...	2.3	3.7	7.0
II. Reproducible tangible assets	37.1	36.4	40.0	42.0
1. Structures	13.8	22.2	22.4	21.9
a) Residential	...	5.7	7.5	7.7
b) Other	...	16.5	15.0	14.2
2. Equipment	3.3	2.8	4.2	4.7
3. Inventories	5.0	5.7	5.6	8.8
4. Livestock	9.2	3.4	5.1	2.8
5. Consumer durables	5.9	2.3	2.8	3.8
III. Tangible assets	78.2	75.6	68.1	60.9
IV. Monetary metals	...	1.1	1.4	0.9
V. Financial assets	21.8	23.3	30.0	37.4
1. Currency and demand deposits	2.3	2.3 (1–2)	3.5 (1–2)	4.3 (1–2)
2. Other deposits	...			
3. Insurance and pension claims	...	...	0.6	1.0
4. Loans by financial institutions	...	4.0	3.6	2.8
5. Consumer credit	...	...	...	...
6. Mortgages	...	1.7	2.1	2.6
7. Government debt	...	4.5	3.2	4.9
a) Central	...	4.5	0.7	3.2
b) Other	...	...	2.5	1.6
8. Corporate and foreign bonds	...	...	2.8	4.2
9. Corporate stock	...	2.3	5.5	9.2
10. Trade credit	19.5 (10–11)	7.4	6.5	5.5
11. Other financial assets		1.1	2.2	2.8
VI. Foreign assets gross	...	...	0.5	0.8
Foreign assets net	...	−4.3	−2.1	−2.5
VII. National assets %	100.0	100.0	100.0	100.0
National assets $bill.[a,b]	0.11	1.72	10.8	63.7
VIII. Gross national product; $bill.[c]	...	0.6	2.6	10.9

[a]Bill. £ in 1774.

[b]In addition, 19.6 for unfree persons in 1774; 8.5 in 1805; 7.4 in 1850.

[c]Year-end rate.

Source of basic data:

Col. 1 Table A20.

Cols. 2–4 Table A21.

Cols. 5–9 Goldsmith, Lipsey, and Mendelson 1963, 2:58–59, 72 ff., omitting equity in unincorporated business enterprises and adding gross foreign assets (*HS* 1975, 869). Line VIII, cols. 7–9, United States, *Economic Report of the President*, 1981, 233.

Cols. 10–11 Goldsmith 1982, table 23, for col. 10, and corresponding print-out for col. 11, omitting equity in unincorporated business enterprises. Line VI based on *HS* 1975, 868–69, and *SA* 1976, 826; line VIII as for cols. 7–9.

1900 (5)	1912 (6)	1929 (7)	1939 (8)	1950 (9)	1965 (10)	1973 (11)	1978 (12)
20.5	19.3	11.8	10.2	9.0	10.7	11.4	12.5
9.6	10.5	3.6	2.7	2.4	2.4	2.5	2.7
10.8	8.8	8.2	7.5	6.6	8.3	8.9	9.8
38.0	35.3	32.0	32.9	37.0	33.1	36.0	37.7
23.1	20.7	19.6	21.7	22.7	19.3	22.0	23.1
10.4	8.4	9.3	9.9	12.0	9.6	10.0	11.1
12.7	12.3	10.3	11.8	10.7	9.8	12.0	11.9
4.3	4.6	4.0	3.9	4.9	5.5	5.4	5.7
4.5	3.7	3.3	2.9	3.6	3.8	3.9	4.2
2.1	1.9	0.7	0.6	0.8	0.3	0.4	0.3
4.0	4.5	4.4	3.7	5.0	4.1	4.3	4.5
58.5	54.6	43.7	43.1	46.0	43.8	47.4	50.2
0.9	0.8	0.5	2.3	1.2	0.2	0.3	0.3
39.9	42.9	53.6	50.5	50.3	53.9	50.2	47.0
4.9	4.7	3.6	8.5	7.4	3.3	2.8	2.3
2.4	3.1	3.6	3.7	3.3	5.6	6.6	6.9
1.0	1.4	2.0	4.2	5.0	4.6	4.3	4.1
3.5	3.8	3.8	1.4	1.5	3.0	3.7	3.6
0.7	1.0	0.9	0.9	1.0	1.8	1.9	1.9
4.5	4.0	4.8	4.1	3.3	5.9	6.3	6.6
2.2	1.9	3.4	7.7	12.7	6.6	5.7	6.2
0.8	0.4	1.7	5.4	11.3	4.8	3.9	4.6
1.3	1.5	1.7	2.3	1.4	1.8	1.8	1.6
3.4	4.8	3.9	3.7	1.9	2.1	2.4	2.4
9.2	12.5	19.4	11.5	8.0	15.8	10.6	7.3
3.8	2.7	2.7	1.7	2.4	2.2	2.7	2.2
4.3	3.1	5.4	3.0	3.8	2.9	3.3	3.4
0.7	1.7	2.2	4.0	2.4	2.1	2.1	2.5
−1.5	−0.7	1.3	2.4	1.6	1.1	0.4	0.4
100.0	100.0	100.0	100.0	100.0	100.0	100.0	100.0
151.1	301.5	964.8	868.2	2230	5684	10788	17887
19.7	39.5	96.8	95.5	309	722	1380	2285

Col. 12:

Line I.1 *SA* 1979, 691.

Line I.2 Rough estimate based on earlier relations between nonagricultural land and structures.

Line II Bureau of Economic Analysis, Department of Commerce print-out. Figures correspond to those in U.S. Department of Commerce, *Survey of Current Business*, April 1976, March 1979, and March 1980.

Line IV Derived from *IFSYB* 1980, 41–43.

Line V Board of Governors of the Federal Reserve System 1979. Estimate for corporate stock increased by 20% for intercorporate stockholdings to preserve comparability with earlier figures.

Line VI U.S. Department of Commerce, *Survey of Current Business*, August 1980, 56.

Line VIII As for cols. 10 and 11.

20. Yugoslavia

The national balance sheet of Yugoslavia (table A23) is considerably more reliable for the first and last benchmark dates for which it can now be constructed—1953 and 1977—than for any intermediate year. This is due to the fact that for 1953 an estimate for all tangible assets has been prepared by Vinski (1959), while for 1977 the National Bank of Yugoslavia has published a detailed statement of financial assets. Even for these two years the complementary figures for 1953 (financial assets) and for 1977 (tangible assets) must be roughly estimated, as must most items in the balance sheets of the two other benchmark years used—1962 and 1972—which are taken in part from estimates made half a dozen years ago (Goldsmith 1975a, which provides a less compact description of the methods of estimation as well as of the Yugoslav financial system). In the case of fixed reproducible assets, new estimates by Vinski (1979) fortunately provide a reasonably firm basis, though they must be shifted somewhat precariously, from gross stock values in 1972 prices to net stock estimates in current prices. So do statements of financial assets in 1972 by the National Bank even though they are not fully comparable to the 1977 figures.

There is little reason to doubt that the estimates, rough as most of them are, correctly reflect the major features of the national balance sheet structure and the important changes in them over the past quarter-century—the sharp drop in the share of land and the lesser though still pronounced decline in that in reproducible assets—both reflecting the sharp increase in the share of financial assets, most of these changes occurring between 1953 and 1962, i.e., in the period when Yugoslavia's economy shifted from a strict Soviet pattern to the present idiosyncratic mixed system. As a result, the size of the financial superstructure relative to the country's infrastructure of income and wealth is now similar to the relations obtaining in developed capitalist countries evidenced in financial interrelations ratios of slightly above unity in the 1970s. The character of the financial superstructure, however, differs in many respects from that of the developed-market economies, particularly in the absence of evidences of private ownership of enterprises and of private claims against enterprises or government and the predominance of assets and liabilities of financial institutions owned by the federal government, the constitutent republics, or communes.

Table A23 National Balance Sheet of Yugoslavia, 1953–1977 (National Assets = 100.0)

	1953 (1)	1962 (2)	1972 (3)	1977 (4)
I. Land	20.9	16.3	12.4	8.4
1. Agricultural[a]	18.4	13.0	10.3	7.0
2. Other	2.4	3.3	2.1	1.4
II. Reproducible tangible assets	60.0	41.3	37.4	37.1
1. Structures and equipment	48.4	32.2	28.6	29.0
a) Residential	12.9	...	...	...
b) Other	35.5	...	...	...
2. Inventories	6.9	5.4	4.8	5.4
3. Livestock	2.2	1.8	1.8	1.3
4. Consumer durables	2.4	1.8	2.3	1.5
III. Tangible assets	80.9	57.6	49.8	45.5
IV. Monetary metals	0.0	0.0	0.1	0.1
V. Financial assets[b]	19.1	42.4	50.1	52.1
1. Currency and demand deposits } 2. Other deposits	7.5	9.8		
1. Currency and demand deposits			4.0	6.0
2. Other deposits			7.0	8.7
3. Loans by financial institutions	7.9	20.6	18.7	17.8
4. Government debt	...	4.3	3.7	1.7
5. Trade credit } 6. Other financial assets	3.8	7.6		
5. Trade credit			10.6	5.9
6. Other financial assets			5.9	12.0
VI. Foreign assets gross	...	...	...	2.3
Foreign assets net	...	...	...	−2.0
VII. National assets %	100.0	100.0	100.0	100.0
National assets bill. dinar	98.3	276	1446	4182
VIII. Gross national product; bill. dinar[c]	13.8	53	323	974

[a]Includes small amounts for forests.
[b]Excluding interfinancial items.
[c]Year-end rate.

Source of basic data:

Col. 1:

Lines I, II — Vinski 1959, 170–71, 190–91. In line II.4 only one-third of Vinski's estimate has been entered, as it includes consumers' stocks of semidurables and nondurables.

Line VIII — Mitchell 1975, 795, plus 20% to shift from net material to gross national product.

Line IV — Derived from *IFSYB* 1979, 40 ff., 446–47.

Line V — Goldsmith (1975), 103 for 1952 increased by 10 percent.

Col. 2:

Line I — Goldsmith 1975a, 103; agricultural land moved in line with prices of agricultural commodities.

Line II.1 — Vinski's estimate in 1972 prices (1979, 181) reduced by 40% to shift from gross to net stock, adjusted by change in prices of producers' goods (Savezni Zavod za Statistiku 1978, 92). Split between lines II.1.a and 1.b based on 1953 ratio and changes in share of housing and communal services in fixed capital stock (Nötel 1980, 18).

Line II.2 — Assumed to bear slightly higher ratio to line II.1 than in 1953.

Lines II.3, 4 — Rough estimates based on movements of agricultural prices assuming annual increase in stock of about 2% (line 3), or on consumer expenditures (line 4).

Line IV	As for col. 1.
Line V	Goldsmith 1975a, 103.
Line VIII	*IFSYB* 1981, 447, plus 20%.
Col. 3:	
Line I	1962 figures moved in line with prices of agricultural commodities or gross material product deflator, *IFSYB* 1979, 343 ff.).
Lines II.1–4	As for col. 2.
Line IV	As for col. 1.
Line V	As for col. 2.
Line VI	National Bank of Yugoslavia, *Quarterly Bulletin*, 1976, 25.
Line VIII	As for col. 2.
Col. 4:	
Line I	As for col. 3.
Line II.1	As for col. 2.
Lines II.2–4	As for col. 3.
Line IV	As for col. 1.
Line V	National Bank of Yugoslavia, *Quarterly Bulletin*, July 1978, 44–45.
Line VI	Based on National Bank of Yugoslavia, *Annual Report*, 1979, 53.
Line VIII	As for col. 2.

Appendix B
Sectoral Balance Sheets for Six Countries

Table B1 **Structure of Sectoral Balance Sheets in France, 1976 (Total Assets = 100.0)**

	All Sectors (1)	Households[a] (2)	Government (3)	Nonfinancial Corporations (4)	Financial Institutions (5)	Rest of the World (6)
I. Tangible assets	59.3	72.8	73.8	78.3	6.4	...
1. Land	6.7	12.1	1.1	6.1	0.0	...
2. Dwellings[b]	23.5	45.6	4.2	14.8	1.2	...
3. Other structures[b]	15.0	3.4	63.8	22.7	3.2	...
4. Equipment	6.8	2.8	2.5	20.7	1.9	...
5. Consumer durables	2.7	6.4	...	...	...	...
6. Inventories	4.2	1.6	2.2	14.0	...	...
7. Livestock	0.4	0.8	...	...	...	...
II. Financial assets[c]	40.7	27.2	26.2	21.7	93.6	100.0
1. Currency and monetary deposits	4.4	6.4	3.2	3.6	2.2	2.1
2. Other deposits	9.3	12.9	1.4	2.3	8.0	42.0
3. Bonds	3.0	1.9	1.6	0.4	9.3	6.0
4. Short-term credits	5.3	0.3	1.8	2.4	21.8	11.7
5. Long-term credits	10.0	0.0	6.8	2.9	44.5	12.1
6. Insurance claims	1.0	2.0	0.0	0.5	...	0.1
7. Shares[d]	6.6	3.8	11.3	9.6	3.0	21.4
8. International means of payment	...	...	0.2	...	4.8	4.6

III. Total assets	100.0	100.0	100.0	100.0	100.0	100.0
IV. Liabilities[e]	34.0	9.1	36.8	33.1	86.2	91.8
1. Currency and monetary deposits	4.4	...	7.5	...	19.3	...
2. Other deposits	9.3	...	3.0	0.6	41.3	32.4
3. Bonds	3.0	...	6.2	3.2	8.1	1.5
4. Short-term credits	5.3	1.6	2.1	12.8	4.6	14.0
5. Long-term credits	10.0	7.5	8.0	16.5	6.7	21.2
6. Insurance liabilities	1.0	...	...	...	5.2	...
7. International means of payment	1.1	...	...	...	1.0	22.6
V. Net worth	66.0	90.9	73.2	66.9	13.8	8.2
VI. Total assets; billion francs[e]	12988[f]	5495	1543[f]	3075	2364	510

[a]Includes "administrations privées" (0.4% of total assets) and unincorporated business enterprises.

[b]Including land underlying structures.

[c]Does not include trade credit.

[d]Includes other participations, particularly donations by government.

[e]Does not include gold held by monetary authorities (68 bill. fr.) or by households (estimated at 175 bill. fr.).

[f]Includes roads (reseau routier) 630.

Source: INSEE, *Le Patrimoine National*, 1979, 18–19, plus estimate of consumer durables based on 1975 figure (op. cit., 78).

Table B2 **Sectoral Distribution of Assets and Liabilities in France, 1976 (National Total = 100.0)**

	All Sectors (Bill. Fr.) (1)	House-holds[a] (2)	Govern-ment (3)	Nonfi-nancial Corpo-ations (4)	Financial Insti-tutions (5)	Rest of the World (6)
I. Tangible assets	7697	52.0	14.8	31.3	1.9	...
1. Land	869	76.3	1.9	21.7	0.1	...
2. Dwellings[b]	3055	82.1	2.1	14.9	0.9	...
3. Other structures[b]	1947	9.7	50.6	35.9	3.9	...
4. Equipment	878	17.8	4.4	72.3	5.2	...
5. Consumer durables	350	100.0	...	...	...	...
6. Inventories	552	16.0	6.3	77.7	0.0	...
7. Livestock	46	100.0	...	...	...	...
II. Financial assets[c]	5291	27.9	8.1	13.1	41.3	9.6
1. Currency and monetary deposits	572	61.3	8.6	19.1	9.1	1.9
2. Other deposits	1207	58.8	1.8	5.6	15.8	17.8
3. Bonds	392	26.2	6.4	3.4	56.3	7.8

4. Short-term credits	693	2.4	3.9	10.8	74.2	8.6
5. Long-term credits	1307	0.0	8.0	6.8	80.5	4.7
6. Insurance claims	124	87.5	0.1	12.0	0.1	0.3
7. Shares[d]	857	24.3	20.2	34.4	8.3	12.8
8. International means of payment	139	...	1.2	...	81.9	16.8
III. Total assets[d,e]	12988	42.3	11.9	23.7	18.2	3.9
IV. Liabilities[e]	4434	10.1	9.3	22.4	45.5	12.8
1. Currency and monetary deposits	572	...	20.3	...	79.7	...
2. Other deposits	1207	...	3.8	1.5	81.0	13.7
3. Bonds	392	...	24.2	25.3	48.7	1.9
4. Short-term credits	693	12.5	4.6	56.9	15.6	10.3
5. Long-term credits	1307	31.3	9.5	38.8	12.0	8.3
6. Insurance liabilities	124	...	...	...	100.0	...
7. International means of payment	139	...	...	...	16.8	83.2
V. Net worth	8554	58.4	13.2	24.1	3.9	0.5

[a]Includes "administrations privées" (0.4% of total assets) and unincorporated business enterprises.
[b]Including land underlying structures and in line 3 roads (630 bill. fr.).
[c]Does not include trade credit.
[d]Includes other participations, particularly donations by government.
[e]Does not include gold holdings of monetary authorities (68) nor of public (estimated at 175).
Source: As for table B1.

Table B3 **Structure of Sectoral Balance Sheets in Germany, 1977 (Total Assets = 100.0)**

	All Sectors (1)	House-holds (2)	Enter-prises (3)	Govern-ment (4)	Finance (5)	Rest of the World (6)
I. Land	13.8	27.6	8.1	5.6	0.7	...
1. Agricultural[a]	7.0	17.6	...	...	...	...
2. Other	6.8	10.0	8.1	5.6	0.7	...
II. Reproducible tangible assets	41.8	41.2	65.2	73.6	2.8	...
1. Dwellings	13.6	30.4	3.8	4.6	...	...
2. Other structures	15.0	...	28.1	66.5	2.4	...
3. Equipment	6.0	...	21.8	2.5	0.4	...
4. Inventories[b]	3.0	...	11.5	...	...	...
5. Consumer durables	4.3	10.8	...	...	...	...
III. Tangible assets	55.6	68.8	73.3	79.2	3.5	...
IV. Gold	0.4	...	...	...	2.0	...
V. Financial assets	44.0	31.2	26.7	20.8	94.5	100.0
1. Currency and demand deposits	2.7	2.7	4.9	0.8	0.4	5.3
2. Time and saving deposits	9.7	15.1	3.5	11.0	4.3	21.6
3. Insurance and pension claims	2.9	6.6	0.8	0.0	...	0.3
4. Short-term loans by financial institutions to private sectors	2.6	...	...	...	12.7	...
5. Long-term loans by financial institutions to private sectors	8.7	...	...	...	42.9	...
6. Government debt	3.4 }	3.4	1.0	0.2	25.7	6.9
7. Corporate bonds	3.6 }					
8. Corporate shares	3.2	1.7	4.7	3.1	1.9	17.2

9. Trade credit	2.9	...	9.0	...	...	16.6
10. Other	4.3	1.6	2.7	5.8	6.6	32.0
VI. Liabilities	40.8	13.2	36.4	32.9	91.4	123.8
1. Currency and demand deposits	2.7	...	...	...	13.3	...
2. Time and saving deposits	9.7	...	...	...	47.7	...
3. Insurance and pension liabilities	2.9	...	...	...	14.0	...
4. Short-term borrowings	2.6	0.9	6.5	...	0.0	15.4
5. Long-term borrowings	8.7	11.6	12.7	...	0.2	22.6
6. Government debt	3.4	...	...	32.1	...	...
7. Corporate bonds	3.6	...	1.3	...	15.4	5.0
8. Trade debt	2.9	...	8.2	...	...	23.8
9. Others	4.3	0.7	7.7	0.8	0.7	57.1
VII. Net worth	59.2	86.8	63.6	67.1	8.6	−23.8
VIII. Total assets; DM. bill.	9994	3972	2600	1077	2025	319

[a]Includes forests.

[b]Includes livestock.

Source of basic data:

Line I.1 — Estimated at twice 1972 figure (Goldsmith 1976, 162) on basis of annual increase of 18% in 1977 and 1978 (Statistisches Bundesamt, Fachserie 3).

Line I.2 — Estimated at 40% above 1972 value (Goldsmith 1976) on basis of increase in price of building land (Statistisches Bundesamt, Fachserie 17, 1979).

Lines II.1–4 — Statistisches Bundesamt, *Statistisches Jahrbuch*, 1979, 527, and *Wirtschaft und Statistik*, 1979, 443*–44*. Total for line II.2 allocated among sectors on basis of structure values excluding substructures (Tiefbau), which is entered on gross rather than net basis because maintenance expenditures are regarded as offsetting depreciation.

Line II.5 — Extrapolated from 1972 figure (Goldsmith 1976) on basis of ratio of private consumption (*SJD* 1979, 358).

Lines V.1–7, 10; VI.1–7, 9; VII — All allocated to col. 5. (Deutsche Bundesbank 1978, 161.) Housing has been transferred from enterprise to household sector and social security from government to finance sector.

Lines V.8–9 — Trade credits and debits from or to foreigners from Deutsche Bundesbank (1978, 161); col. 3 obtained as residual.

Table B4 **Sectoral Distribution of Assets and Liabilities in Germany, 1977 (National Total = 100.0)**

	Total; Bill. D.M. (1)	House-holds (2)	Enter-prises (3)	Govern-ment (4)	Finance (5)	Rest of the World (6)
I. Land	1380	79.4	15.2	4.3	1.1	...
1. Agricultural[a]	700	100.0	...	...	...	...
2. Other	680	58.1	30.9	8.8	2.2	...
II. Reproducible tangible assets	4183	39.1	40.6	19.0	1.3	...
1. Dwellings	1357	88.9	7.4	3.7	...	...
2. Other structures	1496	...	48.9	47.9	3.3	...
3. Equipment	601	...	94.3	4.5	1.2	...
4. Inventories[b]	299	...	100.0	...	...	...
5. Consumer durables	430	100.0	...	...	...	...
III. Tangible assets	5563	49.1	34.2	15.3	1.3	...
IV. Gold	41	...	...	...	100.0	...
V. Financial assets	4390	28.2	15.8	5.1	43.6	7.3
1. Currency and demand deposits	268	40.1	47.2	3.4	3.0	6.3
2. Time and saving deposits	966	62.2	9.4	12.2	9.1	7.1
3. Insurance and pension funds	286	92.4	7.2	0.1	...	0.3
4. Short-term bank loans[c]	257	...	...	...	100.0	...

5. Long-term loans[c]	868	...	...	...	100.0	...
6. Government debt	345	...	...	100.0	...	...
7. Corporate bonds	362	19.2	3.8	0.3	73.6	3.1
8. Corporate shares	319	20.9	39.1	10.2	12.4	17.4
9. Trade credit	288	...	81.5	...	...	18.5
10. Other	430	14.8	16.2	14.4	31.0	23.5
VI. Total assets	9994	39.7	26.0	10.8	20.3	3.2
VII. Liabilities	4075	12.9	23.3	8.7	45.4	9.7
1. Currency and demand deposits	268	...	...	...	100.0	...
2. Time and saving deposits	966	...	...	...	100.0	...
3. Insurance and pension funds	286	...	...	...	100.0	...
4. Short-term borrowing of private sectors	257	14.4	66.2	...	0.3	19.1
5. Long-term borrowing of private sectors	868	53.2	38.0	...	0.4	8.3
6. Government debt	345	...	...	100.0	...	...
7. Corporate bonds	362	...	8.4	...	87.2	4.4
8. Trade debt	288	...	73.5	...	...	26.5
9. Other	435	7.2	45.8	1.8	3.8	41.4
VIII. Net worth	5919	58.2	27.9	12.2	2.9	−1.3

[a]Includes forests.
[b]Includes livestock.
[c]To private sectors.
Source of basic data: As for table B3.

Table B5 **Structure of Sectoral Balance Sheets in Great Britain, 1975 (Total Assets = 100.0)**

	All Sectors (1)	Personal (2)	Companies (3)
I. Tangible assets[a]	45.9	52.7	68.1
1. Agricultural land	1.1	3.3	. . .
2. Dwellings[b]	19.6	43.0	2.6
3. Other structures[b]	12.6	3.4	19.9
4. Equipment	9.3	1.8	30.3
5. Inventories	3.3	1.3	15.3
II. Monetary metals[c]	0.3	. . .	. . .
III. Financial assets	53.8	47.3	31.9
1. Notes and coins	0.7	1.6	0.3
2. Deposits with financial institutions	15.6	15.1	5.6
3. Insurance claims[d]	3.3	11.5	. . .
4. Bank loans	8.7	. . .	. . .
5. Home mortgages	2.4	. . .	. . .
6. British government securities, central	3.1	4.6	0.3
7. British government securities, local	0.6	0.3	0.3
8. British company debentures	0.6	0.6	0.2
9. British company stock	5.6	8.5	3.5
10. Foreign securities	0.6	0.7	. . .
11. Direct investment abroad	2.3	. . .	7.0
12. Trade credit	3.0	2.3	10.9
13. Central government loans[e]	2.6	. . .	. . .
14. Other	4.8	2.0	3.8
IV. Total assets %	100.0	100.0	100.0
Total assets £ bill.	1051	297	181
V. Liabilities	48.2	13.1	38.0
1. Notes and coins	0.7	. . .	. . .
2. Deposits with financial institutions	15.6	. . .	. . .
3. Insurance liabilities[d]	3.3	. . .	. . .
4. Bank loans	8.7	1.9	10.3
5. Home mortgages	2.4	8.4	. . .
6. British government securities, central	3.1	. . .	. . .
7. British government securities, local	0.6	. . .	. . .
8. British company debentures	0.6	. . .	3.3
9. Foreign securities	0.6	. . .	. . .
10. Direct investments abroad	2.3	. . .	. . .
11. Trade credit	3.0	1.6	11.2
12. Central government loans[e]	2.6	. . .	. . .
13. Other	4.8	1.1	13.2
VI. Net worth	51.8	86.9	62.0

[a]Does not include consumer durables estimated at about £43 bill. (based on table A7) equal to 14.5% of assets of personal sector and 4.1% of total assets which would increase share of tangible in personal sector assets to 58.8% and of net worth to 88.5%.

[b]Includes underlying land.

Public Sector				Finance			
Central Govern-ment (4)	Local Govern-ment (5)	Public Corps. (6)	Total (7)	Banks (8)	Other (9)	Total (10)	Over-seas (11)
39.3	93.4	92.0	77.8	2.1	12.6	5.9	...
1.7	0.2	0.2	0.6	...	0.0	0.0	...
2.4	66.2	9.0	30.3	...	...	...	...
31.6	25.0	40.5	31.7	1.8	8.4	4.2	...
2.3	1.7	39.2	13.7	0.3	4.2	1.7	...
1.3	0.2	3.2	1.4	0.0	...	0.0	...
4.0	...	...	1.1	...	...	...	0.5
56.7	6.6	8.0	21.1	97.9	87.4	94.1	99.5
0.1	...	0.4	0.1	0.8	0.2	0.6	0.1
1.0	0.3	0.3	0.5	24.4	5.2	17.1	70.5
...	...	...	...	...	...	...	...
...	...	...	...	61.1	...	38.5	...
0.1	2.9	0.5	1.4	0.9	23.8	9.3	...
...	0.0	0.0	0.0	3.7	11.4	6.5	3.3
0.6	0.3	0.2	0.3	0.7	2.7	1.4	0.7
0.0	0.0	0.0	0.0	0.1	3.5	1.3	0.7
2.8	0.0	0.1	0.8	1.0	25.2	9.9	2.4
0.1	...	...	0.0	0.1	5.4	2.0	...
...	...	0.3	0.1	0.6	...	0.3	10.5
...	1.2	4.4	1.8	...	...	...	...
40.6	...	...	11.4	...	...	...	...
11.7	1.9	1.8	4.6	4.5	10.2	7.3	11.4
100.0	100.0	100.0	100.0	100.0	100.0	100.0	100.0
68	98	77	243	149	86	234	96
68.0	29.2	34.2	41.7	93.7	78.1	88.0	95.2
10.0	...	...	2.8	0.2	...	0.1	0.0
...	...	...	...	92.8	31.0	70.2	...
...	...	...	...	...	40.0	14.6	...
1.5	0.1	2.4	1.2	...	3.5	1.3	63.1
...	...	...	...	...	...	...	...
48.1	...	...	13.5	...	...	...	...
...	6.4	...	2.6	...	...	...	...
...	...	...	...	...	...	...	...
...	...	...	...	...	...	...	7.1
...	...	...	...	...	...	...	24.6
2.0	1.6	4.2	2.5	...	...	...	...
...	11.3	21.7	11.4	...	...	...	...
6.4	9.7	6.0	7.8	0.6	3.5	1.7	0.4
32.0	70.8	65.8	58.3	6.3	21.9	12.0	4.8

[c]Includes net IMF position.
[d]Does not include social security and government pension funds.
[e]To local governments and public corporations.
Source of basic data: Pettigrew 1980, 90–91.

Table B6 **Sectoral Distribution of Assets and Liabilities in Great Britain, 1975 (National Total = 100.0)**

	All Sectors £ bill. (1)	Personal (2)	Companies (3)
I. Tangible assets[a]	483	32.5	25.5
1. Agricultural land	11	86.7	. . .
2. Dwellings[b]	206	62.0	2.3
3. Other structures[b]	133	7.5	27.0
4. Equipment	98	5.6	56.1
5. Inventories	36	10.8	79.0
II. Monetary metals[c]	3	. . .	. . .
III. Financial assets	565	24.9	10.2
1. Notes and coins	7	68.6	7.0
2. Deposits with financial institutions	165	27.3	6.1
3. Insurance claims[d]	34	100.0	. . .
4. Bank loans	91	. . .	. . .
5. Home mortgages	25	. . .	. . .
6. British government securities, central	33	42.0	1.6
7. British government securities, local	6	14.2	8.7
8. British company debentures	6	28.4	6.8
9. British company stock	59	42.9	10.6
10. Foreign securities	7	29.5	. . .
11. Direct investment abroad	24	. . .	53.2
12. Trade credit	31	22.2	63.4
13. Central government loans[e]	28	. . .	. . .
14. Other	50	11.3	13.3
IV. Total assets[a]	1051	28.3	17.2
V. Liabilities	506	7.7	13.5
1. Notes and coins	7	. . .	. . .
2. Deposits with financial institutions	165	. . .	. . .
3. Insurance liabilities[d]	34	. . .	. . .
4. Bank loans	91	6.3	20.5
5. Home mortgages	25	100.0	. . .
6. British government securities, central	33	. . .	. . .
7. British government securities, local	6	. . .	. . .
8. British company debentures	6	. . .	100.0
9. Foreign securities	7	. . .	. . .
10. Direct investments abroad	24	. . .	. . .
11. Trade credit	31	15.5	64.7
12. Central government loans[e]	28	. . .	. . .
13. Other	50	6.7	47.8
VI. Net worth[a]	545	47.4	20.5

[a]Inclusion of consumer durables (about £43 bill.) would increase share of personal sector in tangible assets to 38.1%, in total assets to 31.1%, and in net worth to 51.3%, and reduce shares of other sectors proportionately.

[b]Includes underlying land.

Public Sector				Finance			
Central Govern-ment (4)	Local Govern-ment (5)	Public Corps. (6)	Total (7)	Banks (8)	Other (9)	Total (10)	Over-seas (11)
5.6	19.0	14.6	39.1	0.6	2.2	2.8	...
10.5	1.7	1.1	13.2	...	0.2	0.2	...
0.8	31.5	3.3	35.7	...	...	...	...
16.3	18.5	23.3	58.0	2.0	5.4	7.4	...
1.6	1.7	30.8	34.2	0.4	3.7	4.1	...
2.5	0.6	6.9	10.0	0.1	...	0.1	...
84.1	...	...	84.1	...	...	...	15.9
6.9	1.1	1.1	9.1	25.8	13.2	39.0	16.9
0.6	...	3.7	4.2	17.4	1.8	19.2	1.1
0.4	0.2	0.1	0.7	22.1	2.7	24.8	41.1
...	...	...	...	...	...	...	...
...	...	...	...	100.0	...	100.0	...
0.1	11.5	1.6	13.2	5.2	81.6	86.8	...
...	0.0	0.1	0.1	16.7	29.9	46.6	9.6
6.3	5.0	2.4	13.6	16.7	36.7	53.5	10.3
0.0	0.0	0.2	0.2	2.2	50.4	52.6	11.9
3.3	0.0	0.1	3.4	2.6	36.6	39.2	3.9
0.4	...	...	0.4	2.6	67.4	70.1	...
...	...	0.9	0.9	3.5	...	3.5	42.4
...	3.7	10.8	14.5	...	...	...	...
100.0	...	...	100.0	...	...	...	...
15.4	3.6	2.7	21.6	12.7	20.1	32.8	20.9
6.5	9.3	7.3	23.1	14.2	8.1	22.3	9.1
9.2	5.6	5.2	20.0	27.5	13.2	40.7	18.1
95.2	...	...	95.2	4.5	...	4.5	0.3
...	...	...	...	83.8	16.2	100.0	...
...	...	...	...	...	100.0	100.0	...
1.1	0.2	2.0	3.3	...	3.3	3.3	66.6
...	...	...	...	...	...	...	...
100.0	...	...	100.0	...	...	...	...
...	100.0	...	100.0	...	...	...	...
...	...	...	...	...	...	...	...
...	...	...	...	...	...	...	100.0
...	...	...	...	...	...	...	100.0
4.4	5.1	10.3	19.8	...	...	...	...
...	40.1	59.9	100.0	...	...	...	...
8.7	19.0	9.0	36.8	1.8	6.0	7.8	0.8
4.0	12.8	9.2	26.0	1.7	3.4	5.1	0.9

[c]Includes net IMF position.

[d]Does not include social security and government pension funds.

[e]To local governments and public corporations.

Source of basic data: Pettigrew 1980, 90–91.

Table B7 **Structure of Sectoral Balance Sheets in the Indian Union, 1970 (Total Assets = 100.0)**

	All Sectors (1)	House-holds (2)	Govern-ment[a] (3)	Private Corps. (4)	Financial Institutions (5)	Rest of the World (6)
I. Land	24.6	41.1	3.2	3.1	0.0	...
II. Reproducible tangible assets	39.3	34.5	62.7	71.2	1.8	...
1. Dwellings	9.7	16.8	...	...	...	...
2. Other	29.6	17.7	62.7	71.2	1.8	...
III. Tangible assets	63.9	75.6	65.9	74.3	1.8	...
IV. Gold and silver	5.8	10.0	...	...	...	...
V. Financial assets	30.3	14.4	34.1	25.8	98.2	100.0
1. Currency	1.8	2.8	0.0	0.6	1.3	...
2. Deposits	2.7	3.5	1.0	2.5	3.1	1.0
3. Loans	12.9	0.6	21.9	6.7	46.9	76.5
4. Government securities[b]	5.0	1.3	4.9	0.0	34.2	...
5. Private securities[c]	2.4	0.9	2.3	1.8	10.1	9.2
6. Insurance	1.9	3.3	...	...	...	...
7. Agricultural loans[d]	1.0	1.8	...	...	...	...
8. Other[e]	2.7	0.1	4.1	14.1	2.6	13.3

VI. Total assets	100.0	100.0	100.0	100.0	100.0	100.0
VII. Liabilities	30.3	5.3	61.0	63.2	94.7	15.3
1. Currency	1.8	...	0.6	...	18.4	...
2. Deposits	3.1	...	0.2	0.6	34.6	...
3. Loans	12.3	3.1	32.6	27.6	12.7	...
4. Government securities	5.0	...	21.6	...	...	} 8.2
5. Private securities	2.2	...	...	16.6[d]	7.9	
6. Insurance	2.0	...	2.3	...	16.2	...
7. Agricultural debt[d]	1.0	1.8	...	...	...	...
8. Other[e]	3.0	0.5	3.7	18.4	4.8	7.1
VIII. Net worth	69.7	94.7	39.0	36.8	5.3	84.7
IX. Total assets; bill. R.	2603	1497	616	163	228	98

[a]Includes government enterprises.

[b]Domestic securities only.

[c]Mostly shares.

[d]Noninstitutional loans only.

[e]Includes trade credit.

Source: Venkatachalam and Sarma, 1976.

Table B8 **Sectoral Distribution of Assets and Liabilities in the Indian Union, 1970 (National Total = 100.0)**

	Total bill. R. (1)	House-holds (2)	Private Corps. (3)	Govern-ment[a] (4)	Financial Insti-tutions (5)	Rest of the World (6)
I. Tangible assets	1663	68.1	7.3	24.4	0.2	...
1. Land	640	96.1	0.8	3.1	...	...
2. Reproducible assets	1023	50.5	11.3	37.7	0.4	...
a) Dwellings	252	100.0	...	...	...	...
b) Other	771	34.4	15.0	50.1	0.5	...
II. Gold and silver	150	100.0	...	...	...	...
III. Financial assets	790	27.2	5.3	26.6	28.4	12.4
1. Currency	46	91.3	2.2	0	6.5	...
2. Deposits	71	74.6	5.6	8.5	9.9	1.4
3. Insurance	49	100.0	...	...	...	...
4. Loans and advances	337	2.7	3.3	40.0	31.7	22.3
5. Agricultural noninstitutional loans	27	100.0	...	...	...	...
6. Government securities[b]	129	15.6	0	23.4	61.0	...
7. Other securities[c]	62	21.0	4.8	22.6	37.1	14.5
8. Other assets[d]	69	2.9	32.8	35.7	8.6	20.0
IV. Total assets	2603	57.5	6.3	23.7	8.8	3.8
V. Liabilities	790	10.0	13.0	47.7	27.3	1.9
1. Currency	46	...	...	8.7	91.3	...
2. Deposits	81	...	1.2	1.2	97.5	...
3. Insurance	51	...	...	27.5	72.5	...
4. Loans and advances	321	14.3	14.0	62.6	9.0	...
5. Agricultural noninstitutional debts	27	100.0	...	...	...	...
6. Securities	186	...	14.5	71.5[b]	9.7	4.3
7. Other liabilities[d]	78	9.0	38.5	29.5	14.1	9.0
VI. Net worth	1813	78.2	3.3	13.2	0.7	4.6

[a]Includes government enterprises.
[b]Domestic securities only.
[c]Mostly shares.
[d]Includes trade credit.

Source: Venkatachalam and Sarma, 1976.

Table B9 **Structure of Sectoral Balance Sheets in Japan, 1977 (Total Assets = 100.0)**

	All Sectors (1)	House-holds (2)	Nonfinancial Corps. (3)	General Government (4)	Financial Institutions (5)
I. Land	25.5	44.5	21.7	16.5	1.6
II. Reproducible tangible assets	24.7	20.5	38.1	52.1	1.3
1. Dwellings	5.1	12.0	1.6	...	...
2. Other structures and equipment	15.3	4.0	27.7	52.1	1.3
3. Inventories	3.0	0.7	8.8	...	...
4. Consumer durables	1.4	3.8	...	...	...
III. Tangible assets	50.2	65.0	59.8	68.7	2.9
IV. Financial assets	49.8	35.0	40.2	31.3	97.1
1. Currency	0.9	1.8	0.3	1.1	...
2. Deposits	12.9	22.9	12.3	3.4	0.3
3. Loans	15.5	...	0.0	4.7	69.5
4. Bonds	5.4	2.9	0.5	2.1	18.1
5. Corporate shares	3.3	2.8	3.1	0.0	5.6
6. Insurance and pension funds	1.6	4.1	...	0.3	...
7. Trade credit	6.9	...	22.3	...	...
8. Other	3.4	0.4	1.8	19.7	3.6
V. Total assets	100.0	100.0	100.0	100.0	100.0
VI. Liabilities	46.4	13.4	57.2	37.1	92.5
1. Currency	0.8	...	...	...	3.6
2. Deposits	13.2	...	...	...	60.7
3. Loans	15.5	10.4	32.1	9.9	2.9
4. Bonds	5.6	...	5.1	26.1	7.2
5. Insurance and pension funds	1.6	...	...	...	7.2
6. Trade debt	6.9	3.0	18.6	0.1	0.0
7. Other liabilities	2.8	...	1.3	1.1	10.8
VII. Net worth	53.6	86.6	42.8	62.9	7.5
VIII. Total assets; trill. ¥	1773	671	552	167	384

Source of basic data: Economic Planning Agency, *Annual Report on National Accounts*, 54 (1979) 427 ff., except for distribution of fixed assets between lines II.1 and II.2 in which fairly arbitrarily 90% of dwellings have been allocated to households and 10% to nonfinancial corporations.

Table B10 **Sectoral Distribution of Assets and Liabilities in Japan, 1977 (National Total = 100.0)**

	All Sectors ¥ trill. (1)	House-holds (2)	Nonfinancial Corps. (3)	General Government (4)	Financial Institutions (5)
I. Land	452.1	66.0	26.5	6.1	1.4
II. Reproducible tangible assets	438.9	31.3	47.9	19.8	1.1
1. Dwellings	90.1	90.0	10.0	...	...
2. Other structures and equipment	270.4	9.5	56.5	32.2	1.8
3. Inventories	53.0	8.9	91.1	...	...
4. Consumer durables	25.5	100.0	...	...	...
III. Tangible assets	891.0	48.9	37.0	12.9	1.2
IV. Financial assets	882.2	26.6	25.1	5.9	42.3
1. Currency	15.4	79.7	8.9	11.4	...
2. Deposits	228.6	67.4	29.6	2.5	0.6

3. Loans	274.8	. . .	0.0	2.9	97.1
4. Bonds	95.2	20.5	2.7	3.6	73.2
5. Corporate shares	57.7	33.0	29.8	0.1	37.1
6. Insurance and pension funds	27.8	98.1	. . .	1.9	. . .
7. Trade credit	123.0	. . .	100.0	. . .	. . .
8. Other	59.5	4.9	16.6	55.3	23.2
V. Total assets	1773.0	37.8	31.1	9.4	21.7
VI. Liabilities	822.6	10.9	38.3	7.5	43.2
1. Currency	13.7	. . .	. . .	. . .	100.0
2. Deposits	233.3	. . .	. . .	. . .	100.0
3. Loans	274.9	25.3	64.5	6.0	4.2
4. Bonds	99.6	. . .	28.4	43.7	27.9
5. Insurance and pension funds	27.8	. . .	. . .	. . .	100.0
6. Trade debt	123.0	16.3	83.6	0.1	0.0
7. Other liabilities	50.3	0.2	13.8	3.7	82.3
VII. Net worth	950.4	61.1	24.8	11.0	3.0

Source of basic data: As for table B9.

Table B11 **Structure of Sectoral Balance Sheets in the United States, 1900 (Total Assets = 100.0)**

	All Sectors; $bill. (1)	Nonfarm: Households[a] (2)	Nonfarm: Unincorporated Business (3)	Agriculture (4)	Nonfinancial Corporations (5)	Government: Federal (6)	Government: State and Local (7)	Financial Institutions (8)
I. Land	19.3	13.7	11.0	57.0	5.7	32.1	55.3	1.2
II. Reproducible tangible assets	39.6	39.4	55.7	38.5	54.5	61.3	30.3	2.2
1. Structures	24.1	29.7	22.9	12.8	32.0	61.0	29.0	2.1
a) Residential	12.1	27.7	2.4	6.6	2.9	...	...	...
b) Nonresidential	12.0	2.0	20.5	6.2	29.1	61.0	29.0	2.0
2. Producer durables	4.9	0.2	8.4	4.6	14.6	0.3	1.1	0.1
3. Consumer durables	4.0	9.5	...	3.3	...	...	...	...
4. Inventories[b]	6.6	...	24.4	17.8	7.9	...	0.2	...
III. Tangible assets	58.9	53.1	66.7	95.4	60.2	93.4	85.6	3.4
IV. Monetary metals	1.0	...	...	0.6	0.2	...	0.1	7.1
V. Financial assets	40.1	46.9	33.3	4.0	39.8	6.6	14.3	89.5
1. Currency and demand deposits	5.0	2.8	11.8	1.9	5.5	6.6	1.9	12.0
2. Other deposits	2.5	6.2	...	0.5	0.3	...	0.6	...
3. Insurance reserves	1.0	2.5	...	0.7	...	...	...	...
4. Consumer credit	0.7	...	1.9	...	1.7	...	...	1.4
5. Bank loans	2.6	...	...	...	...	...	...	23.3
6. Loans on securities	0.9	...	...	...	...	...	...	7.6

7. Other loans	0.1	0.2	...	...	...	...	...	0.5
8. Mortgages	4.5	7.0	2.8	0.5	...	...	...	14.8
9. U.S. government securities	0.8	1.1	...	...	...	...	...	3.9
10. State and local securities	1.3	1.0	...	...	0.1	...	10.2	5.3
11. Corporate and other bonds	3.4	6.1	...	...	...	...	...	10.8
12. Corporate stock	9.3	19.5	...	...	8.1	...	...	2.2
13. Trade credit	3.8	...	16.8	...	11.1	...	...	...
14. Other financial assets	4.2	0.6	...	0.3	12.8	...	1.5	7.7
VI. Total assets	100.0	100.0	100.0	100.0	100.0	...	100.0	100.0
VII. Liabilities	29.7	8.3	40.0	13.3	43.0	83.3	37.1	82.4
1. Currency and demand deposits	5.0	...	...	...	...	3.7	...	43.9
2. Other deposits	2.5	...	...	...	...	...	...	21.9
3. Insurance reserves	1.0	...	...	...	...	...	...	9.2
4. Consumer debt	0.4	1.0	...	0.2	...	...	...	...
5. Bank loans	2.4	0.4	14.8	1.9	4.1	...	...	...
6. Loans on securities	0.9	1.7	...	...	0.2	...	...	1.8
7. Other loans	0.2	0.3	...	0.0	0.1	...	...	0.6
8. Mortgages	4.5	4.8	10.0	9.1	2.2	...	...	0.6
9. Bonds and notes	6.9	...	0.1	...	20.2	79.6	37.1	...
10. Trade debt	3.4	...	15.1	1.7	8.8	...	...	...
11. Other liabilities	2.4	0.2	...	0.4	7.3	...	...	4.5
VIII. Net worth	70.4	91.7	60.0	86.7	57.0	16.7	62.9	17.6
IX. Total assets; $bill.	150.1	54.8	10.9	25.5	35.0	5.4	1.6	16.7

[a]Assets of household include the $3 bill. in personal trust funds (R. W. Goldsmith, *Financial Intermediaries in the American Economy since 1900*, 1958, table A16), the equivalent of which for 1975 is shown in table B12 separately in lines 24 and 45.

[b]Includes livestock.

Source of basic data: Goldsmith, Lipsey, and Mendelson 1963, 2:72–73; total for lines I and II in cols. 5–8 given in source, roughly divided between lines I and II.

Table B12 **Sectoral Distribution of Assets and Liabilities in the United States, 1900 (National Total = 100.0)**

	All Sectors; $bill.	Nonfarm		Agri-culture	Nonfi-nancial Corpo-rations	Government		Finan-cial Insti-tutions
		House-holds	Unincor-porated Business			Fed-eral	State and Local	
	(1)	(2)	(3)	(4)	(5)	(6)	(7)	(8)
I. Land	29.00	25.9	4.1	50.3	6.9	1.7	10.4	0.7
II. Reproducible tangible assets	59.42	36.3	10.2	16.4	32.1	1.6	2.7	0.6
1. Structures	36.13	45.1	6.9	9.0	31.0	2.6	4.4	1.0
a) Residential	18.16	83.7	1.4	9.3	5.5	...	...	...
b) Nonresidential	17.97	6.1	12.4	8.7	56.8	5.3	8.8	1.9
2. Producer durables	7.29	1.2	12.4	15.9	69.3	0.1	0.8	0.3
3. Consumer durables	6.05	86.3	...	13.7	...	...	...	...
4. Inventories[a]	9.95	...	26.6	45.6[a]	27.7	...	0.1	...
III. Tangible assets	88.42	32.9	8.2	27.5	23.8	1.6	5.3	0.6
IV. Monetary metals	1.43	21.0	...	10.5	5.0	53.0	...	10.5
V. Financial assets	60.27	42.7	6.0	1.7	23.0	0.2	1.3	25.2
1. Currency and demand deposits	7.46	20.5	17.2	6.7	25.7	1.4	1.4	27.2
2. Other deposits	3.69	92.7	...	3.1	3.3	...	0.9	...
3. Insurance reserves	1.56	88.5	...	11.5	...	...	...	...
4. Consumer credit	1.02	...	19.8	...	56.8	...	...	23.4
5. Bank loans	3.95	...	...	...	...	...	...	100.0

6. Loans on securities	1.29	...	...	...	...	...	...	100.0
7. Other loans	0.19	52.6	...	...	...	...	...	47.4
8. Mortgages	6.78	56.7	4.4	2.1	...	...	...	36.9
9. U.S. government	1.24	46.5	...	...	...	...	...	53.5
10. State and local	2.01	25.9	...	...	2.5	...	27.5	44.1
11. Corporate and other bonds	5.15	64.5	...	...	...	...	...	35.5
12. Corporate stock	13.90	77.0	...	...	20.3	...	...	2.7
13. Trade credit	5.73	31.9	...	...	68.1	...	...	...
14. Other financial assets	6.31	5.4	...	1.3	71.2	...	1.3	20.8
VI. Total assets	150.12	36.5	7.2	17.0	23.3	1.0	3.6	11.3
VII. Liabilities	44.56	10.2	9.7	7.6	33.7	2.9	4.5	31.3
1. Currency and demand deposits	7.49	...	...	...	...	0.8	...	99.2
2. Other deposits	3.71	...	...	...	...	...	...	100.0
3. Insurance reserves	1.56	...	...	...	...	...	...	100.0
4. Consumer debt	0.59	90.9	...	9.1	...	...	...	...
5. Bank loans	3.82	5.2	42.2	12.8	37.2	...	...	2.6
6. Loans on securities	1.29	70.5	...	...	6.3	...	...	23.2
7. Other loans	0.35	52.7	...	2.9	14.9	...	...	29.5
8. Mortgages	6.78	38.4	16.0	34.1	11.5	...	...	...
9. Bonds and notes	10.33	...	0.1	...	68.4	19.5	12.0	...
10. Trade debt	5.13	...	31.9	8.3	59.8	...	...	...
11. Other liabilities	3.50	2.8	...	2.8	72.8	...	...	21.6
VIII. Net worth	105.56	47.7	6.2	21.0	18.9	0.2	3.2	2.8

[a]Includes livestock.

Source of basic data: Goldsmith, Lipsey, and Mendelson 1963, 2:72–73; total for lines I and II in cols. 5–8 given in source, roughly distributed among sectors.

Table B13 **Structure of Sectoral Balance Sheets in the United States, 1975 (Total Assets = 100.0)**

	All Sectors (1)	House-holds (2)	Non-profit Insti-tutions (3)	Nonfinancial Unincorporated Business: Farm (4)	Nonfinancial Unincorporated Business: Others (5)	Nonfi-nancial Corps. (6)	Fed-eral Gov-ern-ment (7)	State and Local Govern-ments (8)	Finan-cial Insti-tutions (9)	Rest of the World (10)
1. Land	12.2	11.0	25.5	64.9	8.7	11.7	11.5	21.8	0.7	...
2. Structures	24.3	21.4	50.4	13.6	69.4	24.3	30.6	62.2	1.3	...
3. Consumer durables	4.3	12.1	...	...	...	...	...	...	...	...
4. Equipment	6.1	...	2.0	9.3	9.9	21.9	21.3	4.1	0.7	...
5. Inventories	3.9	...	...	9.4	3.8	15.8	13.8	0.1	0.0	...
6. Tangible assets	50.8	44.5	77.9	97.2	91.8	73.6	77.1	88.2	2.8	...
7. Demand deposits and currency	2.3	3.6	0.1	1.4	1.9	2.2	2.1	1.2	0.7	7.0
8. Time and savings deposits	7.0	17.0	...	...	...	1.0	0.1	4.1	0.8	10.5
9. Gold and foreign exchange	0.1	...	...	...	...	...	...	...	0.4	...
10. U.S. government securities	3.5	2.2	1.0	...	...	0.7	...	2.6	8.6	33.4
11. U.S. agency securities	1.0	0.2	...	...	...	0.2	1.3	1.9	3.0	...
12. State and local government securities	1.8	1.3	0.2	...	...	0.2	...	0.4	6.2	...
13. Corporate and foreign bonds	2.5	0.7	4.9	...	...	...	...	...	10.3	1.0
14. Corporate stock	6.8	11.2	12.9	...	...	...	...	...	11.1	13.4
15. Mortgages	6.3	1.5	0.6	...	...	...	2.5	1.1	26.9	...
16. Bank loans n.e.c.	2.2	...	...	...	...	...	...	...	10.5	...
17. Other loans	1.3	...	...	...	...	...	12.7	...	3.6	...
18. Consumer credit	1.6	...	...	...	1.9	0.9	...	...	6.3	...
19. Open-market paper	0.6	0.2	...	...	...	1.3	...	...	0.9	4.2
20. Trade credit	2.6	...	...	...	2.7	13.2	1.2	...	0.3	5.8
21. Insurance and pension reserves	4.6	13.0	...	...	...	...	...	...	...	...
22. Direct foreign investment	1.1	...	...	...	...	5.5	...	...	...	11.6

23. Common trust funds	0.1	0.4	...	...	...	...	...	...	...	...
24. Individual trust funds	1.2	3.3	...	...	...	...	...	...	...	...
25. Other financial assets	2.7	1.0	2.5	1.5	1.8	1.3	3.0	0.6	7.6	13.0
26. Total financial assets	49.2	55.5	22.2	22.8	8.2	26.4	22.9	11.8	97.2	100.0
27. Total assets %	100.0	100.0	100.0	100.0	100.0	100.0	100.0	100.0	100.0	100.0
28. Total assets $bill.	12805	4660	243	539	671	2144	535	1178	2637	199
29. Demand deposits and currency	2.6	...	...	...	...	...	...	...	} 45.9	...
30. Time and savings deposits	7.0	...	...	...	...	...	...	...		...
31. U.S. government securities	3.5	...	...	...	...	...	81.8	...	...	...
32. U.S. agency securities	1.0	...	...	...	...	...	...	...	4.6	...
33. State and local government securities	1.8	...	...	...	...	...	...	19.2	...	...
34. Corporate and foreign bonds	2.5	...	...	...	...	11.9	...	...	1.4	12.9
35. Mortgages	6.3	10.6	11.1	9.6	12.1	7.2	0.2	...	0.3	...
36. Bank loans n.e.c.	2.2	0.4	...	3.7	1.7	7.8	...	...	1.5	11.0
37. Other loans	1.4	0.7	...	2.4	4.1	1.6	...	0.5	0.7	23.5
38. Consumer credit	1.6	4.4	...	...	...	...	...	...	...	...
39. Open-market paper	0.6	...	...	...	0.6	0.7	...	...	1.6	5.6
40. Trade debt	2.3	...	3.3	1.0	2.3	10.8	1.0	0.9	...	7.1
41. Insurance and pension reserves	4.6	...	...	...	...	...	17.6	...	18.6	...
42. Other liabilities	3.1	0.5	...	...	...	1.7	2.4	...	11.3	13.4
43. Liabilities (30–44)	40.3	16.6	14.4	16.6	20.7	41.6	102.9	20.6	85.9	73.5
44. Direct foreign investment	0.9	...	...	...	...	...	...	...	...	59.1
45. Common trust funds	0.1	...	...	...	...	...	...	...	0.7	...
46. Individual trust funds	1.2	...	...	...	...	...	...	...	5.6	...
47. Equity in enterprises	11.5	...	...	...	...	58.4	...	...	7.8	...
48. Equities (45–48)	13.7	...	...	...	...	58.4	...	...	14.1	59.1
49. Net worth	46.0	83.4	85.6	83.4	79.3	...	−2.9	79.4	...	−32.6
50. Liabilities, equities, and net worth	100.0	100.0	100.0	100.0	100.0	100.0	100.0	100.0	100.0	100.0

Source: Goldsmith 1982, table 12, after elimination of lines 23–26.

Table B14 **Sectoral Distribution of Assets and Liabilities in the United States, 1975 (National Total = 100.0)**

				Nonfinancial Unincorporated Business						
	Amounts $bill. (1)	Households (2)	Nonprofit Institutions (3)	Farm (4)	Other (5)	Nonfinancial Corps. (6)	Federal Government (7)	State and Local Governments (8)	Financial Institutions (9)	Rest of the World (10)
1. Land	1551	31.9	4.0	22.6	3.7	16.1	4.0	16.5	1.2	...
2. Structures	3078	31.3	4.0	2.4	15.2	16.9	5.3	23.8	1.1	...
3. Consumer durables	546	100.0	...	...	...	...	...	...	...	...
4. Equipment	771	...	0.6	6.5	8.6	60.8	14.8	6.2	2.5	...
5. Inventories	498	...	...	110.4	5.2	68.9	15.0	0.3	0.2	...
6. Tangible assets (1–5)	6582	32.7	2.9	8.0	9.4	24.0	6.3	15.8	1.1	...
7. Demand deposits and currency	290	56.4	0.1	2.5	4.3	16.4	3.8	4.9	6.7	4.8
8. Time and saving deposits	885	87.3	...	...	...	2.5	0.1	5.4	2.3	2.4
9. Gold and foreign exchange	12	...	...	...	...	...	...	...	100.0	...
10. U.S. government securities	437	22.3	0.5	...	...	3.3	...	7.0	51.7	15.2
11. U.S. agency securities	121	7.5	...	...	...	2.6	5.8	18.5	65.6	...
12. State and local government securities	231	24.9	0.2	...	...	1.9	...	1.9	71.1	...
13. Corporate and foreign bonds	317	10.3	3.8	...	...	...	...	...	85.3	0.7
14. Corporate stock	855	59.0	3.7	...	...	...	...	...	34.2	3.1
15. Mortgages	803	8.3	0.2	...	...	...	1.7	1.6	88.2	...
16. Bank loans n.e.c.	277	...	...	...	...	...	...	...	100.0	...
17. Other loans	163	...	...	...	...	...	41.4	...	58.6	...
18. Consumer credit	197	...	...	...	6.4	9.3	...	...	84.3	...
19. Open-market paper	70	15.0	...	...	...	39.8	...	...	33.1	12.0
20. Trade credit	327	...	...	...	5.4	86.7	2.0	...	2.3	3.5
21. Insurance and pension reserves	585	100.0	...	...	...	...	...	...	...	...

22. Direct foreign investment	141	...	...	...	...	83.6	...	...	...	16.4
23. Common trust funds	18	100.0	...	...	...	...	...	...	...	...
24. Individual trust funds	147	100.0	...	...	...	...	...	...	...	...
25. Other financial assets	347	12.6	1.8	2.3	3.4	8.0	4.6	1.9	58.0	7.4
26. Financial assets (9–25)	6223	40.4	0.8	0.2	0.9	9.1	1.9	2.2	41.3	3.2
27. Total assets	12805	35.6	1.9	4.3	5.3	16.9	4.2	9.3	20.8	1.6
28. Demand deposits and currenc	325	...	...	...	...	...	...	...	100.0	...
29. Time and saving deposits	885	...	...	...	...	...	...	...	100.0	...
30. U.S. government securities	437	...	...	...	...	...	100.0	...	...	...
31. U.S. agency securities	121	...	...	...	...	...	...	...	100.0	...
32. State and local government securities	224	...	...	...	...	...	...	100.0	...	...
33. Corporate and foreign bonds	317	...	...	...	...	80.2	...	...	11.7	8.1
34. Mortgages	803	59.9	3.4	6.4	10.1	19.2	0.1	...	0.9	...
35. Bank loans n.e.c.	277	5.9	...	7.3	4.0	60.3	...	...	14.6	7.9
36. Other loans	178	17.7	...	7.2	15.6	19.1	...	3.2	10.9	26.3
37. Consumer credit	197	100.0	...	...	...	...	...	...	...	...
38. Open-market paper	78	...	...	...	5.7	21.0	...	...	56.5	16.8
39. Trade debt	291	...	2.7	1.7	5.3	79.9	1.8	3.7	...	4.9
40. Insurance and pension reserves	585	...	...	...	...	...	16.1	...	83.9	...
41. Other liabilities	395	5.4	...	...	...	9.2	3.2	...	75.4	6.8
42. Total liabilities (28–41)	5105	14.7	0.7	1.8	2.7	17.5	10.8	4.7	44.3	2.9
43. Direct foreign investment	118	...	...	...	...	...	...	...	...	100.0
44. Common trust funds	18	...	...	...	...	...	...	...	100.0	...
45. Individual trust funds	147	...	...	...	...	...	...	...	100.0	...
46. Business equities	1459	...	...	...	...	85.8	...	...	14.2	...
47. Equities (43–46)	1742	...	...	...	...	71.8	...	...	21.4	6.8
48. Net worth	5955	64.8	3.6	7.7	9.1	...	−0.3	16.1	...	−1.1
49. Liabilities, equities, and net worth	12805	40.9	1.8	3.9	4.9	15.6	3.9	8.6	19.1	1.4

Source: Goldsmith 1982, table 14, after elimination of lines 23–26.

Appendix C
Some Statistical Difficulties

This appendix discusses briefly some statistical difficulties encountered in estimating some of the components of national and sectoral balance sheets. The discussion is by no means exhaustive, and does not deal with difficulties specific to individual countries except as illustrations. It may be skipped by readers not interested in technicalities.

Agricultural Land

This is an item for which fairly reliable official census type estimations exist in a few countries, sometimes back well into the 19th century, e.g., the United States, France, and Japan. In others, official or private estimates are available for shorter periods or for a few benchmarks, which can be extended somewhat precariously to other dates by land price indices. For a few countries, however, the available material is very scarce, and the resulting estimates are affected by a large margin of error, e.g., Israel, Russia, and Sweden. These difficulties are intensified by the fact that often estimates are available only for land and buildings combined, so that the separation of the two increases the margin of error.

Nonagricultural Land

For no other important component of tangible assets are the bases of estimation so scarce and unsatisfactory. Comprehensive official or unofficial estimates do not exist for a single country except very recently for France and Japan. Even in the United States data are scattered and limited to the postwar period. It has, therefore, almost always been necessary to use the indirect method of estimating the value of land underlying structures as a proportion of that of the structures, the proportion usually having to be based on fragmentary data and often forcing reliance on information for other dates or even other countries regarded as roughly comparable. As a result, the minority, in terms of value, of nonagricultural land not underlying structures is generally omitted from the estimations.

Structures and Equipment

For the postwar period the estimates are in most countries derived by the perpetual inventory method. With all their limitations, the estimates of residential and nonresidential structures and of equipment generated by this method constitute the least doubtful components of tangible assets, and because of the nature of the method used are at least consistent over time and fairly comparable among countries. The method has been applied in several countries back to the late 19th century, namely, in Denmark, Germany, Great Britain, India, Italy, Japan, Norway, and the United States. In most countries, however, the pre–World War II estimates are heterogeneous and subject to wider margins of error, as they are based on occasional census type enumerations, assessed valuations, or capitalization of earnings.

Under the perpetual inventory method the value of the stock of a category of reproducible tangible assets at one point of time is obtained by cumulating net capital expenditures in constant prices over a period of the past corresponding to the assumed length of life, and then converting this figure into current prices by means of an explicit price index or an implicit deflator. (Cf. e.g., Goldsmith 1954, 2: pt. I; 1962, chap. 3; and mathematically more sophisticated, e.g., Mairesse 1972). The results obviously depend on the reliability of the estimates of capital expenditures in current prices; the adequacy of the price indices used to reduce these expenditures to a constant price level; the treatment or disregard of quality changes; the realism of the choice of length of life; the method of depreciation, usually straight-line but occasionally declining balance, particularly for consumer durables; and the allowance for scrap value. Because of the large differences in the results which follow from even moderate differences in some of the assumptions embodied in the calculations, particularly the choice between straight-line and declining balance depreciation, it is essential to compare them whenever possible with market values, such as periodic census-type evaluations and market price indices for residential structures and secondhand prices for consumer durables. Such checks unfortunately are hardly ever available for nonresidential structures or for equipment which generally constitute well over one-half of the value of all reproducible tangible assets. In international comparisons it is also important to make sure that the same basic method of depreciation has been used.

Consumer Durables

Estimates by the perpetual inventory method exist for only a few countries and generally only for recent years, e.g., in Belgium, France, Germany, Great Britain, Japan, Norway, and the United States. In the majority of cases, therefore, existing heterogeneous estimates had to be used; or resort had to be had to the rule of thumb of estimating the value of the stock of consumer durables at four times the annual rate of purchases at the benchmark date, a relationship based on the cases where perpetual inventory estimates are available.

Inventories

Estimates, of varying degree of reliability and generally unknown method, are available for many of the benchmark or neighboring dates from which they can be extrapolated. They increase over time in number and presumably improve in quality as they are based on combinations of business balance sheets collected for tax or statistical purposes, and as they become parts of the countries' system of national accounts. Not a few of the figures used in this study nevertheless had to be estimated very roughly, particularly for the prewar period, sometimes as ratios to national product or to structures and equipment derived from supposedly comparable situations, and therefore they carry a large margin of error.

Livestock

Estimates of the value of livestock, mostly contemporary, are fairly numerous, and they are likely to be reasonably reliable since most countries have had periodic livestock censuses and prices are not too difficult to ascertain. The need to shift many of the existing estimates from their original dates to the balance sheet dates, however, increases the margin of error.

Gold and Silver

The figures used for the value of monetary gold in the postwar period are probably the most nearly accurate figures used in the study, since the quantities are exactly known, except for the Soviet Union and Hungary, as are the market prices. The figures for earlier dates are almost as good as central banks have regularly reported their holdings, and there were no differences between book and market value. On the other hand, the value of gold and silver coins in circulation before World War I and that of gold coins and bullion hoarded, increasingly important after World War II, is uncertain. For the period before World War I, official or unofficial estimates are available for most large countries. The estimates of nonmonetary nonindustrial holdings of gold and silver after 1913 are too scattered and uncertain to have been included in the national balance sheets used in this study, except because of their relatively very large size in the case of India. They should be significant before the mid-1970s in relation to other components among other countries only in France and possibly Switzerland.

Financial Assets

The situation is radically different between countries and dates for which official estimates of the stock of the different financial assets and liabilities exist, which usually are parts of their flow-of-funds accounts available for about one-half of the countries (Belgium, Canada, France, Germany, Italy, Norway, Sweden, United States, and Yugoslavia) for all or part of the postwar period; and the more numerous cases in which these figures had to be put together item by item from numerous often heterogeneous sources with varying degrees of reliability.

Claims against Financial Institutions

Among financial assets and liabilities, information is generally best, or at least deficient, for those held or issued by financial institutions, though more so for the banking system than for other institutions. Their use was facilitated by the existence of estimates up to 1963 for all the 20 countries except for Hungary (Goldsmith 1969, appendix A). Since the dates of these estimates often did not exactly coincide with the benchmark dates used in this study, interpolations were necessary, generally based on the movements of the assets of central, deposit and savings banks. For the more recent period the information could be obtained for about one-half of the countries from their flow-of-funds accounts. The balance sheets of financial institutions or their condensed statements as published for the postwar period in the *IFSYB* were used to provide data on three important financial instruments—money (currency and demand deposits), nonmonetary deposits, and insurance and pension claims. In some cases, however, the data for these three categories were not separately available, and only one item covering all claims against financial institutions, including their equity, could be shown in the national balance sheet.

For comparisons with financial instruments issued by other sectors, it would be preferable to use a consolidated balance sheet of the financial institutions sector, i.e., to eliminate claims and liabilities, and less importantly holdings of equity securities, among financial institutions. This has not been possible except in the relatively few cases where the basic data are on a consolidated basis, e.g., in the United States for the postwar period, thus introducing some regrettable inconsistencies.

Loans by Financial Institutions

The balance sheets of financial institutions also contain information on their loans, but except when the information is provided as a part of a comprehensive sectorized system of financial accounts, or for the postwar period in *IFSYB*, it often is not in the form required for national balance sheets, i.e., covering all loans to the private sectors. In practice the desired figures often only can be approximated, particularly because of scarcity of information on loans by financial institutions outside the banking system.

Government Debt

This component of the financial superstructure, of considerable size in most cases, can generally be ascertained without much difficulties for the central government. Information is generally scarcer on the debt of local governments, which in most countries and for most dates is considerably smaller. Difficulties arise in some cases, however, with the liabilities of government which do not have the form of securities and are harder to ascertain, such as liabilities to social security organizations. Moreover, it is not always clear whether or to what extent the reported figures have eliminated by consolidation claims among components of the government, and whether and to what extent they include the liabilities of government enterprises. Finally, the figures often do not comprehensively separate domestic from foreign liabilities in the form of either securities originally issued in foreign markets or of originally domestic securities which have been acquired by foreigners. It has not been possible in this study to clarify the exact coverage of the figures for government debt used in the national balance sheets and to apply a standard definition. These figures are, therefore, somewhat vaguer and somewhat less comparable over time and particularly among countries than would be desirable.

Corporate Securities

Comprehensive information on the market value of all corporate securities, particularly on corporate shares, is rarely available, except where it is provided as a part of a system of financial accounts, i.e., essentially only for all or part of the postwar period and for only about one-half of the countries. Otherwise information is generally limited to securities listed on exchanges, so that comprehensive figures must be derived, if at all, by a blowup, often on a precarious basis. An additional difficulty is that it is generally not possible to separate the value of the stock of financial institutions, introducing double-counting in the national balance sheet if the latter uses total assets of financial institutionss in lieu of claims against them. This, however, should generally not exceed 1–2 percent of financial and half as much as of national assets. The situation is somewhat better or corporate bonds, for which information can sometimes be derived from combined corporate balance sheets.

Mortgages

Because of their usually large size, it is desirable to allocate to mortgage loans a separate entry in the national balance sheet. This, however, is often not feasible, because of the absence of specific information, fortunately mostly countries in which mortgages have been relatively less important in the financial structure. A combination of loans and mortgages will generally provide figures more nearly comparable among countries.

Trade Credit

This is probably the most neglected item in the available estimates of financial assets, being omitted or insufficiently covered in even most of the modern flow-of-funds accounts. Because of its size and financial significance it has been regarded as impermissible to ignore this item altogether. The estimates that have been included in the balance sheets of the 20 countries, are, however, of necessity of the roughest. They are based, except where estimates could be found, in most cases on the ratios to inventories or to national product observed in the countries and for the periods for which reasonably reliable figures are available, i.e., mainly the United States since the turn of the century and in Japan and a few other countries in the postwar period.

List of Publications Cited

Alanis, Patino, E. 1955, "La riqueza nacional." In *Investigacion Economica*, Mexico, D.F.

Alphandéry, C. 1968. *Les Prêts Hypothecaires*. Paris: Presses Universitaires de France.

Anderson, R. C. n.d. (ca. 1972). "The valuation of paintings and their return as investments." Unpublished paper.

Aukurst, O., and Bjerke, J. 1959. "Real capital in Norway 1900–1956." In R. Goldsmith and C. Saunders, eds., *The Measurement of National Wealth*.

Australian Bureau of Statistics. *Yearbook Australia*. Canberra.

Babeau, A., and Strauss-Kahn, D. 1977. *La Richesse des Francais*. Paris: Presses Universitaires de France.

Banca d'Italia. *Bolletino* (monthly). Rome.

———. *Assemblea Generale Ordinaria dei Partecipanti* (annual).

———. *Relazione Annuale*. Rome.

Banco de Mexico. *Informe Annual*. Mexico D.F.

———. 1978. "Nota sobre el calculo de las asignaciones para depreciacion en las cuentas nacionales 1950–1977." Unpublished. Mexico D.F.

———. 1979. "Nota metodologica para el calculo de cambio de existencias considerado en el documento de cuentas nacionales consolidadas 1960–1978." Unpublished. Mexico D.F.

Bank of Canada. *Annual Flows and Year-End Financial Assets and Liabilities, 1961–1976*. Ottawa.

Bank of England. *Bank of England Quarterly*. London.

Bank of Israel. *Annual Report*. Jerusalem.

———. *Monthly Statistical Bulletin*. Jerusalem.

Bank of Japan. 1966. *Hundred-Year Statistics of the Japanese Economy*. Tokyo.

———. 1967. *Flow of Funds Accounts in Japan 1963–1966*. Tokyo.

———. 1978. *Flow of Funds Accounts in Japan 1970–1977*. Tokyo.
Banque Nationale de Belgique. *Bulletin d'Information et de Statistique* (monthly). Brussels.
Basch, A. 1968. *El Mercado de Capitales en Mexico*. Mexico: CEMLA.
Becher, A. 1969. *Soviet National Income, 1958–1964*. Berkeley: University of California Press.
Benedetti, A.; Consolo, G.; Fouquet, A. "L'Experience francaise de comptabilité patriomoniale." Paper for 16th General Conference of International Association for Research in Income and Wealth, 1979.
Berry, T. S. 1968. *Estimated Annual Variations in Gross National Product 1789–1909*. Richmond: Bostwick Press.
Biddell, G. 1904. *Loans of Local Authorities (England and Wales)*. London.
Bjerke, K., and Ussing, N. 1958. *Studies over Denmarks National Product 1870–1950*. København, G.E.C. Gads.
Block, H. 1979. *The Planetary Product*. Washington, D.C.: Department of State.
———. 1981. *The PLanetary Product in 1980*. Washington, D.C.: Department of State.
Board of Governors of the Federal Reserve System. 1979. *Flow of Funds Accounts 1946–1978*. Washington, D.C.
———. 1980. *Balance Sheets for the U.S. Economy, 1945–1979*. Mimeo.
———. 1983. *Balance Sheets for the U.S. Economy, 1945–1982*. Mimeo.
Bogachev, V. N. 1979. *National Wealth of the U.S.S.R.: Its Structure, Dynamics and Place in the Balances of National Economy*. Mimeo. Moscow.
Bolsa de Valores (Mexico). *Annuario Financiero y Bursatil*. Mexico D.F.
Bureau of the Census (U.S.A.) *Statistical Abstract* (annually). Washington, D.C.
———. 1975. *Historical Statistics of the United States*. Washington, D.C.
Bureau of Census and Statistics (South Africa). 1960. *Union Statistics for Fifty Years*. Pretoria.
Burns, A. F. 1934. *Production Trends in the United States since 1870*. New York: National Bureau of Economic Research.
Calder, J. R. 1978. "The stock of consumer durables in the U.K." Central Statistical Office. *Economic Trends*, no. 293.
Cameron, R. ed. 1967. *Banking in the Early Stages of Industrialization*. New York: Oxford University Press.
Campbell, D. 1928. "Usury and annuities in the 18th century." *Law Quarterly Review* 44.
Campion, H. 1939. *Public and Private Property in Great Britain*. London: Oxford University Press.
Carré, J-J; Dubois, P.; Malinvaud, E. 1975. *French Economic Growth*. Stanford: Stanford University Press.
Caso Brecht, J. 1971. *El Mercado de Acciones en Mexico*. Mexico D.F.: CEMLA.
Central Statistical Office (Great Britain). *Annual Abstract of Statistics*. London.

———. *Economic Trends*. London.
———. 1978. *Personal Sector Balance Sheets and Current Developments in Inland Revenue Estimates of Personal Wealth*. Studies in Official Statistics No. 35.
Central Statistical Office (Israel). *Statistical Abstract* (annually). Jerusalem.
———. *Monthly Statistical Bulletin*. Jerusalem.
Central Statistical Organization (India). *Statistical Abstract India* (annually). New Delhi.
Chaptal, Comte de. 1819. *De L'Industrie Francoise*. Paris: A. A. Renouard.
Clark, C. 1951. *The Conditions of Economic Progress*. 2d ed. London: Macmillan and Co.
Colson, C. 1927. *Cours d'Economie Politique*. Paris: Gauthier-Villars.
Commissariat General du Plan (France). 1980. *Credit Interentreprises*. Paris: La Documentation Francaise.
Cotula, F., and Caron, M. 1971. "I conti finanzari dell'Italia." Banca d'Italia, *Bolletino*.
Craigie, C. 1902. *Journal of the Royal Statistical Society*. London.
Creamer, D. B., et. al. 1960. *Capital in Manufacturing and Mining*. Princeton: Princeton University Press.
Cunneen, D. J., and Barnes, J. E. M. 1976. "Investing in art." *London Business School Journal*.
Danmarks Nationalbank. *Monetary Review* (monthly). Copenhagen.
Davies, J. B. 1979. "On the size distribution of wealth in Canada." *Review of Income and Wealth*.
Deane, P., and Cole, W. A. 1967. *British Economic Growth 1688–1959*. 2d ed. Cambridge: Cambridge University Press.
De Mattia, R. 1967. *I bilanci degli istituti di emissione italiani dal 1845 al 1936*. Rome: Banca d'Italia.
De Meo, G. 1973. "Sintesi statistica di un ventennio di vita economica italiana, 1952–1971." *Annuali di Statistica*, VIII 27.
Departamento de Agricultura (Mexico). 1975. V. *Censo Agricola-Ganadero y Ejidal 1970, Resumen General*. Mexico D.F.
Department of Commerce (U.S.A.) *Survey of Current Business* (monthly). Washington, D.C.
Department of Statistics (South Africa). *South African Statistics* (annually). Pretoria.
Det Statistiske Departement (Denmark). *Statistisk Årbog* (annually).
———. 1961. *Aktieselskaber 1958–1860*.
———. 1958. *Landbrugets Priser 1900–1957*. Copenhagen.
Division of Agricultural Marketing Research (South Africa). *Abstract of Agricultural Statistics* (annually). Pretoria.
Deutsche Bundesbank. 1976. *Deutsches Geld-und Bankwesen in Zahlen 1875–1975*. Frankfurt am Main: Fritz Knapp.
———. 1978. *Zahlenübersichten und Methodische Erläuterungen zur Gesamtwirtschaftlichen Finanzierungsrechnung der Deutschen Bundesbank 1960 bis 1977*. Frankfurt am Main.

———. *Monatsberichte*.
Dickinson, F. G., and Eakin, F. 1936. *A Balance Sheet of the Nation's Economy*. Bureau of Business Research, University of Illinois. Bulletin No. 54.
Dickson, P. G. M. 1967. *The Financial Revolution in England*. London: Macmillan Co.
Divisia, F.; Pupin, A.; Roy, R. 1954. *A la Recherche du Franc Perdu*. Paris: Socièté d'Edition de Revues at de Publications.
Dominion Bureau of Statistics (Canada). 1967. *Canada One Hundred 1867–1967*. Ottawa.
Dorrance, G. S. 1978. *National Monetary and Financial Analysis*. New York: St. Martin's Press.
Dublin, L. I., and Lotka, A. J. 1946. *The Money Value of a Man*. New York: Ronald Press.
Dument, M. 1962. *Ce que Vaut la Terre en France*. Paris: Hachette.
Dun, J. 1876. "An analysis of joint stock banking in the United Kingdom." *Journal of Royal Statistical Society*.
Economic Planning Agency (Japan). *Annual Report on National Accounts*. Tokyo.
Eilbott, P. 1973. "Estimates of the market value of the outstanding corporate stock of all domestic corporations." In Goldsmith, 1973.
Eisner, R. 1980. "Capital gaims and income: Real changes in the value of capital in the United States, 1946–1977." In D. Usher, ed., *The Measurement of Capital*, Studies in Income and Wealth, vol. 45. Chicago: University of Chicago Press.
English, H. 1827. *A Complete View of Joint Stock Companies Formed during the Years 1824 and 1825*. London: Boosey and Sons.
Epstein, E. J. 1982. *The Rise and Fall of Diamonds*. New York: Simon and Schuster.
Esposito, G. 1973. "Il capitale fisso in Italia per settori di attivita economica nel periodo 1951–71." *Annali di Statistica* 8, no. 27.
Evans, A. W. 1974. "Private sector housing land prices in England and Wales." Central Statistical Office (Great Britain). *Economic Trends*, no. 244.
Feinstein, C. H. 1972. *National Income, Expenditure and Output of the United Kingdom 1855–1965*. Cambridge: University Press.
———. 1976. *Statistical Tables of National Income, Expenditure and Output in the United Kingdom, 1855–1965*. Cambridge: University Press.
———. 1978. "Capital formation in Great Britain." *The Cambridge Economic History of Europe*, vol. 7, p. i. Cambridge: University Press.
Feis, H. 1961. *Europe—the World's Banker, 1870–1914*. New York: A. M. Kelly.
Feldstein, M. 1976. "Social security and the distribution of wealth." *Journal of the American Statistical Association* 71.
Fisher, I. 1909. *Report on National Vitality*. Bulletin 30 of Committee of 100 on National Health. Washington, D.C.: Government Printing Office.

Frankel, S. H. 1969. *Gold and International Equity Investment*. London: Institute of Economic Affairs.
Franzsen, D. G., and Willers, J. J. D. 1959. "Capital accumulation and economic growth in South Africa." In R. Goldsmith and C. Saunders, eds, *The Measurement of National Wealth*. Chicago: Quadrangle Books.
Fuà, G. 1969. *Lo Sviluppo Economico in Italia*. Milan: Giuffre.
Gaathon, A. L. 1971. *Economic Productivity in Israel*. New York: Praeger.
Ganz, A. 1959. "Problems and uses of national wealth estimates in Latin America." In R. Goldsmith and C. Saunders, eds. *The Measurement of National Wealth*. Chicago: Quadrangle Books.
Garland, J. M., and Goldsmith, R. W. 1959. "The national wealth of Australia." In R. Goldsmith and C. Saunders, eds., *The Measurement of National Wealth*. Chicago: Quadrangle Books.
Garvy, G. 1977. *Money, Financial Flows and Credit in the Soviet Union*. Cambridge, Mass.: Ballinger Publishing Co.
Giannone, A. 1964. "Valutazione della ricchezza italiana negli ultimi cinquanta anni." *Moneta e Credito* 17.
Giffen, R. 1970. *The Growth of Capital*. London: G. Bell and Sons, 1889; New York: Augustus M. Kelly.
Gini, C. 1962. *L'Ammontare e la Composizione della Ricchezza delle Nazioni*, 2d ed. Torino: UTET.
Goldsmith, R. W. 1950. "Measuring National Wealth in a System of Social Accounting." In National Bureau of Economic Research, *Studies in Income and Wealth*, vol. 12. New York.
———. 1952. "The growth of reproducible wealth of the United States of America from 1805 to 1950." In S. Kuznets, ed., *Income and Wealth of the United States*. Cambridge: Bowes and Bowes.
———. 1955–56. *A Study of Saving in the United States*. 3 vols. Princeton: Princeton University Press.
———. 1962. *The National Wealth of the United States in the Postwar Period*. Princeton: Princeton University Press.
———. 1964. "The national balance sheet of the Soviet Union." In *Essays on Econometrics and Planning Presented to Professor P. C. Mahalanobis on the Occasion of His 70th Birthday*. Oxford: Pergamon Press.
———. 1966. *The Financial Development of Mexico*. Paris: OECD.
———. 1967. "The Uses of National Balance Sheets." *Review of Income and Wealth*.
———. 1969. *Financial Structure and Development*. New Haven and London: Yale University Press.
———. 1970. "Prolegomènes a l'analyse comparative des structures financières." In *Revue d'Economie Politique*.
———. 1975a. "The Financial Development of Yugoslavia." In *Banca Nazionale del Lavoro Quarterly Review* 28.
———. 1975b. "A Note on the National Balance Sheet of Belgium 1850–1971." In *Tijdschrift voor Economie en Management* 20.

———. 1976. "The national balance sheet of Germany, 1850–1972." *Konjunkturpolitik* 22.

———. 1981. "A tentative secular national balance sheet for Switzerland." *Schweizerische Zeitschrift für Volkswirtschaft und Statistik.*

———. 1982. *The National Blance Sheet of the United States 1953–1975.* Chicago: Chicago University Press.

———. 1983a. *The Financial Development in India, 1860–1977.* New Haven: Yale University Press.

———. 1983b. *The Financial Development of Japan, 1868–1977.* New Haven: Yale University Press.

———, ed. 1973. *Institutional Investors and Corporate Stock.* New York: National Bureau of Economic Research.

Goldsmith, R. W., and Frijdal, A. C. 1975. "La bilan national de la Belgique de 1948 à 1971." In *Cahiers Economiques de Bruxelles.*

Goldsmith, R. W.; Lipsey, R. E.; and Mendelson, M. 1963. *Studies in the National Balance Sheet of the United States.* 2 vols. Princeton: Princeton University Press.

Goldsmith, R. W., and Saunders, C., eds. 1959. *The Measurement of National Wealth.* London: Bowes and Bowes.

Grebler, L.; Black, D. M.; Winnick, L. 1956. *Capital Formation in Real Estate, Trends and Prospects.* Princeton: Princeton University Press.

Helliwell, J., and Boxall, P. 1978. "Private sector wealth: Quarterly estimates in an aggregate model." In *Economic Record* 54.

Heth, M. 1970. *The Flow of Funds in Israel.* New York: Praeger.

Hibbert, J.; Griffin, T. J.; and Walker, R. L. 1979. "Development of estimates of the stock of fixed capital in the United Kingdom." *Review of Income and Wealth.*

Hoffman, W.; with Grumbach, F., and Hesse, H. 1965. *Das Wachstum der Deutschen Wirtschaft seit der Mitte der 19 ten Jahrhunderts.* Berlin: Springer.

Holland, D. M., and Myers, S. C. 1980. "Profitability and capital costs for manufacturing corporations and all nonfinancial corporations." *American Economic Review* 70, no. 2.

Hood, W. C., and Scott, A. 1957. *Output, Labour and Capital in the Canadian Economy.* Ottawa: Royal Commission on Canada's Economic Prospects.

Hunt, F. ed. 1863. *The Merchants' Magazine and Commercial Review.* New York.

Hungarian Central Statistical Office. *Statistical Yearbook.*

———. 1980. *A nemzeti vagyon és az alloeszközallomany.*

Imlah, A. 1958. *The economic Element in the Pax Britiannica.* Cambridge: Harvard University Press.

INSEE (Institut National de la Statistique et des Etudes Economiques) (France). *Annuaire Statistique de la France* (annually). Paris.

———. 1979. *Le Patrimoine National.* Economie et Statistique, 114.

———. 1980. *Les comptes de patrimoine.* Collection de l'INSEE, Series C, no. 89–90.

Institut d'Economie Agricole (Belgium). *Cahiers de l'IEA.* Brussels.

Institut National de Statistique (Belgium). *Bulletin Statistique* (monthly). Brussels.
———. *Statistiques des Mutations Immobilières* (annually).
International Monetary Fund. *International Financial Statistics* (monthly). Washington, D.C.
———. *International Financial Statistics Yearbook.*
Istituto Centrale di Statistica (Italy). *Annuario Statistico Italiano.*
———. *Annuario di Contabiliá Nazionale.*
Joint Economic Committee (U.S.A.). *Measuring the Nation's Wealth.* Washington, D.C.
———. 1964. *Economic Policies and Practices.*
———. 1979. *Soviet Economy in a Time of Change.*
Jones, A. H. 1980. *The Wealth of a Nation to Be: The American Colonies on the Eve of the Revolution.* New York: Columbia University Press.
Jorgenson, D., and Pachon, A. 1980. *Lifetime Income and Human Capital.* Harvard Institute for Economic Research Discussion Paper No. 781.
Joshi, M. J. 1966. *The National Balance Sheet of India.* Bombay: University of Bombay.
Kardwell, J. *Rare Stamps for the Investor.* New York, 1980.
Keene, G. 1971. *Money and Art.* New York: G. P. Putnam's Sons.
Kendrick, J. W. 1976. *The Formation and Stocks of Total Capital.* New York and London: Columbia University Press.
King, G. 1936. *Two Tracts.* Baltimore: The Johns Hopkins Press.
Kravis, I.B., et al. 1975. *A System of International Comparison of Gross Product and Purchasing Power.* Baltimore: The Johns Hopkins University Press.
Kruse, A. 1949. *Die Briefmarke als Wertobjekt.* München: Richard Pflaum.
Kuznets, S. 1966. *Modern Economic Growth.* New Haven: Yale University Press.
League of Nations. *Statistical Yearbook.* Geneva.
Lenti, L. 1978. *I Conti della nazione.* Torino: UTET.
Levasseur, E. 1889–92. *La Population Française.* Paris: A. Rousseau.
Lévy-Leboyer, M. 1976. "L'étude du capital et l'histoire des recensements fonciers en France au XIXe siècle." In INSEE *Pour Une Histoire de la Statistique.* Paris.
———. 1977. *La Position Internationale de la France.* Paris. Editions de l'Ecole des Hautes Etudes et Sciences Sociales.
———. 1978. "Capital investment and economic growth in France, 1820–1930." In *Cambridge Economic History of Europe* I, Cambridge: Cambridge University Press.
Lewis, C. 1958. *America's Stake in International Investments.* Washington, D.C.: Brookings Institution.
Loeser, H. n.d. (ca. 1947). *Sind Briefmarken eine Kapitalsanlage?* N.P. (probably Vienna): Philatelistiche Bibliothek.
Loiter, M. 1976. "Effektivnost'kapitalnikh vlojenii bochradu privodnoi sredi." In *Voprosi Ekonomiki.* Moscow.

London and Cambridge Economic Service. 1967. *The British Economy Key Statistics 1900–1966*. London: Times Newspapers.
Maddison, A. 1979. "Per capita output in the long run." *Kyklos* 32.
Mairesse, J. 1972. *L'Evaluation du Capital Fixe Productif*. Paris: INSEE.
Manfroni, P. 1976. "Flussi e consistense di beni durevoli di consumo in Italia nel periodo 1951–1973." *Rivista Italiana de Economica, Demografia e Statistica*.
Mason, S. 1976. *The Flow of Funds in Great Britain*. London: Paul Elck.
Meyer, I. 1930. *Der Geldwert des Menschenlebens und seine Beziehungen zur Versicherung*. Berlin: E. S. Mittler und Sohn.
Michalet, Ch. A. 1968. *Les Placements des Epargnants Francais de 1815 à nos jours*. Paris: Presses Universitaires de France.
Michel, E. 1925. *Les Evaluations de la Fortune Privée en France*. Paris.
Milot, J-P. 1982. "Le patrimoine en 1979." In INSEE, *Economie et Statistique*.
Ministère des Finances (France). *Bulletin de Statistique et de Legislation Comparée*. Paris.
Ministerio de Hacienda (Mexico). 1977. *Muestra de 5111 Empresas Causantes Maiores*. Mexico D.F.
Mitchell, B. 1975. *European Historical Statistics 1750–1970*. London: Macmillan Press.
Mitchell, B. R. 1982. *International Historical Statistics—Africa and Asia*. New York: New York University Press.
Mitchell, B. R., and Deane, P. 1962. *Abstract of British Historical Statistics*. Cambridge: Cambridge University Press.
Morgan, E. V. 1960. *The Structure of Property Ownership in Great Britain*. Oxford: Clarendon Press.
Morgan, E. V., and Thomas, W. A. 1969. *The Stock Exchange to 1900*. London: Elek Books.
Mulhall, M. G. 1896. *Industries and Wealth of Nations*. London: Longmans, Green and Co.
———. 1899. *The Dictionary of Statistics*. London: G. Routledge and Son.
———. 1909. *The Dictionary of Statistics*. London: G. Routledge and Son.
Musgrave, J. C. 1980. "Government-owned fixed capital in the United States, 1925–79." *Survey of Current Business* 3.
———. 1981. "Fixed capital stock in the United States: revised estimates." *Survey of Current Business* 2.
National Bank of Hungary. 1971, 1979. *Information Memorandum for International Loans*. Budapest.
National Bank of Yugoslavia. *Annual Report*. Belgrade.
———. *Quarterly Bulletin*.
Nationwide Building Society. *Occasional Bulletin*. London.
Necco, A. 1915. *Il Corso dei Titoli di Stato in Italia dal 1861 al 1912*. Suppl. to *Riforma Sociale*. Torino.
Nesterov, L. 1972. "National wealth estimation in socialist countries." In *Review of Income and Wealth*, ser. 18.

Neufeld, E. P. 1972. *The Financial System of Canada*. Toronto: Macmillan.
Newmarch, W. 1851. "An attempt to ascertain the magnitude and fluctuations of the amount of bills of exchange . . . 1828–1847." *Journal of the Royal Statistical Society*. London.
Neymarck, A. 1903. "La statistique internationale der valeurs mobilières." *Bulletin de l'Institut International de Statistique* 13 no. 3. Rome: J. Bertoro.
Nötel, R. 1980. *Capital and Labour in the Development Process*. Papers in East European Economics No. 59. Mimeo. Oxford: St. Anthony's College.
OECD (Organization for Economic Cooperation and Development). *Financial Statistics* (annually). Paris.
Ohkawa, K., et al. 1965. *Estimates of Long-Term Economic Statistics of Japan since 1868*. Tokyo: Toyo Keizai Shimposha.
Perroux, F. 1955. "Prise de vue sur la croissance de l'economie francaise 1780-1950." In S. Kuznets, ed., *Income and Wealth*, ser. 5. London: Bowes and Bowes.
Petroleos Mexicanos. *Memoria de Labores* (annually). Mexico D.F.
Pettigrew, C. W. 1980. "National and sector balance sheets for the United Kingdom." In Central Statistical Office (Great Britain) *Economic Trends*, 321. London.
Pick's Currency Yearbook.1977–79. New York: Pick Publishing Corporation.
Powell, R. P. 1952. "Monetary statistics." In V. G. Treml and J. P. Hardt, *Soviet Economic Statistics*. Durham: Duke University Press.
———. 1979. "The Soviet capital stock from census to census, 1960–73." *Soviet Studies* 31.
Pupin, R. 1916. *La Richesse de la France davant la Guerre*. Paris: M. Rivière et Cie.
Reserve Bank of Australia. 1978. *Statistical Bulletin* (Company Supplement). Sydney.
———. 1979. *Statistical Bulletin* (Financial Flow of Funds Supplement).
Reserve Bank of India. *Reserve Bank of India Bulletin* (monthly). Bombay.
Reserve Bank of South Africa. *Quarterly Bulletin*. Pretoria.
Retti-Marsani, S. 1936. "Variazioni annuali della ricchezza italiana dal 1901 ai giorni nostri." *La Vita Economica Italiana* (1936).
Revell, J. 1967. *The Wealth of the Nation*. Cambridge: Cambridge University Press.
Revell, J., and Roe, A. R. 1971. "National balance sheets and national accounting—A progress report." In Central Statistical Office (Great Britain). *Economic Trends*, 211. London.
Reynders, H. J. J. 1963. "The geographical income of the Bantu Areas in South Africa." In L. H. Samuels, ed., *African Studies in Income and Wealth*. London: Bowes and Bowes.
Reynolds, C. W. 1970. *The Mexican Economy*. New Haven: Yale University Press.

Rostow, W. W. 1980. *Why the Poor Get Richer and the Rich Slow Down*. Austin: University of Texas Press.

Rothman, J. 1974. *The Wealth of the United Kingdom*. London.

Royal Commission on the Distribution of Income and Wealth (Great Britain). 1977. *Third Report on the Standing Reference (CMD 6999)*. London.

Ruggles, R., and Ruggles, N. D. 1982. "Integrated Economic Accounts for the United States 1947–1980." In *Survey of Current Business* (based on the more detailed Working Paper No. 841 of Institute for Social and Policy Studies, 1981, Yale University.

Salomon, R. S. 1980. *Tangible Assets vs. Financial Assets*. Investment Policy Stock Research Department. New York: Salomon Brothers.

Savezni Zavod za Statistiku (Yugoslavia). *Statisticki Godisnjak Jugoslavija*. (Annually).

Scott, W. R. 1910–12. *The Constitution and Finance of English, Scottish and Irish Joint Stock Companies to 1720*. Cambridge: Cambridge University Press.

Secretaria de Presupuestos y Programacion (Mexico). *Anuario Estadistico de los Estados Unidos Mexicanos* (annually). Mexico D.F.

———. 1979. *Informacion Financiera de Empresas Mexicanas 1975–1978*. Mexico D.F.

Sheppard, D. K. 1971. *The Growth and Role of U.K. Financial Institutions 1880–1962*. London: Methuen and Co.

Siesto, V. 1973. *Teoria e Metodi di Contabilitá Nazionale*. Rome: Libera Universitá degli Studi Sociali Pro Deo.

Silaev, E. D., and Shimov, V. N. 1977. "Ekonomitsheskaia otsenka prirodno-resoursnovo potentsia regiona." In *Vestnik Akademii Nauk, Seria Ekonomitsheskaia*.

Skånland, H. 1967. *Det Norske Kreditmarked siden 1900*. Oslo: Statistisk Sentralbyrå.

South African Reserve Bank. *Quarterly Bulletin*. Pretoria.

Spånt, R. 1979. "Den svenska förmögenhetsfordelningens utveckling." In *Lontagarna och kapitalväxten* 2. Stockholm: Statens Offentiliga Utrednigar 1979:9.

Statesman's Yearbook. London: St. Martin's Press.

Statistics Canada. 1977. *Financial Flow Accounts, Annual Flows and Year-End Financial Assets and Liabilities 1961–1976*. Ottawa.

———. 1979. *Fixed Capital Flows and Stocks, 1926–1978*.

Statistisches Bundesamt (West Germany). *Wirtschaft und Statistik* (monthly). Wiesbaden.

———. *Statistiches Jahrbuch für die Bundesrepublik Deutschland* (annually).

———. Fachserie 3.2 *Kaufwerte für landwirtschaftlichen Grundbesitz* (quarterly).

———. Fachserie 17.5 *Kaufwerte für Bauland* (quarterly).

Statistisk Sentralbyrå (Norway). 1978. *Historisk Statistisk*. Oslo.

———. *Kreditmarkedstatistikk* (annually).

———. *Statistisk Årbok* (annually).

———. *Statistiske Översikter* (monthly).
Statistiska Centralbyrån (Sweden). *Allman Manadstatistik* (monthly). Stockholm.
———. *Statistisk Årsbok för Sverige* (annually).
———. *Statistiska Meddelanden* (monthly).
Stein, J. P. 1977. "Monetary appreciation of paintings." *Journal of Political Economy* 85.
Stone, R., and Roe, A. 1971. *The Financial Interdependence of the Economy, 1957, 1966*. Cambridge: Chapman and Hall.
Studenski, P., and Kroos, H. 1952. *Financial History of the United States*. New York: McGraw-Hill.
Summers, R.; Kravis, I.; and Heston, A. 1980. "International comparison of real product and its composition: 1950–77." *Review of Income and Wealth* 26.
Sutch, R. C. 1983. "The Value of the Slave Population, 1805–1860." Unpublished memorandum. Berkeley, Calif.
Swanepoel, C. J., and Van Dyk, J. 1978. "The fixed capital stock and sectoral capital-output ratios in South Africa." In South African Reserve Bank, *Quarterly Bulletin*. September.
Tagliacarne, G. 1961. "La bilancia internazionale dei pagamenti della Italia nel primo centenario del'Unitá." In *L'Economia Italiana del 1861 al 1961*. Milan: Giuffré.
Théry, E. 1911. *La Fortune Publique de la France*. Paris: C. Delagrave.
Tostlebe, A. S. 1957. *Capital in Agriculture: Its Formation and Financing since 1870*. Princeton: Princeton University Press.
Triffin, R. 1964. *The Evolution of the International Monetary System: Historical Reappraisal and Future Perspectives*. Princeton: Princeton University Press.
Tsentralnoie Statisticheskie Upravlenie (USSR). *Narodnoie Khosiaistvo SSSR* (annually). Moscow.
———. 1977. *Narodnoie Khosiaistvo S.S.S.R. sa 60 let.*
Ulmer, M. J. 1960. *Capital in Transportation, Comunication and Public Utilities*. Princeton: Princeton University Press.
United Nations. *Statistical Yearbook*. New York.
———. *Yearbook of National Accounts Statistics*.
United Nations, Department of Economic and Social Affairs. 1968. *A System of National Accounts*.
———. 1977. *Provisional International Guidelines on the National and Sectoral Balance-sheet and Reconciliation Accounts of the Systems of National Accounts*. Statistical Papers, Series M, No. 60. New York.
United Nations Statistical Commission. 1978. *Draft International Guidelines on Statistics of Tangible Assets* (E/CN, E/508). New York.
United States, Bureau of the Census. 1975. *Historical Statistics of the United States: Colonial Times to 1970*. Washington, D.C.
———. *Statistical Abstract of the United States* (annually).
United States, Congress, Joint Economic Committee. 1964. *Economic Policies and Practices*. Paper No. 3.
———. *Economic Report of the President* (annually).

United States, Department of Commerce. *Survey of Current Business* (monthly).
United States, National Foreign Assessment Center. 1980. *Estimating Soviet and East European Hard Currency Debt.*
Urquhart, M. C., and Buckley, K. A. 1965. *Historical Statistics of Canada.* Cambridge: Cambridge University Press.
Van der Weide, T. 1959. "Statistics of national wealth for eighteen countries." In R. Goldsmith, and C. Saunders, eds., *The Measurement of National Wealth.*
Venkatachalam, T. R., and Sarma, Y. S. R. 1976. "Structure and Trends in the National Balance Sheet of India." Paper for Tenth General Conference of Indian Association for Research in National Income and Wealth.
Vinski, I. 1959. "The national wealth of Yugoslavia at the end of 1953." In R. Goldsmith, and C. Saunders, eds., *The Measurement of National Wealth.*
———. 1979. "Fiksni fondovi u privredi Jugoslavije ed 1953 do 1976 godine." *Sovremeni Ekonomiski Problemi* 5. Zagreb: Jugoslavenska Akademija Znanosti i Umjetnosti.
Vitali, O. 1968. *Nuova Stima Dissaggregata dello Stock di Capitale in Italia.* Rome: Instituto Nazionale per lo Studio della Congiuntura.
Vliebergh, E. 1899. *Le Crédit Foncier.* Paris.
Wheatley, H. B. 1898. *Prices of Books.* London: G. Allen.
Ward, N. 1976. *The Measurement of Capital.* Paris: Organization for Economic Cooperation and Development.
World Bank. 1981. *World Development Report, 1980.* Washington, D.C.
Woytinski, W. W. 1925. *Die Welt in Zahlen.* Berlin: Rudolf Mosse.

Index

This Index does not identify the numbers of the comparative tables in the text in which asset ratios for individual countries are shown, namely, tables 8–20, 22–26, 31, 33, 38–64, 66–63, and 70; nor those of the country tables in which ratios for individual assets and liabilities are shown, namely, tables 1–6 and 34–37 in the text, and all tables in Appendices A and B; nor the sectors for which balance sheets are shown in tables 60–67 in the text or in Appendix B. References to individual countries or to individual assets and liabilities in the text are identified only when they are substantial. References to sources in the text or in Appendix C and in text tables are included in the Index but not those in the notes to the tables in Appendix A. All sources used, however, are included in the List of Publications Cited. Tables are identified by an asterisk.